TOPIC	LESSON FOCUS	EXAM SKILLS	GRAMMAR	VOCABULARY
Unit 8 **Urban jungle** 66–71 City living	8.1 Reading and Vocabulary 8.2 Grammar and Vocabulary 8.3 Listening, Speaking and Vocabulary	Reading and Use of English: 4 and 7 Speaking: 3	Inversion	Compound adjectives Phrases with *place*
Writing folder 4 72–73		Writing: 2 Set text question: Film tie-in		
Revision Units 5–8 74–75				
Unit 9 **Fitting in** 76–81 Attitudes	9.1 Listening and Vocabulary 9.2 Grammar and Vocabulary 9.3 Reading into Writing	Reading and Use of English: 2 and 4 Writing: 1 Linking Listening: 4	Gerunds and infinitives	Phrases with *come* Prefixes Linking words and phrases Personal appearance, personality
Exam folder 5 82–83		Reading and Use of English: 6 Gapped text		
Unit 10 **Globalisation** 84–89 Language and culture	10.1 Reading and Vocabulary 10.2 Grammar and Vocabulary 10.3 Listening and Speaking	Reading and Use of English: 1, 3 and 4 Listening: 1 Speaking: 2	Reference devices Expressing wishes and preferences Pronunciation: word stress	Expressions with *turn*
Writing folder 5 90–91		Writing: 2 Article		
Unit 11 **For better, for worse** 92–97 Relationships	11.1 Listening and Vocabulary 11.2 Grammar 11.3 Reading into Writing	Reading and Use of English: 2 and 3 Writing: 1 Reformulation 2 Listening: 3	Gradability	Phrasal verbs Idioms to do with relationships
Exam folder 6 98–99		Listening: 4 Multiple matching		
Unit 12 **At the cutting edge** 100–105 Scientific advances	12.1 Reading and Vocabulary 12.2 Grammar 12.3 Listening and Speaking	Reading and Use of English: 1, 4 and 6 Speaking: 3	Passive structures Pronunciation: stress and emphasis	Idioms with technical words Phrases with *set*
Writing folder 6 106–107		Writing: 2 Report		
Revision Units 9–12 108–109				
Unit 13 **Save the planet** 110–115 The environment	13.1 Listening and Vocabulary 13.2 Grammar 13.3 Reading into Writing	Reading and Use of English: 1 and 2 Writing: 1 Giving opinions Listening: 1	Reported speech	Vocabulary – the environment Register Synonyms
Exam folder 7 116–117		Reading and Use of English: 5 Multiple-choice text		
Unit 14 **Get fit, live longer!** 118–123 Sport and health	14.1 Reading and Vocabulary 14.2 Grammar and Vocabulary 14.3 Listening and Speaking	Reading and Use of English: 4 and 7 Listening: 3 Speaking: 2	Articles review Pronunciation: noun/verb/ adjective stress	Register Phrases with *live* Phrases with nouns and no article Prepositions Word formation
Writing folder 7 124–125		Writing: 2 Letter		

Content of Cambridge English: Proficiency (CPE)

Cambridge English: Proficiency, also known as *Certificate of Proficiency in English (CPE)* consists of four papers. The Reading and Use of English paper carries 40% of the marks while the Writing, Listening and Speaking papers each carry 20% of the marks. It is not necessary to pass all four papers in order to pass the examination. If you achieve a grade A, B or C in the examination, you will receive the *Cambridge English: Proficiency* certificate at Level C2. If your performance is below Level C2, but falls within Level C1, then you will receive a *Cambridge English* certificate stating that you have demonstrated ability at C1 level.

As well as being told your grade, you will also be given a Statement of Results – a graphical profile of your performance, i.e. it will show whether you have done especially well or badly on some of the papers.

Reading and Use of English 1 hour 30 minutes

There are seven parts to this paper and they are always in the same order. For Parts 1 to 4, the test contains texts with accompanying grammar and vocabulary tasks, and separate items with a grammar and vocabulary focus. For Parts 5 to 7, the test contains a range of texts and accompanying reading comprehension tasks. The texts are from books (fiction and non-fiction), non-specialist articles from magazines, newspapers and the internet.

Part	Task Type	Number of Questions	Task Format	Objective Exam Folder
1	Multiple-choice cloze	8	You must choose which word from four answers completes each of the gaps in a text.	**3** (48–49)
2	Open cloze	8	You must complete a text with eight gaps using only one word in each gap.	**2** (30–31)
3	Word formation	8	You need to use the right form of a given word to fill each of eight gaps in a text.	**1** (14–15)
4	Key word transformations	6	You must complete a sentence with a given word, so that it means the same as the first sentence.	**2** (30–31)
5	Multiple-choice text	6	You must read a text and answer the questions by finding the relevant information in the text.	**7** (116–117)
6	Gapped text	7	You must read a text from which paragraphs have been removed and placed in jumbled order, together with an additional paragraph, after the text. You need to decide from where in the text the paragraphs have been removed.	**5** (82–83)
7	Multiple matching	10	You read a text or several short texts, preceded by multiple-matching questions. You must match a prompt to elements in the text.	**4** (64–65)

Writing 1 hour 30 minutes

There are two parts to this paper. Part 1 is compulsory, you have to answer it. In Part 2 there are five questions and you must choose one. Each part carries equal marks and you are expected to write 240–280 words for Part 1 and 280–320 words for Part 2.

Part	Task Type	Number of Tasks	Task Format	Objective Writing Folder or Unit
1	Question 1 An essay with a discursive focus	1 compulsory	You are given two short texts and you must write an essay summarising and evaluating the key ideas contained in the texts.	**WF 1** (22–23); **WF 3** (56–57); **U1** (12–13); **U3** (28–29); **U5** (46–47); **U7** (62–63); **U9** (80–81); **U11** (96–97); **U13** (114–115); **U15** (130–131); **U17** (148–149); **U19** (164–165)
2	Questions 2–4 • an article • a letter • a report • a review Question 5 Choice of two questions – one on each of the specified set texts: article, essay, letter, review, report	5 choose one	You are given a choice of topics which you have to respond to in the way specified.	Article **WF 5, 9** and **10** (90–91; 158–159; 174–175) Letter **WF 7** and **10** (124–125; 174–175) Review **WF 2** (38–39) Report **WF 6** (106–107) Set text: Film tie-in **WF 4** (72–73) Set text: Review **WF 8** (140–141)

Listening about 40 minutes

There are four parts to this paper. Each part is heard twice. The texts are a variety of types either with one speaker or more than one.

Part	Task Type	Number of Questions	Task Format	Objective Exam Folder
1	Multiple-choice questions	6	You hear three short, unrelated extracts, with either one or two speakers. You must answer two questions on each extract, choosing from A, B or C.	9 (150–151)
2	Sentence completion	9	You must complete spaces in sentences with information given by one speaker.	8 (132–133)
3	Multiple-choice questions	5	You will hear two or more speakers interacting. You must choose your answer from A, B, C or D.	9 (150–151)
4	Multiple matching	10	There are two tasks, each task containing five questions. You must select five correct options from a list of eight.	6 (98–99)

Speaking about 16 minutes

There are three parts to this paper. There are usually two of you taking the examination and two examiners. This paper tests your accuracy, vocabulary, pronunciation and ability to communicate and manage the tasks.

Part	Task Type	Time	Task Format	Objective Exam Folder
1	The interviewer asks each candidate some questions	2 minutes	You will be asked some questions about yourself and asked to express personal opinions.	10 (166–167)
2	Two-way conversation between candidates	4 minutes	You will be given visual and written prompts which are used in a decision-making task.	10 (166–167)
3	A long turn for each candidate followed by a discussion on related topics	10 minutes in total	You will be given a written question to respond to. You will then be asked to engage in a discussion on related topics.	10 (166–167)

Ring the changes

Listening

2 **1 02** You will hear five different people talking about a key change in their lives. Tick each speaker's life-changing moment. There is one extra that you will not need.

life-changing moment	1	2	3	4	5
being made redundant					
gaining media attention					
meeting 'Mr Right'					
heading the wrong way					
losing something special					
stepping in for someone					

3 **1 02** Listen again to check your answers. Then choose one of the speakers and describe what happened to him or her.

Speaking

1 Everyone goes through changes, whether by choice or because of something outside their control. Talk about changes that have happened to you or might happen in the future, relating them to these phrases.

- a change for the better
- the earliest change you can remember
- a new location
- a change of direction in your life
- a change of heart

Which two phrases above are examples of idioms? Find a third idiom on this page.

Vocabulary

Phrasal verbs

🌀 Idiom spot

At C2 level, you need to understand and use phrases and idioms where the meaning is not transparent. You will probably know the individual words used, but this may not help! Some examples of common idioms are given below. Choose the correct option (a or b) to complete each definition. These idioms are used in the Listening section.

EXAMPLE: If something happens **out of the blue**, it is
a) unexpected b) creative. *Answer a)*

1 When things **fall into place**, events happen to a) change the order of a list b) produce the situation you want.
2 If something **goes downhill**, it a) gradually becomes worse b) picks up speed.
3 If something is **on the cards**, it is a) likely to fail b) likely to happen.
4 When you are talking about a change in your life and you say **the rest is history**, you mean that a) it happened a long time ago b) you are sure that people know what happened next.

🌀 Exam spot

Phrasal verbs are tested in Parts 1, 2 and 4 of Reading and Use of English. Remember that their use is generally informal, so they should be used with care in Writing, where the tasks mostly require a more neutral or formal register.

You will already have come across many phrasal verbs, but now you need to add to this knowledge. If there are gaps in your learning, try to fill them in. How many phrasal verbs can you come up with from the recording in 2? Remember that some phrasal verbs contain two particles rather than one (an adverb and a preposition), as in the last example.

4 Match the verbs to the correct particle(s) to form phrasal verbs that were used by Speakers 1–5. Four of them are 'three-part' phrasal verbs.

EXAMPLE: *break up (3)*

verbs			
break	catch	cheer	come
cut	end	get	hang
help	jump	pay	run
settle	take	track	turn

particles	
around	at
back	down
in	off
on	out
up	with

5 Now complete these sentences using a phrasal verb from 4 in a suitable tense. Sometimes the passive form will be needed.

EXAMPLE: The whole family moved to Switzerland last month and their two children *are settling in* well at school there.

a Their lives changed completely once the loan .... as it meant they could treat themselves to meals out and weekends away.

b An old school friend .... me .... on the Internet and we met up recently to compare our life stories.

c The company offered Maria a post in the New York branch and she .... the chance.

d During the last recession, local businesses .... recruitment and no graduate trainees .... as a result.

e Jeff explained that shortly after they bought the house together, he and his wife .... and she moved to another town.

f People often manage to advance their careers by .... the right people and telling them what they want to hear.

g Everything fell into place – she was offered the scholarship at Harvard, the flight was booked and her missing passport .... just in time!

h My brother has had a change of heart and is willing to .... me .... with decorating the flat after all.

◎ Exam spot

Part 1 of Reading and Use of English is a short text with eight gaps. Don't panic if you find unfamiliar words in options A–D. Try the other words in the gap first. If you're sure they don't fit, choose the word you don't know.

6 Read the text below, which is from the introduction to a book on *feng shui*. Decide which answer (A, B, C or D) best fits each gap.

The ancient Chinese philosophers who considered *feng* (wind or air) and *shui* (water) to be the **(1)** .... of mankind also understood that these were not the only supportive elements flowing through the **(2)** .... They perceived a subtler **(3)** .... , calling it *chi* or 'cosmic breath'. This life force is well-known to acupuncturists, who have **(4)** .... elaborate maps of the 'meridians' or channels it uses to flow through the body. Kung Fu masters believe that *chi* can be concentrated in the human body, allowing someone to **(5)** .... almost supernatural feats, such as the breaking of concrete blocks **(6)** .... by using the edge of their hand. A real feng shui master is able to **(7)** .... the flow of *chi* in a site, and may advise changes to the environment to **(8)** .... health, wealth and good fortune.

1	**A** sustainers	**B** providers	**C** keepers	**D** promoters
2	**A** background	**B** location	**C** outlook	**D** landscape
3	**A** vigour	**B** weight	**C** energy	**D** stimulus
4	**A** shown up	**B** built up	**C** put up	**D** laid up
5	**A** perform	**B** play	**C** act	**D** conduct
6	**A** barely	**B** merely	**C** hardly	**D** slightly
7	**A** suspect	**B** realise	**C** sense	**D** endure
8	**A** set about	**B** come about	**C** go about	**D** bring about

1 Read these short texts about alternative ways of approaching city life. The highlighted parts illustrate some of the grammar areas that C2 learners continue to have problems with. What are they?

2 Tick any grammar areas below that you feel you need to work on. Add your main grammar problem if it is not listed.

- [ ] Modal verbs
- [ ] Passives
- [ ] Conditionals
- [ ] Perfect tenses
- [ ] Relative clauses
- [ ] Reported speech
- [ ] Uncountable nouns
- [ ] ....

Corpus spot

Correct the errors in perfect tenses in these sentences, which were written by exam candidates.

a Three years ago I have been to Germany on a cultural exchange.
b Tourism is a word that is being used for the last 50 years.
c In England last year, I was able to appreciate things I have never seen in my entire life.
d The noise levels have been measured in our suburb the other day and are twice the acceptable level.
e All these years I'm practising basketball, I'm trying to become a better player.
f When you will have bought your train tickets, you should take one each and put it into the machine.
g Supposing they would have got married, wouldn't the day have come when they got bored with each other?
h Nowadays, almost every disease has a cure and people have been caring more about their health.

A LIFE LESS ORDINARY

« Knit the City

From knitted graffiti to guerrilla crocheting – needle crafts have exploded in ways entirely unforeseen by previous generations. Our grandmothers would no doubt approve of twenty-somethings knitting something similar to a tea cosy (which they used to cover their teapots), even when it is large enough to keep a London phonebox warm! This original item of knitwear has been made by Knit the City, a subversive group of knitters who also operate in other capital cities. In Berlin, for example, a woolly 'Currywurst' was created entirely out of yarn recently. For those not in the know, the Currywurst is a popular fast food item – over 800 million of the sausage treats are sold every year!

Pink Lady Flamingo »

You may have come across the extravagantly dressed Pink Lady Flamingo, whose real name is Maryanne Kerr, busking on the underground in London. She auditioned for an official licence to perform her music, having experimented with many previous careers. "I've been busking since I broke a recording contract with a major record company," said Maryanne, "because I refused to be dictated to." She added that she became a busker more than forty years ago and announced that she is in her late seventies now and still busking.

3 Explain how tense choice alters the meaning in these sentences. In which two sentences is there no change in meaning?

a Mirek *has gone / went* to Gdansk on business.
b Our society *has been suffering / was suffering* from high unemployment for decades.
c We *were given / have been given* more time to complete the task.
d Top government ministers *have been dealing / have dealt* with the problem.
e Matt and James *have played / have been playing* golf all day.
f I've *thought / been thinking* about what you said.
g Is there anything else we *could have done / will have done*?
h Come October, we *will have lived / will have been living* here for eleven years.

4 Answer these questions so that they are true for you, using perfect tenses.

a How long have you been learning English?
b What have you never done that you would like to do?
c What change has been made to your town or city recently that you don't approve of?
d Which single change would most improve your quality of life at home?
e What may have changed in your life by this time next year?

G → page 178

5 Complete the text below, using the words in brackets in such a way that they fit the space grammatically.

Innovation
in our lives

Across the centuries, people's daily lives **(1)** .... (continually transform) by innovation. One of the most obvious characteristics of the 20th century was the rapid growth of technology, with individual quality of life **(2)** .... (improve) immeasurably as a result. Basic labour-saving appliances such as washing machines, refrigerators and freezers were commonplace in the home by the 1960s and the demand for these and other 'white goods' **(3)** .... (further stimulate) by the availability of cheap electricity and noticeable increases in personal wealth during that decade.

Personal computers first made their appearance in the home in the 1970s, but surely few people **(4)** .... (be able to) imagine then that the home computer could evolve into the super-fast, super-sleek machines of today. Nor could they **(5)** .... (even think) that handheld mobile gadgets would **(6)** .... (use constantly) by all of us, in our desperation to keep up with everything from office correspondence to world news.

So what lies ahead of us? By 2025, will we **(7)** .... (embrace) even more sophisticated technological aids – or will the world's resources **(8)** .... (deplete) by mankind to such an extent that there will be insufficient electricity to support these advances? Only time will tell.

3 For sentences a–j, replace the words in italics with a single adjective formed from one of the verbs or nouns given. What adjectives are formed from the four remaining words?

adventure	alternate	disaster	dispose
exhaust	experiment	flaw	hope
identify	mass	notice	philosophy
predict	speech	understand	

EXAMPLE: I've been given this *very lengthy and complete* list of all the repairs needed in the flat. *Exhaustive*

a My boss's response to my plea for changes to my job description was *exactly what I was expecting*.

b If the weather is unfavourable, do you have any *other suggestions to replace our original* plans?

c Both sides in the conflict are *expressing their optimism* that the ceasefire will hold.

d Jeremy seems *to have calmly accepted the news* about the break-in.

e That play I went to see last night was *trying something new* in its use of dialect.

f I was *incapable of any reply* when Ella told me she had quit her job.

g It's *really easy to see* how much fitter Liam has become since he started swimming regularly.

h Your last piece of writing was *without any mistakes whatsoever*.

i Many of today's products are *used only once and then thrown away*, which is having an impact on the environment.

j The updating of the university's computer system has had *extremely bad and far-reaching* consequences.

1 What changes do you notice in the world around you? Identify the changes shown in the pictures and categorise them, choosing from the adjectives below. Then suggest other changes that could be classified under these categories.

commercial	environmental	physical
political	social	technological

Vocabulary

Word formation

2 The adjectives above are formed from nouns. Generally, the suffix *-al* is added to the noun, as in *environmental*. Explain the formation rules for *commercial* and *technological*.

The suffixes *-able* and *-ive* frequently combine with verbs to form adjectives, as in *favourable* and *supportive*. Explain the formation rules for *creative* and *variable*.

The suffix *-ous* combines with nouns, as in *courageous*. Give two more examples.

Other common adjectival suffixes added to nouns are *-ful* and *-less*, as in *meaningful* and *harmless*. Give two more examples of each.

In the Writing, Part 1 compulsory task, you will read two short texts in order to summarise and evaluate them. You will need to reproduce different ideas concisely, using your own words wherever possible.

4 In extracts 1 and 2, important information has been underlined. Do the same in 3 and 4. Then answer questions 1–3 below the texts.

1

We pick up on <u>health</u> and <u>social status</u> from <u>facial features</u>, as shown by a recent research project where people were <u>unconsciously attracted</u> to healthy females and wealthy men, even when they only had a picture of a face (without make-up or jewellery) to judge them by.

2

It was in 1856, while working in his tiny laboratory at home, that William <u>Perkin produced</u>, quite by <u>chance</u>, the colour <u>mauve</u>, which not only <u>revolutionised the dye industry</u> but also led to important <u>innovations</u> in perfume, photography and, <u>most</u> <u>significantly</u> for modern <u>medicine</u>, to the development of <u>aspirin</u>.

3

Rather than burgers and fries being a product of the social changes seen over the last fifty years in America, the author suggests that fast food brands were to a large extent responsible for these changes, as they profoundly affected both lifestyle and diet.

4

Tiny holes found in human teeth estimated to be over 8000 years old are now believed to be the earliest evidence of dentistry, for when these holes were examined with an electron microscope, researchers found their sides were too perfectly rounded to be caused by bacteria and have therefore proposed that they were drilled by prehistoric dentists.

1 Which information in text 1 is summarised in the following sentence?
   People form opinions of others by looking at their faces.
   What has been omitted?
2 Which phrase in text 1 could be replaced by the verb *assess* or *evaluate*?
3 Which underlined words in text 2 could be replaced by others?

5 Choose from a–f the best summary sentence for text 2, judging it by the inclusion of information, use of alternative words, choice of register and conciseness. Say why the remaining sentences are less successful.

   a Mauve not only radically changed the dye industry but also led to new discoveries of anything from perfume to aspirin.
   b By cooking up mauve in his lab, Perkin pushed the dye industry forward and set the ball rolling in other industries too, such as perfume and photography and aspirin.
   c In accidentally discovering mauve, Perkin transformed dyeing and many other areas, notably medicine.
   d Perkin discovered a special pale purple colour and this discovery was revolutionary for the dye industry and also for the pharmaceutical industry, since it led to the innovation of aspirin.
   e Aspirin owes its development to Perkin, who found mauve by chance in his laboratory at home.
   f Commercially-speaking, Perkin's chance discovery was very important, as other innovations followed, for example the development of aspirin.

6 Now write summary sentences for texts 3 and 4, referring to the parts you have underlined and using between 12 and 20 words for each. Use your own words wherever possible.

Exam folder 1

Reading and Use of English, Part 3 Word formation

In Part 3 of the Reading and Use of English paper, you will be asked to read a text and complete the eight numbered gaps with a form of the word in capitals at the end of the line. There is an example at the beginning of the text.

There are three main categories of changes that are tested. These are affixation (suffixes and prefixes), compound and grammatical changes. Unlike lower level examinations, at Proficiency level there is no limit to the number of changes which might be required to the root word.

Below are some examples of the changes you might need to make.

Affixes

noun to adjective *flaw* to *flawless*
noun to negative adverb *effect* to *ineffectively*
adjective to negative adverb *definite* to *indefinitely*
verb to noun *act* to *interaction*
verb to plural noun *apply* to *applicants*
adjective to verb *deep* to *deepened*

1 Do the following for practice. Make sure you check the following:

- do you need to make the word plural?
- is a prefix needed?
- does any prefix need to be negative?

a There are a number of
.... activities now **CURRICULUM**
being offered at the school.

b People have always enjoyed the
.... effects of sea air. **BENEFIT**

c Tony is a really .... **OPINION**
person.

d The animal .... really **KING**
fascinates my young daughter.

e Stefan was a .... **COMPEL**
collector of gadgets throughout his life.

f It was rapidly becoming
.... that we would have **APPEAR**
to make changes to our plans.

g There have been a number of
female .... in the **INNOVATE**
field of aircraft design.

h There were a number of
....................................built into the **CONSTRAIN**
contract.

i The .... of fast food **CONSUME**
is increasing at a frightening rate.

j .... seems to suit Ella **DOMESTIC**
– she's really happy with her home life.

k The side wall of the house had to
be .... **STRONG**

l I believe she had the .... **FORTUNE**
to have been seriously ill as a child.

m The broken vase turned out to be
totally .... **REPLACE**

n She showed her deep
.... by slamming the **APPROVE**
door in our faces.

o The police tried to evict the three
.... from the building. **OCCUPY**

Compounds

Compounds are often tested at this level.
EXAMPLE:

a The .... of the meeting **COME**
was rather inconclusive.
Answer: outcome

b His brother had a second-hand car
which was barely .... **ROAD**
Answer: roadworthy

2 Match a word from A with one from B to form a compound noun or adjective. The words in B can be used more than once.

A	B
frame	worthy
up	fall
out	date
wind	work
rain	break
credit	turn
down	proof

EXAM ADVICE

● Read through the text carefully and decide which form of the given word you need to use.

● Be careful as you will need to use a negative prefix or another form of prefix at least once.

● Check to see if a noun needs to be plural.

● All the words must be correctly spelled. American spelling is acceptable.

● Write your answers in CAPITAL LETTERS on your answer sheet.

3 Read the Exam advice and then do the task below.

Use the word given in capitals at the end of some of the lines to form a word that fits in the gap in the same line. There is an example at the beginning (**0**). Write your answers **IN CAPITAL LETTERS**.

Example: | 0 | W | I | L | F | U | L | L | Y | | | | | | | | | | |

IT'S ONLY SKIN DEEP

We are the only animal that chooses what it will look

like. True, the chameleon changes colour – but not

(0) WILFULLY . Unlike us, it doesn't get up in the morning   **WILL**

and ask itself, 'What shall I look like today?', but we can and

do. Indeed, the **(1)** .... of body decoration points to the   **ANTIQUE**

conclusion that it is a key factor in our development as the

(2) .... life-form on our planet.   **DOMINATE**

By **(3)** .... their physical appearance our ancestors   **CUSTOM**

distanced themselves from the rest of the animal

kingdom. Within each tribe this helped them to mark out

differences of role, status, and **(4)** .... Our ancestors   **KIN**

(5) .... developed extraordinary techniques of body   **APPEAR**

decoration for practical reasons. How to show where one

tribe ends and another begins? How to **(6)** .... in a   **LINE**

lasting way the significance of an individual becoming an

adult member of society? **(7)** .... , without the expressive   **ARGUE**

capabilities of such 'body language' we would have been

(8) .... less successful as a species.   **FINITE**

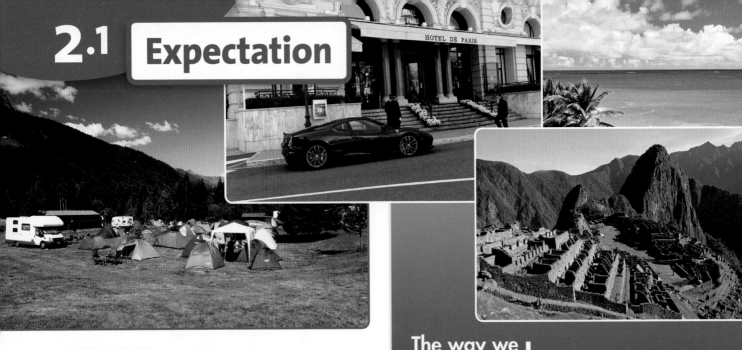

2.1 Expectation

The way we travel now

Speaking

1 Work with a partner. Look at the photos. What expectations would you have of a holiday in each of the places?

On which holiday might you

- get off the beaten track?
- be able to chill out?
- possibly have to rough it?
- end up spending a fortune?
- get by on a shoestring budget?
- enjoy being a culture vulture?
- get back to nature?
- be in the lap of luxury?

If you have had such a holiday, did it live up to your expectations? Have you ever had a holiday which exceeded/didn't live up to your expectations?

 Exam spot

In Part 7 of Reading and Use of English there are a number of short texts or one long text divided into sections. You need to read the sections carefully and then look at the questions. Underline your answer when you have found it. Make sure that your underlined text fully answers the question.

Reading

2 You are going to read an article about holidays and what we expect of them. Read through the article quickly to get a general idea of what it is about, ignoring the highlights for now. What does the writer think about holidays?

A

The prospect of a holiday is liable to persuade even the most downcast that life is worth living. Few events are anticipated more eagerly, nor form the subject of more complex and enriching daydreams. They offer us perhaps our finest chance to achieve happiness – outside of the constraints of work, of our struggle for survival and for status. The way we choose to spend them embodies, if only unknowingly, an understanding of what life might ideally be about. However, holidays almost always go wrong. The tragicomic disappointments of travel are a staple of office chat; the half-built hotel, the sense of disorientation, the mid-afternoon despair, the dreary fellow travellers, the lethargy before ancient ruins.

B

I remember a trip to Barbados a few years ago. I looked forward to it for months. But on my first morning on the island, I realised something at once obvious and surprising; that my body proved a temperamental partner. Asked to sit on a deckchair so that the mind could savour the beach, the trees and the sun, it collapsed into difficulties; the ears complained of an enervating wind, the skin of stickiness and the toes of sand lodged between them. Unfortunately, I had brought something else that risked clouding my appreciation of my surroundings; my entire mind – not only the part that had planned the journey and agreed to pay for it, but also the part committed to anxiety, boredom, self-disgust and financial alarm. At home, as I had pored over the photographs of Barbados, I had felt oblivious to anything besides their contents. I had simply been in the pictures; alone with their elements. But melancholy and regrets were my bedfellows on that Caribbean isle, acting like panes of distorting glass between myself and the world.

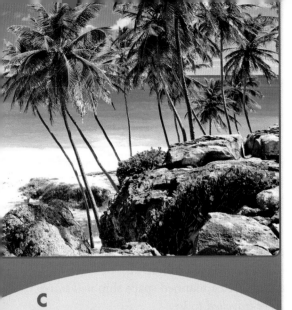

C

There was a trip to a hotel in France a friend took with his wife. The setting was sublime, the room flawless – and yet they managed to have a row which, for all the good the room and setting did them, meant that they might as well have stayed at home. The row (it started with who had forgotten the key in the room and extended to cover the whole of the relationship) was a reminder of the rigid, unforgiving logic to which human moods seem subject – and which we ignore at our peril. Our capacity to draw happiness from aesthetic or material goods seems critically dependent on first satisfying a more important range of emotional or psychological needs, among them the need for understanding, for love, expression and respect.

D

It may be necessary to accept that the anticipation of travel is perhaps the best part about it. Our holidays are never as satisfying as they are when they exist in an as-yet-unrealised form; in the shape of an airline ticket and a brochure. In the great 19th-century novel, *Against Nature*, by JK Huysmans, the narrator goes on a few holidays which go wrong and then decides never to leave home again. He has the itineraries of the major shipping companies framed and lines his bedroom with them. He fills an aquarium with seaweed, buys a sail, some rigging and a pot of tar and, with these aids is able to experience the most pleasant sides of a long sea voyage without the inconveniences such as sea-sickness, storms or uncongenial fellow passengers. I continue to travel myself but there are times when I too feel there might be no finer journeys than those provoked in the imagination by remaining at home slowly turning the pages of an airline timetable.

3 You need to decide in which part of the text you will find the answer to the questions. Do the following question for practice.

Which section mentions a number of unanticipated problems faced by the writer? [1][   ]
You will see that there are problems mentioned in sections A, B, C and D (highlighted). However, which section mentions problems which are 'unanticipated' and 'faced by the writer'?

Now do questions 2–8.

Which section mentions

the possibility of the writer altering a previous pattern of behaviour? [2][   ]

negative emotions being ever present? [3][   ]

the fact the some conditions must be met for other aims to be achieved? [4][   ]

the frequency of a certain topic being raised? [5][   ]

the possibility that an unfulfilled objective may be more desirable? [6][   ]

the writer finding it impossible to achieve his goal? [7][   ]

the belief that the selection of a holiday is a product of an unconscious desire? [8][   ]

Vocabulary

Collocations with *traveller*

4 The writer in the article talks about 'dreary fellow travellers'. Circle the most suitable collocation in these sentences.

a Dr Parr was a *frequent / recurrent* traveller to Dublin.

b There has been a rise in the numbers of *self-contained / independent* travellers as opposed to those on packages.

c *Seasoned / Practised* travellers know exactly how to get an upgrade on their bookings.

d I'm fed up with reading about all these *intrepid / heroic* travellers going up the Amazon river in a canoe.

e The hotel offers *fatigued / weary* travellers an excellent opportunity to recharge their batteries.

f LuxVac is the resort for *judicious / discerning* travellers – ones who know how to appreciate the good things in life.

g My father has always been more of a / an *armchair / sofa* traveller, much to my mother's disgust!

h Susie is the kind of *inveterate / habitual* traveller who will probably never settle down in one place.

i The hotel touts lie in wait for *unguarded / unwary* travellers and then take them to unsuitable lodgings.

5 Discuss with a partner.

• Do you agree with the ideas put forward by the writer? Why / Why not?

• Do you think it's better to travel hopefully than arrive? Why / Why not?

1 When we want to talk about the future in English we have to use a variety of tenses, modals and expressions, not just *will do*. The context of the sentence is what tells us which aspect of the future to use.

For example, there are many different variations possible for the verb in brackets here: *What you (do) tonight?*

Answers

a What are you doing tonight?
b What will you do tonight?
c What are you going to do tonight?
d What will you be doing tonight?
e What will you have done tonight?
f What were you going to do tonight?

Before you can decide which aspect of the future to use, you need to know the context. With a partner, discuss when each of the forms above would be used.

G → pages 178–179

Note – the present simple is also used to express the future when talking about travel arrangements, e.g. *The ship leaves on Saturdays*, and also about facts that can't be changed, e.g. *Tomorrow is Wednesday.*

2 Choose the best alternative in sentences a–s.

EXAMPLE: I think I *will* / *'m going to* faint – let me get some air!

a He never does any work, I'm sure *he's going to get* / *he's getting* the sack.
b That *will be* / *is going to be* the postman – he usually comes round at this time.
c The plane for Zurich *leaves* / *will leave* at 16.00 on Fridays.

d Sue *is going to get* / *is getting* her visa next week, if she has time.
e It's a lovely day – I think *I'll go* / *I'll be going* to the beach.
f I rang her up to tell her that *I won't go* / *I'm not going* to the party because I'm already busy that night.
g I'll see you on Saturday. What *will you do* / *will you be doing* in the afternoon?
h By the year 2040 a manned space ship *will travel* / *will have travelled* to Io.
i The hotel *is not to allow* / *is not allowing* guests to use the car park this week, while building work goes ahead.
j I *will do* / *am doing* my packing this afternoon, if I can find my suitcase.
k Peter *will have been painting* / *will have painted* that portrait for three weeks by Saturday.
l This time next year we *will have finished* / *will finish* our exams.
m Don't let him read in the coach – *he'll feel* / *he's going to feel* sick.
n What *will you be doing* / *will you do* if the flight is delayed tomorrow?
o Tomorrow *is* / *will be* Tuesday.
p I *will have* / *am having* caviar tonight – it's already in my fridge!
q I'll ring you on my mobile when I *will arrive* / *arrive*.
r Stop worrying – the train *is arriving* / *will be arriving* soon.
s *Will* / *Shall* I help you?

3 With a partner, decide what you would say in the following situations.

EXAMPLE: Your birthday tomorrow. *I'm 22 tomorrow.* / *I'll be 22 tomorrow.* (fact/ neutral future)

a Your intention to clean your car tomorrow.
b You see dark clouds in the sky.
c The weather next week.

d Your dinner tonight – salmon and salad already in the fridge.

e Your government – a solution to pollution by the year 2050.

f Your future job in 10 years' time.

g An airline timetable – Singapore 6.00 Fridays.

4 The following expressions are used to express probability:

- *to be bound to* + infinitive
- *to be certain to* + infinitive
- *to be likely/unlikely to* + infinitive

Using a suitable tense or one of the expressions above, talk to your partner about the following:

a The effects the growth in the speed of travel will have on your life.

b The goals you will have achieved by the middle of the century.

c It's your English friend's first day on holiday in your town. Tell him/her what to expect.

5 The following expressions can be used for the very near future.

- *to be about to* + infinitive – more informal use, everyday situations and spoken English
- *to be on the brink of* + noun; *to be on the point/ verge of* + gerund/noun – more formal use, usually in written English

EXAMPLE: *The government is on the brink of collapse.*

She was on the verge of bursting into tears.

I'm about to make a cup of coffee.

Make sentences using one of the expressions above and including one of these words or phrases. Think carefully about formal/informal use.

disaster	leave home	get married
bed	extinction	revolution
a scientific breakthrough		

Vocabulary
Prepositional phrases

6 Complete sentences a–i with the following prepositional phrases. (Use each phrase once only.)

in the region of	on behalf of
on the brink of	in vain on the verge of
to some extent	on the grounds (of)/(that)
in conjunction with	with the exception of

a The judge closed the club .... there was too much noise being made.

b The speech to the assembly was made .... the Prime Minister who, unfortunately, couldn't attend.

c I think you, ..., bear some responsibility for making her leave home.

d Tom was .... downloading the file when he realised it might have a virus attached.

e The journalist reported that the city was .... a crisis.

f The staff pay rise was .... 3%.

g Tom looked .... for the photos he had put away in the attic.

h The book was released .... a TV special and a DVD.

i Everyone here, ... Agnes and Liam, has tickets for the trip.

Have no ...

7 *Have* is often used in expressions with an abstract noun with *no*. With a partner, use these expressions to say what is true for you. Take care with prepositions.

EXAMPLE: I don't object to staying at home instead of travelling abroad.

I have no objection to staying at home instead of travelling abroad. No, this isn't true for me. I really enjoy going on holidays and dislike having to stay at home.

a I'm not interested in going somewhere like Las Vegas.

b I don't regret spending too much money on my last holiday.

c I can't remember childhood holidays.

d I wouldn't hesitate to book a cruise.

e I will have to stay at home this year rather than go away.

f I don't intend to ever go to Disneyland.

g I don't have time to look at lots of travel brochures.

 Exam spot

Parts 1–4 of Reading and Use of English test a broad range of vocabulary, so you should learn vocabulary in an organised way. Write down new words and phrases in your vocabulary notebook under headings such as *prepositional phrases*, *adjective–noun collocations*, *phrasal verbs* and so on. Try to include an example sentence to show meaning and usage.

In Part 1 of Speaking you may be asked questions about your expectations and ambitions in life. Here you are going to hear three short extracts which are all concerned in some way with expectations.

1 The words and phrases in italics below occur in the extracts. Before you listen, work with a partner and explain their meaning.

  a Conservative ideas about women in the workplace really *get my goat*.
  b I got a bit *carried away* when I went shopping and spent far too much money.
  c How much did you *fork out* for your new shoes?
  d The credit card bill was pretty *hefty* this month – I'll have to watch my step in future.
  e My sister was on a *tight* budget when she was at college.
  f She let her imagination *run wild* when she painted her room.
  g I'm *dead set on* going to university and getting my degree.
  h His ideas for expanding the company are very much *in line with* mine.

2 **1 03** You will hear three different people talking about their expectations. For each extract, choose the answer (A, B or C) which fits best according to what you hear.

Extract One

You hear a woman talking about her expectations of a round-the-world trip. How does the speaker say she felt when planning her trip?

A shocked by the potential cost
B happy to make compromises
C doubtful whether she could go

Extract Two

You hear a student talking about someone who has influenced him. What does he think is the most important factor in becoming successful?

A having a supportive family
B having academic qualifications
C having high expectations of yourself

Extract Three

You hear a radio newsreader talking about a new survey of young people. What does he say about young people's expectations now?

A They continue to rise with their age.
B They are slightly more realistic than previously.
C They are different to those of a previous generation.

🌀 Phrase spot

In the first listening extract, the speaker said:
I didn't intend to be thumbing lifts.

If you 'thumb a lift', you signal with your thumb for a vehicle to stop and give you a free lift. Many nouns for parts of the body have related verbs that are used in phrases or idioms.

Match the verbs 1–6 with a–f to form phrases or idioms. Which verb can be used twice?

1 elbow	a the burden
2 face	b the bill
3 foot	c the idea
4 shoulder	d the line
5 stomach	e the music
6 toe	f people aside

Use the phrases to complete these sentences, changing the verb form where necessary.
a It is part of a manager's job to .... of complaints made by guests.
b Don't worry about paying for your hotel – I'm happy to ....
c On his return to Canada, he finally .... and told his wife about his debts.
d At the resort, I always .... on company policy, even if I disagreed with it.
e Jenny couldn't really .... of moving to a big city, so she turned the job down.
f The woman .... in the queue so she could get on the plane first.

3 Discuss these questions with a partner.

a Do you have much opportunity to travel? Where would you go if you had the choice?

b How would you feel about a round-the-world trip?

c What are your expectations of a job and salary?

d How important to you is it to do well academically?

e How do you feel about the idea of becoming an entrepreneur?

f What would your priorities be if you were bringing up children?

Pronunciation

4 A homophone is a word which is pronounced in the same way as another word but has a different meaning or a different spelling or both, for example *they're/their/there*.

Replace the wrong word in each of the sentences with its homophone and write a sentence which shows how the other word is used.

EXAMPLE: I don't ~~no~~ *know* what to expect from this new government.

> *There were no strawberries in the market today.*

a Can you tell me the weigh to the centre of town, please?

b How many pears of trousers do you own?

c Let's meat for lunch tomorrow.

d His new girlfriend is air to a fortune.

e Walking down the isle was the scariest thing Ellen had ever done.

f The school principle is going to speak to everyone at midday.

g Great the cheese over the vegetables and bake for twenty minutes.

h The horse tossed its main and neighed.

i This fish bar does the best place and chips in town.

Writing folder 1

Part 1 Essay

Part 1 is the compulsory question on Writing. You have to write an essay based on two short texts, which either present opposing or complementary viewpoints. There will be two main points in each text. You must summarise and evaluate the ideas expressed, using your own words as far as possible and adding your own ideas on the topic where relevant.

The essay should be between 240 and 280 words in length. Remember that you will only have 90 minutes to complete the whole of Writing, so use your time wisely. It is better to spend some time planning what you are going to write, rather than attempting to do a rough copy of a whole answer.

1 Read the two texts below and say whether they contain opposing or complementary ideas about museums today.

Text 1

Even in our information-rich digital age, when there are diverse ways of occupying our leisure time, museums continue to play a fundamental role in society. Over the last decade in particular, museums have become more community-orientated, and the majority seek to be inclusive rather than elitist, reaching out to everyone. This change of heart has necessitated a degree of creativity in the presentation of information. Objects rarely 'speak for themselves' and, where a low reading age must often be assumed, museum curators have looked to modern technology to breathe more life into exhibits, whether through interactive techniques, or accompanying audio-visual effects.

Text 2

The purpose of a museum is to stimulate learning and broaden the horizons of its visitors, yet many museums nowadays appear to neglect this responsibility in an attempt to entertain rather than educate. The dumbing down of exhibitions is widespread – in short, the medium has become more important than the message. Learning is all too often compromised by technological wizardry, which may impress on a superficial level but essentially trivialises, and provides a content-lite 'experience'. Whether this is in response to government cuts or merely reflects a trend among museum directors, it is undoubtedly a change for the worse.

2 Decide on the four main points that are covered in the texts, choosing from a–f. Underline the parts of each text that confirm your choices.

a Given the wealth of information online, museums are no longer relevant.

b Judicious use of technology has made museums more accessible to the public.

c Many museums create innovative displays but this is at the expense of substance.

d Museums have had to reduce the number of objects displayed due to a lack of funds.

e In contrast to their former position in society, museums now seek to engage a wider audience.

f The recent shift in policy is undesirable as museums have lost sight of their core role in society.

3　Using the sentence openers below, rewrite your four choices
　　from a–f in 2, in your own words.

　　The first text suggests that …
　　The second text raises the issue of …
　　The writer is of the opinion that …
　　Additionally, it is argued that …

4　Read the sample answer below, thinking about these questions.

　　Does the writer
　　☐ summarise all four points from the texts?
　　☐ evaluate each of the four points?
　　☐ use their own words throughout?
　　☐ add relevant ideas of their own?

EXAM ADVICE

- Read the texts carefully.
- Underline the four key points.
- Decide how far you agree with these points.
- List some relevant ideas of your own.
- Plan your answer in four or five paragraphs.
- Select one or two important phrases to quote from the texts.
- Remember to use your own words where possible.

> The texts consider the role of museums in our modern world. Both texts identify a
> shift in museum policy, which has had an impact on how museums are seen by the
> general public.
>
> 　The first text views museums positively and the writer suggests that a real
> attempt has been made to attract a more diverse audience. In order to support
> this, museum curators have had to come up with alternative ways of displaying
> the objects in their possession and have relied on new technology to "breathe more
> life" into them. This is an interesting point of view that justifies the use of innovative
> technology as a way of engaging people's interest in museum exhibits, especially
> those who are less literate.
>
> 　In contrast, the second text raises the issue of "dumbing down" and its writer
> claims that those in charge of museums have lost their way. They have forgotten
> that the purpose of a museum is to stimulate learning and broaden the horizons
> of its visitors and the writer is of the opinion that this is a change for the worse,
> because the medium has become more important than the message.
>
> 　The first text outlines how museums have taken steps to maintain their role in
> our "information-rich digital age", while the second text complains about the use of
> technology in museums nowadays.

5　Rewrite the second sentence of Paragraph 3 in your own words.
　　You may find some of this alternative vocabulary useful.

　　purpose – aim, function, objective
　　stimulate – encourage, promote
　　a change for the worse – less desirable, an unfortunate outcome
　　the medium – the method of delivery
　　the message – the subject matter, the content

6　Write a final paragraph of about 60 words, including your own
　　ideas about the points made in the texts.

3.1 Strange behaviour

Speaking

1 Look at the following sayings about the weather and discuss them with a partner. Do you think they are true? Do you have similar sayings in your country? Do sayings such as these have any place in our modern world?

- Red sky at night, shepherd's delight, Red sky in the morning, shepherd's warning.
- Cows lying in the field means rain is on its way.

Listening

2 **1 04** You are going to hear a writer called Peter Watkins being interviewed by the programme presenter, Sue Manchester. He is talking about his book, which discusses the behaviour of animals and birds in relation to the weather.

For questions a–j decide whether these statements are true or false.

a Sue has little faith in the accuracy of sayings about the weather.

b Peter says that nowadays people are less interested in sayings than in previous times.

c Peter says that low-flying birds suffer badly in storms.

d Peter believes that there is a logical explanation for why certain birds change their habits.

e According to Peter, insects have difficulty in sensing changes in the atmosphere.

f Sue concludes that the rain goose's behaviour is surprising.

g Peter says that weather sayings used to be confined to the farming community.

h Peter says that the sayings fulfilled a basic human need for control.

i Sue agrees with Peter about the contradictory nature of some of the sayings.

j Peter says that in the past people relied on animal and bird behaviour to predict the weather.

Phrase spot

In the recording, Peter Watkins uses the phrase: *life and death*.

Pairs of words used like this are fixed – you cannot say *death and life*.

Using a dictionary to help you, decide whether these pairs are in the right order and explain how you would use these phrases.

give and take	black and white
again and time	thick and thin
high and dry	go and touch
fortune and fame	blood and flesh
first and foremost	soul and life

Complete the sentences below with the correct phrase.

a Jenny promised to live with Nigel through ....

b When Joe was 18 he left home to find ....

c It was .... whether we would get to the airport in time.

d .... , we need to solve the budget problem and then we can move on to other issues.

e .... , we see this pattern of behaviour repeating itself.

f There needs to be a bit of .... in every relationship.

g My brother James is the .... of any family party.

h My aunt treats her relatives really badly, considering they are her own ....

i When the company closed down I was left .... without a job.

j How could you not understand? Look at this letter – it's all there in ....

Vocabulary

Modifiers

3 Both speakers in the recording used words such as *quite*, *rather* and *fairly*, which are adverbs of degree, to modify what they were saying.

- *fairly* means 'moderately'
- *rather* can be used before negative adjectives to mean 'moderately'; it can also be used before positive adjectives to mean 'more than expected'
- *quite* has a variety of meanings, ranging from 'moderately' to 'totally', depending on the tone of voice that is used.

1 05 Listen to some sentences which include *quite* being read and then match the speakers 1–5 with the appropriate meaning, a or b.

a totally   b moderately

> Note that *quite* means 'fairly' before a gradable adjective. These are adjectives which can be modified, such as *good*, *clever*, *helpful*. *Quite* means 'completely' before an ungradable adjective. Ungradable adjectives are those which can't be modified, such as *fantastic*, *brilliant*, *dreadful*, etc.
>
> **G → page 184**

4 Use the following adjectives and the adverb of degree specified to talk about the sayings below.

- to be dubious of/about; cautious about; sceptical of (use *rather*)
- mystified by/about; annoyed by/about; convinced by/about (use *quite* meaning 'completely')
- certain of/about (use *fairly*)

EXAMPLE: Youth is wasted on the young.

> *I'm quite mystified by what is meant by 'Youth is wasted on the young'. After all, young people usually make the most of the time they are young. I think this is just something old people think because they're jealous.*

a Money is the root of all evil.

b Early to bed, early to rise, makes a man healthy, wealthy and wise.

c If you give a man a fish you feed him for a day, but teach him to fish and you feed him for life.

d A friend in need is a friend indeed.

e Don't count your chickens before they are hatched.

Exam spot

In Reading and Use of English, Part 2, make sure you read through the whole text before attempting to fill in the spaces. Quite often the answer to a space is dependent on information later on in the passage.

5 Read through the article quickly, ignoring the spaces for now. What is the article about?

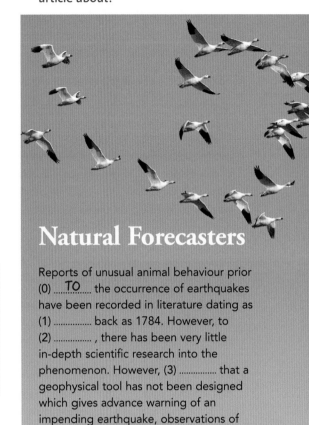

Natural Forecasters

Reports of unusual animal behaviour prior (0) ....TO.... the occurrence of earthquakes have been recorded in literature dating as (1) .... back as 1784. However, to (2) .... , there has been very little in-depth scientific research into the phenomenon. However, (3) .... that a geophysical tool has not been designed which gives advance warning of an impending earthquake, observations of animal behaviour might (4) .... out to be a useful tool.

Animals and birds could act as geosensors. It is well known that the Earth's electromagnetic field is used by birds and fish as an aid to navigation and migration. Sharks (5) .... use of low or high frequency electro-receptors to detect objects and to communicate. Perhaps it is time to (6) .... this sensitivity to good use?

Animals may have the means to understand the signal that says 'leave this place' or 'fly-away now' or (7) .... is necessary to survive the coming catastrophe. It comes (8) .... no surprise, therefore, that animals have the potential to act as accurate geosensors, to detect earthquakes before they occur.

6 Read the article again and decide where the following words should go.

whatever	far	as	given
make	put	turn	date

Review of conditional clauses

1 How does the weather affect your mood? Do you think people's characters are influenced by where they live and the weather they are used to? Give some examples.

2 Read this article about the effect of the wind on mood.

There's an old English saying: *When the wind is in the east, 'tis good for neither man nor beast*. Whether you believe in folklore or not, this one's got a grain of truth in it. Winds have been associated with a rise in the levels of serotonin, a compound which occurs in the brain and which controls mood, sleep and blood circulation. This rise in serotonin has been found to occur in the Swiss population during a Föhn wind. The Föhn is said to be responsible for traffic accidents rising by fifty per cent and a rise in industrial injuries by twenty per cent.

It's not only the Swiss who suffer. Los Angeles is occasionally buffeted by the Santa Ana, a hot dry wind named after the canyon it sometimes blows through. One study found that murders rose by up to a half during a Santa Ana, no matter if it blew during winter or summer. In California's early days, defendants in crimes of passion were able to plead for leniency, citing the wind as an extenuating circumstance.

The quality of the air can be a force for good, however. The Victorians especially prized sea air for its health-giving properties. Sea air is charged with negative ions which makes it feel invigorating. To get a similar effect you can stand next to a waterfall, or even under a domestic shower.

Now, with a partner, complete the sentences using information from the article.

a When the Föhn blows, …
b If you go to the seaside, …
c Even if the Santa Ana blew at a different time to normal, …
d I wouldn't have murdered my wife …
e You are less likely to have an accident if …
f If I were you, …

3 What kind of conditional is used in each sentence in 2? When do we use these forms?

EXAMPLE: People can be adversely affected if a certain wind is blowing. *Zero conditional (present tense + present tense). This is used to express a universal truth or habitual action.*

◎ Corpus spot

The *Cambridge Learner Corpus* shows that even at C2 level, learners still make mistakes with basic conditional clauses. Be careful to use the right tense and check whether a negative or positive verb form is needed. The learner example below contains a common mistake – what is it?

EXAMPLE: *If someone treats these two things equally, he can easily succeed in both, unless he does not succumb to the temptation of laziness.*

G → pages 179–180

4 There are other forms of the conditional besides the four basic patterns. Look at the following examples and discuss how they are formed and what they express.

EXAMPLE: But for my father's help, I wouldn't have been able to complete my course.

'But for' is used in third conditional sentences and has the meaning of 'If it hadn't been for'.

a Should you happen to see Lucy, tell her to ring me.

b If you would sit down, I'm sure Mr Peterson will see you soon.

c I'll diet if you will.

d You can borrow the money from me as long as you pay me back.

e Had I known about the weather conditions, I wouldn't have ventured out.

f Provided that you tell the truth, nothing will happen to you.

g You could be a lot thinner now, if you hadn't given up your diet so easily.

h Were the Prime Minister to announce lower tax increases, the country would be delighted.

i You can't come unless you have an invitation.

5 *If* isn't the only conjunction used in conditional sentences. Complete the sentences using the following conjunctions.

given that	on condition that
but for / without	even if
provided that / as long as	suppose/supposing
unless	

a .... lightning tends to strike the nearest high point, you would do well not to stand under a tall tree during a thunderstorm.

b .... you learn to drive better, I won't be getting in your car again.

c .... you use a sun screen, you shouldn't get burnt.

d .... the support of my boss, I wouldn't have been promoted.

e .... you do say you love me, I'm not marrying you.

f I'll give you a lift to school .... you wash the car for me at the weekend.

g .... there was an air traffic controllers' strike, what would you do?

6 Rewrite each sentence, beginning with the words in italics, without changing the meaning.

EXAMPLE: I didn't drown because my instructor knew how to help me.
Had my instructor not known how to help me, I would have drowned.

a Could you tell her my address if, by any chance, you see her.
Should ....

b As people were dependent on farming for their livelihood, it's not surprising that they used animal behaviour to predict the weather.
Given that ....

c You can borrow my bike but you must take care of it.
Provided that ....

d Kindly have a seat as I'm sure Mr Johnson won't be long.
If ....

e My advice to you is to get another job.
If ....

f I'm not earning much money because I didn't work hard enough to pass my diploma.
If ....

g I wouldn't have been able to afford to go to university except that my grandmother left me some money.
But for ....

h Climatic changes may, in due course, render weather lore obsolete.
Were ....

Speaking

7 In groups, ask and answer these questions.

What will you do if

a you can't get home tonight?

b you get more homework than you expect?

c your Internet stops working?

d the fire alarm goes?

What would you do if you

e won the lottery?

f lost your mobile?

g were on a plane which was hijacked?

h had the chance to take six months' holiday?

What would you have done if you'd

i been born with a mathematical or musical gift?

j been given the opportunity to study in the USA?

k been born poor?

1 What makes you angry? Look at this list. With a partner, put them in order with the most infuriating at the top. Justify your decisions.

a People talking loudly on their mobiles
b Being overtaken by a sports car
c Rude shop assistants
d Computers that keep crashing
e Jokes which are in bad taste
f Poor government decisions
g Being overcharged

2 The nouns in the box express extreme emotions. Decide which emotion (a–f) they express.

rage	dejection	revulsion	tedium
bliss	sorrow	fury	dread
incredulity	terror	loathing	astonishment
apathy	delight		

EXAMPLE: disgust – *revulsion, loathing*

a anger   d sadness
b fear   e surprise
c happiness   f boredom

3 Read through the article below on anger and answer the questions that follow.

New psychological research suggests that air rage, road rage and other seemingly irrational outbursts of wild-eyed, foaming–at-the-mouth fury could be extreme responses to the violation of a set of unwritten rules that choreographs our every waking moment without our even realising it. Apparently, we walk around in a sort of invisible bubble which is egg-shaped – this is because we allow people to come closer from in front than from behind – an entire language is expressed via the amount of distance we choose to keep between each other. In northern Europe and North America (lovers, close friends and wrestling partners aside) the average depth of the bubble is about a metre. When it's intruded upon the physiological responses can range from feelings of mild annoyance and tension to a pounding heart, raised blood pressure, sweating and severe anxiety. Tension levels increase hugely when someone comes too close and you get a feeling of being invaded, and responses fall into two categories. The first kind are blocking tactics when you avert your gaze, put your hand up at the side of your head or just make yourself immobile; then there are the tension and anxiety-reduction responses, hair-pulling, foot-tapping, getting red in the face and ultimately leaving the scene.

1 Where do you think you would read this article? What evidence is there to support your decision?
   A in a magazine or newspaper
   B in a psychology textbook
   C in an advertisement
   D in a health awareness leaflet

2 Why does the writer describe air and road rage as 'seemingly irrational'?

3 List both the inward and the outward signs which may occur when one's space is invaded.

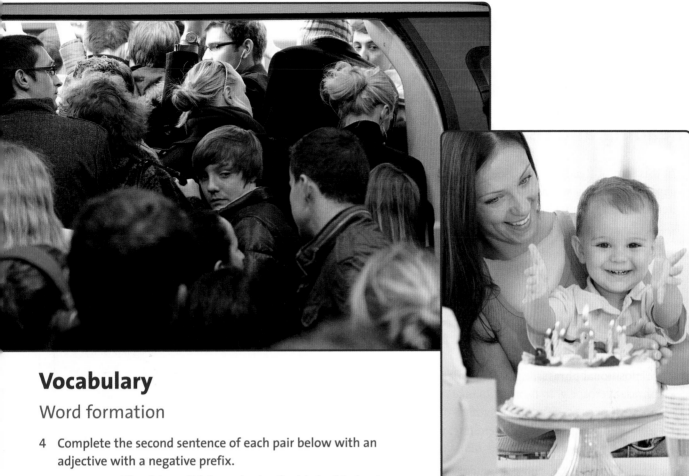

Vocabulary

Word formation

4 Complete the second sentence of each pair below with an adjective with a negative prefix.

EXAMPLE: The driver didn't apologise for his bad behaviour.

The driver was unapologetic about his bad behaviour.

a It's very hard to predict the results of the meeting, I'm afraid.

The outcome of the meeting is .... , I'm afraid.

b You can't deny that global warming is becoming a real threat.

It is .... that global warming is becoming a real threat.

c There is a real need to raise consciousness about the influence of the media on our lives.

Many of us are still largely .... of the influence of the media on our lives and this needs to change.

d The damage to the car was of no significance.

There was an .... amount of damage to the car.

e It won't be possible to replace that vase, I'm afraid.

Unfortunately, that vase is ....

f My father never seemed to exhaust his supply of jokes.

My father seemed to have an .... supply of jokes.

g Liz never tries to assert herself in tricky situations.

Liz is a very .... type of person.

h The solicitor's advice didn't help me form any conclusions about my situation.

The solicitor's advice was rather .... about my situation.

 Exam spot

In Part 1 of Writing, you will need to summarise some information. Summarising will use new language and not incorporate large amounts of the original. It is important to manipulate words, especially as you have to write a summary within a set word limit. One way of doing this is to use a negative adjective.

5 Read through the text in 3 again and then write a summary sentence using no more than 18 words. Where possible, try to use different words from the ones in the text and try to use some of the vocabulary from 2 and 4.

Exam folder 2

Reading and Use of English, Part 2 Open cloze

In this part of Reading and Use of English, you will be asked to complete a text which has eight numbered gaps. The missing words will have a mainly grammatical focus, although there might be a few vocabulary items. Each gap must be filled with **one word only** and must be correctly spelled.

It is very important to read through the whole text carefully before you decide to write anything down. Some answers may be dependent on a sentence which comes later in the text. Awareness of the writer's train of thought and logical argument is often tested at Proficiency level.

The areas which are often tested are:

- fixed phrases, e.g. *as a rule, to all extent and purposes*
- relative pronouns, e.g. *who, which*
- linkers, e.g. *moreover, let alone*
- prepositional phrases, e.g. *out of order*
- phrasal verbs, e.g. *to turn up, to take over*
- prepositions, e.g. *result in, regardless of*
- collocations, e.g. *seriously interesting, widely read*
- reflexive pronouns, e.g. *myself, himself*
- articles, e.g. *the, a*
- comparison, e.g. *fewer, many*

EXAM ADVICE

- First of all read through the whole article carefully and go back and decide which type of word is missing from each gap, e.g. a verb, a noun or a preposition, etc.
- Make sure that your word makes sense in the text and fits grammatically.
- Use only one word in each gap.
- Write your answers in CAPITAL LETTERS on your answer sheet.

Example: 0 AS

Read the Exam advice and then do the task.

Read the text below about French photographer Henri Cartier-Bresson and think of the word which best fits each gap. Use only **one** word in each gap. There is an example at the beginning (**0**). Write your answers **IN CAPITAL LETTERS**.

Example: **0** | A | S | | | | | | | | | | | | | | | | | | | |

HENRI CARTIER-BRESSON

Henri Cartier-Bresson helped establish photojournalism (**0**) ....AS.... an art form. He believed that photography (**1**) .... capture the meaning of outward appearance and so his camera accompanied him (**2**) .... he went in the world.

In his twenties, he travelled in Africa, recording his experiences with a 35-millimetre Leica. Its portability and the ease with (**3**) .... one could record instantaneous impressions were hugely advantageous. This type of camera was particularly relevant to Cartier-Bresson. It lent (**4**) .... not only to spontaneity but to anonymity as well. To such an extent (**5**) .... Cartier-Bresson wish to remain a silent, and even unseen, witness, that he covered the bright chromium parts of his camera with black tape to render it less visible.

Cartier-Bresson travelled unceasingly, but there was (**6**) .... compulsive or hurried about his travels or his photography. One story tells of how Cartier-Bresson was present during the student riots in Paris in 1968. Undeterred (**7**) .... the explosive nature of the riots, he continued to take photographs at the (**8**) .... of about four per hour.

Reading and Use of English, Part 4 Key word transformations

There are six key word transformations in Reading and Use of English, Part 4. Read the Exam advice and then complete the exam task.

Complete the second sentence so that it has a similar meaning to the first sentence, using the word given. **Do not change the word given**. You must use between **three** and **eight** words, including the word given. Here is an example (**0**).

Example:

0 It's unlikely that the product would have taken off, if they hadn't run such a massive TV campaign.

likelihood

Without such a massive TV campaign, there
.... the product taking off.

0	WOULD HAVE BEEN LITTLE LIKELIHOOD OF

EXAM ADVICE

- Read both sentences very carefully.
- Make sure that you actually use the word given and that you don't change its form in any way.
- Don't add anything which isn't necessary.
- Make sure your sentence means the same as the first sentence.
- You will often need to use the words in the first sentence in a different form. For example, you may have to change a verb to a noun.
- Remember to count the number of words you write. Contractions count as two words.

---

1 The group leader's poor judgement jeopardised the safety of the climbers.

put

The climbers' safety .... by the poor judgement of the group leader.

2 Paula and I have been friends since 2008.

dates

My .... to 2008.

3 'It wasn't my fault that the window got broken,' Gary said.

responsibility

Gary denied .... the window.

4 My grandmother has finally got used to living alone.

terms

My grandmother .... living alone.

5 I am not expecting an increase in summer sales this year.

upturn

I have .... in summer sales this year.

6 The students were told to either keep quiet or leave the art gallery.

no

The students .... keep quiet or leave the art gallery.

4.1 Sweet rituals

1 Identify the ritual that is taking place in each picture. How common are ceremonies like these where you live? Give another example of ritual behaviour involving special food or drink.

2 **1 06** Listen to a man talking about ritual family meals. What happens before the event and on the day itself? Describe a family gathering you have had to attend.

Reading

3 This extract is from the novel *Reef* by Romesh Gunesekera, a Sri Lankan author. Read it once to form an overall impression. What is the relationship between the narrator and Mister Salgado?

Before Miss Nili first came to our house on the *poya*-holiday of April 1969, Mister Salgado only said to me, 'A lady is coming to tea.' As if a lady came to tea every week. It had never happened before in his life, or mine, and yet he acted as if it were the most
5 natural thing in the world. Luckily he gave me some warning. He was concerned to make sure there was plenty of time to prepare, even though he acted so nonchalant. I made everything – little coconut cakes, patties, egg sandwiches, ham sandwiches, cucumber sandwiches, even *love-cake* … I made enough for a horse. It was just
10 as well: she ate like a horse. I don't know where she put it; she was so skinny then. So hungry-looking. I expected her to bulge out as she ate, like a snake swallowing a bird. But she just sat there on the cane chair, one leg coiled under her, her back straight and her face floating happily in the warm afternoon haze while huge chunks of the richest,
15 juiciest love-cake disappeared into her as into a cavern.
'You like cake?' he asked her stupidly.
She made a lowing sound between bites. It made him happy, and although I didn't approve of her being quite so uninhibited so soon in our house, I was touched too.
20 'Where did you get this, this cake?' Her lips glistened with my butter, and one corner of her mouth had a line of golden semolina crumbs which smudged into a dimple as she spoke.
'Triton made it,' my Mister Salgado said. *Triton made it.* It was the one phrase he would say with my name again and again like a
25 refrain through those months, giving me such happiness. *Triton made it.* Clear, pure and unstinting. His voice at those moments would be a channel cut from heaven to earth right through the petrified morass of all our lives, releasing a blessing like water springing from a river-head, from a god's head. It was bliss. My coming of age.
30 'Your cook? He makes a lovely cake,' she said, endearing herself to me for the rest of my life.
After tea she said she had to go. I went to get a taxi for her. She stayed with him alone in the house while I went up to the main road. It didn't take long. A black tortoise of a taxi with a butter-coloured
35 top came along, and I rode in it like a prince back to the house. The driver croaked the old horn warning them of our approach. We rolled in right up to the porch. I got out and held the door open while Mister Salgado helped her in. 'Bye-bye,' she said to him and then turned to me. 'That cake was *really* good.'
40 The taxi rolled down to the gate and veered to the left. The wheels wobbled, making the whitewalls around the rim go fuzzy. Mister Salgado watched the vehicle slowly disappear.
'The lady ate well,' I said brightly.
'Yes.'
'Sir, the love-cake was good? *Really* good?' 45
'Yes.'
'And the patties also she liked?'
'They were good.'
They were more than good. I knew, because I can feel it inside me when I get it right. It's a kind of energy that revitalises every 50
cell in my body. Suddenly everything becomes possible and the whole world, that before seemed slowly to be coming apart at the seams, pulls together. But however confident I was about the perfection of what I produced, like everybody else, I needed praise. I needed his praise and I needed her praise. I felt stupid to need it, 55 but I did.
She came again the following *poya*-day and then regularly almost every weekend after that for months. I made mutton patties and a small cake every time, and she always said how wonderful they were. Mister Salgado ate nothing: he watched her eat as if he were 60 feeding an exotic bird. He drank tea. He always drank lots of tea: estate-fresh, up-country broken orange pekoe tip-top tea. He looked completely content when she was there. His face would be bright, his mouth slightly open with the tips of his teeth just showing. It was as if he couldn't believe his eyes, seeing Nili sitting there in 65 front of him. I would bring the patties in four at a time, fried only after she arrived to ensure they came fresh and hot-hot, straight from the pan. When she finished the last of the first batch, I would wait a minute before bringing in a second plate. 'Nice and hot-hot, Missy,' I would say, and she would murmur her approval. After she 70 finished a couple of the new patties, I would come again with fresh tea. 'More patties?' She would shake her head – I would always ask when her mouth was full. This allowed Mister Salgado to speak on her behalf. 'No, bring the cake now.' It was our little ritual. I would nod, she would smile and he would look longingly. I would 75 give her enough time to savour the aftertaste of the patties and feel the glow of coriander inside her. Let the tea slip down to cleanse her palate and subdue the nerves that had been excited by the spice and fattened by the meat, and only then bring out the cake on a small salver for Mister Salgado to cut. 80

4 Now read the text carefully to answer questions 1–6.

1 What was Mister Salgado's state of mind before his first tea-party with Miss Nili?

A He felt confident, as it was a role he was accustomed to performing.

B He appeared relaxed, but inwardly, he was worrying about the event.

C He wished he had told his cook about the visit more in advance.

D He became nervous about his cook's obvious lack of experience.

2 What effect did Miss Nili's large appetite have on the narrator?

A He felt rather sorry for her because she was so hungry.

B He suspected that she was hiding some of the food.

C He had mixed feelings about her unconventional way of eating.

D He thought she should take more care when she ate.

3 Why did the narrator derive so much satisfaction when he heard the phrase 'Triton made it'?

A It gave him a sense of purpose in his life.

B Mister Salgado said the phrase so rarely.

C Miss Nili didn't believe the cake was home-made.

D The words improved the atmosphere at the tea-party.

4 How did the narrator feel about his taxi ride back to the house?

A He was annoyed that it was such a slow vehicle.

B He was concerned about Miss Nili during his absence.

C He appreciated being helped out of the taxi.

D He enjoyed the relative luxury of the experience.

5 What do we learn about the narrator in the penultimate paragraph?

A His successes in the kitchen dictated his general mood.

B He thought it reasonable to expect praise for his cooking.

C He knew he would benefit from some help in preparing the food.

D His feelings had been hurt by Nili and Mister Salgado.

6 Which phrase best describes Mister Salgado's behaviour at subsequent tea-parties?

A feverishly eating and drinking

B full of praise for Triton's wonderful efforts

C slightly incredulous at Nili's regular presence

D nervously monitoring the supply of food

Vocabulary

Collocations

5 Explain the precise meaning of the words in italics below.

I would give her enough time to *savour the aftertaste* of the patties …

Savour is a verb that is commonly used in other contexts apart from food. Underline the nouns or noun phrases that collocate with this verb in a–e.

EXAMPLE: At 37, the Oscar-nominated actress is savouring every <u>moment</u> of her new status.

a After years in the wilderness, the band were finally savouring success.

b His father, Pat, should have been savouring freedom alongside them, but had died in prison.

c She has decided to retire at 33 and savour the memories of her career.

d Its more recent past can be savoured just by wandering aimlessly through the streets.

e Laurence was now savouring every word quite as much as the wine.

6 Identify the collocations by matching each verb to two nouns from the box. Write a sentence for each one.

a consume **c** relish
b devour **d** swallow

books	challenge	equivalent
news	pill	pride
quantity	thought	time

EXAMPLE *consume + equivalent*

Each of us consumes the equivalent of two trees a year in paper use alone.

1 What implements would people have been using 2,000 years ago when eating their food? How long ago was the first metal cutlery made, do you think? Why has the recent design of the Swedish 'spork' proved so successful (see picture below)?

2 Read the text, ignoring any underlining. Then explain briefly how the appearance and use of the fork has changed over the past 400 years.

Fork-like implements for spearing food <u>have been used for over 2000 years</u>. For example, the Ancient Romans <u>used to use special spoons</u> with one prong or two at the end of the handle for winkling out shellfish.

5 The first 'modern' fork is thought to have been used in the eleventh century by the wife of the Venetian Doge. Forks are mentioned again three centuries later, in 1361, in an inventory of the plate owned by the Florentine Commune. However, the first real evidence

10 that forks had spread as eating tools came some two hundred years later, in a 1570 engraving of a knife, fork and spoon. In 1605, King Henri III of France and his companions were satirised for their fork-wielding effeminacy. 'They would rather touch their mouths

15 with their little forked instruments than with their fingers,' wrote Thomas Artus, who claimed that they looked especially silly as they strove to capture the peas and broad beans on their plates – <u>as well they might have done</u>, since early forks had long, widely

20 separate prongs and <u>scooping with them must have been impossible</u>.

On returning home from Italy in 1611, the Englishman Thomas Coryat bore the news that he had seen forks in Italy and had decided to adopt them. The reason

25 for the Italian custom was, he explained, that these extremely fastidious, ultra-modern people considered that any fingering of the meat that was being carved at table was a transgression against the laws of good manners,

30 'seeing all men's fingers are not alike cleane'.

However, even Coryat did not regard forks as being for eating with, but for holding the meat in place while carving.

Although in the course of the seventeenth century there was some use of individual forks, <u>people would 35 more often share forks with others</u>, wiping them carefully on their napkins as they would spoons. It was only in the nineteenth century that eating with a fork truly began to proliferate, and at this time there were important modifications to its basic 40 design. Craftsmen had been making forks with three prongs, but these were now shortened, moved closer together, and a fourth 'tine' commonly added. With the fork's design in transition, one-handed eating was increasingly in vogue: <u>the knife was put down once 45 the food had been cut up</u> and the fork was then used to take the food to the mouth. Diners with yet more elaborate manners sought to perform this manoeuvre for every mouthful consumed. This form of 'zig-zag' eating was still customary among the French 50 bourgeoisie in the 1880s, though the English were successfully introducing a new fashion, where the knife was kept in the right hand and the fork held in the left, much as we have been doing ever since.

3 Find examples of the following ways of talking about the past, choosing from the underlined parts of the text and completing statements a–d.

a reference to an earlier point in past time, using the .... tense

b two ways of referring to habitual past action: .... and ....

c two examples of speculating about the past, using ....

d talking about something that continues to be true today, using the .... tense

Find the following past forms or form elsewhere in the text and explain the choice of tense or form.

e one past passive infinitive

f two different past tenses in the passive

g three different continuous tenses

h four irregular past verb forms in the active (name their infinitives)

 G → page 180

G → page 180

Exam spot

Proficiency texts are bound to contain words you don't know, so you need to develop ways of guessing meaning from context clues.

4 Line 43 contains the technical term *tine*. Work out its meaning by looking at the words around it. Which words help you?

Now explain the meaning of these words and phrases.

a implements (line 1)
b inventory (line 8)
c effeminacy (line 14)
d scooping (line 20)
e fastidious (line 26)
f transgression (line 29)
g in place (line 32)
h proliferate (line 39)
i in transition (line 44)
j in vogue (line 45)

5 Complete these sentences using the verbs in brackets in a suitable tense. Sometimes you will need to use a passive (P) or a modal (M).

a In seventeenth century France, a nobleman's education .... (think: P) to be incomplete until he .... (master) the art of carving.

b From the sixteenth century, women seem to .... (carve) meat at British tables, though by the mid-nineteenth century, carving at formal meals .... (carry out: P) mainly by servants.

c The French .... (insist + *always*) that salad .... (tear: M + P) rather than cut with a knife, a rule which probably .... (arise) in order to eliminate the taste of metal – lettuce .... (dress: P) with oil and vinegar or lemon, which .... (react: M) with some metals.

d Arriving in Athens pursued by the Furies because he .... (murder) his mother, Orestes .... (give: P) dinner, but so horrified were the other diners that they .... (eat) in silence and .... (drink) from a separate pitcher.

e Although live-in household staff .... (continue) to be the norm in America up until the 1920s, their numbers .... (start) to decline in Europe much earlier.

f For the last hundred years, the separate tiers of a British wedding cake .... (support: P) by pillars, although more recently, upturned champagne glasses .... (choose: P) by some couples as a variant.

6 The text refers to *fork-like* implements and *fork-wielding* effeminacy. Combining words like this helps to show your language range. Answer these questions.

1 Who or what might be *spoon-fed* by
   a a vet?   **b** an academic?   **c** a manager?

2 Why might the following be on a *knife-edge*?
   a a president   **b** the economy   **c** a top athlete

3 If a salver is *silver-plated*, name an object that is
   a copper-plated.   **b** chrome-plated.   **c** gold-plated.

4 Why might each of the following have been *foil-wrapped*?
   a soft cheese   **b** smoked fish   **c** baked potatoes

5 Sweets are often *sugar-coated*. Can you name a food that is
   a vanilla-flavoured?   **b** vitamin-rich?   **c** fat-free?

6 Who or what would you describe as
   a flesh-eating?   **b** beer-swilling?   **c** blood-sucking?

7 What might be
   a oven-proof?   **b** foolproof?   **c** tamper-proof?

8 How would someone look or behave if they were
   a clown-like?   **b** doll-like?   **c** owl-like?

1 Identify the fruit below and classify their appearance, flavour and effect on your taste buds according to these adjectives.

fleshy	luscious	juicy	sour
sensuous	fibrous	bitter	heavenly
chewy	sharp	exquisite	soft
watery	appetising	pulpy	sweet
tender	sugary	overripe	

2 **1 07** Now listen to a journalist's report on the growing of mangoes in India. Take notes under these headings and review the main points in pairs.

- Ideal temperature for ripening
- Chief mango-growing area
- Facts about the mango tree
- History of mango-growing in India

3 **1 07** Listen again and explain the meaning of these phrases.

a perfect wilting weather
b stacked up according to variety
c exotic foliage
d the Moghul dynasties
e amazing diversity

4 The journalist talks about people in India eating *seasonally*. With the variety of choice offered by supermarkets, it is often possible to buy produce *out of season*. Is this a good thing?

Discuss the following related points.

- Big supermarkets offer maximum diversity, but minimal flavour.
- Local food producers do not get a fair deal from multinational companies.
- There should be larger government subsidies for organic farming.
- People should eat to live and not live to eat.

◎ Idiom spot

There are many common English idioms to do with food. Use the pictures on the opposite page to complete idioms a–j. Then use some of these idioms in sentences describing the situations in a–h opposite.

a the .... on the ....
b have a .... on your ....
c put all your .... in one ....
d have bigger .... to fry
e sweeten the ....
f take something with a .... of ....
g spill the ....
h sell like ....
i get .... on your ....
j eat humble ....

EXAMPLE: Jack told us he had flown to Los Angeles for the weekend and had had dinner with Carey Mulligan, but we didn't believe him.

We took Jack's story about flying to Los Angeles and having dinner with Carey Mulligan with a pinch of salt.

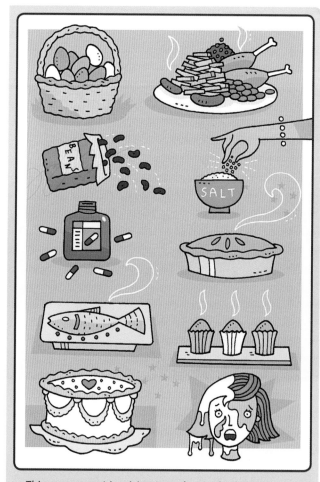

a This government is raising taxes but is also bringing in additional benefits for employees.

b Although I'm freelance, I'm only working for one company – if they closed down, I'd be left high and dry.

c Not realising that Professor Samuels was in front of him in the canteen queue, Harry started imitating his Australian accent – when the professor turned round, Harry felt really embarrassed.

d Valentina had decided to stay on here as a student, but now she's been offered a scholarship at Harvard, so she's off to the US.

e Journalists have been criticising the rugby team all season but after this amazing victory, they will have to admit they were wrong.

f I finally managed to persuade Simon to tell me his big secret – he's getting married!

g Sharon is studying for an MBA and running a big department – and she has building work going on at home too.

h The earrings Maria has designed are doing really well on the market stall.

5 Pictures A–D show four different aspects of current food consumption. First, discuss the issues illustrated in A and B, using the phrases below and your own ideas.

Picture A: *air miles, seasonal produce, the buying power of supermarkets*
Picture B: *shrink-wrapped, rubbish disposal, health implications*

6 Now talk together about all four pictures, suggesting how lifestyle choices could be modified to promote a greener future.

Writing folder 2

Part 2 Review

In Part 2 of Writing, you may be asked to write a review of a book, film, TV programme, concert, or other media event. In addition to reviewing your particular choice, you are likely to have to comment in a more general way, as in the sample task below. Read the question carefully, so you know exactly what is required.

1 Look at the photograph and write three descriptive sentences about the sea.

2 Read this exam task and look at the paragraph plan.

Your college magazine has invited students to contribute a film review to a special feature entitled *Special effects: essential nowadays – or distracting?* Write a review of a film you have seen that uses special effects and say whether you think they are an important aspect of today's films.

- Lead in to review
- Introduce film - 'The Perfect Storm'
- Describe its special effects
- Evaluate importance of special effects in general

EXAM ADVICE

- When writing a review, provide a balance of information and opinion.
- Do NOT describe the whole plot, as this is inappropriate.
- Introduce your opinions with a variety of linkers.
- Use rhetorical questions to preface opinions and ideas.
- Show your range of vocabulary, including specialist terms.
- Name the film (book, play, etc.) early in the review.

3 Decide how well the sample answer on page 39 follows the plan. What improvements would you make in terms of content and organisation?

This is a very good example to consider. In one way, it is not a typical Hollywood film, as there is no happy ending, but in other ways - the actors used, the money spent, the special effects - it is.

Why is it 'perfect'? It is actually a weatherman who uses this word. As he tracks the worsening weather out at sea, we see him getting genuinely excited about the unique set of weather conditions. This was an interesting part for me. The captain of the fishing boat, acted by George Clooney, does not care about the safety of his men. He only wants to find more fish and make lots of money. So he goes to sea, turning off the weather forecasts and ignoring the sensible advice of another captain (a very attractive woman), who is in love with him and doesn't want him to risk his life. And yes, they catch lots of fish, but then the ice-machine on board breaks down, which means that he needs to return to harbour quickly before the fish go bad, so he decides to go back right through the worst weather. This is where the special effects start. They are really very good, and include some clever use of computers. You feel as though you are in the boat with them, facing those big waves. * At the end, the ship goes down and we see one of the sailors - the film also has Mark Wahlberg - drifting on an empty sea, thinking beautiful thoughts about his girlfriend. Then the film shows the girlfriend, looking out to sea with an anxious look on her face.

Are special effects an essential part of all films today? **
In this film, the special effects were probably its best thing.

Based on the sentences you wrote earlier about the sea, write a phrase or a sentence to follow the (*), describing the waves.

4   In Part 2, it is important to demonstrate your range of language. Use these words and phrases as replacements in the text. They are in text order.

a	blockbuster	**i**	outstanding
b	budget	**j**	digital imaging
c	sub-plot	**k**	gigantic
d	portrayed (by)	**l**	stars
e	heads out	**m**	cuts to
f	crew	**n**	scanning the horizon
g	eye of the storm	**o**	prerequisite
h	kick in	**p**	feature

5   The final paragraph contains an example of a rhetorical question. This is a useful stylistic device for introducing opinions and works particularly well in essays and articles – and, as here, in the general comment in reviews.

The writer should have followed up the rhetorical question with some relevant opinions on the use of special effects. For example:

Speak to most Hollywood producers and they would probably argue the case. Yet they are no substitute for an original storyline or engaging dialogue. Used wisely, special effects blend into a film seamlessly, as demonstrated in Peter Jackson's Oscar-winning 'The Lord of the Rings: The Fellowship of the Ring'. If not, they will only irritate.

Write about 50 words of your own to follow the rhetorical question (**).

6   Now answer this exam task in 280–320 words, following the advice on page 38. Make a paragraph plan and check useful vocabulary in a dictionary before you start writing.

An international film magazine wants readers around the world to contribute a review to a special edition entitled *The Art of Advertising: Selling Products through Film*. You decide to write a review of a particularly memorable advertisement. In your review, you should evaluate the visual impact of the advertisement, outline its other features, and assess how much influence such advertisements have on us.

Units 1–4 Revision

Use of English

1 For questions 1–8, read the text below. Use the word given in capitals at the end of some of the lines to form a word that fits in the space in the same line. There is an example at the beginning (0).

VENICE

I first arrived in Venice by train. My parents and I had driven from

Milan, but they had very **(0)** _THOUGHTFULLY_ left the car at Mestre, because they   **THINK**

knew how vital first impressions were. That afternoon my father **(1)** .... to show   **TAKE**

me Venice. The thing to remember, he told me, was that however **(2)** ....   **GLORY**

its churches and palaces, the greatest miracle was the city itself, **(3)** .... by sea   **CIRCLE**

and marsh.

You might ask why anyone in their right mind would build a settlement in so **(4)** ....   **INVITE**

a location. In fact, the reason was fear. In the days of **(5)** .... , Venice did not   **ANTIQUE**

exist; but then, in the fifth and sixth centuries, the Barbarians swept into Italy, and

the panic-stricken **(6)** .... of the great mainland cities fled to the lagoon. And the   **INHABIT**

lagoon continued to protect Venice throughout her history, separating her from the

(7) .... feuding cities of the mainland. Today, more than ever, we have cause for   **PERPETUATE**

(8) ....: it is thanks only to the lagoon that Venice has been spared the motor car.   **GRATEFUL**

2 For questions 1–6, complete the second sentence so that it has a similar meaning to the first sentence, using the word given. **Do not change the word given.** You must use between three and eight words, including the word given.

1 I'm afraid the only option open to me is to ask you to leave the restaurant.
alternative
I .... you to leave the restaurant.

2 If I had known the flight was going to be late leaving, I wouldn't have bothered rushing to the airport.
delay
Had I .... to my flight, I wouldn't have bothered rushing to the airport.

3 The authorities made the landlord take on the financial burden of looking after the building.
shoulder
The landlord .... looking after the building.

4 David looked as if he was about to cry when he saw the damage to his motorbike.
verge
David looked like
.... when he saw the damage to his motorbike.

5 If you need to contact me urgently, then ring this number.
necessary
Should .... , ring this number.

6 I'm sure that the hotel will be good, as it was recommended by Pablo.
bound
The .... recommended it to me.

3 For questions 1–8, read the text and decide which answer (A, B, C or D) best fits each gap.

EXAMPLE: (A) carried out   B put across
         C taken over   D caught up

1 A arms
   B parts
   C forces
   D roles

2 A fruition
   B life
   C action
   D book

3 A held
   B deemed
   C said
   D regarded

4 A model
   B equivalent
   C measure
   D standard

5 A degree
   B scale
   C margin
   D quantity

6 A shorten
   B discount
   C minimise
   D abbreviate

7 A expectations
   B associations
   C regulations
   D implications

8 A comes down to
   B sets off against
   C lives up to
   D gets over with

Too much on your plate? Waste not, want not!

Recent research (0) ..... *carried out* ..... in Ireland amongst chefs and consumers found that 48% of people admitted to regularly over-ordering in restaurants. A campaign has been launched as a result, calling for the food-service industry to join (1) .... with chefs and consumers to address the issue of food waste.

To bring the research findings to (2) .... , the owner of a restaurant in Dublin is creating a "Great Irish Waste" menu, reconsidering food ingredients that have been thrown away, rejected or (3) .... inedible and turning them into imaginative dishes that are both appetising and of a suitable (4) .... to serve his customers. He says that while there will always be some (5) .... of waste in the kitchen, due to elements such as bones or fat trimmings, there's an opportunity to (6) .... wastage in the restaurant itself through better communication. "Even though so much food comes back on customers' plates and goes in the bin, the majority of diners aren't aware of the environmental or cost (7) .... of that waste. Without consumers shifting their mindset, restaurants will struggle to reduce food waste significantly."

Tackling this problem as a consumer is straightforward. Ultimately, it (8) .... smart shopping, clever cooking and shrewd storage.

Writing

4 Add punctuation and capital letters to the following book review where necessary. Then divide the review into suitable paragraphs. The first sentence is done for you.

No one has yet written 'Froth: the Trend that Changed History', but *Universal Foam* comes pretty close to being the definitive example of publishing froth. The book blends two recent publishing trends the newer of which is the wacky science subject. If there is a market for books on cryptography chronometry or cod and books on all these subjects have sold well in the last decade then there is no reason why any subject should seem boring. Once you have discovered a subject so obscure that no other publisher has come across it before all that remains is to prove that it holds the key to universal understanding. Cod a biography of the fish that changed the world is a pretty good example but universal foam the story of bubbles from cappuccino to the cosmos outdoes it since it permeates the universe from the smallest to the largest scale. After all there arent any galaxies stretched on the skin of unimaginably vast cod nor do physicists speak of the world arising from fluctuations in the quantum codfish. So the boys bumper book of froth might contain as every best-seller should everything you need to know about the universe. Then again it might contain everything else.

Thats pretty frothy too. In fact universal foam runs into another current publishing style the book of lists. Among the subjects covered here are volcanoes shaving foam champagne fire fighting equipment and meringues. Then you list everything you know about everything in the first list 101 important facts about galaxies 20 things you never knew about the cappuccino and so on. Finally all this is wrapped up in the academic style as old as exams where you simply cram in all the knowledge that you can possibly get hold of and regurgitate it with the echoing solemnity of a tv anchorman on the simpsons suggesting a rhetorical question can everyday foams like milk foam ever be fully understood and controlled. At which point there is foam flecking this reviewers lips. You cant really blame the author sidney perkowitz who has worked hard and writes clearly. It is not his fault that he has nothing particular to say after he has got through the bits that particularly interest him the fairly technical discussions of how to measure foams and describe them mathematically. However the fact is there is no sound reason for this book to have been written in the first place.

5.1 The consumer society

Speaking

1 Discuss these topics with a partner.

- What is a shopaholic? Do you think you're one? What percentage of items that you buy are things you *want* rather than *need*?
- How often do you buy clothes, CDs, shoes, computer games, books and chocolate?
- How important are designer labels for you?
- Do you think it's necessary to keep in fashion?
- Have you ever had to complain about something you've bought? What happened?
- Would you prefer a refund or an exchange if you took an item back to the shop?
- Do you know what legal rights you have as a consumer? If not, who would you turn to for advice?

◎ Exam spot

In Part 2 of Listening, you need to complete nine sentences with information you hear on the recording. There is no need to write very much, just **a word or short phrase**. You should write down the words you hear – there is no need to use your own words.

Listening

2 **1 08** You will hear an interview between a radio presenter called Paula and her guest, Mike James, who is the presenter of a programme called *Pricewise*. This is a TV programme which champions consumer rights. For questions 1–9, complete the sentences with a word or short phrase.

In 2002, Mike James began working on a (1) .... for a nightly news programme.

Mike says that the programme keeps all correspondence on a (2) .... for future use.

Mike says that it's important that (3) .... read the script carefully.

Mike gives the example of an advert which offered to sell people a (4) .... and some land.

Mike says a researcher was shown a table next to the (5) .... in a restaurant.

Mike talks about a story about ordering food (6) .... from a supermarket.

A supermarket customer was sent (7) .... instead of what they had ordered.

Mike mentions people complaining about trainers which (8) ....

Mike says that manufacturers and retailers are worried about poor (9) ....

Vocabulary

Phrasal verbs

3 **1·08** Listen to the conversation again and write down the phrasal verbs you hear which mean the following. (They are all in the order in which you will hear them.)

a	to intend	**f**	to discover
b	to agree to do	**g**	to test
c	to investigate	**h**	to mention
d	to make inquiries	**i**	to tolerate
e	to be highlighted	**j**	to concede

◎ Phrase spot

Mike James talked about *Pricewise* becoming a programme 'in its own right'. *In its own right* means by itself, without being part of another programme.

There are many other expressions that use *right*.

the right way round	by rights
to serve someone right	in the right
to be right under your nose	as right as rain
to make all the right noises	right on time
to be within your rights	the film rights

Choose one of the above expressions to complete the sentences below. (You might need to put it in a different form.)

a .... you should be in bed at 9.00 pm.
b I've had a cold but I'll be .... when I've had a holiday.
c I refused to apologise because I knew I was ....
d The police never found the murder weapon, even though it was ....
e His book has been very successful and it looks like he's all set to sell .... too.
f Helena turned up to the meeting .... for a change.
g You'd be well .... to take that dress back to the shop – it's torn at the collar.
h Dave .... so I expect he'll be promoted ahead of me.
i Turn it the other way, you can't read it if it isn't ....
j It'll .... Michelle .... if no one ever speaks to her again!

4 For questions 1–8, read the text and decide which answer (A, B, C or D) best fits each gap.

A BRIEF HISTORY OF the mall

Standardized shopping malls have become the new Main Streets of the USA according to one **(1)** .... on the subject. Along with antibiotics and personal computers, the shopping mall has been **(2)** .... as one of the top 50 wonders that have revolutionized the lives of people today. But shopping malls didn't just happen out of the blue. The mall was originally **(3)** .... of as a community center where people would **(4)** .... for shopping, cultural activity, and social interaction. It is safe to **(5)** .... that the mall has achieved and surpassed those early expectations.

The first enclosed mall was developed in a suburb of Minneapolis in 1956 and was designed to get the shopper out of the harsh weather. The phenomenal growth and development of shopping centers was a natural **(6)** .... of the migration of population out from the cities and **(7)** .... the growth of the use of the automobile. The success and impact of the shopping mall may have something to do with their potential to **(8)** .... community life.

	A		B		C		D	
1	A	scholar	B	master	C	body	D	authority
2	A	put forward	B	set up	C	picked up	D	brought out
3	A	imagined	B	devised	C	conceived	D	formulated
4	A	cluster	B	converge	C	group	D	rally
5	A	say	B	tell	C	speak	D	remark
6	A	sequel	B	upshot	C	follow-up	D	consequence
7	A	corresponded	B	paralleled	C	correlated	D	equated
8	A	raise	B	magnify	C	enhance	D	heighten

5 Talk about the following with a partner.

- Where do you like to shop – in a town centre or in an out-of-town mall?
- What do you think of the threat to small independent shops from large chains?
- Why do you think shopping centres or malls are so popular?

Corpus spot

Several of the sentences below, some from the *Cambridge Learner Corpus*, contain common mistakes connected with countable and uncountable nouns. Correct the sentences which are wrong and leave the ones which are correct.

EXAMPLE: *It gives you new* ~~informations~~ ^options^, *I would say a larger window on the world.*

Information is uncountable and should be singular.

a The acoustics in this room are terrible.
b How many luggages did you bring with you?
c Doctors and scientists, with their researches, have managed to give us a better life.
d The news this morning were terrible – more price rises and a teachers' strike.
e Thanks to the revolution in transports, travelling has become easier.
f Marco Polo set off on his travels from Venice.
g Drivers should watch out for roadworks on the M25 this morning.
h Equipments such as the tape recorder and stereo are very outdated.
i My advice to you is to keep quiet about what is happening in the office.
j The future behaviours of our children will depend on a good upbringing.
k I live on the outskirt of the city.
l The fishmonger weighed out three kilos of fishes.
m I was never much good at statistics.
n The sceneries in New Zealand are spectacular.
o Traffic is becoming a problem in most cities nowadays.
p The police is aware of the break-in.
q My father is a Professor of Economic.

G → page 181

1 Some nouns have different meanings according to whether they are used uncountably or with *a* or *an* or in the plural. Write sentences which show the two meanings of the following nouns.

EXAMPLE: damage

The fire did enormous damage to the town.

The judge awarded her £1 million in damages.

a work
b iron
c disorder
d speech
e room
f language
g comfort
h experience
i capital
j coffee

2 Some uncountable nouns can be made singular if they are used with *a bit of* or *a piece of*. They can also be made plural by adding *bits of* or *pieces of*. However, many uncountable nouns have special words to make them singular or plural, for example *a loaf of bread*.

Match the noun with its special word.

a a burst of   glass
b a pane of   smoke
c a stroke of   abuse
d a grain of   dust
e a gust of   thunder
f a speck of   luck
g a stream of   emergency
h a ray of   wind
i a source of   sunshine
j an item of   applause
k a rumble of   sand
l a puff of   amusement
m a state of   clothing/news

3 You must spell correctly in the examination. Read through the following advertisement and find the nouns which are spelled wrongly. Use your dictionary to help you.

Look around. You're in the midst of a global maelstrom. A swirling mass of converging technologies and new business oportunities unleashed by the Internet. All waiting to be harnessed by large IT service providors. As one has said: 'We've focused our energy and resauces on creating technology to solve the unique problems of thousands of individual businesses. Last year alone we invested $2.5 bilion of our global IT and telecomunications revenus on R & D. Innervations that keep your company one step ahead of the Internet. And light years ahead of the competition.'

4 There are three ways of showing possession in English:

A The apostrophe
- used with people, e.g. *customers' rights* (NB the customer's rights refers to one customer; the customers' rights refers to more than one.)
- used with time and distance, e.g. *a day's pay*

B Using 'of'
- usually used with objects, e.g. *the price of petrol*
- used to talk about position, e.g. *the back of the room*

C Using a noun as an adjective
e.g. a table leg, a travel agency

Complete the following sentences using one of the forms above, A, B or C.

a (seat, back) Can I sit in the
.... on the way home?

b (boss, wife) His .... is in hospital having a baby.

c (room, corner) The boy was sitting in the ....

d (day, pay) When is .... ?

e (week, holiday) Mary only had one .... last year.

f (wine, glass) Would you prefer a .... or a tumbler for your drink?

g (delay, moment) The decision was taken without a ....

h (Anne, best friend) .... has just got a job in Milan.

i (door, handle) Take care with that .... – it's loose.

j (field, sports) The team went out onto the .... , wearing their new strip.

G → page 181

Vocabulary

Prepositions

5 Read the article and fill the spaces with a suitable preposition.

SPOILT FOR CHOICE

There has been a huge rise **(1)** .... the number of sports 'superstores' on the High Street. You go in and are faced **(2)** .... a giant wall, consisting entirely **(3)** .... shoes, each model categorised **(4)** .... either sports affiliation, basketball star, economic class or consumer niche.

I noticed a boy **(5)** .... even greater awe **(6)** .... the towering selection of footwear than I was. His eyes were glazed **(7)** .... a psycho-physical response **(8)** .... the overwhelming sensory data. This phenomenon, known as the 'Gruen Transfer', is commonly observed **(9)** .... a shopping mall or High Street store.

Having finished several years **(10)** .... research **(11)** .... this exact psychological state, I knew to proceed **(12)** .... caution. I slowly made my way **(13)** .... the boy's side and gently asked him, 'What is going **(14)** .... in your mind right now?'

He responded **(15)** .... the slightest hesitation, 'I don't know which trainer is me and I'm no good **(16)** .... making choices!'

1 Discuss these questions in groups.

- Is there a certain advertisement that has appealed to you more than others? Why?
- What do you think makes a good advertisement?
- Do you think admen can sell anything? Think of some things that might be difficult to sell.
- Should advertising be curbed in any way? Should there be restrictions on, for example, junk food being advertised on TV?
- Do you think some people are more vulnerable to advertising than others?

2 Read the texts below on advertising. Think about:

- where you would find these texts, e.g. in a newspaper, magazine, research paper, novel, encyclopaedia, leaflet, brochure, etc.
- what style the writer is using, e.g. formal, informal, journalistic, academic, personal, narrative, etc.

Text 1

Advertising and young people

It's been estimated that young people today shell out nearly £50 a week on clothing, entertainment, and fast food. And that's not all. It's now beginning to dawn on advertisers that, through nagging power, young people not only influence the purchases of the goods and services that appeal to them, but they also influence many of the purchases in the entire household, even down to the family car. This is an advertiser's dream. People, especially in the 13–19 age group, buy on impulse. They are less likely than others to weigh up price differences or get recommendations. They buy based on what their friends are buying, what will make them more popular with their peer group, or what a celebrity they are into says they need.

Text 2

Advertising: exploiting the vulnerable?

Concern about young people's lack of life skills and cognitive ability to evaluate advertisements has provided much scope for research and heated debate. Embedded within the discussion is the contention that advertising to this group is inherently 'unfair'. However, many now believe that the vulnerabilities of young people are often overstated and that, having grown up with the constant barrage of advertising, they are able to pay it little or no attention. There is also the argument that, by providing product information, advertising helps young people make more informed choices.

3 Find words in the texts which mean the same as the following in the context. (They are in text order.) Use an English–English dictionary to help you.

Text 1	Text 2
occur to	assess
pester	extent
including	claim
whim	essentially
evaluate	exaggerated

4 Read through the sentences below and decide which are the two main points that each text is making.

Text 1

a Young people like to buy the same things that everyone else does.

b Young people do not spend time carefully considering what to buy.

c Young people have more money than ever to spend nowadays.

d Young people have a great deal of influence on what is bought by their friends and family.

Text 2

a Young people pay little attention to advertising as they are used to it.

b There has been increased concern about the amount of advertising that is aimed at young people.

c Advertising can be helpful to young people by providing them with product information.

d Young people don't have the background knowledge to be able to make sensible choices.

5 Write two paragraphs, summarising and using your own words as far as possible, the information in the two texts. Begin with a sentence which tells the reader what the texts are generally about, for example:

The two texts discuss the pros and cons of advertising to young people.

Then continue, summarising the two points that each text makes. Begin:

Text 1 claims that …
Text 2 argues that …

Vocabulary

Abstract nouns

6 Being able to manipulate words is a very useful skill for both the Writing and Reading and Use of English papers. Complete these sentences by changing the word in brackets into an abstract noun. Use a dictionary to help you.

EXAMPLE: I value her (friend) greatly. *friendship*

a They quarrelled out of sheer (bored).

b Some new products have built-in (obsolete).

c Environmental (aware) has increased dramatically over the last decade.

d He felt great (proud) when his youngest daughter won first prize.

e He's got the (confident) to walk into an interview and get the job.

f The government believes that its (austere) programme will reduce inflation.

g His friends take advantage of his (generous), and borrow his things without asking.

h Now she is 18, she is keen to have her (independent) from her parents.

i He complained that the (inefficient) of the bus service was having an impact on employment.

j His feelings of (insecure) made him desperate to get other people's approval.

k Scrooge is a character in Charles Dickens' book *A Christmas Carol* who is famous for his (mean).

l (Individual) is the idea that freedom of thought and action for each person is the most important quality of a society, rather than shared effort and (responsible).

m Louise's (aspire) to help others come from her own misfortune as a child.

n I think it's important to treat his articles with a degree of (sceptical).

Exam folder 3

Reading and Use of English, Part 1 Multiple-choice cloze

This part of the Reading and Use of English paper is composed of a text drawn from a range of different sources of written English, for example from advertisements, newspaper articles, encyclopaedia entries, literary texts, etc. The text contains eight gaps and is followed by eight four-option multiple-choice questions.

The questions test your knowledge of the following.

Idioms

They had a terrible row, all because Mike had got hold of the wrong end of the .... when Sonia was explaining what had happened at the beach.

A line   **B** stick   **C** rope   **D** ruler

The answer is **B**. *To get hold of the wrong end of the stick* means *to misunderstand* something. Idioms are expressions which cannot be changed.

Collocations

Primary education has been .... underfunded in this area of the country for many years now, and it is about time something was done about it.

A seriously   **B** deeply   **C** highly   **D** remarkably

The answer is **A**. *Seriously* and *underfunded* are often used together. Words that are often used together in this way are called collocations.

Fixed phrases

Everyone quickly .... their places on the stage in readiness for the curtain to go up.

A made   **B** had   **C** saved   **D** took

The answer is **D**. *To take one's place* is a fixed phrase. This means that it contains elements that can change with the sense of the sentence, e.g. *he took **his** place, they took **their** place*s.

Complementation

The menu .... of various starters, main courses and desserts, all, in my opinion, designed to please the eye rather than the palate.

A consisted   **B** composed   **C** contained   **D** comprised

The answer is **A**. *Consist* takes the preposition *of*. Your knowledge of prepositions, reflexives and verb patterns is tested in this type of question.

Phrasal verbs

Pete didn't bother to .... up until nearly the end of the lesson, and then he just slouched into the room and flung himself into a seat with no apology.

A come   **B** show   **C** catch   **D** go

The answer is **B**. *To show up* means *to put in an appearance*.

Semantic precision

The rain down slowly under his coat collar, making him feel thoroughly damp and miserable.

A crept   **B** waded   **C** trickled   **D** teemed

The answer is **C**. *Trickled* is the only option which refers to slow movement of water. The precise meaning of a word in relation to the whole context, either at sentence or whole text level, is tested.

Read the Exam advice and then do the task below.

EXAM ADVICE

- Read the whole text carefully before looking at the options.
- Think carefully about your choice of answer. Remember that you are often being tested not just on choosing a word which is grammatically correct, but also one which best fits the sense or tone of the text.
- Always choose an answer, even if you are not sure you are right. You are not penalised for wrong answers. You have a 25% chance of getting an answer right, even if you really have no idea what the answer is!

For questions **1–8**, read the text below and decide which answer (**A**, **B**, **C** or **D**) best fits each gap. There is an example at the beginning (**0**).

0   **A** brought   **B** given   **C** shed   **D** shown

0	A	B	C	D

MERCHANT@FLORENCE

An Italian academic, Giorgio Stabile, has (0) ....A.... to light the fact that the ubiquitous symbol of Internet era communication, the @ sign used in email addresses, is actually a 500-year-old invention of Italian merchants. He claims to have (1) .... on the earliest known example of the symbol's use, as an indication of a measure of weight or volume. He said the @ sign (2) .... an amphora, a measure of capacity based on the terracotta jars used to transport grain and liquid in the ancient Mediterranean world. The first known (3) .... of its use occurred in a letter written by a Florentine merchant on May 4, 1536.

The ancient symbol was (4) .... in the course of research for a visual history of the 20th century. (5) .... , the sign had made its way along trade routes to northern Europe, where it (6) .... on its contemporary accountancy meaning: 'at the price of'. According to Professor Stabile, the oldest example could be of great value as it could be used for publicity purposes and to (7) .... the prestige of the institution that has it in their (8) ....

1	**A** encountered	**B** stumbled	**C** run	**D** fallen
2	**A** substituted	**B** represented	**C** described	**D** typified
3	**A** instance	**B** occasion	**C** precedent	**D** illustration
4	**A** uncovered	**B** unwrapped	**C** unearthed	**D** unmasked
5	**A** Outwardly	**B** Actually	**C** Logically	**D** Apparently
6	**A** put	**B** took	**C** set	**D** came
7	**A** enhance	**B** lift	**C** elevate	**D** embellish
8	**A** tenure	**B** proprietorship	**C** possession	**D** custody

Speaking

1 Give your opinion on the following statements.

- Listening to music helps me to concentrate, especially when studying.
- Every child should have the opportunity to learn an instrument.
- Some instruments are easier to learn than others.
- Listening to pop music improves my mood.
- Classical music is far superior to pop music.

Reading

2 You are going to read an extract from an article. Seven paragraphs have been removed from the extract. Choose from the paragraphs A–H the one which fits each gap (1–7). There is one extra paragraph which you do not need to use.

To help you, the first two answers have the links highlighted. Underline the links which give you the answers to the other gaps.

The enduring myth of music and maths

As a mathematician with strong musical interests who grew up in a family of musicians, I have been asked about the connection between music and maths many times. And I have bad news: although there are some obvious similarities between mathematical and musical activity, there is (as yet) no compelling evidence for the kind of mysterious, almost magical connection that many people seem to believe in. I'm partly referring here to the 'Mozart Effect', **the hypothesis** that children who have heard music by Mozart are supposedly more intelligent, including at mathematics, than children from a control group.

1 _____

Of course, **this conclusion** does not show that there is no interesting connection between mathematics and music. It was always a little implausible that lazily listening to a concerto would earn you extra marks on that maths test you are taking tomorrow, but what about learning to read music or **spending hours practising** the piano? That takes genuine effort.

2 _____

Demonstrating **a connection** of this kind is not as easy as one might think. To begin with, there are plenty of innumerate musicians and tone-deaf mathematicians, so the best one could hope to demonstrate would be a significant positive correlation between aptitudes at the two disciplines. And then one would face all the usual challenges of establishing a statistical connection.

3 _____

And yet, the belief that the two are interestingly related won't go away without a fight. I cannot help observing that among the mathematicians I know, there do seem to be a surprising number who are very good indeed at the piano.

4 _____

Indeed, yes, we can. For a start, both mathematics and music deal with abstract structures, so if you become good at one, then it is plausible that you become good at something more general – handling abstract structures – that helps you with the other. If this is correct, then it would show a connection between mathematical and musical ability, but not the kind of obscure connection that people hope for.

5 _____

Of course, abstract structures are not confined to mathematics and music. If you are learning a foreign language then you need to understand its grammar and syntax, which are prime examples of abstract structures. And yet we don't hear people asking about a mysterious connection between mathematical ability and linguistic ability.

6 _____

In an effort to dispel this air of contradiction, let me give one example of a general aptitude that is useful in both mathematics and music: the ability to solve problems of the "A is to B as C is to D" kind. These appear in intelligence tests (car is to garage as aircraft is to what?) but they are also absolutely central to both music and mathematics.

7 _____

I take the view that the general question of whether mathematical ability and musical ability are related is much less interesting than some similar but more specific questions. Are musicians more drawn to certain composers (Bach, for instance)? Are musical mathematicians more drawn to certain areas of mathematics? One can imagine many interesting surveys and experiments that could be done, but for now this is uncharted territory and all we can do is speculate.

Read the introduction to get an idea of what the text is going to be about. Then read the text and the missing paragraphs.

Read through the paragraphs on either side of the gap very carefully. Don't just read the paragraph before the gap as this might not give you any clues to the missing text. This part of the exam is testing understanding of content as well as reference devices.

A I feel that it would be more like the straightforward link between ability at football and ability at cricket. To become better at one of those then you need to improve your fitness and co-ordination. That makes you better at sport in general.

B For example, identifying and controlling for other potentially influential factors is difficult, and as far as I know, there has been no truly convincing study of that type that has shown that musical ability enhances mathematical ability or vice versa.

C The second phrase is a clear answer to the first. But one can be more precise about what this means. If you try to imagine any other second phrase, nothing seems 'right' in the way that Mozart's chosen phrase does.

D Could it be that the rewards for **that time-consuming dedication** spill over into other areas of intellectual life, and in particular into mathematics? Is there any evidence that people who have worked hard to become good at music are better at mathematics than people who are completely unmusical? And in the other direction, are mathematicians better than average at music?

E My guess is that that is because the link exists but not the uncertainty: grammar feels mathematical. Music, by contrast, is strongly tied up with one's emotions and can be enjoyed even by people who know very little about it. As such, it seems very different from mathematics, so any connection between the two is appealingly paradoxical.

F It is not hard to see why **such a theory** would be taken seriously: we would all like to become better at mathematics without putting in any effort. But the conclusions of the original experiment have been grossly exaggerated. If you want your brain to work better, then not surprisingly, you have to put in some hard graft; there is no such thing as an intellectual perpetual-motion machine. Mozart CDs for babies and toys that combine maths and music might help, **but not much, and the effects are temporary**.

G I believe that there is a study waiting to be done on this: are mathematicians more drawn to this rather than to other instruments? Of the mathematicians I can think of who are superb instrumentalists, all but one are pianists. While we wait for scientific evidence to back up the anecdotal evidence, can we at least argue that it is plausible that there should be a connection?

H Music is full of little puzzles like this. If you are good at them, then when you listen to a piece, expectations will constantly be set up in your mind. Of course, some of the best moments in music come when one's expectations are confounded, but if you don't have the expectations in the first place then you will miss out on the pleasure.

3 What do you think about the idea that people who are good at music are also good at maths? Do you think listening to music or learning an instrument can improve your overall intelligence?

⊚ **Phrase spot**

Phrases with the verb *take* are often tested at this level. In the text there was *take a test, take effort* and *take seriously*.

Complete the gaps with one of the following words or phrases:

part	exception to	
the view	for granted	
place	a stand	by surprise
issue	advantage	
notice	into account/consideration	
account of	second place	

a Alicia took great .... the fact that her name had been left off the guest list.
b Don't take any .... of what Sue says – she's just in a bad mood.
c The seminar will take .... in the new lecture room on the fourth floor.
d He rarely took .... in proceedings, preferring rather to have a backseat role.
e This institution takes .... that all employees should be treated fairly.
f When you add up your business expenses don't forget to take .... hotel tips.
g The Minister took .... with the interviewer over whether the government was sticking to its manifesto pledges.
h Mark took .... of the breeze and went windsurfing.
i His sudden appearance took me ....
j Fathers tend to have to take .... when a new baby comes along.
k We need to take .... the neighbours if we're going to have a party.
l Luisa was fed up with being taken .... and decided to leave both her husband and family.
m The teacher decided it was time to take .... on school uniform and not allow the children to wear trainers in class.

6.2 Modals: Degrees of likelihood

Likelihood ranges from absolute certainty to complete impossibility and can be expressed in a number of ways:

- with modal auxiliaries *can, may, could, might, should, ought to, must be, can't be* in the present and with a perfect infinitive in the past
- with a sentence beginning with *It* and followed by a *that*-clause
- by an adverbial such as *perhaps, without a doubt*, etc.

G→ page 181

1 **Which of the sentences below express the following?**

  A complete certainty (negative and positive)
  B strong probability/possibility
  C weak probability/possibility
  D general or theoretical probability/possibility

  a The chances are it will rain tonight.
  b He can't have got home already, as I think the trains are delayed.
  c He couldn't have looked less enthusiastic if he'd tried.
  d Caroline is bound to pass her violin exam.
  e You shouldn't have gone swimming off the rocks, because you really could have had an accident.
  f You definitely won't have any problem with your application, as it looks fine.
  g The package ought to arrive in a couple of days.
  h The postman must've already called – look there's a letter on the table.
  i I may very well see you on Saturday.
  j There's every likelihood of rain this afternoon.
  k It can be interesting to re-read books you read as a child.
  l She's certain to get lost when she goes to Tokyo.
  m There's a faint chance I'll get a car for my birthday.

2 **In pairs talk about the likelihood of the following happening.**

  a The birth of another Mozart.
  b An asteroid hitting Earth.
  c People having brain transplants.
  d English no longer being the language of the Internet.
  e New Zealand winning the football World Cup.
  f Electric cars taking over from petrol-driven ones.

3 **In groups decide what person or event the speaker might be talking about in these extracts from radio news bulletins.**

  EXAMPLE: '… and as the car slows down for him to wave to the crowds a shot is heard …'

    It may be a movie star.
    The chances are it's a politician.
    It's bound to be someone famous because he's waving at the crowds.

  a '… he's coming down the steps slowly, and with a final movement that looks like a small jump because of the atmosphere, he …'
  b '… and the crowds are standing outside waiting for the happy couple to come out onto the balcony …'
  c '… and she has been successful in both her singing and acting careers, having number one singles for the past twenty years …'
  d '… he's won more championships than anyone else in his field and, though he's near retirement age now, I think he still has some more cups to win …'
  e '… And scientists are saying that because of this breakthrough the world will soon be free of this disease …'

◎ Exam spot

In Reading and Use of English, Part 4
transformations, you must use between three
and eight words including the key word.
Contractions (*can't*, *won't*, etc.) count as two
words. Check your answers for length and
accuracy before transferring them to the
answer sheet.

4 Complete the second sentence so that
it has a similar meaning to the first
sentence, using the word given. **Do
not change the word given.** You must
use between **three** and **eight** words,
including the word given.

1 In all probability Alan will get a
place to study music at Oxford.
chances
The ....
accepted to study music at Oxford.

2 Professor Potts is unlikely to retire
before she has to.
doubtful
It ....
early retirement.

3 Unless there is a last-minute hitch,
the Head's job is his for the taking.
bound
He's ....
there isn't a last-minute hitch.

4 It's possible that the fire was caused
by an electrical fault in the gym.
likelihood
In ....
of the fire in the gym was an
electrical fault.

5 It's pretty certain that we'll win a gold
medal this year in the 100 metres.
foregone
It's ....
is ours for the taking in the 100
metres this year.

6 There's a strong possibility the
audience will ignore any mistakes
she makes at the concert.
take
It's highly

....
of any mistakes she makes at the
concert.

5 Quickly read through this extract from an article about pop music
to get some idea of what it is about. Don't fill in any spaces at this
stage. When you've read it, answer the questions below.

Band Manufacture

The fate of any pop band is a question that **(0)** ....NO........
longer is of interest to its fans alone. **(1)** .... only have
economists recognised pop music's importance **(2)** ....
a business, pointing **(3)** .... that it contributes more
(4) .... export earnings than the steel industry, but
strange as it **(5)** .... seem, people in some countries
spend more on pop than they do on fruit and vegetables.
(6) .... such serious money washing around, the
question of **(7)** .... will be the next big thing is
(8) .... too important to be left to random factors such
as chance and talent. **(9)** .... the great names of rock in
the 60s and 70s formed bands spontaneously **(10)** ....
they were discovered and then marketed, their successors are
increasingly **(11)** .... to be brought
(12) .... by marketing men. Many groups, often sold
as four young men or women in **(13)** .... of their own
destiny, were in **(14)** .... dreamed up and promoted by
middle-aged men. Designing a band is much the same as designing
(15) .... other product: take a basic, successful model
and adapt it. The challenge, when everything has been tried already, is
to persuade consumers that what you
are doing is in some way innovative.

a What is the writer's attitude to the pop industry?
b What comparison does the writer make in the article?
c What conclusion does the writer draw?

Now fill the spaces with one word only.

1 Link the following instruments with the category they belong in.

brass	electronic	keyboard
percussion	string	woodwind

violin	clarinet	drum
saxophone	cello	flute
triangle	piano	synthesizer
guitar	trumpet	xylophone

2 You are going to hear an interview with Sue Pearson, who teaches violin-making at a college. For questions 1–9, complete the sentences with a word or short phrase.

Steps to
making a violin

The interviewer describes violins as being elaborately **(1)** ....

Sue prefers to have wood which has grown in a **(2)** .... climate.

It's important for the grain to be uniform so that the violin will have **(3)** .... as well as strength.

Sue explains that there is a great deal of **(4)** .... when she makes a violin.

The thickness of the wood is reduced to make what Sue refers to as the **(5)** .... of the violin.

(6) .... is used to attach the top and bottom of the violin.

Students find the **(7)** .... the hardest part of the violin to make.

Sue believes the **(8)** .... can alter the sound of the violin.

Sue hopes that in the future the **(9)** .... of one of her violins will be enhanced.

Style extra

In the interview you've just heard, wood was described as
finely grained
and
incredibly strong
This kind of adverb–participle and adverb–adjective collocation is fairly common in English and you should try to familiarise yourself with them. Below are some more common collocations.

seriously ill	widely believed
strongly worded	carefully chosen
singularly successful	staggeringly expensive
keenly priced	

Write a sentence which includes the following words and one of the collocations above.

EXAMPLE: *sister / food poisoning*

My sister is seriously ill with food poisoning.

My sister sent a strongly worded letter to the restaurant when she got food poisoning.

a a monster / Loch Ness
b boyfriend / birthday present
c designer clothes / out-of-town retail outlets
d seats / rock concert
e new album / number one

Idiom spot

Complete the following sentences using one of these words. One is used more than once:

tune	chord	song	string	note	score

a It was clear from people's reactions that the newcomer was someone of ....
b The new college principal would appear to be in .... with most of the students.
c I put in a bid for that old piano because it was going for a ....
d Rachel did an advanced IT course before she started work, to make sure she had a second .... to her bow.
e The fight occurred when the youths decided they needed to settle the .... with the other gang.
f The speech seemed to strike the right .... with the crowd and they clapped loudly.
g Her biography struck a .... with quite a few elderly people who had had a similar experience.

Exam spot

In Part 2 of Speaking, there is a two-way conversation between the candidates: a one-minute task, followed by a three-minute related task. In Unit 4 you looked at the one-minute task. In the three-minute task you are given visual material and asked to speculate, evaluate, compare, give your opinions and make decisions.

3 Look at photographs A–D. You need to imagine that a television documentary is being produced on music today. These pictures show some of the aspects that are being considered. You have about three minutes to decide which aspect is most representative of music today.

Try to include some mention of the following:

accessibility	popularity
sound quality	value for money

Pronunciation

4 **1 10** In 6.2 you looked at modals. The tone of voice that is used with certain modal auxiliaries can change the meaning. Listen to these sentences. What feeling is the speaker expressing? For example, irritation, anger, surprise, being reproachful, etc.

  a You could have rung me from the station.
  b You could have rung me from the station.
  c You might ask before you borrow the car!
  d You might ask Pete if you can borrow his car.
  e Liz should have got here an hour ago.
  f Liz should have got here an hour ago.

5 **1 11** You are going to hear other examples of contrastive stress. Underline the word which is stressed in the sentence you hear and answer the question that follows.

  EXAMPLE: I wanted <u>white</u> wine with the meal.
  Did she get white wine? *No.*

  a I thought you'd gone home.
    Is the person at home?
  b I thought you'd gone home.
    Is the person at home?
  c She's an English teacher.
    Does she teach English?
  d She's an English teacher.
    Does she teach English?
  e I'm not buying a car.
    Is he buying a car?
  f I'm not buying a car.
    Is he buying a car?
  g She's not pretty.
    Is she pretty?
  h She's not pretty.
    Is she pretty?
  i I had wanted to see the paintings.
    Did he see the paintings?
  j I had wanted to see the paintings.
    Did he see the paintings?

Writing folder 3

Part 1 Essay

Look back at Writing folder 1 on pages 22–23 for basic facts about this compulsory question. An essay is a discursive task that expresses an argument. Clear organisation is required, together with a logical sequence of ideas. The register used should be 'unmarked' – that is, neither formal nor informal – and impersonal in tone, as there is usually no reference to personal experience.

1 Read the two texts below, which contain complementary ideas on the status of music in society. Express these ideas in sentences, using your own words.

Text 1

Music is something that we perhaps take for granted in our daily lives, particularly when it exists in the form of background music in public places or advertising jingles, and with the huge availability of downloadable music, we now have ready access to whatever we desire. However, do we as a society take music as seriously as we should? Professional musicians are highly-skilled individuals, yet many of them struggle to find regular work and their talent is seldom recognised. In most countries, they receive no state support and many are forced to abandon a career in music altogether. What a waste!

Text 2

Music has been downgraded in importance in our schools and is often the first subject to be withdrawn from the curriculum, with more and more emphasis placed on core subjects. Yet research has shown that those who learn music from a young age benefit in different ways. Music lessons are creative and engage children in a collaborative activity that has a real outcome. Even if parents are reluctant to contribute additional funding for instruments, they will usually come to see their offspring perform in the school concert. Let's give music back the status it deserves in education.

2 Choose sentences from a–f that are closest to your own wording. Decide whether the remaining sentences represent ideas in the texts.

   a Music should have a special place in the school curriculum because it allows children to participate in something productive.
   b The best-known performers earn a great deal, so state support cannot be justified.
   c It is short-sighted to cut the study of music in schools, given its proven positive effects.
   d Despite the widespread presence of music in the modern world, it tends to be under-valued.
   e Parents should pay for their children's music tuition throughout their schooling.
   f It is scandalous that promising young musicians are often unable to develop in their field.

3 Read these exam instructions, paying attention to the highlighted parts. Note down additional ideas of your own that are relevant to the topic.

Write an essay summarising and evaluating the key points from both texts. Use your own words throughout as far as possible, and include your own ideas in your answer.

4   When writing an essay, there are various ways of introducing an argument. Read these sentence openers and choose one from each section to preface your different ideas.

Generalising

It is often said that …
It is usually the case that …
People tend to regard …
The reality is that …

Specifying

From the classical performer's point of view, …
Professional musicians are seen as …
In terms of the school curriculum itself, …
As far as parents are concerned, …

Raising an argument

Considering …
On the question of …
No one would dispute …

Giving one side

One argument in favour of this is …
In support of …
It is true that …

Giving the other side

At the same time …
In actual fact …
On the other hand, …
In contrast to …
Set/Weighed against this is …
This is not to say that …

5   Plan your essay, organising your ideas in a paragraph plan. Then draft an introduction that outlines the scope of the essay.

EXAM ADVICE

- Refer to the four key points clearly in your answer.
- Introduce the main argument at the outset.
- Include ideas of your own that are relevant.
- Organise your ideas in logical paragraphs.
- Make sure your argument is coherent.
- Include an effective conclusion.
- Use a variety of sentence openers and linkers.
- Write in an unmarked register, using an impersonal tone.
- Use your own words wherever possible.

6   Now write your essay, following the Exam advice and the instructions in 3. You should write 240–280 words.

7.1 Before your very eyes

Listening

1 Identify each of the pictures opposite. What do they have in common with the unit title?

Exam spot

Part 1 of Listening contains three short extracts, each with two multiple-choice questions. Read through the questions before you listen, to predict what to listen out for.

2 🔊 **1 12** You will hear three different extracts. First, read the questions and check any difficult words in your dictionary.

For questions 1–6, choose the answer (A, B or C) which fits best according to what you hear. There are two questions for each extract.

Extract One

You hear a woman being interviewed on the radio about the eye.

1 What is the woman's profession?

   A zoologist   **B** psychologist   **C** journalist

2 What point does she make about staring?

   A Humans have to resort to less direct forms of intimidation.

   B False eye spots on animals prove that the eye is irreplaceable.

   C Animals make eye contact to signal they are about to attack.

Extract Two

You hear a woman talking about when her son was very young.

3 Why did the woman choose not to tell her son off when he drew on the wall?

   A She felt guilty as she had not been keeping an eye on him.

   B She thought his pictures added some much-needed colour.

   C She believed it was wrong to put a stop to his creativity.

4 Now that he is grown up, how does she feel about the action she took?

   A sceptical   **B** justified   **C** regretful

Extract Three

You hear a man talking on the radio about Percy Shaw, an inventor.

5 What prompted Percy Shaw to work on his invention?

   A He was involved in a serious car accident.

   B Something on which he had relied disappeared.

   C His eyesight was no longer as keen as it once was.

6 Which part of his invention is likened to an eyelid?

   A the pad   **B** the base   **C** the assembly

3 Explain the meaning of the phrases in bold in the recording scripts for Extracts Two and Three in your own words.

Extract Two

'It was always the same wall and he appeared to be attempting pictures, as well as showing a definite **sense of colour** … As soon as Sam completed one **magnum opus** I would take it down and replace it with a fresh canvas, so to speak … You see, he has absolutely **no leanings towards** art, being heavily into information technology!'

Extract Three

'Driving home through the unlit outskirts of Halifax at night, he found **the perfect substitute** for night vision, following the glint of his headlights in the metal tramlines. But he ran into a problem: no longer in use, these rails were soon taken up for good. With this **serious setback**, Shaw decided it was time to come up with something that would help him – and others – to steer in the dark. His now **ubiquitous invention**, modelled on the eye of a cat, consists of a mirror and a spherical lens mounted on a rubber pad.'

Idiom spot

Which of these idioms was used in the recordings? What do the others mean?

catch someone's eye
look someone in the eye
have an eye for

turn a blind eye (to)
see eye to eye (with)
be in the public eye

Use your imagination to the full to finish these sentences.
a The thing that really caught my eye was …
b I shouldn't have turned a blind eye to …
c My boss looked me in the eye and said …
d I've never seen eye to eye with …
e You definitely have an eye for …
f People who are in the public eye should …

 Exam spot

The Reading and Use of English, Part 3 word formation task tests related parts of speech and compound words. Read the text carefully – a space may require a plural or negative form.

4 Read the text about the French artist Georges Seurat. Use the word given in capitals at the end of some of the lines to form a word that fits in the space in the same line. There is an example at the beginning (0).

The Pointillist Georges Seurat

(1859–1891)

Few artists discover a **(0)** ....MEANINGFUL.... direction so young in life. Barely into his twenties, Georges Seurat did just this, developing one of the most lucid classical styles since the fifteenth century, the **(1)** .... of which was the dot.   **MEAN**

ESSENTIAL

This was a radical departure from the style of Impressionist artists such as Pissarro and Renoir. **(2)** ...., the unit of Impressionism had been the brush-stroke, always **(3)** .... in form – fat or thin, clean or smeared, streaky, squidgy or transparent – and **(4)** .... mixed to conform with the facts of sight. Seurat wanted something with greater **(5)** .... than that. A child of late nineteenth-century positivism and scientific optimism, Seurat drew on studies of visual colour analysis to generate his own **(6)** .... style. The most **(7)** .... work of this nature was 'The Law of Simultaneous Colour Contrast', written by Eugène Chevreul. According to Chevreul, colour recognition was a matter of **(8)** .... – a web of connected events – rather than the simple presentation of one hue after another to the eye. Seurat resolved to make this process explicit on canvas by making his colour patches tiny, reducing them to dots: hence the name, 'Pointillism'.

HITHER
PREDICT
INTUITION
STABLE

COMPARE
INFLUENCE

ACT

 Style extra

Look at this example from the text.
A child of late nineteenth-century positivism and scientific optimism, Seurat drew on …

The use of an extended noun phrase to preface a sentence like this is common in biographical and other academic writing.

Complete the sentences a–d, which start with noun phrases, writing about people of your choice.

EXAMPLE: *One of the most creative artists of the 20th century, Picasso produced many different styles in the course of his working life.*

a A highly-regarded and ground-breaking film-maker,
b Best-known for their awe-inspiring poetry,
c The most significant political thinker of his generation,
d A leading innovator in her field of expertise,

Write two more complete sentences on subjects of your choice.

1 a Identify the part of speech of each underlined word in the following sentence, which is from one of the recordings in 7.1.

You may see a pair of <u>dazzling</u> headlights <u>eyeballing</u> you.

b Identify the participle and say what it refers to in these examples, also taken from 7.1.

   i Driving home through the unlit outskirts of Halifax at night, Percy Shaw would follow the glint of …

   ii His invention, modelled on the eye of a cat, consists of …

c Sometimes the position of the participle clause in the sentence alters the meaning. Explain the difference in meaning of these two sentences.

   i I saw our cat sitting precariously on the roof.
   ii Sitting precariously on the roof, I saw our cat.

2 Compare the two pictures. One is by the 19th-century British artist J.M.W. Turner and the other was taken by the Hubble Space Telescope.
Would you describe each as *beautiful*? Why? / Why not?
How else might you describe these pictures? Would you use any of these words?

awe-inspiring	dazzling	flamboyant
indistinct	natural	spectacular
unimaginable		

3 Now read the article, ignoring the use of italics. Why does the writer draw a parallel between the Hubble image and Turner's work? What idea is expressed about art and beauty?

4 Say whether the italicised participles in the article are used actively or passively. Does each one refer to simultaneous action or to previous action? For example, *Gazing* is an active use, referring to the same time as the action in the main clause of the sentence (*we are savouring*).

ⓖ→ page 182

Beauty written in the stars

Gazing at the smoky, glowing gas clouds of the 'starburst' galaxy shown here, we are savouring a beauty that is the accidental product of events that happened in a distant time and part of the universe. The result looks like a great painting. To be precise, it is reminiscent of the work of Turner, that masterly nineteenth-century British artist. For John Ruskin, Turner's champion and near-contemporary, the object of art was to reveal the divine hand in nature. That was what he meant by beauty. What might he have said today, *having viewed* the pictures *taken* by the Hubble Space Telescope?

Having been launched in 1990 with an inaccurately ground lens, Hubble was initially a huge embarrassment, *sending* back indistinct images that impressed no one. However, the picture changed, quite literally, in 1993. On *being* successfully *repaired* by shuttle astronauts, the telescope proceeded to relay the most spectacular images to us. Hubble is now like an eye with a cataract removed, *seeing* into deep space with a hard, bright precision that is almost uncomfortable.

There has never been a more gratuitous addition to our store of beauty. Ultimately, when we call a work of art beautiful we are comparing it to nature. The underlying structures of nature *imitated* by artists from ancient Greece until the middle of the twentieth century were chosen because nature was perceived as beautiful. If we don't talk much about 'beauty' in contemporary art, it is due to the fact that art is no longer concerned with the representation of nature. Arguably, the photographs taken by Hubble are the most flamboyantly beautiful artworks of our time.

5 Join a sentence from 1–6 with one from a–f, starting each new sentence with a participle clause. Think about timing in the two sentences you are joining. An example (0 + g) is given.

EXAMPLE: *Having slashed the half-finished canvas with a knife, the temperamental artist threw his paints out of the seventh-storey window one by one.*

0 The temperamental artist slashed the half-finished canvas with a knife.
1 The exhibition includes some rather shocking images.
2 Andy Goldsworthy's sculptures often occur in open landscape.
3 Physicists want to create order from chaos.
4 The photographer took quite a few warm-up shots.
5 People come in from the street for an hour's rest.
6 I have already bought two previous works by this artist.

a They don't realise that the beds – and they themselves – are part of an installation.
b They are constantly trying to reduce the universe to a set of basic principles.
c It has received mixed reactions from members of the public.
d I am looking out for a third.
e Then he caught the model unawares in a more relaxed pose.
f They are particularly effective during dramatic weather conditions.
g He threw his paints out of the seventh-storey window one by one.

6 Complete the sentences with a suitable passive participle, formed from one of the verbs below.

announce	choose	damage	make
search	sell	show	

a The sculptures .... for the exhibition will all have to travel to New York by sea.
b Many of the images .... in advertisements at the moment are based on original artists' work.
c The colourful posters .... at the gallery could themselves become collectors' items one day.
d Jewellery .... from recycled glass and plastic is particularly popular.
e Delays have mainly been caused by visitors' belongings .... at the exhibition entrance.
f The shortlist .... yesterday has already provoked strong criticism.
g The museum basement .... by flooding last November will remain closed to visitors.

1 What is a visual *cliché*? Decide which of the images shown are the most clichéd, giving your reasons. Then describe something that is a cliché for you.

2 Read the two texts about clichéd images. Do they give complementary or opposing arguments? How far do you agree with the points made?

Text 1

When does a photographic style become a cliché? There can be little doubt that those images now deemed clichés were once powerful and stimulating photographs when they first appeared in the clubs, salons and magazines. Clearly, they merited the awards, and influenced many other photographers, and so photography could be seen to be moving forward. Such is the way of progress. But when an innovative winning image is copied by numerous others, hell-bent on walking off with the annual club trophy, a cliché is born. While the slavish copying of any image or existing style is the road to ultimate ruin, we should actively look at those images to find seeds of stimulation.

Text 2

When is a picture worth a thousand words? Some of nature's most remarkable images become clichés through familiarity, thanks to the commercial world we live in. Transferred to a squat greetings card or popular poster, the once exceptional representation of a radiant sunset over tranquil sea is rendered mundane. For consumer-driven websites, it is visual rather than verbal impact that counts, at least at the outset. The use of original, intriguing photos suggests creativity and innovation, while certain stock photos have become overused clichés, a disincentive to would-be customers. Images are more influential than ever in our digital age.

3 Which text gives specific examples of clichéd images? Why is this done, do you think? The comments in Style extra may help you.

 Exam spot

In Part 1 of Writing, the texts are a starting point for your own ideas. Although you need to summarise and evaluate the points made, you should move beyond any specific examples given in the texts, to include different examples of your own. Spend five minutes before you start writing, listing other things you can mention to support your evaluation.

 Style extra

Many adjectives carry disapproval, as in these examples from the two texts:
- *slavish copying* – the idea of copying is reinforced by the adjective and a lack of originality suggested
- *squat greetings card* – the adjective describes something that is small and ugly, so a contrast is emphasised between the exceptional and the mundane.

Here are other adjectives used to show disapproval, some of which occurred in earlier units.

childish behaviour   a **fatuous** remark
florid poetry/speeches   **glaring** errors/faults

4 Read these paragraphs, ignoring spaces 1–8 for the moment. Where does the writer make reference to specific examples? Underline the phrases used to introduce these.

> Both texts consider the negative effect of clichéd images. The first text is concerned with photography as an art form and the important point made is that **(1)**............. remains vital, in the search for truly original photographic images. **(2)**.............portrait shots, such as those by Irving Penn and Diane Arbus among others, should be viewed by others in the profession as **(3)**............. triggers for new developments and techniques, rather than merely being replicated – the "slavish copying" that is referred to so **(4)**............. by the writer.
>
> The second text outlines the pivotal position of imagery in our modern world, especially in relation to the use of photographs to sell goods and services on the Internet. Take for instance the cliché-ridden use of visuals like the business handshake or the world as a globe that appear on **(5)**............. marketing websites. Given that these images are ubiquitous, how can they be sufficiently **(6)**............. ? As the saying goes, "familiarity breeds contempt" – such a degree of overuse totally **(7)**............. what was initially a powerful image, making it banal and **(8)**.............

5 Use the words given in capitals below to form suitable words to fit in spaces 1–8 in the text in 4. Questions 2 and 8 require a compound.

1 EXPERIMENT	5 COUNT
2 LAND	6 PERSUADE
3 INSPIRE	7 VALUE
4 DISMISS	8 PLACE

6 Select suitable phrases from a–d to insert in the final paragraph opposite, to produce an answer of the target exam length (240–280 words).

a one of the most crucial aspects
b innovative visual material
c genuinely creative excellence
d photography in its own right

> Central to both these texts is a consideration of the role of **(1)**............. in the 21st century. The first text is quite specialist in its subject matter, focusing solely on **(2)**............. The second text is far more relevant to contemporary life. It rightly argues that "visual impact" is **(3)**............. to achieve – any company seeking to engage new customers via its website has no alternative but to invest in **(4)**............. and cannot afford to be satisfied with second-best.

Reading and Use of English, Part 7
Multiple matching

This part of the Reading and Use of English paper focuses on your ability to retrieve specific information from a text. You are given 10 questions and you must find the answers either in a group of texts or in one which has been divided into sections.

Read the Exam advice and then do the task below.

You are going to read an extract from an article about paintings. For questions **1–10**, choose from the sections (**A–E**). The sections may be chosen more than once.

In which section are the following mentioned?

the inscrutable nature of the subjects	1
the artist's ability to give an insight into temperament	2
the integrity of the image portrayed	3
the view that the artist was an innovator	4
delight in a painting's ability to endure	5
the background to a painting being well documented	6
the view that a painting's impact depends on its surroundings	7
a painting which gives an image of a lost world	8
admiration for an artist who dared to challenge conventional ideas	9
conflicting opinions about the subject of a painting	10

EXAM ADVICE

- Read the title and, if there is one, the subtitle carefully.
- Skim the sections quickly to get an idea of the subject matter. Don't worry about vocabulary that you aren't familiar with.
- Read through the questions carefully.
- Scan the text to find the specific information that answers the questions. When you find an answer in the text, underline it and put the question number next to it.
- Don't spend too much time looking for an answer to a question. Leave it until the end and go on to the next question.
- At the end, go back to the questions you have no answer to or the ones which you are unsure of. Never leave a blank on your answer sheet.
- The questions ask you to locate words/ phrases/sentences that mean the same as the ones used in the questions – a paraphrase. Often, an idea will be repeated in more than one section, but only one section really answers the question.
- Don't just look for a word in the question being repeated in the text. This will not be the answer, just a distractor.
- Check to make sure that the part of the text where you think the answer is fully answers the question. Sometimes the question comes in two parts, for example, *a surprising view held on the integrity of a subject*.

Mr and Mrs Andrews, by Gainsborough

Henry VII, 29 October 1505, by unknown artist

Paintings which inspire

Art experts give their opinions

A Luisa Sutton

A Bar at the Folies-Bergère, by Edouard Manet

Manet was inviting some kind of response in the way in which he presented women in his work and he succeeded in bridging the gap between classical traditions and painting modern life. Above all, I have tremendous respect for the fact that he was a breakthrough artist: a champion of realist modernism who was censured for breaking the mould. Through the medium of painting, Manet constantly reassessed the prevailing attitudes of the world he was living in. Today we are used to multiple perspective – seeing the same image from different angles. This was not so in Manet's time, and in this painting we see him crossing boundaries as he switches reality by employing a mirror to reflect his subjects.

B Paul Harris

Henry VII, 29 October 1505, by unknown artist

Visually, this is a stunning portrait; Henry moves towards the viewer from the parapet wearing the red robes of Lancaster, his hands on the ledge. It is immediately exciting and emotive. Henry VII was on the lookout for a new bride and this was painted to be sent to the court of Maximilian, much as we would send a photo today. So the provenance is clear. Portraits of other English monarchs, Richard III in particular, are, in comparison, stiff and remote. Henry VII's portrait speaks in a very particular way. His eyes look at one. He is Renaissance Man but, at the same time one sees a shrewd, wise and wily man who, throughout his reign, managed to amass the fortune of the Tudor dynasty.

C Tom Newman

James VI and I, 1618, by Paul Van Somer

I used to work for an art handling company in New York, and I came to realise how wonderful paintings are as entities. Old paintings last for so long because of the materials used – the oil is so robust, it expands or contracts depending on the heat. They can be rolled up and taken around the world, they'll never die. This portrait, in particular, made a huge impression on me. Works of art often lose their power as soon as they're placed in a museum. This painting is where it belongs – in a palace. Subject to who you speak to, James is either a buffoon or a tactical genius, but in this work he looks so stately. The painting was clearly commissioned to convey regality – and it worked on me, 400 years later.

D Paula Smith

Mr and Mrs Andrews, by Gainsborough

I chose this painting as it has personal relevance for me. I grew up in my grandmother's house in London. She was an excellent copyist of Gainsborough. We had copies of all of his paintings, except for this one, which my grandmother didn't approve of. I've always found it incredibly beautiful though. The two figures in this wonderful painting have very enigmatic expressions. What are they up to? What are they thinking? And then what are we to make of the landscape? It's an agricultural scene, in the middle of the day, but there are no agricultural workers anywhere to be seen. Where on earth is everybody? What a strange atmosphere the place has, a long ago era that will never be recaptured.

E Lynn D'Anton

An Old Woman Cooking Eggs, 1618, by Velàzquez

What is most striking about this painting is surely its veracity. One gets the feeling that one is looking into a room in which there are no obstacles to understanding. Nothing comes between the subject and the observer. The artist here is the perfect observer. When I saw it a few years ago in the National Gallery of Scotland, set alongside many other works from Velazquez's youth, there was no doubt in my mind that it was a masterpiece. I think that it is easy for many people to empathise with this painting in one way or another.

Urban jungle

1 Rank these factors according to their likely importance for city residents. What would be the most important benefit for you?

diverse employment opportunities
low levels of pollution
sufficient open spaces

effortless access to amenities
spacious living accommodation

Reading

2 You are going to read an extract from an article on urban planning (see page 67). First, look at questions 1–10 and check you understand the key words and phrases that have been highlighted.

In which section are the following mentioned?

the interrelationship between metropolitan
amenities and good conduct | 1 | |

the failure to see through a project
according to its original design | 2 | |

an indication of the expectations
held by a majority of citizens | 3 | |

the lack of transport infrastructure
in one development | 4 | |

the avoidance of urban
development on the periphery | 5 | |

the apparent failure to foster
sufficient urban renewal | 6 | |

an experiment in mixed-use
communities prior to the CNU | 7 | |

an inability to identify adequate
sites of a certain type | 8 | |

the slow pace of change due to
relatively recent construction | 9 | |

an unforeseen environmental
consequence of planning policy | 10 | |

3 For questions 1–10, choose from the sections (A–E) in the text opposite. The sections may be chosen more than once.

Vocabulary

Compound adjectives and their collocations

> Several compound adjectives are used in the article, such as *mixed-use*, *car-dependent*. Compound adjectives are often formed from a present or past participle with a preposition, as in *boarded*-**up**, an adjective, as in **slow**-*paced*, or an adverb, as in **forward**-*thinking*.

4 Make compound adjectives using these lists and suggest noun collocations for each one. For example, *well-constructed (house)*; *smashed-up (car)*; *quick-thinking (politician)*.

Adjectives	Adverbs	Participles	Prepositions
quick	well	constructed	down
long	far	smashed	up
short	poorly	sighted	out
		blown	through
		fitting/fitted	
		running/run	
		thinking/thought	

The *New Urbanism* architectural movement

A The Congress for the New Urbanism (CNU) was founded two decades ago by a group of talented architects in the USA, who were looking to create sustainable, walkable, mixed-use neighbourhoods. One of their most ambitious projects, by founder member Peter Calthorpe, was Laguna West, south of Sacramento. However, during the grim California recession of the 1990s, the original developer for this scheme went bankrupt and the entire project was taken over by a less sympathetic developer, who contravened virtually all of CNU's principles. Had Laguna West been completed as Calthorpe planned it, it would have been one of the great visionary new towns of the late 20th century. As things have turned out, it is just another conventional, car-dependent suburb. And the current extent of New Urbanist communities in terms of population absorption implies that if they are regarded as a solution to metropolitan problems, all the usual clichés – shuffling the deckchairs on the Titanic, fiddling while Rome burns, etc. – must apply.

B The key principles of the CNU remain unchanged. They seek to promote neighbourhoods that are diverse in terms of use and have mixed populations in terms of age, race and income. They believe in giving communities transportation alternatives – especially walking, cycling and public transit. They have a strong preference for 'infill' development – that is, the use of land within a built-up area, especially as part of a community redevelopment project – rather than the endless expansion of cities sometimes referred to as 'urban sprawl'. They give some priority to accessible public spaces, community institutions and a variety of parks and other green spaces, in order to foster exemplary civic behaviour.

C New Urbanist communities are intended to be more than residential subdivisions, with shops, a wide range of personal and consumer services, and workplace sites all conveniently accessible on foot. This is one of the plans for Kentlands, perhaps the most successful of the NU communities to date, and yet commercial development in terms of employment opportunities is lagging far behind. The same idea of 'self-containment' was one of the principles behind the creation of the British new towns of the 1960s, such as Milton Keynes and Telford. Job prospects were certainly good in these towns, though unfortunately the vacancies did not cater to the resident population, due to skill mismatch and other reasons. The overwhelming tendency was for residents to work elsewhere, with the jobs available in the new towns filled by commuters from outside, with the net result being more use of fossil fuels rather than less.

D Critics of the CNU say that it embraces pie-in-the-sky social engineering based on a false diagnosis of society's urban problems, an excessive faith in the ability to change the world, and the prescription of policies that are implementable only under very special circumstances. Urban capital stock is already largely in place and remains a constant, while much of the residential housing in the US has been built in the last 40 years, so innovation through renewal is off the agenda for the time being. Hence, the practical consequences of New Urbanism continue to be a small number of relatively small communities accommodating a miniscule proportion of metropolitan population growth. The US government-sponsored company Fannie Mae's research into housing preferences shows that up to 80% of US households would hope to live in a single-family dwelling with a garden, regardless of income, race or current tenure status. It is only possible to meet these preferences through high-density developments in the suburbs.

E As for the idea that somehow New Urbanism can contribute to the stability, if not revival, of city centers, it remains just that – an idea. Most NU communities are being built on green field sites some distance away from the central city, and infill development has been limited – probably of necessity because of land scarcity – to tiny pockets. Hence, there is no identifiable relationship between NU communities and the fate of central cities and those who live there. If there is some consensus for tackling the social problems found in the central cities (and it is by no means clear that this consensus exists), it would be far better to deal with these problems via direct, tightly-targeted measures rather than via land use controls and social experiments on the metropolitan fringe. The real issue for the city of today is how to counter or accommodate the obvious loss of commercial investment from its heart to its suburbs, which has created run-down central neighbourhoods supported by few amenities. The New Urbanists are largely silent on this.

8.2 Inversion

1 This sentence from the article in 8.1 is an example of inversion.

> ...s. Had
> Laguna West been completed as Calthorpe planned it, it would
> have been one of the great visionary new towns of the late 20th
> century. ...

Inversion is often used in formal English, but in fact also appears in less formal writing and spoken English, to emphasise or contrast something.

The example above shows inversion in a conditional sentence with the past perfect. The fixed expression *Had it not been for...* also uses the past perfect, to talk about the reasons for changed results:
Had it not been for Ben, we would have got totally lost in Madrid.

Inversion is also commonly used after a time adverbial, like the next two examples.
No sooner had we left the building than it started to pour with rain.
Barely had Janie recovered from her operation when she was promoted.

Sometimes a full time clause precedes the inversion.
Only after a rigorous security check were we allowed to enter the building.

G → page 182

2 Finish the sentences using your own ideas and the tenses specified.
  a Never before … (present perfect)
  b Only once in my life … (present perfect)
  c Scarcely … (past perfect) when … (past simple)
  d No sooner … (past perfect) than … (past simple)
  e Hardly … (past perfect) when … (past simple)
  f Not until last month … (past simple)
  g Seldom … (present simple)
  h Rarely … (future simple)
  i Had it not been for the fact that … (past perfect / past simple and would have + past participle)

Inversion also occurs in written description after adverbials of place (usually prepositional phrases).
Opposite the gallery entrance stands an imposing bronze statue.
Under the table sat a tiny mouse with bright, beady eyes.

Notice how the verbs used in these examples are to do with location. Verbs of movement, for example, *come, go, run*, are also used in this way.
Up the hill crawled the number 77 bus.
Alongside the road runs the River Avon.

3 Complete the short description in the grey panel using these verbs in a suitable past tense. Use each verb once only.

| be   do   hang   have   sit   stand   stretch |

At the very end of a dead-end street (1) .... a rather run-down hotel. Jan and I approached it in trepidation – in spite of the torrential rain, it looked neither warm nor welcoming. Just inside the door on a rickety bar stool (2) .... an old man, probably the night porter. Above his head (3) .... the keys to all the rooms – not a single one taken, or so it seemed. We looked at each other, conscious of the rain lashing down outside. Only by chance (4) .... we come this way in the first place, but there was nothing for it: we steeled ourselves and checked in.

At the top of three flights of stairs (no lift) (5) .... a long, dark corridor, that eventually led to our room. How could they put us so far away when every room was vacant? We decided to go down and ask to be moved. However, scarcely (6) .... we back in the lobby when six or seven taxis drew up outside,

---

Here are some other types of inversion:

after prepositional phrases with *no*
On no account should children be left unsupervised in this play area.
In no way can a goalless draw be seen as a good result for United.
Under no circumstances was Sally going to admit defeat.

after *not*
Not only did the team win the county cup, they also came top of their league.
Not one grain of encouragement did she show him throughout the course.

discharging hordes of well-dressed, happy individuals, including a bride and groom. It seemed the old man's niece had just got married and the entire wedding party was staying over at her uncle's hotel. Jan didn't sleep a wink that night, and neither (7) .... I. It was the best party we'd ever been to!

after *little*
Little did I think then that I would miss the bright lights in years to come.
Little was she expecting Sam to walk through that door.

with *so/such … that*
So popular has the system become that it now carries nearly two million passengers each day.
Such was the outcry that the advertisement had to be withdrawn.

with *neither* or *nor*
Yasmin doesn't relish living in a high-rise apartment and neither do I.
Jenny hasn't been asked to work overtime and nor should you be.

4 For questions 1–8, complete the second sentence so that it has a similar meaning to the first sentence, using the word given. **Do not change the word given.** You must use between **three** and **eight** words, including the word given.

1 That week, the train was late every day except for Friday.
   run
   Only .... that week and that was Friday.

2 Shortly after Sue and Brian met, he announced they were getting married.
   had
   Scarcely .... he announced they were getting married.

3 You are not staying out late tonight!
   no
   Under .... stay out late tonight!

4 They left their car and almost immediately heard a deafening crash.
   sooner
   No .... they heard a deafening crash.

5 Kerry didn't send us any postcards during her travels through Argentina.
   one
   Not .... she was travelling in Argentina.

6 It wasn't long before the bus company increased their prices for a second time.
   put
   Hardly .... before they increased them again.

7 The demand for tickets is so high that the play has been extended by a month.
   has
   So .... the play has been extended by a month.

8 There are beautiful buildings in Barcelona and it has a wonderful climate too.
   only
   In Barcelona, not .... is also wonderful.

Vocabulary

Phrases with *place*

1 What is the meaning of the idiom below? How might it apply to living in a village as opposed to a city, or vice versa? Use the pictures for ideas.

The grass is always greener …

2 **1 13** Listen to three people discussing where they live. What is their relationship? What are the pros and cons of their *lifeplan*?

3 **1 13** As you listen again, note down the idioms you hear that include these key words. Then match them to explanations 1–6.

a	blue	**1**	only benefits
b	frame	**2**	to summarise
c	roses	**3**	reduce your options
d	burn	**4**	not possible
e	nutshell	**5**	by chance
f	worlds	**6**	things aren't perfect

◎ Idiom spot

How can idioms be learned most efficiently? They can be grouped in various ways:
- as pairs of words: *high and dry, touch and go*
- by topic: *eat humble pie, spill the beans*
- by form: *out of (the blue / this world), in (a nutshell / the bag)*
- by key word: *strike (it lucky / a chord / gold)*

One of the key words in 3 is used in many other idioms. Which one? Use it in a suitable form to complete these idioms and then give an example situation to explain the meaning of each.

a … *a hole in your pocket*
b … *the midnight oil*
c *get your fingers* …
d *fiddling while Rome* …
e *have money to* …
f … *your bridges*

4 Look at this sentence from the recording.

Everything's fallen into place.

The noun *place* has several meanings and is used in many common phrases. Complete sentences a–e to check how many you know.

a During the festival, there are a lot of exciting events .... place in different parts of the city.

b Traffic restrictions have been .... place for several months in an attempt to reduce pollution levels in the urban area.

c The amount of litter on our streets is appalling – there are empty drinks cans and discarded packaging .... the place!

d The city of Derry has been awarded .... place and is the UK City of Culture for next year.

e I felt really .... place at the party as everyone else had dressed down for the occasion, while I was still in my office clothes!

5 Read the text about an organisation called PLACE. Select nouns from the box to complete spaces 1–8.

acronym	aspirations	consultation
demolition	network	neighbourhood
occupancy	regeneration	sector spaces

PLACE was established in 2004 and is an architecture centre based in Belfast, Northern Ireland – the name is the **1** .... of Planning, Landscape, Architecture, Community and Environment. PLACE belongs to a large, loosely-connected **2** .... of centres and organisations across the world, from Canada to Japan.

PLACE does not design buildings or public **3** .... – its role is to engage people in how architecture and design affects their lives. For example, they have embraced the education **4** .... , reaching out to young people in order to increase their understanding of good design.

Exam spot

In Speaking, Part 3, each candidate has an individual long turn of two minutes. You will be given a prompt card containing the question you have to speak about. Below the question are three ideas, which you can include or not, as you wish. The emphasis is on your ability to speak fluently and to organise your ideas into a coherent whole. Before you start speaking, use the ten seconds allowed to order your thoughts.

6   Look at the prompt card below. In groups of four, brainstorm and note down possible ideas, starting with the three areas listed but also including other aspects. Remember to think of both positive and negative points.

> Are there more benefits or drawbacks to living in a city nowadays?
>
> ● employment   ● amenities   ● housing

7   Now form two pairs. Each pair should select three of the group's ideas and then decide how to organise these ideas into a short talk.

Things to consider are:

Balance
Both benefits and drawbacks need to be mentioned.

Discourse management
What is the clearest order of ideas?
How will you introduce the topic?
How can you signal a new point?
How will you round off?

Exemplification
Can you give examples to underline your point of view, either personal or general?

Since the sectarian troubles in Belfast, the city has undergone many changes and improvements, and PLACE has recently played a part in this **5** .... At the junction of the Falls and the Glen Road in West Belfast lies the site of the former Andersonstown Barracks, an oppressive presence in the **6** .... for many years. Following the **7** .... of the original building and several failed attempts to invest in the site, PLACE was asked to run a programme of public **8** .... and participation, which was very successful.

Which organisational aspect does each of these phrases relate to? Write B, D or E beside each one.

EXAMPLE: *Speaking personally …*   E

a *The question is complex …*
b *All things considered …*
c *… is a separate issue.*
d *One definite disadvantage is …*
e *That is not to say that …*
f *The third and perhaps most important …*
g *Take the area of …*
h *To evaluate this …*
i *By way of illustration …*
j *Moving on to …*
k *Taking everything into account …*
l *More specifically …*

8   One person in each pair should now run through their long turn, with the second person time-keeping and taking notes as to where an idea could be developed or should be cut down. Aim for 30 seconds on each of three ideas, with a short introduction and conclusion.

 Exam spot

Following each long turn in Speaking, Part 3, the second candidate is asked a question by the interlocutor that relates to what they have been listening to, so you must pay attention during the two minutes when your partner is speaking, and listen carefully to what is said. One minute is allowed for your response to the interlocutor's question and further discussion with the other candidate.

9   Give your long turn to the rest of the group. One student in the second pair should take on the role of the interlocutor, asking Student B one of the questions below after Student A's long turn. The fourth student in the group should time the performance and indicate when the time allowed has elapsed (see Exam spot for details).

> Choice of questions for Student B:
>
> ● What is the main drawback to city living, in your opinion?
> ● Do / Would you enjoy living in a big city, on the whole? (Why? / Why not?)
> ● If you could make one improvement to your neighbourhood, what would it be and why?

Writing folder 4

Part 2 Set text question: Film tie-in

Question 5 of Writing offers two options, a) and b) – one on each of the specified set texts. At least one of these texts will have a film version and it is acceptable to study the film in place of or alongside the book. This Writing folder suggests ways of approaching the set text through film, and includes an essay task. Writing folder 8 focuses on writing a book review.

1   Read the suggestions below about how to start out on the set text. Is there anything you would add?

Tips for the set text

- Use the Internet to familiarise yourself with the story you are going to study.
- Watch trailers of the film to get an impression of the main characters.
- Visit a bookselling website to find out more – check out any sample pages and customer reviews.
- Read online comments from people who have seen the film.
- Do an Internet search on the author's name to see whether s/he has an official website.

2   *The Secret Life of Bees* by Sue Monk Kidd was chosen as a set text for the Proficiency exam. Read this description of the story, taken from the author's website. Does the story interest you? Why? / Why not?

The Secret Life of Bees

It is the summer of 1964 in South Carolina, USA. Living on a peach farm with her harsh, unyielding father, 14-year-old Lily Owens has shaped her entire life around one devastating, blurred memory – the afternoon her mother was killed, when Lily was four. Since then, her only real companion has been the fierce-hearted, and sometimes just fierce, black woman Rosaleen, who acts as her 'stand-in mother'.

When Rosaleen insults three of the deepest racists in town, Lily knows it's time for them both to leave. They take off in the only direction Lily can think of, to a town called Tiburon – a name she found on the back of a picture amid the few possessions left by her mother. Lily and Rosaleen are given refuge in Tiburon by a trio of black sisters who run a bee-keeping business from their home, the Pink House.

3   While you are watching the film, think about the following questions.

1   Dakota Fanning, the young actor who plays Lily, was born in the southern state of Georgia. She was only 14 when the film was released. How might her age and background have helped her performance?

2   The character of Rosaleen was recast as a younger woman in the film. Why do you think this was done?

3   Through the book and film, we learn a great deal about the process of bee-keeping. Why is this theme important to the story?

4   How do the three sisters, August, June and May, differ in character?

5   The author, Sue Monk Kidd, has commented on the film's accuracy in terms of scene setting. What examples of this do you notice in the Pink House and its surroundings?

4   Read the exam task below and the sample answer on page 73, ignoring the spaces for the moment. How would you conclude the essay?

Your teacher has asked you to write an essay discussing how events and details included in *The Secret Life of Bees* reflect the historical period in which the story is set. You should give specific examples based on your knowledge of the book or the film.

Write your **essay**.

The story of 'The Secret Life of Bees' takes place in South Carolina in the summer of 1964, against the backdrop of the desegregation of the American south. It is clear through the many examples of meticulous 1 .... that the director and the other members of her 2 .... researched the historical background to the story thoroughly, in order to breathe life and authenticity into the story. The brilliant 3 .... adds tremendous atmosphere, suggesting a long hot summer through its portrayal of harsh daylight and sultry nights.

Early on in the film at T. Ray's peach farm, we see President Johnson talking about the Civil Rights Act on a fuzzy black and white TV screen. This brief clip places the story very precisely in time. Other aspects that confirm the period of the 4 .... are the 1960s cars, the commemorative plates of President Kennedy displayed on the parlour walls of the Pink House (the 5 .... excelled itself in sourcing these), the old washing machine that sits out on the porch, and also snatches of popular music from the time. The 6 .... must have spent a considerable number of hours researching the dresses and hats, as well.

One particularly moving event that highlights the continuing reality of segregation is when Zach and Lily go to see a film together. They buy their tickets separately and have to enter the cinema through separate doors – Zach goes through the one marked 'COLORED' – but once inside, they sit together upstairs and watch the film. However, this is not tolerated by some of the racist townspeople, who manhandle Zach and take him off to jail, where he is beaten up.

Rosaleen's thwarted attempt to register to vote on July 4 is the key event that prompts her and Lily to flee. During the scene, the state of Mississippi is mentioned, which is where the most brutal attacks on would-be black voters occurred. Here, the 7 .... has decided to depart slightly from the book in transferring the mention of Mississippi from Lily's thoughts into Rosaleen's mouth, but it seems a valid change from book to 8 .... , which serves to underline the reality of Rosaleen's position and the very real risk she is taking in a bigoted southern town.

5 Now complete spaces 1–8 with the correct word or phrase to do with film-making, choosing from the box. There are two extra words that you do not need to use.

action	cast
cinematography	crew
producer	props department
scene setting	screenplay
script writer	wardrobe manager

6 Now write an essay based on the exam task in 4. If you have not read *The Secret Life of Bees*, refer to the book and film tie-in of your choice. Follow the advice given below.

EXAM ADVICE

- Don't be afraid to refer exclusively to the film of the book – you will not be penalised for doing this.
- Plan your answer, noting down specific examples that you can mention.
- Use an appropriate register for the task type required – this will be unmarked to formal for an essay.
- Summarise your views in a conclusion.
- Demonstrate a wide range of language, including vocabulary relevant to novels and film-making.

Units 5–8 Revision

Use of English

1 Read this extract from the book *No Logo*. Decide which answer
   (A, B, C or D) best fits each gap.

   1 **A** tokens   **B** emblems   **C** marks   **D** signs
   2 **A** elegance   **B** countenance   **C** flamboyance   **D** resemblance
   3 **A** scurried into **B** put onto   **C** tucked into   **D** latched onto
   4 **A** caused   **B** kept   **C** served   **D** made
   5 **A** flap   **B** bill   **C** note   **D** tag
   6 **A** branch   **B** accessory   **C** annexe   **D** extension
   7 **A** discover   **B** uphold   **C** reveal   **D** pioneer
   8 **A** leading   **B** prevalent   **C** dominant   **D** outstanding

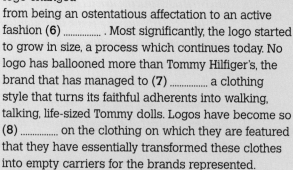

Logos on clothes used to be generally hidden from view, discreetly placed on the inside of the collar. Small designer **(1)** .... did appear on the outside of shirts, but such sporty attire was pretty much restricted to the golf courses and tennis courts of the rich. In the late 1970s, when the fashion world rebelled against the **(2)** .... of the hippie era, Lacoste's alligator escaped from the sports club and **(3)** .... the streets, dragging the logo decisively onto the outside of the shirt. These logos **(4)** .... the same social function as keeping the item of clothing's price **(5)** .... on: everyone knew precisely what premium the wearer was willing to pay for style. Gradually, the logo changed from being an ostentatious affectation to an active fashion **(6)** .... Most significantly, the logo started to grow in size, a process which continues today. No logo has ballooned more than Tommy Hilfiger's, the brand that has managed to **(7)** .... a clothing style that turns its faithful adherents into walking, talking, life-sized Tommy dolls. Logos have become so **(8)** .... on the clothing on which they are featured that they have essentially transformed these clothes into empty carriers for the brands represented.

2 For questions 1–6, complete the second sentence so that it has a similar meaning to the first
   sentence, using the word given. **Do not change the word given.** You must use between **three**
   and **eight** words, including the word given.

   1 Many people used to believe that they would
         lose their soul if their photo was taken.
         widespread
         There was once ....
         taken would mean losing your soul.

   2 I'm quite sure that Bill hasn't left yet as I saw
         him yesterday.
         set
         Bill .... as I saw
         him yesterday.

   3 Bridgton is very proud of its new shopping mall.
         takes
         Bridgton .... its
         new shopping mall.

   4 We weren't aware at the time that we were
         making a big mistake.
         know
         Little .... big
         mistake we were making.

   5 I had only just come back from the supermarket
         when I realised I had forgotten to buy any milk.
         returned
         No sooner ....
         I realised I had forgotten to buy any milk.

   6 I've often thought of you when listening to that
         sonata by Barsanti.
         come
         Many's .... when I
         have been listening to that sonata by Barsanti.

Vocabulary

3 Decide which word or phrase is correct in the following sentences.

EXAMPLE: You're well within your *right/rights* to complain to the manager.

The correct expression is 'be within your rights'.

a Pablo couldn't find his credit card anywhere, even though it was right under his *chin/nose* all the time.

b A *burst/puff* of applause greeted his entrance onto the stage.

c Toni has been *seriously/singularly* unsuccessful in her attempts to sell her range of clothes.

d It was a *grain/stroke* of luck that the plane was delayed because of bad weather, otherwise we would've missed it.

e I'm fed up with being taken *for granted/by surprise* by my flatmates, who seem to expect me to do all the washing up.

f Celebrities complain bitterly about being in the public *eye/purse*, but this is the price they pay for fame.

g My neighbour took *exception/part* when I left my car parked outside his house.

h His speech when he came on stage certainly struck a *note/chord* with the audience, who loved it.

i It is *widely/staggeringly* believed that glaciers are not melting because of climate change.

j A rumble of *thunder/wind* could be heard in the distance.

k I think the festival succeeded because it was in *chord/tune* with what the audience expected.

l Stefan takes the *stand/view* that people should be responsible for their own actions.

m I have never *been/seen* eye to eye with my boss.

n Lisa's behaviour at the party was incredibly *childish/youthful*.

o I always knew that my sister would turn out to be someone of *note/score*.

Writing

4 Insert rhetorical questions A–E into this essay about modern art and music.

A Is the world of contemporary music any better?

B Yet is there genuine technical skill in Damien Hirst's sheep, pickled in formaldehyde?

C What has happened to good judgement and common sense?

D So should we look again to nature to provide us with the beauty that we crave?

E Have these composers really nowhere left to go?

1 [ ] In my opinion, the art world lacks both. It has, moreover, abandoned its traditional role, that of being pleasing to the senses. Modern artists are merely out to shock, to be sensationalist. Bound up with this ruthless modernism is intense commercialism. Prices are inflated by urban galleries and urbane collectors, whose 'discerning' purchases appreciate by the day, as mediocre artists are successfully hyped as the latest Andy Warhol or Georgia O'Keeffe.

2 [ ] Here, too, we are no longer given works we can enjoy, but 'difficult' music with no discernible melody, that jangles the nerves and leaves us with a dreadful headache.

3 [ ] Yet perhaps I am making the very same mistake as contemporary critics of Georges Seurat's, who shunned his masterpieces and saw him die at the age of 31, poor and unappreciated. Maybe in another twenty years, the music that I personally cannot fathom will be regarded as safe and conventional; the art installations seen as old hat.

4 [ ] The jury's still out. Living in our post-industrial society, the vast majority of today's artists and musicmakers fail to give us any beauty in their work, exhibiting only their own creative frustration. **5** [ ] Or at least, as Andy Goldsworthy has proved, art could be transported to a more meaningful setting, where commercialism does not hold sway.

Speaking

1 Discuss the photos with a partner. Why do you think the people have chosen to wear those particular clothes?

2 What would you wear on the following occasions? Make sure you justify your decisions.

- to a classical concert
- to a rock festival
- on a long-distance plane trip
- on a first date
- at a club
- at a job interview
- to a wedding
- to the gym

Vocabulary

3 You are going to hear five people talking about what they wear. Before listening, complete the sentences below, which contain some of the words and expressions you will hear in the recordings. Choose the word or phrase in italics which best fits the meaning of the sentence. Use a dictionary to help you.

a The office manager decided that Friday should be dress-*down/off* day.

b I hated the thought of being *glued/stuck* behind a desk all day.

c The *outlay/outgoings* on my wedding dress was huge.

d I would steer *clear/straight* of having your hair dyed, if I were you.

e When I read about lip piercing, I was absolutely *caught/hooked* on the idea.

f My wearing jeans to the interview really raised some *eyebrows/looks*.

g Turning up to my ex-girlfriend's wedding in trainers really got up her *nose/face*.

h Alicia wasn't sure which pair of jeans to *take/opt* for as both fitted well.

Listening

4 **1 14** You will hear five short extracts in which different people are talking about the way they dress. Read the Exam spot and complete Tasks One and Two.

◎ Exam spot

In Listening, Part 4, you are tested on whether you can identify gist, attitude, main points and interpret context. You need to complete two tasks as you listen. Sometimes you will hear the answer to Task Two before you hear the answer to Task One. You hear the recording twice.

TASK ONE

For questions **1–5**, choose from the list **(A–H)** what caused each speaker to choose a particular way of dressing.

TASK TWO

For questions **6–10**, choose from the list **(A–H)** what each speaker mentions is the benefit of the way they dress.

While you listen, you must complete both tasks.

A feeling a distinct
  pressure to conform   Speaker 1 | 1 |
B being bullied at school   Speaker 2 | 2 |
C being influenced by
  a colleague   Speaker 3 | 3 |
D seeing an article   Speaker 4 | 4 |
E attending a music festival
F visiting another country   Speaker 5 | 5 |
G wanting to rebel
  against society
H needing to make a
  good impression

A increased
  comfort   Speaker 1 | 6 |
B less expense   Speaker 2 | 7 |
C instant recognition
D improved safety   Speaker 3 | 8 |
E more authority   Speaker 4 | 9 |
F faster promotion
  at work   Speaker 5 | 10 |
G higher self-esteem
H greater acceptance
  by others

5 With a partner, talk about how you made your decisions.

6 What do you think about different ways of dressing? What would make you change the way you dress? Talk about your ideas with a partner.

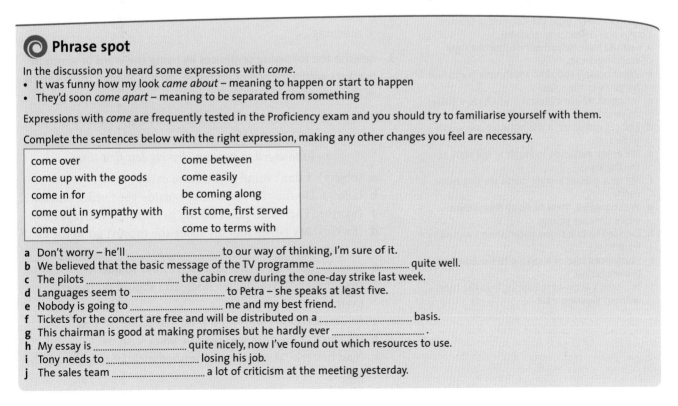

◎ Phrase spot

In the discussion you heard some expressions with *come*.
- It was funny how my look *came about* – meaning to happen or start to happen
- They'd soon *come apart* – meaning to be separated from something

Expressions with *come* are frequently tested in the Proficiency exam and you should try to familiarise yourself with them.

Complete the sentences below with the right expression, making any other changes you feel are necessary.

come over	come between
come up with the goods	come easily
come in for	be coming along
come out in sympathy with	first come, first served
come round	come to terms with

a Don't worry – he'll .... to our way of thinking, I'm sure of it.
b We believed that the basic message of the TV programme .... quite well.
c The pilots .... the cabin crew during the one-day strike last week.
d Languages seem to .... to Petra – she speaks at least five.
e Nobody is going to .... me and my best friend.
f Tickets for the concert are free and will be distributed on a .... basis.
g This chairman is good at making promises but he hardly ever ....
h My essay is .... quite nicely, now I've found out which resources to use.
i Tony needs to .... losing his job.
j The sales team .... a lot of criticism at the meeting yesterday.

9.2 Gerunds and infinitives

1 It is important to realise that verbs cannot be learned in isolation. You should always learn what follows a verb in order to use it accurately.

Finish these sentences with the correct form of the words in brackets. There may be more than one answer.

a I stopped (wear) any sort of uniform the day I left school.

b My brother used (wear) a grey sweater and black trousers to school.

c I prefer (you/wear) a suit to work.

d Tom prefers (wear) jeans at the weekend.

e His boss forced (him/shave) his beard off.

f Her mum let (her/wear) high heels to the party.

 G → page 183

Corpus spot

One of the biggest problems students have when writing at Proficiency level is the use of gerunds and infinitives. Look at the following sentences taken from the *Cambridge Learner Corpus* and correct any mistakes.

a I would have helped her finding the right wedding dress.

b We shouldn't spend so much time try to find bargains in the sales.

c I suggest to use a plaster if you have a blister on your foot.

d The old uniforms in the museum are worth to be seen.

e We enjoy ourselves to laugh at the stars at the Oscars.

f My new glasses enable me to reading more easily.

g We should let them to enjoy themselves while they are young.

h I missed to talk to my sister when I was away from home.

i I convinced him of applying to the Editor of the magazine.

j You aren't allowed to coming into the hotel without wearing a tie.

2 Some verbs take either a gerund or an infinitive, but change their meaning accordingly. With a partner, discuss the difference in meaning of the following pairs of sentences.

EXAMPLE: Sheila stopped having a break at work. – *'stopped' means 'ceased', i.e. she didn't have a break any more*

Sheila stopped to have a break before continuing her work. – *the reason she stopped was to have a break*

a I mean to mark all these essays before ten o' clock.

b It will mean having to start earlier.

c We regret to inform you that you haven't been accepted at fashion college.

d I regret wearing stiletto heels when I was young.

e I remember going for long walks in the snow.

f Remember to buy the milk, will you?

g I hope you didn't forget to post my letter.

h I can't forget meeting my first boyfriend.

i Try to understand my feelings, will you?

j Try opening the window, if you're feeling sleepy.

k Professor Winters went on to speak about *Paradise Lost* after he'd introduced everyone present.

l My mother goes on talking even when no one appears to be listening.

m Roger came to accept she wouldn't marry him.

n She came rushing into the room in some alarm.

o I was lucky enough to hear Muse sing in London.

p I heard the birds singing in the tree outside my room every morning.

3 Rewrite the following sentences by using the word or words in brackets with a gerund or infinitive. Do not change the meaning of the sentence.

EXAMPLE: (manage) I succeeded in passing my driving test first time.

I managed to pass my driving test first time.

a (object) I don't mind if you leave early.

b (allow) Do they let you smoke outside your office entrance?

c (worth) There's no point asking her out, she's always busy.

d (forbid) My father told my sister she mustn't go to the club in town.

e (avoid) Book early and you won't have to queue.

f (recommend) His doctor said, 'You should do more exercise.'

g (promise) Don't worry, I'll post that letter for you.

h (suggest) I propose we take our bikes with us.

i (had better) 'Move your car immediately or else I'll call the police!'

j (deny) Peter said he hadn't caused the accident.

k (make) His mother forced him to apologise.

4　**1 15** Listen to this woman talking about her time at school. What does she say about:

- the uniform?
- the teachers?

With a partner, talk about what you remember about the time you were at primary school. Talk about: the teachers, the building, your friends, what you wore, what was popular.

Vocabulary

Prefixes

5　In the listening for 4 you heard the speaker talk about feeling 'self-conscious' and her teacher was 'undervalued'. Look at the expressions below and decide how the prefix changes the word it is attached to.

EXAMPLE: redo – *to do again*

a self-conscious	**g** superhuman
b misheard	**h** anti-smoking
c counter-productive	**i** pre-arranged
d pro-government	**j** outdo
e overworked	**k** undervalue
f sub-zero	

6　Complete the sentences below using a prefix from 5 and the correct form of the word in brackets.

EXAMPLE: The experts managed to (construct) the three-hundred-year-old dress using information from a painting.

The experts managed to reconstruct the three-hundred-year-old dress using information from a painting.

a There's a shortage of (contain) flats in my neighbourhood.

b The local swimming pool is advertising itself as a '(tropic) swimming paradise'!

c I think this printer (live) its usefulness and should be sold.

d Never (estimate) the cunning of a black bear – he is very clever.

e Apparently, it was all a (understand) and they are now good friends.

f Lisa prefers to buy her vegetables (pack) rather than from the market.

g This detergent is (concentrate) so you should use much less than normal.

h My car is fitted with (lock) brakes.

i I didn't mean to (hear) the argument, but it was hard to avoid.

j As I didn't have a suitable (argue) I decided to back down and apologise.

k Their teacher is very (America), and is always praising that educational system.

7　Quickly read this extract from an article about dress to get some idea of what it is about. Don't fill in any spaces at this stage. Answer the following question.

What changes does the writer say have occurred in the way we dress?

SUITABLY DRESSED

Today the notion of 'suitable clothing' is dying **(0)** ...OUT... . It **(1)** .... now appear that, to all **(2)** .... and purposes, anything goes. At one **(3)** .... , it was possible to **(4)** .... at a glance the difference **(5)** .... someone dressed for work and someone en route to a nightclub. And, needless to **(6)** .... , the same clothes would never have been worn to both.

However, in the last thirty years, we have undergone a sea change in **(7)** .... ideas of what a dress code consists of. Even well **(8)** .... the 1960s, male air travellers were expected to wear a suit; these days it would **(9)** .... as no surprise to find them in shorts and trainers.

In fact, **(10)** .... has been the revolution in our own dress codes that we may find **(11)** .... dressing down to go to work and dressing up to go **(12)** .... in the evening. That **(13)** .... said, there are occasions, a wedding or a funeral, for example, **(14)** .... only certain clothes will **(15)** ....

Now fill in the spaces. Having a good idea of what the text is about will help you.

8　Do you think that clothes are as important as personality? How do you respond to people who dress very differently to you? How do you respond to the way people in government or celebrities dress?

Speaking

1 With a partner, talk about the following.

- How important is it to look attractive?
- What do you think makes a face attractive?
- What's your opinion of
  — cosmetic surgery
  — nose and lip piercing
  — make-up
  — wigs

- How important are good looks to a politician?
- Would you describe yourself as a) immaculate, b) smart or c) neither?
- Do you ever look a) scruffy or b) unkempt?

2 Read both texts. With a partner, decide which points the writer is making in each.

Text 1

Recently, a politician was mocked in the press for having a digitally enhanced poster of himself produced. Gone were the receding hairline and wrinkles and a younger, more attractive face peered down from the hoarding. However, there does seem to be evidence that, although they may be unaware of it, a considerable number of people vote according to a candidate's looks. A scientific experiment which used photos of just under 2,000 political candidates and over 10,000 voters took place recently. It found that if a candidate was attractive, then both men and women were more likely to believe that he or she was trustworthy and very able. When a candidate's educational background and occupation were included as an additional check, it was found to have no effect.

Text 2

The images we see on magazine covers today are not what they used to be. A few clicks of the mouse on Photoshop can easily transform models and celebrities into living Barbies. It seems as if advertisers and photojournalists are on the quest to define and sell 'ideal beauty'. Female models have their spots and wrinkles airbrushed out, their legs and eyelashes are made to look longer than they really are and faces magically become more symmetrical. Perhaps the time has come for legislation prohibiting editors from using these techniques? Or, maybe, as some people think, all this is nothing new. Artists have been doing something similar for centuries and we have accepted it as normal.

3 Now look at this summary of the two texts. There are five linking words missing. Decide which answer A, B or C, best fits each space. Use the information in the Phrase spot to help you.

According to the first text, research has shown that both people involved in the political process and, (1) .... , the public at large, unconsciously give more weight to a candidate's attractiveness than to their background skills. (2) .... , good-looking candidates were seen to possess very positive personal qualities.

Text B puts forward the opinion that (3) .... , modern technology enables people in the media to idealise faces and bodies. It (4) .... goes on to question whether this is really a problem and (5) .... it asks whether this issue is entirely modern.

1 **A** thus   **B** additionally   **C** finally
2 **A** Moreover   **B** Then   **C** On the other hand
3 **A** although   **B** besides   **C** firstly
4 **A** besides   **B** then   **C** therefore
5 **A** finally   **B** equally   **C** although

4 Now write two paragraphs of about 120 words each, giving your opinion on the points mentioned in the two texts. Try to link your sentences effectively.

Phrase spot

In Writing, Part 1, it is important to use linking devices effectively. This means choosing your words with care. Avoid beginning a sentence with these words – *And, Or, But*.

Link your points together using a variety of linking words and phrases, such as the following.

Introducing	Adding	Conceding
First of all,	Besides,	however
Firstly,	Moreover,	even though
Secondly,	In addition,	although
At the same time,	Additionally,	on the other hand
	Above all,	then again
	Not only, ... but also	

Equation	Summarising	Result
Equally,	Finally,	therefore
Likewise,	In short/brief,	thus
Similarly,	In conclusion,	consequently
In the same way,	To conclude,	so

5 The following are definitions of personality types. With a partner, decide if the definition is correct or not. If you think the definition is wrong, write a correct version.

EXAMPLE: An observant person is one who is always interested in everyone else's business.

Wrong. An observant person is one who is good at noticing things.

a A morbid person is one who is interested in unpleasant subjects, especially death.

b Someone who is opinionated has a lot of excellent suggestions to make when there is a problem.

c A pompous person is one who is full of their own importance.

d Someone who is vivacious is likely to get angry quickly.

e An acquisitive person likes to buy lots of presents for their friends.

f A meticulous person checks everything they do very carefully.

g A discriminating person is racially prejudiced.

h A complacent person is one who is easy-going and pleasant to be with.

i Someone who is unobtrusive is shy and introverted.

j A manipulative person likes making things by hand.

k Someone who is boastful is inclined to tell everyone about their possessions and successes.

Exam folder 5

Reading and Use of English, Part 6 Gapped text

This part of the Reading and Use of English paper consists of one text, from a range of sources, which has had seven paragraphs removed and placed in jumbled order after the text. You must decide from where in the text the paragraphs have been removed. This part tests knowledge of cohesion (the relationship of the words/sentences and paragraphs to each other), text structure and global meaning.

Read the Exam advice and then do the task below.

Questions 1, 2 and 3 have some clues to help you. Some words have been underlined in both the main article and the missing paragraphs. When you have the answers to questions 1, 2 and 3, do the same with the other questions. Find the words which tell you which paragraph goes where and underline them. Some words will be topic words and others grammatical links.

You are going to read an article about telling lies. Seven paragraphs have been removed from the extract. Choose from the paragraphs **A–H** the one which fits each gap (**1–7**). There is one extra paragraph which you do not need to use.

Would I lie to you?
Blatant dishonesty has invaded our culture. Sue Jackson explains how to spot a liar.

Who hasn't told a lie? Even the most upstanding individual probably utters one occasionally to help the day to run more smoothly. But, according to experts, the extent to which people regularly tell serious untruths has exploded. Lying has pervaded every aspect of our lives.

1

Research in California reveals that people lie up to 20 times a day, while in a poll last year, a quarter of respondents admitted being untruthful on a daily basis. Only 8 per cent claimed they had never lied – although there is always the chance that even then they weren't being honest. Many of these will be sweet little lies, the type psychologists refer to as 'false positives' and the sort we are all guilty of committing when we want to appear more enthusiastic about something than we really are.

2

Until recently it was thought that only manipulative and Machiavellian characters were prone to excessive fabrication of this sort, but research has proved otherwise. According to experts, anyone under pressure or with a big enough incentive is prepared to say something that isn't true.

3

That figure rose to one in three among people with university qualifications. Apparently, this sort of background gives people the vocabulary and the confidence to deceive. The lies are more sophisticated and plausible than you might find elsewhere in society.

4

The proliferation of lying in corporate culture means that there are huge profits to be gained by companies who can weed out real-life fraudsters before employing them. Numerous studies have been conducted, including some using video cameras, to analyse people who lie. There are two main methods of ousting liars, although one, the mechanical lie detector or polygraph, requires subjects to be trussed up in electrodes, so it hardly lends itself to interviews. That leaves body language and psychological testing.

5

However, sometimes the subconscious takes over. Liars often start blinking fast, a visual sign that the brain is concentrating hard on the task in hand, and are likely to frequently touch their body and face with their hands. Liars are also more likely to tap or swing a foot as they speak.

6

Everyone seems to agree that good liars don't show non-verbal signals, so you need to know what to look for. Lying takes a lot of effort, so often they will rely on past experience to see them through and reduce the cognitive load.

7

Experts, however, agree that the one person you shouldn't deceive is yourself – and that, once you begin to do so, it is a sure sign that your untruthfulness is getting out of hand.

A This makes detecting the charlatan who fibs his way through a CV very difficult. In the film *Liar, Liar* the comedian Jim Carrey played a smooth-talking lawyer and consummate liar who specialises in dealing with untrustworthy clients whom no one else will take on. Only when his young son made a wish to see his father get through an entire day without lying was Carrey's character forced to tell the truth. Mayhem ensued.

B Things like 'That was delicious, thank you', 'You look great in that dress' and 'Of course I want to see you'. They are mostly considered harmless social lubricants. But at the other end of the spectrum are the compulsive liars who are effortlessly dishonest.

C Visual clues are not wholly reliable, as experienced deceivers are aware of the common give-away signs and take calculated measures to avoid them. Shifty eyes, for instance, are traditionally thought to be a sure way to tell whether someone is being dishonest, but experienced fabricators will capitalise on this myth.

D So, for instance, people who are lying about where they have been may declare they were at the cinema or the gym so that their untruth doesn't take too much mental planning. It is easier to make up a story about something they know well and have done many times.

E 'We are experiencing an <u>epidemic</u> of lying,' says Professor Leo Damak, an expert in lie detection at a leading university. 'It has always been around, but we are much more aware of it now.' <u>In one study of college students, 85 per cent of couples reported that one or both of them had lied about past relationships or recent events. In another, it was found that dating partners lie to each other in about a third of their conversations.</u>

F A recent study found that pathological liars are just as likely to be self-confident, attractive and popular as they are introverted and withdrawn. It also seems that the better educated a person is, the higher their level of deceit. It was found that falsehoods typically occurred in <u>one fifth</u> of all ten-minute conversations they have.

G Obviously, many won't stand for ambiguity any more. By being more aware of how and why someone will tell a lie, they have more chance of catching him before he tells another and causes real harm.

H However, vocabulary and sounds are generally considered more reliable indicators than body movements. Liars tend to use fewer words, take longer to start answering a question and pause a lot as if to mentally rehearse what they are about to say. Their voices may adopt a high pitch and they are prone to repetition.

EXAM ADVICE

- Read through the base text for general meaning and then read the removed paragraphs very carefully. Go back and read the base text more carefully.

- Highlight any words which will help you to find which paragraph goes where.

- You need to fully understand what is going on in each paragraph to be able to do this task. However, both subject and grammatical links are important.

- Try to find a suitable paragraph for each gap. Check it fits by reading both the paragraph before and the paragraph after.

- Go back at the end and check that the whole passage makes sense.

- As a last check, make sure the extra paragraph wouldn't fit in any of the gaps. If it would, you will need to check all your answers carefully again to see where you have gone wrong.

Cześć, co słychać?

Γειά σου. Τι κάνεις;

Merhaba. Nasılsın?

您好！

Здрасти. Как си?

szia! hogy vagy?

Speaking

1 Before reading the article, talk about these questions with a partner.

- Look at the words above. Can you recognise the languages?
- Roughly how many languages are there in the world?
- Approximately how many languages do you think die out every year?
- Which language is spoken more than any other?
- Do you think your language is worth learning by other people?

Reading

2 Read through the article quickly and then answer these questions.

a Why do you think the writer chose the title *Death sentence* for this article?

b Do you think the writer is in favour of or against having a world language? Underline the part of the text which gives you the answer.

3 Read the article again more carefully and then answer the questions which follow.

DEATH SENTENCE

A language dies only when the last person who speaks it dies. One day it's there; the next it is gone. Here is how *it* happens. In late 1995, a linguist, Bruce
5 Connell, was doing some fieldwork in the Mambila region of Cameroon. He found a language called Kasabe, which no westerner had studied before. *It* had just one speaker left, a man called Bogon. Connell had no
10 time on that visit to find out much about the language, so he decided to return to Cameroon a year later. He arrived in mid-November, only to learn that Bogon had died on November 5.

15 On November 4, Kasabe existed as one of the world's languages; on November 6, it did not. The event might have caused a stir in Bogon's village. If you are the last speaker of a language, you are often considered
20 special in your community. You are a living monument to what the community once was. But outside the village, who knew or mourned the passing of what he stood for?

There is nothing unusual about a single
25 language dying. Communities have come and gone throughout history, taking their languages with them. But, judged by the standards of the past, what is happening today is extraordinary. It is language
30 extinction on a massive scale. According to the best estimates, there are now about 6,000 languages in the world. Of *these*, about half are going to die out during this

century. *This* means that, on average, there
35 is a language dying out somewhere in the world every two weeks or so.

A survey published by SIL International, formerly known as the Summer Institute of Linguistics, established that there were 51
40 languages with only one speaker left – 28 in Australia alone. There are almost 500 languages in the world with fewer than 100 speakers; 1,500 with fewer than 1,000 speakers; more than 3,000 with fewer
45 than 10,000 speakers; and a staggering 5,000 languages with fewer than 100,000 speakers. Ninety-four per cent of the world's languages are spoken by only 6% of its people. No wonder so *many* are in danger.

50 Many languages die as a result of cultural assimilation. When one culture assimilates another, the sequence of events affecting the endangered language is usually characterised by three broad stages. The first
55 is immense pressure on the people to speak the dominant language. The second stage is a period of bilingualism; people become increasingly efficient in their new language while still retaining competence in their old.
60 Then, often quickly, bilingualism starts to decline, with the old language giving way to the new. This leads to the third stage, in which the younger generation increasingly finds its old language less relevant.

65 Is language death such a disaster? Surely, you might say, *it* is simply a symptom of more people striving to improve their lives by joining the modern world. So long as a hundred or even a couple of thousand
70 languages survive, that is sufficient. No it is not. We should care about dying languages for the same reason that we care when a species of animal or plant dies. *It* reduces the diversity of our planet. In the case of
75 language we are talking about intellectual

and cultural diversity, not biological diversity, but the issues are the same.

Increasing uniformity holds dangers for the long-term survival of a species. The
80 strongest ecosystems are those which are most diverse. If the development of multiple cultures is a prerequisite for successful human development, then the preservation of linguistic diversity is essential, because
85 cultures are chiefly transmitted through spoken and written languages. Encapsulated within a language is most of a community's history and a large part of its cultural identity.

90 Sometimes what we might learn from a language is eminently practical, as when we discover new medical treatments from the folk medicine of an indigenous people; sometimes *it* is intellectual, as when the
95 links between languages tell us something about the movements of early civilisations. Sometimes it is literary. Every language has its equivalent – even if only in oral form – of Chaucer, Wordsworth and Dickens, and of
100 course, very often it is linguistic: we learn something new about language itself – the behaviour that makes us truly human, and without which there would be no talk at all. Ezra Pound summed up the core intellectual
105 argument: 'The sum of human wisdom is not contained in any one language, and no single language is capable of expressing all forms and degrees of human comprehension.'

110 Not everyone agrees. Some people believe that the multiplicity of the world's languages is a curse rather than a blessing. If only we had just one language in the world – whether English, Esperanto, or whatever
115 – we would all be better off. World peace would be established. Or so *they* think.

4 What do the words in italics in the article refer to?

  a Here is how *it* happens. (lines 3–4)

  b *It* had just one speaker left (lines 8–9)

  c Of *these*, about half are going to die out (lines 32–33)

  d *This* means that, on average (line 34)

  e No wonder so *many* are in danger. (line 49)

  f Surely, you might say, *it* is simply a symptom (lines 65–66)

  g *It* reduces the diversity of our planet. (lines 73–74)

  h sometimes *it* is intellectual (line 94)

  i Or so *they* think (line 116)

 Exam spot

A good understanding of reference devices will help you in the Reading parts of the exam.

---

5 Read the article again and answer these questions.

  a What does the writer mean by 'caused a stir' in line 17?

  b Explain in your own words what happens during 'cultural assimilation'? (lines 50–51)

  c What point is the writer making when he gives a comparison between languages and animals? (lines 71–73)

  d Why does the writer believe that 'linguistic diversity' (line 84) is important?

  e What examples does the writer give of what we can learn from a language?

  f Explain in your own words what Ezra Pound stated. (lines 105–109)

6 Esperanto is an artificial language, based on Western European languages, which was once believed to have a future as a world language. It has never become popular. Why do you think that is? Do you think that your first language could be a world language? Why? / Why not?

7 Read through the text below. Where would you find this type of text? Give your reasons.

Pidgin and Creole

Just as a language may develop varieties in the form of dialects, languages as a whole may change. Sometimes rapid language change occurs as a result of (1) .... between people who each speak a different language. In such circumstances a pidgin language may (2) .... Pidgins usually have low (3) .... with respect to other languages. They are grammatically (4) .... on one language but are also influenced, especially in vocabulary, by others; they have relatively small sound systems, reduced vocabularies and simplified and altered grammars, and they rely (5) .... on context in order to be understood.

Pidgins are often the result of traders meeting island and coastal peoples. A pidgin has no native speakers: when speakers of a pidgin have children who learn the pidgin as their first language, that language is then called a creole. (6) .... the creole has enough native speakers to form a speech community, the creole may (7) .... into a fuller language. Many Creole speakers think of their languages as dialects of some colonial language (e.g. dialects of French or English). Linguists nearly always disagree with this view – from our (8) .... , Creoles have independent grammars and all the equipment of full, proper languages.

For questions 1–8, read the text above and decide which answer (A, B, C or D) best fits each gap.

	A	B	C	D
1	A approximation	B acquaintance	C link	D contact
2	A issue	B stem	C spring	D arise
3	A prestige	B credit	C esteem	D stature
4	A based	B derived	C built	D hinged
5	A decisively	B thoroughly	C closely	D heavily
6	A Whereas	B Promptly	C Once	D Presently
7	A increase	B expand	C enlarge	D swell
8	A perspective	B outlook	C context	D view

10.2 Expressing wishes and preferences

Wish and if only

1 Read this business anecdote and then answer the question below.

> The British company was chasing a multimillion-pound deal to sell slate from a quarry that it mined to a Spanish customer. The meeting was arranged, the plane arrived and the guests were whisked off to a smart restaurant. Everything was in place – but the interpreter failed to turn up. The directors managed to say the five words of holiday Spanish that they knew between them – several times – but most of the meal passed in embarrassed silence. The guests returned to Spain the next day and, needless to say, there was no deal.

One of the directors might have said to his colleague during the meal 'I wish I had learned Spanish' or 'I wish the customers could speak English'. What else might have been said using *wish*?

2 What verb form do you use after *wish* when you want to talk about

  a the present?
  b the past?
  c something that is annoying you?

3 What difference does it make if you begin a sentence with *If only ...* rather than *I wish*?

> *Hope* and *wish* are often confused. If you want something to be true or to happen in the future and you believe it's possible, then a structure such as *I hope* is required. *Wish* is used for things which you want to happen but think may not happen.

G → page 183

Corpus spot

Look at the following sentences. They are all taken from the *Cambridge Learner Corpus* and contain errors that Proficiency candidates have made in the exam when using *wish*. Work with a partner to correct them.

  a I do wish I will turn out to be a good doctor.
  b I wish I will be able to suppress my laughter when he speaks, but I can't.
  c She wishes she would be more positive about the future.
  d I wish you like the present I've got you for your birthday.
  e I hope you to have a pleasant stay.
  f I wish they allowed us to enter the club last night.
  g He hopes he would remember things more easily.
  h I really wish to hear from you soon.
  i I wish her children can be as well-behaved as yours.
  j I wish they stopped smoking; it's making me cough.
  k I wish there'll always be green hills and rivers.
  l We spent hours in the forest wishing to see an elk.

4 What do you wish for? Talk with your partner about things that you wish for now, in the past and in the future:

- your family
- your job/studies
- your country
- the world

Would rather, It's time, etc.

5 With a partner discuss how you would complete these sentences. Give reasons for your choice.

  a It's time (go) home. (said as a general statement)
  b It's time (go) home. (said to a particular person)
  c I'd rather (spend) my money on clothes than cigarettes.
  d I'd rather Michael (leave) his bicycle somewhere else.
  e I'd rather she (give) me some flowers instead of chocolates yesterday.
  f It's high time (do) his own ironing.
  g It's about time (take) a more serious attitude to her job.

G → page 183

6 For questions 1–8, complete the second sentence so that it has a similar meaning to the first sentence, using the word given. **Do not change the word given.** You must use between **three** and **eight** words, including the word given.

1 I really think you should be more assertive about your rights.

up

It's about time .... more.

2 You should really stop behaving like a child.

though

It's high time .... a child.

3 They should do a proper review of teachers' salaries.

out

It's time .... a proper review of teachers' salaries.

4 I think it preferable for all students to write in ink.

rather

I .... in ink.

5 I regret now spending so much money on that car.

splashed

I wish now .... so much money on that car.

6 It's a pity that he turned up without warning me.

let

I wish .... he was coming.

7 It's a shame she wasn't aware how much I cared for her.

strength

If only .... of my feelings for her.

8 Please don't wear shoes in the house.

rather

I .... your shoes in the house.

 Phrase spot

The interpreter failed to turn up to the meal with the British company. *Turn up* is a phrasal verb that means 'to come or arrive rather casually'. *Turn* is often tested at Proficiency, as a phrasal verb, a phrasal noun or in an expression.

The following are all expressions with *turn*. Read the sentences below and rewrite them using one of the expressions in the box.

to take a turn for the better	not to turn a hair
to have a nice turn of phrase	to toss and turn
not to know which way to turn	to take it in turns
to turn as red as a beetroot	a turn-up for the books
the turn of the century	

a Well, there's a surprise – I never thought he'd get a girlfriend.
b He expresses himself well.
c He went scarlet when she asked him to dance.

d From 1900 we see a change in attitudes towards the countryside.
e I didn't know what to do when the airline told me they'd lost my luggage.
f I couldn't sleep last night for worrying.
g My dad was ill in hospital but he's suddenly improved so he'll be home at the weekend.
h Muriel wasn't the least bit put out when we told her the awful news.
i Now, everyone must wait to have a go with the new computer game.

10.3 Listening and Speaking

1 With a partner, look at the photos and talk together about whether or not you think that the photos show positive aspects of globalisation. You have about a minute to do this.

2 Now, you have three minutes to talk together about the aspects of global culture that the photos show.

Things to think about:
- Does it make you feel excited or depressed when people say we live in a 'global village'?
- In what ways do you think it affects culture in your country – for example, in music, food, education, work, family life, language?
- Does global culture widen or cross the generation gap?

3 You will hear three different extracts. For questions 1–6, choose the answer (A, B or C) which fits best according to what you hear. Read through the questions carefully before you listen. After listening, discuss your answers with your partner.

Extract One

You will hear part of an interview with a politician called Steven Bright, in which globalisation is being discussed.

1 Steven Bright is concerned that globalisation means a country
   A losing employment opportunities.
   B having a lack of economic control.
   C losing its sense of individuality.

2 Which aspect of loaning money to developing countries does Steven Bright disagree with?
   A the reasons for giving out loans
   B the unrealistic amount of money loaned
   C the imposition of certain conditions

Extract Two

You hear a woman called Paula Drinkwater talking about her research into bilingualism.

3 Why did Paula do research into bilingualism?
   A She needed a research project for her psychology doctorate.
   B It was a natural development of a project she was involved in.
   C She was keen to get into a new and exciting field.

4 What does Paula say about the experiment she did?
   A She thought it was too dangerous to repeat.
   B She realised that any results would be questioned.
   C She wasn't particularly surprised by the outcome.

Extract Three

You will hear a man called Bob talking about learning Chinese.

5 What is Bob doing when he speaks?
   A justifying the learning method he used
   B criticising the way languages are often taught
   C advising other people to learn Chinese

6 What does Bob say about some of Elena's ideas?
   A Some of them were more useful than they first appeared.
   B They were based on what she had picked up in Spain.
   C They didn't help with every aspect of learning Chinese.

Pronunciation

4 In the recording in this unit you heard the words *homework* and *bookshelves*. Where is the main stress in these words? Make as many combinations as you can from the following words and say where the main stress should go. Some combinations are written as one word, some as two words and others take a hyphen. Use a dictionary to check.

EXAMPLE: old <u>house</u>

     <u>boat</u>house

old	seat	back	tea	house	woman
carpet	bag	horse	dog	red	boat
wine	sheep	road	sign	glass	race

5 For questions 1–8, read the text below. Use the word given in capitals at the end of some of the lines to form a word that fits in the space in the same line. There is an example at the beginning (0).

Remember the words must be spelled correctly. Use your dictionary to check.

MODERN
CULTURE?

When people talk about contemporary culture they are just as
(0) .... **LIKELY** .... to be talking about fast cars, trainers or high heels as
they are to be talking about Shostakovich or Shakespeare.   LIKE

Goods have become as **(1)** .... a measure and marker of   MEAN
culture as the Great and the Good. The word 'culture' can now cover just
about anything. Culture is no longer merely the beautiful and singular.

It wasn't until the late twentieth century that a **(2)** ....   SCHOOL
interest in objects began to replace the traditional interest in -isms, with
historians, **(3)** .... critics and philosophers all suddenly   LITERATE
becoming fascinated by the meaning of objects, large and small. Is this a
sign, perhaps, of a society cracking under the strain of too many things?

Our current **(4)** .... with material culture, one might argue,   OBSESSIVE
is simply a **(5)** .... to the Western crisis of abundance. There   RESPOND
are obvious problems with this materialist **(6)** .... of culture.   CONCEPT
If our experience of everyday life is so **(7)** .... , then how   SATISFY
much more so is the **(8)** .... of our everyday things under   SPECTATE
scrutiny?

Writing folder 5

Part 2 Article

For Part 2 of Writing, you may have to write an article on a certain topic or discussion point. Real-world articles carry an eye-catching title, open with a thought-provoking statement and use stylistic devices to hold the reader's interest throughout.

1 These quotes are all to do with globalisation. Match each one to the organisation or product to which it refers.

a 'It can locate thousands of sites on your chosen topic within seconds and operates at country-level, so you won't need to wade through lots of irrelevant American stuff.'

b 'Name me one bar in the whole world where you can't get this or its local equivalent – they'll be serving it on the moon next!'

c 'Their innovation revolutionised the music industry and led to a worldwide collapse in CD sales.'

d 'The company has a high profile and its logo pops up everywhere, even at sports events – driving one is a real status symbol.'

2 Read the article below and choose the best title, a, b or c.

a *GLOBALISATION MEANS STANDARDISATION*

b *LIKE IT OR LUMP IT*

c *DON'T WORRY, BE HAPPY*

Nowadays, we hear a lot about the growing threat of globalisation, accompanied by dire warnings that the rich pattern of local life is being eroded, and that its many dialects and traditions are on the verge of extinction – but stop and think for a moment about the many positive aspects that globalisation is bringing. Read on and you are bound to feel comforted, ready to face a global future.

Consider the Internet, that prime example of our shrinking world. Leaving aside the all-too-familiar worries about pornography and political extremism, even the most parochial must admit that immeasurable benefits are offered by it, not just in terms of education, the sector for which the Internet was originally designed, but more importantly, the dissemination of news and comment worldwide. With global internet access and Smartphone technology, it is increasingly difficult for dictators to maintain regimes of misinformation, and any oppressed group is able to organise themselves quickly and effectively.

Is the world dominance of brands like Nike and Coca-Cola so bad for us, when all is said and done? Sportswear and soft drinks are innocuous products when compared to the many other things that have been globally available for a longer period of time – dangerous drugs, for example. In any case, just because Nike trainers and Coke cans are for sale, it doesn't mean you have to buy them – even globalisation cannot negate the free will of the individual.

Critics of globalisation can stop issuing their doom and gloom statements. In the final analysis, life goes on, and undoubtedly has more to offer for many citizens of the world than it did for their parents' generation.

3 Do you agree with the views expressed? Why? / Why not? Note down some counter-arguments to this positive viewpoint.

4 Look back at the article to find these expressions, which are used to underline an opinion.

when all is said and done (line 25)
in the final analysis (lines 37–38)

Do you know these similar expressions? Fill in the missing words.

a at the .... of the day
b .... things considered
c when you .... to think of it
d in the .... light of day
e .... in all

5 Read this rhetorical question, which introduces the third paragraph of the article.

Is the world dominance of brands like Nike and Coca-Cola so bad for us, when all is said and done?

Turn statements a–c into rhetorical questions, using one of the expressions from 4 and making any changes necessary.

EXAMPLE: The net effect of globalisation is to standardise everything.

Isn't the net effect of globalisation to standardise everything, when you come to think of it?

a American products impose a way of life that many of us regard as alien.
b Globalisation could bring more equality to the world.
c It's very depressing to find a McDonald's in every town.

Write two more rhetorical questions on the negative aspects of globalisation, referring to the notes you made in 3.

6 Write a paragraph of 50 words to insert into the article, to give a more balanced answer. Start your paragraph with a rhetorical question.

7 Use the advice above to answer the following Part 2 task. Write 280–320 words.

An international current affairs magazine has invited readers to contribute articles entitled 'Globalisation – good news or bad?' for its next issue. You decide to write an article explaining your personal views on this topic.

Write your **article**.

EXAM ADVICE

- Read the question carefully.
- Spend a few minutes making notes of ideas to include.
- Order these ideas logically and to best effect.
- Present a balanced argument or personal view.
- Use rhetorical questions to maintain interest.
- Write in an appropriate register.
- Include a punchy final message.

11.1 For better, for worse

Speaking

1 What causes ups and downs in relationships? What external factors can put stress on a marriage or partnership? What character traits and personal attributes contribute to a successful long-term relationship?

2 Rank these aspects from 1 to 7, with 1 being the most important factor. Then summarise what counts in a relationship, justifying your ideas.

- sharing a sense of humour
- being honest and trustworthy
- lending emotional support
- taking the lead in a crisis
- being willing to compromise
- having interests in common
- being loyal and dependable

⊚ Exam spot

In Listening, Part 3, the multiple-choice task, you have to understand detail and infer meaning. This will include identifying attitude or opinion in what is said. Read the five questions carefully before the recording starts and read them again before the second listening. They provide clues on what to listen out for.

Listening

3 **1 17** You will hear an interview with Steve, who talks about the love of his life, Abby. For questions 1–5, choose the answer (A, B, C or D) which fits best according to what you hear.

1 How did Abby feel about Steve five years ago?
 A She felt the same way as Steve did about her.
 B She was uncertain about starting any relationship.
 C She thought he was fun to be with occasionally.
 D She looked up to Steve, but didn't love him.

2 How did Steve explain Abby's change of heart initially?
 A He saw it as an aberration, brought on by boredom.
 B He thought she was having a laugh at his expense.
 C He put it down to her being lonely and unattached.
 D He decided something at work must have upset her.

3 What did Steve's work colleagues suddenly notice about him?
 A He was putting in longer hours than he had done.
 B He was showing more commitment to his work.
 C He seemed preoccupied by a personal problem.
 D He spent less time chatting with them in the office.

4 On hearing Steve's declaration, the first thing Samantha did was to
 A get some flowers for Abby.
 B tell Steve's office he was sick.
 C burst into tears at his news.
 D rush round to Abby's place.

5 At the family wedding, Steve
 A announced his plan to get married to Abby.
 B showed an American how to drive a British car.
 C was given advice by someone he didn't know well.
 D was attacked by his mother for ditching Samantha.

4 Will Steve and Abby's marriage work out? Why? / Why not?

5 Steve says Abby has always had a *streak of theatricality*. What does he mean by this?

Many adjectives collocate with *streak*, for example *jealous*, *nasty*, *romantic*, *ruthless*, *sadistic*, *vicious*. Are all of these attributes negative?

Fill the spaces in the 'problem page' letter with words from the recording. Then decide what advice you would give Christine.

Can too much romance be a bad thing? I'm beginning to think so! I met Max at my local gym seven months ago and it was love at **(1)** .... I soon discovered his deeply romantic **(2)** .... , which I absolutely revelled in to begin with. He would bombard me with chocolates and fluffy toys, turn up on my doorstep with champagne and roses and text me every day with really **(3)** .... messages. The trouble is, he still does. I feel our relationship should have moved beyond these excessively romantic **(4)** .... , but he obviously sees it differently. I'm sure Max is the **(5)** .... for me, and I'd say 'yes' immediately if he **(6)** .... the question. But I really can't take much more romance. It's suffocating! What should I do? I don't want to hurt his feelings.

Christine (22)

Vocabulary

Phrasal verbs

6 Look at these examples of nouns that collocate with phrasal verbs.

To fend off <u>the problem</u>, I threw myself into my <u>job</u>.
I couldn't keep up <u>the pretence</u> any longer.

Make similar expressions, choosing from the lists below. Some of the nouns will be used more than once. Suggest other noun collocations for each phrasal verb if you can.

blurt out	an argument
bottle up	a problem
choke back	a secret
fend off	criticism
keep up	appearances
shoot down	emotions
sweep aside	tears
tease out	rage
tone down	blows
whip up	accusations

Now use some of these expressions in sentences of your own based on the following situations.

a You have seen your best friend arm-in-arm with someone other than their partner.

b A publisher doesn't want to hurt a new writer's feelings but thinks their novel is rubbish.

c At a protest rally, a student is giving a passionate speech to the crowd.

d Two teenagers are having an argument which has degenerated into physical violence.

e You had to give some disappointing news to your family and it has affected them, though they don't want to show this.

f A politician is demolishing a member of the opposition party's reasoning in a debate.

Idiom spot

Explain the meaning of these idioms from the recording.

a tying the knot	**g** rolled up her sleeves
b cast my net	**h** at death's door
c bolt from the blue	**i** giving me the cold
d time on her hands	shoulder
e calling the tune	**j** get a grip
f carrying a torch for	

Now complete these idioms, four of which contain keywords from a–j.

k The union *has its* .... *tied*, as it can no longer support any form of industrial action.

l The party has been *losing its* .... on those middle class voters who have traditionally been so loyal.

m I've got a cunning plan *up my* .... which I think you're going to approve of.

n We're .... *at straws* here – there's no way a deal is going to be struck.

o Once again, it seems that the government has failed to .... *the nettle* on transport.

p I haven't quite *got to* .... *with* Jack's eccentric behaviour, though I'm learning fast!

q Marion *played right into* management's .... by voicing her concerns so blatantly.

r There are several jobs *up for* .... in the marketing department.

11.2 Gradability

1 How many new friends have you made via the Internet? What are the advantages and disadvantages of social networking sites that you have used?

2 Skim the text below to find out why the Internet was especially important for Richard and Cindy. Ignore spaces 1–8 for the moment.

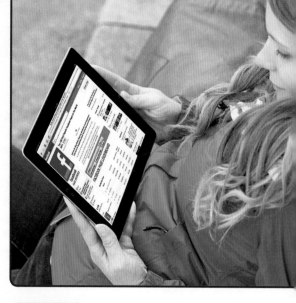

♥ Love on the INTERNET ♥

Richard and his American wife Cindy are extremely affectionate towards **(0)** ....EACH........ other and talk constantly – using sign language. Cindy has been deaf **(1)** .... birth, but Richard lost his hearing only recently. He had had problems as a child, although doctors failed to find **(2)** .... amiss. However, on finishing university, his hearing difficulties became acute. He was so depressed he **(3)** .... ate and his weight dropped to 44 kilos. **(4)** .... been surrounded by sound his whole life, he found living in this new silent world completely devastating.

Richard learnt sign language so **(5)** .... to be able to communicate again and his audiologist suggested finding new friends online. **(6)** .... hours of getting this advice, Richard was in contact with other deaf people. For the **(7)** .... part, he chatted to Americans, finding them particularly upbeat. No **(8)** .... had he got chatting to Cindy than he was bowled over. Their signed wedding took place on a Mississippi riverboat only a few months later.

Now complete 1–8, using only one word in each space.

3 Look back at the beginning and end of the first paragraph. Are the degree adverbs _extremely affectionate_ and _completely devastating_ interchangeable? Why? / Why not?

Which degree adverbs can only modify the adjectives in column A? Which only relate to column B? Three adverbs can be used with both sets of adjectives. Which ones?

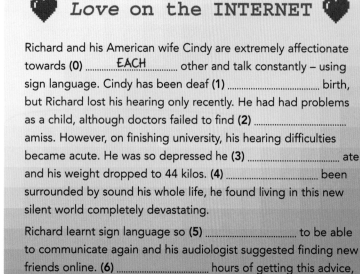

entirely
deeply   fairly
                          immensely
A   **B**
angry   awful
absolutely   cheerful   broken-hearted
             hurt   impossible   pretty
very   irritable   terrible
             upset   wonderful   quite
utterly   rather
        really

G → page 184

4 Choose adverb–adjective combinations from the box to complete sentences a–f. Use each one once only. Then make two sentences of your own with the remaining phrases.

> absolutely staggering
> doubly disappointing
> fairly laid-back
> highly suspicious
> remarkably accurate
> slightly embarrassed
> somewhat envious
> utterly miserable

a It's been .... around here without Tom, but we're all putting on a brave face until he gets back.

b I missed out on a trip to the States because I was ill – and what makes it .... is that they were going to fly me business class!

c The guys are .... by their poor performance in front of the home fans and hope to play better in Australia next month.

d Since the phone-hacking scandal, many celebrities have become .... of the press and its motives.

e I find it .... that anyone manages to have a proper social life, given the hours we work here!

f Both girls were .... of their brother's trip to Mauritius and would have liked to accompany him.

94 UNIT 11

5 Although adjectives are generally classified as either *gradable* or *ungradable*, some are used in both ways, often with a change in meaning. Consider these examples of the adjective *dead*.

The tiny bird had fallen from its nest and was dead. (Literal use – ungradable – a bird is either dead or alive.)
The town centre is completely dead after eight o'clock at night. (Figurative use – gradable, with degree adverb used for emphasis.)

Compare the use of *British* in these examples. Which is ungradable?

Richard is British by birth but moved to Spain 20 years ago.
Despite living in Spain, Richard remains very British in his behaviour.

6 Comment on the differences in meaning in these pairs of examples. Which pairs include a meaning that is restricted to informal use?

a I couldn't get to the market today, so we'll have to use frozen spinach instead.
It's minus 15 outside and I had to walk home – I'm absolutely frozen!

b Your glass is empty. Shall I get you another drink?
Margit's life is totally empty without him.

c Brad won't listen to me – he's being utterly impossible!
It was impossible to drive the car as all four tyres were flat.

d The crowd went absolutely insane when the band came on stage.
He was finally diagnosed as insane and remained in an institution until his death.

e Right now, Shirley feels she has an utterly bleak future ahead of her.
The house stands on a bleak, windswept moor and is very isolated.

f They eventually dished up a pretty tasteless bowl of lukewarm soup.
George's jokes in the wedding speech were fairly tasteless in my view.

Ⓖ → page 184

7 Choose suitable suffixes from the box to make adjectives from these verbs and nouns, making any necessary changes to the base word and being careful with spelling.

EXAMPLE: adore *adorable*

| -able -ary -ible -ical -ive -ous -some |

a alternate   **f** labour   **k** tenacity
b caution   **g** loathe   **l** theatre
c collapse   **h** hypocrisy   **m** virtue
d detest   **i** philosophy   **n** volunteer
e honour   **j** repel

8 For questions 1–8, read the text below. Use the word given in capitals at the end of some of the lines to form a word that fits in the space in the same line. There is an example at the beginning (0).

MAKING CONTACT IN TOMORROW'S WORLD

The *Lovegety* is a matchmaking device that has become a (0) .... MASSIVE .... hit in Japan, selling **MASS**
well over a million units. It is a pendant-shaped radio transmitter that sends out simple offers of activities, from rather (1) .... things, **DETERMINE**
such as 'fun', to more specific invitations, like 'movie'. When a pink plastic female *Lovegety* approaches a blue one on the same (2) .... , green lights flash. **SET**

Even as a gimmick, this is a (3) .... **DECIDE**
empowering social experiment. Indeed, Regan Gurung, a professor of human development and psychology, argues that badge technology could be designed to (4) .... highly significant **CLOSE**
information. He suggests that (5) .... **ALLY**
based on similar levels of self-esteem are absolutely (6) .... to lasting relationships. **CRUX**

Gurung postulates that sophisticated matching software might achieve a 60 to 65% success rate in terms of partner (7) .... **OUT**

Bullish though this statement may be, social engineering technology looks set to make (8) .... into our lives. **ROAD**

1 Why do people feel the need to conform in society? How important is it for an individual to feel part of a group? What is the attraction of belonging to a particular club – or a gang?

2 Read these two texts about belonging to a group. Where do they overlap in subject matter?

Text 1

There are between 100 and 200 gangs in London alone, and their members are getting younger – down to ten years old in some cases. In an inner-city area dominated by gangs, it's almost impossible to improve people's quality of life, so addressing gang culture is a critical element in tackling social breakdown.

There is a need for more male role models in schools, as constructive fatherhood has disappeared in many of these communities. The original value set has collapsed and often, a gang provides a kind of structure, promoting a sense of belonging and a perverse sense of purpose.

Text 2

A group is a collection of individuals, and the prejudices and shortcomings of individuals are likely to be found at group level too. However, groups often behave bullishly, reaching more polarized decisions than individuals. Irvin Janis has studied the rationality of group decision-making, using the Orwellian term 'groupthink' to refer to poor group thinking.

Janis identifies three aspects to groupthink: a tendency to overestimate the group, giving rise to the illusion of invulnerability; a lack of open-mindedness in decision-making, disregarding additional (outside) information; a craving for uniformity, leading to self-censorship, with direct pressure being exerted on dissenters in the drive towards unanimity.

3 Which two statements below accurately reflect the content of text 1? Identify where the ideas come in the text.

1 Damaged communities will only be rebuilt once gang culture is dealt with.
2 With so few male teachers, schools need to seek positive parental support.
3 In the absence of a social code, gangs offer a substitute group dynamic.

4 Reformulate phrases a–h from text 2 concisely, including some of the words below.

absent/absence	biased/bias
deceive/deceptive(ly)/deception	desire/desirability
extreme/extremist	failings/failure
homogenous/homogeneity	inclined/inclination
inflexible/inflexibility	invincible/invincibility
oppose/opposition	radical/radically
rigid/rigidity	suppress/suppression

a the prejudices and shortcomings of individuals
b groups often behave bullishly
c a tendency to overestimate the group
d the illusion of invulnerability
e a lack of open-mindedness
f a craving for uniformity
g self-censorship
h direct pressure being exerted on dissenters

5 Read the sample answer below. How successfully does it summarise and evaluate both texts? Identify examples of where the writer has reformulated the original wording. Replace any 'lifted' words and phrases in red with your own words.

Becoming an accepted member of a group is a natural human desire that is present in all walks of life, from football supporters and music societies to the hardest of street gangs. Both texts raise the phenomenon of the group mentality – the first considers the social context, while the second is possibly more rooted in the commercial world.

The first text is a simple description of the harsh realities of 21st century inner-city life, where children from broken homes join gangs in their search for acceptance and a perverse sense of purpose. The writer believes that only by addressing gang culture will society be improved.

The second text reflects complex ideas about the dynamics of a group, suggesting that any prejudices or shortcomings that an individual has will also be present in a group. This text cites the work of Janis on group decision-making, which he terms "groupthink". According to Janis, groups often behave bullishly when making decisions. He identifies a trio of "groupthink" characteristics: the illusion of invulnerability, a lack of open-mindedness in decision-making and a craving for uniformity.

The second text offers a plausible scenario in the world of business, where poor boardroom decisions are often the result of blinkered vision and where disregarding external advice often leads to poor decisions. However, do Janis's ideas extend outside the realm of business? Up to a point: two of his three criteria could even be applied to gang culture, where there may well be a feeling of invincibility and a desire to conform. However, decision-making itself is unlikely to form part of gang mentality, where actions are taken largely on impulse.

Exam folder 6

Listening, Part 4
Multiple matching

This part of the Listening paper consists of five short themed monologues, lasting approximately 35 seconds each, with ten multiple-matching questions. In Part 4 you will need to identify gist, attitude, main points and interpret the context. It is divided into two tasks, each with a different focus. Each task contains five questions and requires you to select the correct option from a list of eight. You hear the information to complete each task in random order – i.e. you might hear the information for Task One before you hear the information for Task Two. You hear the recording twice.

1   **Read through both tasks extremely carefully.**

You will hear five short extracts in which different people are talking about their relationships.

TASK ONE

For questions **1–5**, choose from the list (**A–H**) each speaker's reason for being initially attracted to their partner.

TASK TWO

For questions **6–10**, choose from the list (**A–H**) which quality each speaker appreciates most in their partner now.

While you listen, you must complete both tasks.

A	having a sense of humour			**A**	their conscientious approach to work	
B	being tolerant of others	Speaker 1	1	**B**	their determination	Speaker 1 6
C	being clever	Speaker 2	2	**C**	their ability to judge character	Speaker 2 7
D	being shy around others	Speaker 3	3	**D**	their grasp of detail	Speaker 3 8
E	being outgoing	Speaker 4	4	**E**	their attitude towards money	Speaker 4 9
F	being well-dressed	Speaker 5	5	**F**	their affectionate nature	Speaker 5 10
G	having lots of energy			**G**	their patience	
H	being good-looking			**H**	their loyalty	

2 **[1] 18** Now, you are going to hear Speaker 1. Look at both Task One and Task Two and decide which answers are true for the first speaker. You will hear the recording twice.

The answer for 1 is E and the answer for 6 is H. With a partner, look at the recording script for Speaker 1 below. Underline the parts containing the answers. Also look to see where distraction is being used.

Speaker 1

I was at a 21st birthday 'do'. I'd just broken up with a beautiful girl who I'd been head over heels in love with and my loyal friends thought it was time to find me someone else. I'm quite shy but I was instantly taken with this girl they introduced me to, called Sarah. She struck me as really fun and sparkling, ready to chat to anyone, even me! Anyway, we were married a year later. She's a wonderful person – she must be to have stayed married to me all these years. She's been there through thick and thin, and I can tell you there have been times when money's been extremely tight.

---

3 **[1] 19** Now listen to Speaker 2 and, with a partner, decide on the answers for questions 2 and 7. When you have decided what the answers are, look at the recording script below and underline the part of the text which gave you the answers. You will hear the recording twice.

Speaker 2

I'm a bit of a workaholic and so actually finding someone to have a relationship with was always tricky. I'm at the top of my game, head of a large fashion house, and I've found that men find me a bit intimidating because I'm so determined to succeed. I guess that's why I've always liked older men – they are usually less insecure. My partner is great, so shrewd about people, much better than me, although when I first met him, even though he was as stylish as everyone around me, it was his intellect that drew me to him. I like to think we're really well matched.

---

4 **[1] 20** You will notice that the order in which the information is given to complete the tasks is different. Speaker 1 mentions information for Task One first whereas Speaker 2 mentions information for Task Two first. The order in the exam can vary so you need to keep both tasks in mind when you are listening. Now listen to the other three speakers and for questions 3–5 and 8–10, choose from the lists A–H. Use each letter only once. There are three extra letters which you do not need to use. You will hear the recordings twice.

1 **Discuss these questions on the role of science today.**

- How have the lives of ordinary people been affected by recent scientific advances?
- In what areas are scientific discoveries likely to be made in the near future?
- Should scientific research be subject to tighter governmental controls?

Reading

2 **You are going to read an extract from a 'popular science' book that gives information about living cells and DNA. This is presented as a gapped text, as in Reading and Use of English, Part 6. First read the text, ignoring the missing paragraphs. How has the writer tried to simplify the subject for the non-scientific reader?**

THE MIRACLE OF LIFE

Some years ago, scientists at Cornell University released photographs of a guitar no larger than a human blood cell, its strings just one hundred atoms thick. This Lilliputian instrument was sculpted from crystalline silicon, using an etching technique involving a beam of electrons. The implications of being able to develop machines that are too small to be seen with the naked eye are breathtaking, but we should not lose sight of the fact that nature got there first. The world is already full of nanomachines: they are called living cells. Each cell is packed with tiny structures that might have come straight out of an engineer's manual. Minuscule tweezers, scissors, pumps, motors, levers, valves, pipes, chains and even vehicles abound.

1

Individually, atoms can only jostle their neighbours and bond to them if the circumstances are right. Yet collectively, they accomplish ingenious marvels of construction and control, unmatched by any human engineering. Somehow nature discovered how to build the intricate machine we call the living cell, using only the raw materials to hand, all jumbled up. Even more remarkable is that nature built the first cell from scratch.

2

Like any urban environment, there is much commuting going on. Molecules have to travel across the cell to meet others at the right place and the right time in order to carry out their jobs properly. No overseer supervises their activities – they simply do what they have to do. While at the level of individual atoms life is anarchy, at this higher level, the dance of life is performed with exquisite precision.

3

Even nowadays, some people flatly deny that science alone can give a convincing explanation for the origin of life, believing that the living cell is just too elaborate, too contrived, to be the product of blind physical forces alone. Science may give a good account of this or that individual feature, they say, but it will never explain how the original cell was assembled in the first place.

4

It would be wrong, however, to suppose this is all there is to life. To use the cliché, the whole is more than the sum of its parts. The very word 'organism' implies cooperation at a global level that cannot be captured in the study of the components alone. Without understanding its collective activity, the job of explaining life is only partly done.

5

With the discovery of DNA, however, this mystery was finally solved. Its structure is the famous double helix, discovered by Crick and Watson in the early 1950s. The two helical strands are attached by cross-links and we can imagine the whole shape unwound and laid out to make a ladder, where the handrails are the two unwound helices and the rungs the cross-links.

6

Each rung is actually a pair of bases joined end to end and it is here that geometry comes in. A is tailor-made to butt neatly with T, while C and G similarly slot together snugly, though the forces that bind these base pairs in their lock-and-key fit are in fact rather weak. Imagine the two handrails being pulled apart, breaking all the base pairs, as if the ladder had been sawn up the middle. Each would be left with a row of complementary projecting arms.

7

So long as the base-pairing rules work correctly, this is guaranteed to be identical to the original. However, no copying process is perfect, and it is inevitable that errors will creep in from time to time, altering the sequence of bases – scrambling up the letters. If the message gets a bit garbled during replication, the resulting organism may suffer a mutation. Viewed like this, life is just a string of four-letter words, for we are defined as individuals by these minuscule variations in DNA.

3 Now read paragraphs A–H and use the underlined parts to help you fit them into the text correctly (there is one extra). Remember to look for links before and after a gap.

A Can <u>such</u> a magnificently self-orchestrating <u>process</u> be explained or might the mystery of life be, in the end, impenetrable? <u>In 1933</u>, the physicist Niels Bohr, one of the founders of quantum mechanics, <u>concluded that</u> life hides its secrets from us in the same way as an atom does.

B <u>It is this templating</u> that is the basis for the replication process and ultimately, the recipe for life. If a DNA molecule is pulled apart and if there is a supply of free base molecules – As, Gs, Cs and Ts – floating around, they will tend to slot in and stick to these <u>exposed stumps</u> and thereby automatically reconstruct <u>a new strand</u>.

C <u>Near the top of my list of its defining properties</u> is reproduction. Without it, and in the absence of immortality, all life would sooner or later cease. <u>For a long time</u>, scientists had very little idea how organisms reproduce themselves. Vague notions of invisible genes conveying biological messages from one generation to the next <u>revealed little</u>.

D Of course, <u>there's more to it than</u> just a bag of <u>gadgets</u>. The various components fit together to form a smoothly functioning whole, like an elaborate factory production line. The miracle of life is not that it is made of nanotools, but that these tiny diverse parts <u>are integrated in a highly organised way</u>.

E <u>Boiled down to its essentials</u>, this secret can in fact be explained by molecular replication. The idea of a molecule making a copy of itself may seem rather magical, but it actually turns out to be quite straightforward. The underlying principle is in fact an exercise in <u>elementary geometry</u>.

F <u>I beg to differ</u>. Over the past few decades, molecular biology has made gigantic strides in determining which molecules do what to which. Always it is found that nature's nanomachines operate according to perfectly ordinary physical forces and laws. No weird goings-on have been discovered.

G <u>The former</u> perform a purely scaffolding role, holding the molecule together. The business part of DNA lies with <u>the latter</u>, which are constructed from four different varieties of molecules or bases, with the chemical names adenine, guanine, cytosine and thiamine – <u>let's use their initials</u> for simplicity's sake.

H As a simple-minded physicist, when I think about life at the molecular level, the question I keep asking is: How do all these mindless atoms know what to do? The complexity of the living cell is immense, <u>resembling a city</u> in the degree of its elaborate activity. Each molecule has a specified function and a designated place in the overall scheme so that the correct objects get manufactured.

4 At the end of the first paragraph, the writer refers to a set of technical things, from tweezers to chains. Decide which is suitable for these actions.

a The floodwater was extracted by means of ....
b A trumpet is played by shutting off a series of ....
c Julie's hair had been hastily lopped off with ....
d The splinter was finally pulled out with ....
e The bike had been secured to the railings with ....

◎ Idiom spot

Many technical words are used in other contexts, for example, *a negotiating **lever**, a **chain** of supermarkets*. They also occur in some idioms. Choose the correct word to complete idioms a–j and explain their meanings.

bolt	chain	fuse	gear	knife
nail	spade	strings	tubes	wires

a the final .... in the coffin
b to call a .... a ....
c to go down the ....
d a weak link in the ....
e to blow a ....
f with (no) .... attached
g to get your .... crossed
h to shoot your ....
i to get into ....
j to twist the ....

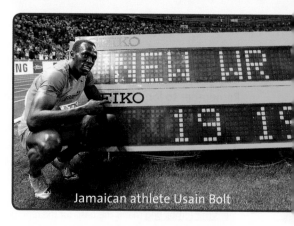

Jamaican athlete Usain Bolt

When should the passive be used? In this example from 12.1, it is not important to know who made the nano-guitar – the emphasis is on the innovation itself.

This Lilliputian instrument was sculpted from crystalline silicon.

1 When is it more appropriate to use a passive rather than an active form? Match examples a–e to the explanations 1–5 below.

a The world record for the men's 200 metres was broken by Usain Bolt in 2009.

b Over a thousand people have been affected by the recent flooding.

c Kerstin's knee is being operated on tomorrow at the City Hospital.

d The front of the building has been severely damaged.

e Jonathan's apartment was broken into twice last year.

1 the action is emphasised, but the sentence still mentions *who* is or was responsible for it

2 *who* is or was responsible for the action is not important or not known

3 the action is emphasised, but the sentence still mentions *what* was responsible for it

4 *what* is or was responsible for the action is not important or not known

5 *who* or *what* is or was responsible for the action is obvious so does not need to be mentioned

2 Rewrite these sentences in the passive, making the underlined words the subject of each sentence and deciding whether the agent needs to be mentioned.

G → page 184

a They gave the Nobel Prize for Chemistry to <u>Marie Curie</u> for her discovery of radium.

b Lengthy power cuts have affected <u>homes</u> in and around the city all this week.

c Researchers found that the <u>'miracle' drug</u> had unpleasant side-effects.

d Scientists have found <u>meteorites</u> in Antarctica which they believe have come from the Moon.

e Astronomers say that there is <u>dark matter</u> in the universe, but they haven't been able to detect this as yet.

f Due to recent global restructuring, they will no longer manufacture <u>the car</u> in Europe.

g Mark McGurl won the <u>Truman Capote Award for Literary Criticism</u> in 2011.

h You should install the <u>latest version of Adobe Flash</u> to get the best from this application.

3 In the rewritten sentence h in 2, the use of the passive reflects not only the chosen emphasis, but also a shift in register, producing a more formal sentence and an impersonal tone. Rewrite these sentences in the passive to change their register.

EXAMPLE: You must supervise young children on this play equipment.

Young children must be supervised on this play equipment.

a You mustn't bring food and drink into the lab.

b You can't take any photographs inside this museum.

c They're using infra-red equipment to search for further survivors.

d Three postgraduate students will share the award for best innovation.

e They are to carry out thorough safety checks immediately.

 Corpus spot

Example e in 3 requires a passive infinitive. The *Cambridge Learner Corpus* shows that even at C2 level, candidates sometimes find it difficult to use passive infinitives and participle forms accurately. Correct the errors in these sentences.

a I did not have to be remind of what had happened on that day.

b If your boss doesn't mind you delaying some mornings, public transport could be a solution.

c Protect tender plants from being damage by frost.

d It was strange to been invited by his brother rather than by John himself.

e Despite asked to attend a second interview, I wasn't offered the job.

f Even though it may prove impossible for all the reasons to discover, research continues.

4 Complete the text below using suitable passives. Where a modal passive is required, be careful with the tense choice.

THE END OF THE DINOSAURS

In 1990, ten years after Nobel prizewinner Luis Alvarez first suggested a link between the extinction of the dinosaurs and an asteroid collision, a huge impact crater **(1)** .... (discover) underground, near the village of Chicxulub in the Yucatan, Mexico. Recent research has shown that this crater **(2)** .... (could not + cause) by volcanic activity. This is because a significant quantity of the element iridium, which is extremely rare on earth, **(3)** .... (detect) at the crater site, supporting the view that the crater **(4)** .... (must + form) by an asteroid. 65 million years ago, iridium-enriched dust **(5)** .... (would + throw) up into the atmosphere, causing the sun **(6)** .... (blot out) for many weeks. As a result, the temperature would have plummeted and the plants which **(7)** .... (eat) by the dinosaurs **(8)** .... (would + kill) by the accompanying acid rain. With the removal of their food chain, the dinosaurs could not have survived.

5 Rewrite these sentences using a noun formed from the underlined verb. You should add a new verb of your choice in the passive, making any other changes necessary.

EXAMPLE: They will only <u>confirm</u> a place on the course upon full payment.

Confirmation of a place on the course will only be issued upon full payment.

a They won't <u>publish</u> these scientific papers until next year.
b They have just <u>announced</u> big job losses on the local news.
c They are <u>considering</u> the planning application for a new sports centre.
d They will <u>recommend</u> the immediate closure of the hospital.
e They are to <u>investigate</u> the case in more depth.
f They didn't <u>explain</u> how much the project would cost.

6 For questions 1–6, complete the second sentence so that it has a similar meaning to the first sentence, using the word given. **Do not change the word given.** You must use between **three** and **eight** words, including the word given.

1 The European Space Agency's *Rosetta* mission aims to land a probe on a comet.
for
The aim of the European Space Agency's *Rosetta* mission is
.... on a comet.

2 It will be necessary to wear safety gloves throughout this experiment.
duration
Safety gloves
.... of this experiment.

3 Using electron beams, it is possible to manufacture machines that are too small to see.
naked
Tiny machines that cannot
.... are manufactured by means of electron beams.

4 Recently, astronomers have been finding more and more planets outside our solar system.
increasing
Recently, an
.... outside our solar system.

5 Advances in science should soon yield a cure for cancer.
brink
Scientists are thought
.... finding a cure for cancer.

6 Although they tried to dissuade Josh from continuing with it, he has opted for physics as a career.
advised
Despite
.... Josh has chosen a career in it.

1 You are going to listen to a recorded task for Speaking, Part 3, where one candidate will speak for two minutes and a second candidate will be asked a question. First, look at the prompt card below and decide what aspects might be covered in the recording.

> What are the implications of scientific research today?
> ___
> ● career opportunities
> ● commercial interests
> ● moral issues

2 **1 21** Now listen to the recording. How many of your ideas are covered? Do you agree with the speakers? Why? / Why not?

Pronunciation

3 Here are some expressions that Jana could have used to show more advanced language. Match them to their meanings 1–6.

a in the vanguard
b a double-edged sword
c the lay person
d for its own sake
e subject to enough regulations
f the greater good

1 as an end in itself
2 effectively controlled by law
3 at the cutting-edge
4 having advantages and disadvantages
5 non-expert
6 the benefit of society at large

1 22 Now listen to Jana using these expressions. Notice how she stresses certain words and slows down or pauses when making an important point. This can be quite effective in a two-minute talk – and will allow you time to think about what you want to say next.

4 **1 23** Practise using the following words, building them up into the phrases and sentences you hear on the recording.

a concern
b duty
c repercussions
d significance
e cusp
f reservations

◎ Phrase spot

In the recording Jana used the idiom *set the ball rolling*, which means initiate a course of action. Make further idioms and expressions with *set*, choosing from the phrases below.

Which two other common verbs combine with the remaining phrases?

the wheels in motion
your teeth on edge   the world on fire
your sights on   rings round
a fast one   the scene
in stone   (set)   the risk of
a tight ship   out your stall
the strings   your weight
counter to   your heart on
the other one   your socks up
a dangerous precedent   the record straight

5 Use expressions with *set* to describe the situations below.

EXAMPLE: The investigation has found Peter Gresham to be entirely innocent and will publish their findings.

   *The investigation will **set the record straight** about Peter Gresham.*

a As soon as Jenny spotted the new gadget in the shop window, she was determined to buy it.

b The consultant explained in detail to the whole department how she could help them.

c Allowing her teenage son to stay out late last Wednesday night has given him an argument for doing so again.

d No contract has yet been signed and both sides are keen to be flexible.

e The vivid description of the Martian landscape at the beginning of the book helps the reader to visualise it better.

f The sound of a young child attempting to play the violin never fails to irritate me.

g No sooner had the brilliant young scientist finished his PhD than a leading biotech company took steps to recruit him.

h Carla's a good singer, but she's never going to be outstanding.

6 Read this extract about scientific risk and decide which answer (A, B, C or D) best fits each gap. There is an example at the beginning (0).

The Precautionary Principle

How far should members of the public have to run the risk of personal **(0)** ....**A**.... where scientific or technological innovation is concerned? In some legal systems, including European Union law, the **(1)** .... of the 'precautionary principle' is a statutory requirement. The precautionary principle advises society to be **(2)** .... about a technology or practice where there is scientific uncertainty, ignorance, gaps in knowledge or the likelihood of **(3)** .... outcomes.

This runs **(4)** .... to the optimistic notion that any adverse effects that **(5)** .... unintentionally can be addressed. Indeed, some claim these may provide an opportunity to develop new solutions, and in this way **(6)** .... to economic growth. For this reason, the US Chamber of Commerce dislikes the precautionary approach and prefers: 'the use of sound science, cost–benefit analysis, and risk assessment when assessing a particular regulatory issue.' Its **(7)** .... is therefore to: 'Oppose the domestic and international adoption of the precautionary principle as a basis for regulatory decision making.' Yet history reminds us that asbestos, halocarbons and PCBs seemed like miracle substances at first, but **(8)** .... to be highly problematic for human and environmental health.

0 **A** harm	**B** abuse	**C** hurt	**D** damage
1 **A** exercise	**B** application	**C** function	**D** commitment
2 **A** discreet	**B** anxious	**C** cautious	**D** prudent
3 **A** unforeseen	**B** unsolved	**C** undeniable	**D** unimaginable
4 **A** opposite	**B** versus	**C** counter	**D** fast
5 **A** come	**B** issue	**C** stem	**D** arise
6 **A** supply	**B** contribute	**C** lend	**D** assign
7 **A** strategy	**B** manner	**C** scheme	**D** theory
8 **A** sprang up	**B** came out	**C** caught up	**D** turned out

Part 2 Report

If you choose to write a report for Part 2 of Writing, make sure you use impersonal language and adopt a neutral tone. It is appropriate to include passive structures to achieve this. Sub-headings and other organising devices such as bullets will make your report easier to read.

1 Look at the sub-headings opposite, then read the report below, which is on career opportunities for science graduates. Decide where the sub-headings fit, and suggest where bullets would be helpful for readability.

Exciting new opportunities

A more unconventional path

Academic research

Next steps

A broad scope of employment

Education as a career

This report summarises the current career opportunities for science graduates, drawing largely on the experiences of past and present students. Many final-year students have already been invited to interviews and some have even been offered jobs, conditional on graduation.

The first point to stress is that interesting opportunities exist outside the specialist scientific fields. This is dealt with in the final section of the report.

Returning to pure science, it has been estimated that there will be over a thousand post-graduate posts available for the next academic year, countrywide. Students should consult their tutor for advice in the first instance. High-achievers should contemplate applying for scholarships to the U.S.A., where so much research is at the cutting edge. Students wishing to follow up on specific research possibilities in the States are advised to consult Professor Grimbleton.

The fast-moving developments in biotechnology and genetics look set to provide good job opportunities, as many companies are being expanded in their bids to become market leader. Four local companies have specifically requested graduate trainees from this college. They are Bio-futures, Genotech, PJF Seed Research and Railton Systems. Application forms can be obtained from the Administration Secretary.

Several past students have opted for jobs in teaching and it is recommended that anyone considering such a career should attend the information day planned by this department. At this event, it will not only be possible to meet Head Teachers and Science Coordinators from schools in the region, but also former college students who are now qualified and practising teachers.

As indicated above, any report on current opportunities would be incomplete without mentioning other non-scientific jobs that past students have taken up with relish. While none of these jobs can be said to demand the recall of actual science, the generic skills that students have been given through their undergraduate courses are directly relevant. Here are some of the more unusual career moves: accountancy, stockmarket brokering, counselling, air-traffic control and casino management.

More details can be found on the student website. A booklet is also in preparation.

2 The report contains some 'signposting' devices, for example, *As indicated above*. These are included to help the reader to process the report without undue effort. What other examples of signposting can you find in the report?

Here are some more useful signposting devices. Which are looking forward and which refer back?

a As already discussed …
b Alongside this decision …
c Below is a different interpretation of …
d The previous statement confirms that …
e Further ideas will be elaborated in the next two sections.
f As mentioned at the outset …
g It should now be considered whether …
h It would appear then that …
i The aspects covered earlier suggest …
j This does not necessarily mean that …

3 Find examples of the following in the report opposite.

a compound nouns
b compound adjectives
c prefixes
d suffixes
e topical expressions, e.g. *market leader*

4 Now look at the following exam task.

> You belong to an international film club and have been asked to write the club's annual report this year. This report is written for club members and has to include information about the main events held over the last twelve months, to present plans for activities in the coming year and to summarise the current financial position of the club in respect of money received and payments made.

To plan your report, make a spider diagram like the one below. Spend at least five minutes thinking of what to include under each of the three areas, adding to the ideas given. Then draft suitable sub-headings, further dividing the three main sections if necessary.

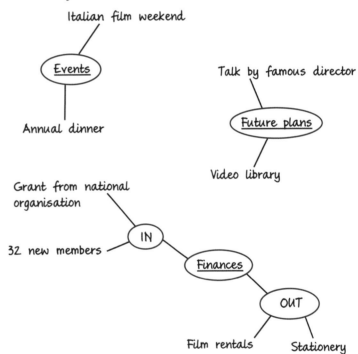

5 Now use this advice to write your report, in 280–320 words.

Use of English

1 Read this extract from an article about socks. For questions 1–14, think of the word which best fits each space. Use only one word in each space. There is an example at the beginning (0).

SOCKS

Mr Twenty-First Century strikes a pose on (0) ....**THE**........ pages of a 1939 issue of British *Vogue* magazine. He wears a jump-suit, belt and waistcoat festooned (1) .... hardware. His hat is 'an antenna snatching radio out of the ether', *Vogue* tells (2) .... (3) .... quite today's mobile-phone man, (4) .... close. However, as we reach his socks, the best *Vogue*'s futurologist can (5) .... up with is 'disposable'.

Throwaway insults are (6) .... new for socks. And that's not (7) .... they have to put up with. Over a day, the average human foot (8) .... off at least half a cup of moisture – manna from heaven for those odour-causing micro-organisms. Yet socks are (9) .... the most ancient of human inventions – an Egyptian mummy's knitted socks are arguably the oldest surviving examples, (10) .... hand-sewn versions may (11) .... back to the Bronze Age. They surely deserve a better future than consignment to the bin.

Not (12) .... appreciates the sock's versatility, though. Albert Einstein famously eschewed socks altogether, apparently regarding them as an unnecessary luxury. I too go sockless in the summer. (13) .... the frost begins to bite, I can't help wondering, (14) .... Einstein have been wrong?

2 For questions 1–6, complete the second sentence so that it has a similar meaning to the first sentence, using the word given. **Do not change the word given.** You must use between **three** and **eight** words, including the word given.

1 The children agreed they would each tidy the playroom on alternate days.
turns
The children .... the playroom.

2 Professor Smith talked firstly about living on Mars, and then discussed the Space Lab.
went
After talking about living on Mars, Professor Smith .... the Space Lab.

3 It's a shame Peter didn't wear a suit to the wedding.
put
If only .... the wedding.

4 Everyone remembers my great-uncle because he was always having arguments with his wife.
having
My great-uncle .... arguments with his wife.

5 We must always bear in mind that many scientific breakthroughs are due to luck.
sight
We must .... plays a large part in many scientific breakthroughs.

6 When it comes to friendship, I prefer having a few close friends to many acquaintances.
rather
As far .... a few close friends than many acquaintances.

Vocabulary

3   For questions a–n, decide which word is correct.

a His plans *came in for/came up with* fierce criticism at the meeting.

b My English teacher always had a nice *turn/set* of phrase when he commented on essays.

c Lisa is such a bright, *meticulous/vivacious* girl, always fun and cheerful.

d That new girl is never going to *set/put* the world on fire, I'm afraid.

e I'm sorry to say that Pete is the one weak link in the *wires/chain*.

f Karen gave me the cold *elbow/shoulder* when we were introduced.

g The little girl just stood there, trying to *choke back/fend off* the tears.

h Tom's really *pompous/morbid* now he's been promoted – he never lets you forget he's boss.

i Eating really cold ice-cream *puts/sets* my teeth on edge.

j The news of his engagement to Elisa arrived like a bolt from the *sky/blue*.

k My brother admires anyone who calls *a knife a knife/a spade a spade*.

l The dress I'm making is *coming along/round* well and will be ready for the weekend.

m I really think the council needs to grasp the *thistle/nettle* and decide whether to have more rural buses or not.

n I have a terrible habit of *whipping up/blurting out* the first thing that comes into my mind.

Writing

4   Improve this report on an exchange visit by inserting suitable compound adjectives where the symbol * appears, choosing from the list below.

deep-sea	record-breaking	long-standing	glass-bottomed	wider-ranging
inter-continental	easy-going	trouble-free	meticulously-planned	half-day

Here is my report on our club's recent exchange visit to Australia. Without exception, members who participated in this trip were highly appreciative of the * itinerary, not to mention the warm welcome extended by our * Australian hosts. This * relationship continues to flourish and we will be hosting a * number of visitors this summer (see below).

Travel

The * flights went smoothly and we arrived in Melbourne on schedule. A coach had been organised to transport us to the civic reception, where our individual hosts awaited us. Travel within Australia was mostly by plane – unfortunately, our visit coincided with industrial action, so our transfers were not entirely *.

Trips

The highpoint was the Great Barrier Reef, where two exhilarating days were spent * diving. Those members who chose not to dive were given the alternative of a * cruise in a * boat, which was said to be very enjoyable for all concerned.

Some members have suggested that the visit to the Kakadu National Park could have been extended, as it was rather rushed. In subsequent years, it might also be more informative to visit during the dry season, which would allow * access to the park.

Return visit

There will be 48 visitors to us in July, including six families with young children. In view of this, it will be necessary to find extra hosts. Strategies for achieving this should be agreed at the next club meeting. In anticipation, could the following suggestions be tabled:

- advertising in relevant journals
- feature in local newspaper
- posters in public places, e.g. library
- mailshot to schools and colleges
- interview on KJY radio
- club website?

Perhaps other members should be asked for further suggestions in advance of the meeting.

13.1 Save the planet

Vocabulary

Environment collocations

1 Match a word in A with one in B to make the correct collocation. Some words may be used more than once.

A	B
fossil	resources
severe	environment
pristine	sea levels
finite	famine
greenhouse	density
water	ice cap
climate	expectancy
solar	gases
population	shortages
melting	energy
rising	fuel
life	change

Speaking

2 Are we doing enough to save the planet? Look at the photos and discuss the problems shown. Try to think of some solutions. Use some of the collocations above.

3 Think about your daily routine and make a list of ways you could help the environment. With a partner, choose three things that you would both find the easiest to put into practice.

Listening

4 **1 24** You are going to hear three different extracts on subjects relating to the environment.

Read through questions 1–6 opposite. Choose the answer (A, B or C) which fits best according to what you hear. There are two questions for each extract.

Extract One

You hear a woman talking about her job.

1 How does the woman get her message across to the school children?
A She helps teachers to make their lessons more relevant.
B She takes advantage of their interests.
C She believes in getting them out of the classroom.

2 What does she find frustrating?
A The lack of time she has in the classroom.
B That more waste could be recycled.
C The low prices paid for recycled waste.

Extract Two

You hear part of an interview with a climate change expert.

3 What does the man say about solar and wind as sources of energy?
A They are often unreliable.
B They are costly to install.
C They are unlikely to be adopted in some countries.

4 What is the man's attitude to biomass energy?
A It wouldn't supply enough of the world's energy needs.
B It may be politically more unacceptable than other renewables.
C It is untenable in the long term.

Extract Three

You hear two people talking on the radio about a controversial theory.

5 What does the man say about the theory?
A It was ahead of its time.
B It wasn't a very scientific theory.
C It has never been acknowledged by the government.

6 What do the speakers agree about?
A Lovelock's approach was too amateurish.
B Lovelock was rather an odd person.
C Lovelock alienated fellow scientists.

5 **1 24** The extracts you heard illustrate different registers. Listen again, and then with a partner decide whether the extract is formal, informal or unmarked in tone. Give reasons for your decisions.

6 The following are all examples of words which have been used inappropriately by Proficiency candidates. The words are either formal, informal or unmarked. Decide when it would be appropriate to use each word.

EXAMPLE: kids / children

> *'Kids' is informal and used mainly in speaking; 'children' is unmarked.*

a people / persons
b amelioration / improvement
c bloke / man
d stuff / things
e frequented / went to
f reckon / think
g boozing / drinking
h mates / friends
i fellow / guy
j snaps / photographs
k pluses / advantages
l lousy / terrible
m prudent / careful
n mad / annoyed

The words in the exercise above are all synonyms – that is words with the same or similar meaning. Synonyms can rarely be used interchangeably, either because of difference in register (as above), or because of a difference in use. For example, *rife* and *widespread* have a similar meaning – 'existing in many places':

*Many illnesses are **rife** in areas with a poor water supply.*

*There is **widespread** flooding of coastal areas.*

However, *rife* suggests something unpleasant, whereas *widespread* is a more unmarked or neutral word.

---

7 Decide which of the words in italics in each sentence below fits best. Justify your answers and think of a sentence using the alternative word.

a I can't afford to buy a new car this year – I'm *broke/destitute*.
b Her grandmother is always telling her she should eat more, as she's much too *slender/skinny*.
c Dr Pitt has made many *opponents/enemies* because of his rudeness.
d I have a feeling my horrible sister's been *sneaking into/ entering* my room and reading my diary while I'm out.
e The evening will *commence/kick off* with a short speech, given by Sir John Bertram.
f The left back *lost his cool/became displeased* with his opponent and socked him in the jaw.
g Pablo *struck/touched* the jammed window forcibly with his fist to make it open.
h I felt the rain *trickling/flooding* slowly down the back of my collar.

8 For questions 1–8, read the text below and decide which answer (A, B, C or D) best fits each gap.

THE FUTURE

The environmental **(1)** .... for the future is mixed. In spite of economic and political changes, interest in and **(2)** .... about the environment remains high. Problems such as acid deposition, chlorofluorocarbons and ozone depletion still require solutions and **(3)** .... action is needed to deal with these. Until acid depositions **(4)** .... , loss of aquatic life in northern lakes and streams will continue and forest growth may be affected. Water pollution will remain a growing problem as an increasing human population puts **(5)** .... stress on the environment. To reduce environmental degradation and for humanity to save its habitat, societies must recognise that resources are **(6)** .... Environmentalists believe that, as populations and their demands increase, the idea of continuous growth must **(7)** .... way to a more rational use of the environment, but that this can only be brought **(8)** .... by a dramatic change in the attitude of the human species.

1 A outline	**B** outset	**C** outcome	**D** outlook
2 A concern	**B** attention	**C** responsibility	**D** consideration
3 A affiliated	**B** shared	**C** concerted	**D** pooled
4 A wane	**B** diminish	**C** depreciate	**D** curtail
5 A untold	**B** uncounted	**C** unrelated	**D** undreamed
6 A finite	**B** restricted	**C** confined	**D** bounded
7 A make	**B** force	**C** give	**D** clear
8 A on	**B** about	**C** off	**D** in

13.2 Reported speech

1. **1 25** You will hear part of a radio interview with a woman who helped save a type of rhino from extinction in the wild. Before you listen, read through the notes below.

Area visited:	1
Habitat of rhino:	2
Susan was there to	3
She found a	4
People she met:	5
People who gave her a lot of help:	6
Condition of rhino today:	7

Now, listen and complete the notes.

2. With a partner take it in turns to report verbally to each other what you heard in the interview. Try to put in as much detail as possible.

   EXAMPLE: *The man said that we were all aware of the need for biodiversity.*

G → page 185

- When reporting, it's usual to go back one tense. This is called 'backshifting'.
  'I saw her yesterday.' She said she had seen her the day before.
  'I'll email her now.' He said he would email her then.

- In conversations, people sometimes don't backshift if what they are reporting happened not long ago.
  'I saw Rachel this morning. She says she'll meet us at the cinema at seven, if that's OK?'

  Backshift also doesn't need to happen if a fact is still true or the speaker believes it is true.
  He said that elephants are still in danger today.

- There are some structures which are more difficult than others when reported because they do not always follow either of the patterns outlined above.

3. Report the following. Begin each sentence with *She said ...* .

   EXAMPLE: 'I shall see you at the meeting.'
   She said she would see me at the meeting.

   a 'My grandmother could walk to school without worrying about traffic.'
   b 'You must come to tea sometime!'
   c 'You must remember to recycle the rubbish.'
   d 'You mustn't smoke in the restaurant.'
   e 'Companies which pollute rivers must be fined.'
   f 'If I were mayor, I'd make public transport free.'
   g 'If the children picked up the rubbish regularly, I'd pay them.'

> When reporting, it is often possible to use a verb or a verb plus an adverb which carries much of the meaning of the sentence.
> *'I hate you! You're scum!' she said to Tom and then she walked out of the door.*
> *She screamed abuse at Tom before walking out of the door.*
> *'Shh! You're not supposed to talk in here!' the librarian scolded us.*
> *The librarian sternly told us off for talking.*

4. Use the following verbs to convey the meaning of the sentences below. Take care with these verbs – some are followed by a gerund, others by an infinitive and others by a clause. Sometimes a preposition is required.

claim	decide	declare	insist
object	refuse	sigh	suggest

   a 'What about going to Crete this year for our holiday?' Tina said.
   b 'I will always love you, Daphne!' Fred said.
   c 'I've made up my mind – I'm going to take the job, but I'm not keen!' Colin said.
   d 'It can't be helped. I know you didn't mean to drop it,' my mother said.
   e 'Leave that window shut. We don't want to catch our death of cold,' the old man said.
   f 'That's my book you've got in your school bag!' Rose said.
   g 'I'll go out if I want to!' my brother said.
   h 'I have no intention of going by train, thank you very much,' Lucy said.

5   Which of the following adverbs would fit with the reporting verbs on page 112? Insert one
    adverb in each of the sentences you wrote in 4.

passionately	confidently	categorically	peevishly
tentatively	reluctantly	resignedly	stubbornly

6   Write a sentence in direct speech which ends with these adverbs. (Use a dictionary to help you.)

   a ‘...’ the shopkeeper exclaimed angrily.
   b ‘...’ the police officer said sarcastically.
   c ‘...’ the teacher stated pedantically.
   d ‘...’ my grandfather muttered absent-mindedly.
   e ‘...’ Theresa said decisively.
   f ‘...’ the doctor murmured reassuringly.
   g ‘...’ my neighbour retorted rudely.
   h ‘...’ his boss said cautiously.

7   For questions 1–15, read the text below and think of the word which best fits each space. Use
    only one word in each space. There is an example at the beginning (0).

The first naturalists

There came a time, maybe 20,000 years ago,
(0) ....**WHEN**........ man, instead of being
merely a hunter, started to domesticate animals.
The dog helped in his hunting activities and
geese and ducks were kept and bred
(1) .... a source of food, which
was easier than **(2)** .... to go out
and hunt them. Once humans had domesticated
animals they **(3)** .... their attention
to plants. Instead of being nomads, drifting from
place to place following the game animals, they
began to create farms and thus enter upon a more
settled **(4)** .... of life. Villages and
towns sprang **(5)** .... in places where
previously there had been only a hamlet. Now
animals and plants began to be kept
(6) .... merely for food but also for
interest's **(7)** .... or for their beauty.

   The first writers on animal life were Aristotle,
in 335 BC, and Pliny, in 75 AD, but for many
hundreds of years after Pliny the subject of natural
history, in **(8)** .... with many
other areas of knowledge, **(9)** ....
progressed at all. For the most part
(10) .... zoos as existed were
in the hands of the dilettante nobility and were
no **(11)** .... than second-rate
menageries, **(12)** .... any scientific
purpose.

   However, in the seventeenth century, naturalists
began to realise that they needed a system for
classifying living things **(13)** .... ,
as more plants and animals were discovered,
(14) .... was difficult to
(15) .... track of them all.

8   In the recorded interview, it was pointed out that
    biodiversity was important for a healthy planet. In
    groups, talk about which of these methods you think
    is the best way to maintain biodiversity. Present your
    ideas to the rest of the class.

   • Keeping animals in zoos.
   • Having more national parks.
   • Having egg and sperm banks of endangered
     species or collecting and preserving the DNA of
     endangered species.

1 How much do you know about endangered species? The five animals above are examples of animals which are or have been endangered. With a partner, decide which animal you think is no longer endangered.

2 All these words are useful when talking about the environment. Complete the table with the correct form of the word given.

Noun	Verb	Adjective
predator predation a	b	c ....
demography	✗	d ....
e	sustain	f ....
✗	g	domestic
conifer	✗	h ....
i .... j	diversify	k ....
evolution	l	m ....
n	✗	inevitable

3 Complete the sentences using a preposition from the box.

in	to	of	into	on

a The impact .... climate change has been greatest in the polar regions.
b The attitude of this community .... recycling has been very positive.
c Research .... solar power has shown it can be cost effective.
d Analysis .... the data will be done later in the year.
e What the outcome .... the scientific report will be, no one yet knows.
f The rise/increase .... the cost of petrol continues to trouble the government.
g An increase/rise .... 12% on heating bills will prove unsustainable.
h A change .... the law against polluting streams is long overdue.
i The impact .... polar bears of the ice cap melting will be huge.
j The objection .... the legislation was not based on scientific evidence.

4 In Writing, Part 1 you will need to write a well-structured essay summarising and evaluating the main points of two short texts and also giving your own opinions. Read the two texts below and decide what are the key points in both texts.

Text 1

THE NEED TO SAVE THE TIGER

Tigers are an important part of the planet's rich diversity of life. As top predators in their food chain, they feed on a variety of prey species and help maintain the structure and functioning of the ecosystems they inhabit. Tigers, therefore, are considered a keystone species. If tigers disappear, there will be far-reaching and negative consequences for other parts of the ecosystem. Protecting tigers, therefore, helps many other species as well. For example, protecting tiger habitats in India and Bangladesh has helped to protect human habitats by reducing land erosion, stabilising ecosystems and encouraging wise land use. It has also led to an increase in global awareness of climate change and the problem of rising sea levels.

Text 2

Conservation: Is it worthwhile?

A majority of professional conservationists believe it is time to consider shifting efforts away from some of the world's most famous species, such as the polar bear, to concentrate on others which have a greater chance of survival. The scientists believe a serious loss of biological diversity is 'likely, very likely or virtually certain'. Some experts have rejected the idea on the grounds that it is impossible to make judgments about one species at the expense of another, given the complexity of the ecological interactions in the natural world. However, others are starting to question the value of spending millions of pounds on one celebrated species, such as the panda, or a big predator such as the tiger, where loss of habitat is almost inevitable.

5 With a partner, brainstorm ideas that you can use in the personal opinion part of the essay. There are some suggestions in the box below.

> tigers/polar bears/useful symbols
> people attracted to cuddly animals/good publicity
> important to save unattractive animals too
> global warming/unlikely to decrease

Exam spot

In Writing, Part 1, as well as summarising the information from two texts, you are asked to give your own ideas. You gain higher marks for linking your points clearly and for showing that you can use a range of phrases to do so.

6 Now, write an essay summarising and evaluating the key points from both texts. Use your own words as far as possible, and include your own ideas in your answers. Use the sentence openers below and some of the phrases from the Useful language in your answer.

Sentence openers
The two texts contrast differing views of …
According to the first passage …
Personally, I …
The second text puts forward …
I believe that …
In conclusion, it is my opinion that …

Useful language
Linking points and arguments

as opposed to – *African elephants, as opposed to Indian elephants, tend to have larger ears.*

in the sense that – *The study has been somewhat discredited, in the sense that it won't be published in a reputable magazine.*

For this reason – *Conservation of natural resources is at the forefront of policy. For this reason, we are introducing a law concerning logging in the area.*

Making generalisations – on the whole, in general, for the most part, as a rule

Being specific – with respect to, in the case of, as regards, in terms of, with the exception of

Attitude – personally, unfortunately, obviously, evidently, presumably, naturally, fortunately

Quantity – a great deal of, to some/a large extent, a large number of

Exam folder 7

Reading and Use of English, Part 5
Multiple-choice text

This part of the Reading and Use of English paper consists of a text from a range of sources with six four-option multiple-choice questions. The questions may test any of the following: detail, opinion, attitude, tone, purpose, main idea and implication. They may also test organisational features such as exemplification, comparison and reference.

Read the Exam advice and then do the task below.

EXAM ADVICE

- Read through the text carefully.
- Read through the questions very carefully to make sure you really understand what the question is asking. Then find the answer in the text.
- Underline your answer in the text and then find the option, A, B, C or D, which best matches your answer.
- Read the text again to check you are right.
- Don't spend too much time worrying about a word you can't guess the meaning of.

You are going to read an extract from an article where two books are reviewed. For questions **1–6**, choose the answer (**A**, **B**, **C** or **D**) which you think fits best according to the text.

Wild flowers

The journalist Simon Jenkins considers two books on wild flowers.

We all find solace in flowers. I go when times are hard to the wild dune church of Aberdaron in north Wales, where is pinned up (or was) a list of flowers that battle against the wind in the graveyard outside. Here is an uplifting array of thrift, vetch, yarrow and dozens more that toss and chatter, apparently immune to the salty south-westerlies. I hardly know these flowers, let alone could recognise them. Nature's wilderness is a foreign land, yet its tongue is strangely comforting. It is a realm of unrivalled colour and richness, defying time and order.

Hence when Sarah Raven's colossal new compendium, *Wild Flowers*, thudded into my lap, it was not to the pictures that I turned but to the index. The names are, in truth, the pictures, recording how country people down the ages have seen in nature a mirror of their lives. Here are adder's tongue, autumn lady's-tresses and betty-go-to-bed-at-noon. Flower names can be peculiar down to individual parish, corrupted by geographical accent and dialect. They can be vulgar, poignant and romantic. What pain yielded traveller's-foot? What anguish went into heartsease, love-in-a-mist and love-lies-bleeding? The poet and botanist Geoffrey Grigson traced more than 6,000 English common names for plants. There are 50 for dandelion alone and 90 for lords-and-ladies: starchwort, cuckoo pint and jack in the pulpit. Only the dreariest Linnaean sergeant-major could want to dragoon all these into *arum maculatum*.

Raven cries for us to save the homesteads of her beloved friends. Ninety-seven percent of England's lowland wilderness has gone in the last sixty years.

A quarter of all hedgerows have been destroyed since 1980 alone. Marshes are drained, woods conifered, meadows concreted. In South Africa an appeal is being launched this week to save the world capital of wild flowers, the Cape's unique Fynbos landscape, threatened with mass development spreading out from Cape Town. Fynbos is the most florally diverse ecology on earth. Yet wild flowers are wild. They are nature's flotsam, survivors, anarchists, freelances, defying the horrors of modern life. I am drawn to a different botanical lifestyle, that of the weed-seekers. While Raven wanders her moors, urban geeks are scrambling over rubbish tips and railway sidings in search of vagabond exotics. Their champion is the naturalist Richard Mabey, whose *Defence of Weeds* must be the most eye-opening book I have read. De-industrialisation has led to a new, mostly urban British landscape which is fertile ground for the invaders.

Mabey tears back the city's familiar curtain to reveal a jungle of migrant species beneath. They bear with pride the seedsman's definition of weeds as 'plants in the wrong place'. They are tramps, rebels, defying the laws of municipal authority. Moving in among the empty factories and canal banks are giant hogweeds, buddleias and rosebay willowherbs. They come with sinister names such as winy Jack and stinker Bob. Exotics arrive from round the globe, spilling from cargos on to roads and railway lines. Mabey finds specimens from Africa dropped from the hems of Commonwealth conference visitors in Buckingham Palace gardens.

Wild flowers have evolved a class system of their own: effete respect is shown to Raven's country cousins while war is declared on Mabey's 'vegetable guerrillas that have overcome the dereliction of the industrial age'. Many wild flowers are protected so that roads and footpaths must be diverted round them. Biodiversity grants are awarded for endangered species such as corn buttercup and pheasant's eye.

Despite the damage they do to other flora, that splendid weed, the daffodil, is planted out 'wild' by councils to give 'a splash of spring colour' to verges. Yet even weeds must conform. When a friend of mine drove round the M40–M25 interchange after it was built, hurling poppy seeds from his car and delighting in the subsequent harvest of red, he found a year later that it had fallen foul of ministry herbicide. Mabey even admires those mighty bolsheviks who are determined to defy humankind's occupation of the earth. Buffel grass, tumbleweed, hogweed, Indian balsam, Japanese knotweed and kudzu grow a metre and more overnight. They can upheave motorways and tear down houses in days. Acts of parliament have been passed against Japweed, the cost of clearing it now exceeding £150m a year. 'Weeds are the tithe we get for breaking the earth,' cries Mabey. They are feral biology.

1 How does the writer react to the church at Aberdaron?

A He finds consolation in the barren appearance of its surroundings.

B He is embarrassed that he knows so few of the names of the flowers.

C He is cheered by the abundance of flowers in such a windswept place.

D He takes pleasure from the care that has been lavished on the flowers.

2 What point is the writer making about wild flower names in the second paragraph?

A They are more evocative than the correct botanical names.

B They can differ from one period of time to another.

C There are a few which keep the same name throughout the UK.

D There are still many that haven't yet been recorded.

3 What is the writer's attitude to wild flower habitat destruction?

A He is pleased that Raven has made a very clear case for calling a halt to it.

B He is saddened that wild flowers have to work so hard to survive nowadays.

C He is concerned that the threat to Fynbos is inevitable, given the circumstances.

D He is enthusiastic about the possibility of there being another viewpoint.

4 What does the writer say about the contents of Mabey's book?

A It contains a number of anecdotes about the introduction of new species.

B It is groundbreaking in its attempt to put a name to unusual species.

C It includes plants which are unintentional immigrants to the UK.

D It charts the evolution of a number of plants of foreign origin.

5 What does the writer suggest about wild flowers in the fifth paragraph?

A They are only to be found nowadays in rural areas.

B They are treasured but weeds are vilified.

C They are easier to protect than other types of plant.

D They are too expensive to preserve.

6 What point is the writer making in the final paragraph?

A More money is needed to stem the tide of seriously destructive weeds.

B People should be encouraged to sow seeds in unlikely places.

C It is hard not to respect the tenaciousness of some plants.

D The authorities have a contradictory attitude towards weeds.

Get fit, live longer!

Speaking

1 Work with a partner and decide whether the following statements are true or false.

a Most people get enough exercise from their normal daily routine.

b The younger you are, the less active you need to be.

c It's a good idea to eat pasta or a banana before you exercise.

d It's better to eat a large meal at lunchtime than in the evening.

e Running is the best form of exercise.

f To live longer you need to give up smoking, drinking alcohol and coffee and become a vegetarian.

g You will only really get fit if you have a personal trainer.

Reading

2 You are going to read a magazine article about health and fitness. For questions 1–10, choose from the sections (A–D). The sections may be chosen more than once.

Which person

mentions being disconcerted by their lack of ability when faced with a completely new activity?	1
was grateful for having been spurred on in their efforts?	2
suggests that prior experience of the exercise method can be advantageous?	3
suggests that they have overreached themselves during their first session?	4
is sceptical about whether a way of exercising would really appeal to them?	5
suggests that their chosen exercise programme seemed to be based on a slightly eccentric premise?	6
rejects the idea that they are following an exercise programme to improve fitness?	7
comments on the relentless nature of the trainer?	8
contrasts the amount of pleasure to be gained from different types of exercise?	9
suggests that the outcome of their exercise programme was not wholly positive?	10

A I'll be honest, I have never felt the natural high which scientists claim follows a bout of intense exercise. The empirical evidence of my own body tells me that the only thing exercise releases in my brain is loathing. So I scoff when the people at the gym tell me I'll be hooked on a new type of Pilates in two sessions. My first session is an hour's one-on-one with Daniel, my trainer; a good idea for any beginner. Although I, disappointingly, don't actually lose any weight over my six sessions – personally, I find it rather ups my appetite – I can attest to its toning abilities. The classes themselves – which take a maximum of six people – are entertaining, and as agreeable as enforced muscle fatigue can ever be. It definitely helps if you'd already got to grips with some basic Pilates techniques before you start, but, once you've got the hang of commands such as 'squeeze that imaginary grape under your armpit', it provides a great variety of exercise.

Chloe: New Pilates

B A month of sessions with a personal trainer three times a week seems like the perfect springboard to a better future. My personal trainer, Tony, asks me what I hope to achieve. I mutter something about losing a few pounds and toning up a bit, but the truth is I want to get back into my tailormade suits. It's the gap between my expectations and reality that is hardest to contend with. I know that no matter how healthy I become at the age of 36, I will still be less fit than I was as a lazy 18-year-old who did no exercise at all. But if I'm honest, I secretly believed I wouldn't actually be all that bad at this. The problem is weights. I've never bothered with them before. I take it slowly for the first few sessions but it's hard going and I eventually pull a muscle in my right arm. It's time for a few days off. I greet a four-day respite with enthusiasm, but actually find myself in the gym, running faster and longer than before and lifting weights well.

Mark: Personal training

C I go along to my nearest fitness centre and decide to try out the DVD of Sport Active, which has more than 70 different exercises on it. The programme can measure and display your heart rate, thanks to a monitor that straps to your forearm which sends information to the console. I start with tennis and get an enormous kick out of hitting balls into an onscreen net. I quickly move on to mountain biking, or, as I now call it, 'total physical punishment'. However, even though I am an old hand at cycling, by halfway round, I have clearly lost all ability to show off. On screen, my heart rate has rocketed up to 178. 'You're definitely getting a good cardio workout here,' encourages Robert, the fitness centre trainer. Could these games damage people by suggesting the wrong positions? Robert is dismissive: 'It's unlikely you're going to hurt yourself.' I decide to carry on and after a few weeks begin to see the benefits.

Ben:
Sport Active

D Wild Fitness is more than a form of exercise, Matt, my trainer, told me that it was a whole philosophy of life: to transform yourself by learning to move and eat in the way of our hunter-gatherer ancestors and to become strong, fast and agile. It all sounded a bit bizarre but I was more than happy to give it a go. The first session began at 8am on a Monday morning in Regent's Park, London, with some introductory exercises. The hardest session came the next week when Matt told us we would sprint around the 400-metre running track four times, with a short rest in-between – no excuses allowed. I did my best and then discovered that the so-called rest was going to involve squat thrusts; 20 of them. Matt didn't stop there. It was thanks to him that I did far more than I would ever have done exercising alone and I looked thinner and was far more toned as a result, especially around my thighs and stomach.

Tasha:
Wild fitness

health&fitness

3 Which of the ways of exercising mentioned in the texts would appeal to you? Why / Why not?

4 The choice of verb you make will often change the tone of what you are saying. For example, in the first text, the writer talked about 'loathing' exercise. This is a more emphatic way of saying *dislike*.

For each sentence, replace the words in italics with one of the verbs in the box and make any other necessary changes. Decide what difference the new verb makes. Use a dictionary to help you.

yank	harangue	resolve	swear	seethe
unearth	crave	flout	scrounge	

a She *lectured* me for over an hour about the need to keep fit.
b Laura *decided* to give up chocolate at New Year.
c I *promise* I won't use your bike again without asking first.
d 'Can I *borrow* £5 from you, do you think?'
e My sister really *wanted to eat* coal when she was pregnant.
f Jo *was very angry* when his mobile was stolen.
g Don't *pull* the door open like that – you'll only break it.
h The boys *found* some interesting old photos.
i Trevor *ignored* the rules of the gym and used the new equipment without permission.

⊙ Phrase spot

Read the sentences below and replace the words in italics with one of the phrases with *live*. Use an English–English dictionary to help you.

live through	live it up	learn to live with
live down	live by your wits	live up to your expectations

a James really *had a good time* when he was in Ibiza last summer.
b The neighbours are the original neighbours from hell, but short of moving, we have to *get used to* them.
c The yoga class was brilliant – it *was everything we wanted*.
d No one will let me *forget* my tennis skirt falling down.
e We *experienced* two revolutions while we were abroad but survived both.
f Tom lived on the streets from an early age, but *cleverly managed to survive through his ingenuity*.

1 With a partner, do the quiz below to see how much you know about articles. When you have finished, check your answers with the Grammar folder on page 185.

1 Which of the following do not need an article?

the USA, the Indonesia, the Netherlands, the Gambia, the Antarctic, the Hague, the Berlin, the North Pole, the Europe, the European Union, the Oxford University, the Sahara, the Sierra Nevada, the Times, the Olympics

2 Which of these words requires *a* rather than *an*?

European, apple, university, hour, one-day ticket, household, union, MP, hotel

3 Decide which of the sentences below is correct, i) or ii), and say why. If both are correct, then say what the difference in meaning is.

a   i   Ken is a personal trainer.
    ii   Ken is personal trainer.
b   i   I've been to the gym.
    ii   I've been to a gym.
c   i   My coach makes a great energy drink.
    ii   My coach makes great energy drink.
d   i   I love rich food.
    ii   I love the rich food I had at the festival.
e   i   Japanese enjoy sumo.
    ii   The Japanese enjoy sumo.
f   i   Come to dinner.
    ii   I went to the dinner on Saturday.
g   i   I play violin.
    ii   I play the violin.
h   i   I play tennis.
    ii   I play the tennis.
i   i   I want a drink of water.
    ii   I want one drink of water.
j   i   The weather is wet at the moment.
    ii   Weather is wet at the moment.
k   i   You need to wash the face.
    ii   You need to wash your face.
l   i   Go to bed!
    ii   If you look under the bed you might find the book.

2 Read through this article and fill in the spaces with a suitable article: *a*, *an*, *the* or – (no article). There is sometimes more than one possibility, depending on meaning.

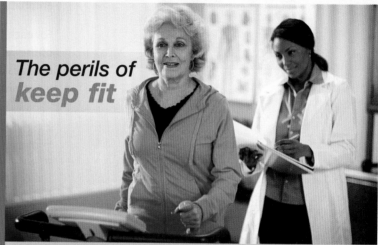

The perils of keep fit

(1) .... exercise season is upon us and January is **(2)** .... busiest time at any gym as **(3)** .... old members work off **(4)** .... excesses of **(5)** .... holiday period and new ones **(6)** .... excesses of **(7)** .... past five years. But **(8)** .... experts warn that we should proceed with **(9)** .... care; throwing yourself too vigorously into **(10)** .... new fitness regime can make you vulnerable to **(11)** .... number of **(12)** .... health risks.

'**(13)** .... exercise is **(14)** .... stress on the body,' says Dr Nick Webborn, **(15)** .... medical advisor to **(16)** .... National Sports Medicine Institute. 'That's how it makes you fitter. You stimulate your body and it adapts to this stimulus by building **(17)** .... muscle and strengthening **(18)** .... heart and lungs.'

Done correctly, this will be one of **(19)** .... most potent things you can do for your health – **(20)** .... moderate exercise has been shown to lower **(21)** .... risk of **(22)** .... endless day-to-day ailments.

G → page 185

3 Many nouns require no article when used as part of an idiom or expression, for example *to take something to heart*.

Write a sentence to show you know how to use the following idioms or expressions. Use a dictionary to help you.

a by word of mouth
b to lie face downwards
c to set foot on
d to have a heart to heart
e to walk hand in hand
f to stroll arm in arm
g to be nose to tail
h to come face to face with
i to live from hand to mouth
j to be made by hand
k to fight tooth and nail
l to see eye to eye

Vocabulary

Prepositions

Corpus spot

The *Cambridge Learner Corpus* shows that prepositions often cause problems at Proficiency level. Complete the sentences with a suitable preposition. There may be more than one possible answer.

a Most sportswear commercials are produced by companies that specialise .... this type of advertising.

b Town planners have not paid enough attention .... the need for recreational areas such as parks.

c You shouldn't laugh .... Tony, he can't help being a slow runner.

d Melissa shouted .... the player to look behind him.

e What are you thinking .... right now?

f If I catch you throwing your ball .... my house again, I'll tell your father.

g I don't object .... you watching the Olympics, as long as you don't stay up all night.

h His professional approach is typical .... our team.

i The Sports Council voted .... the amendment late last night.

j You can't insist .... a refund of your gym membership you know.

k Let me congratulate you .... your fine achievement.

l Sal certainly doesn't care .... running, but enjoys long walks.

m We discussed it for ages before we finally agreed .... a solution.

4 With a partner, ask and answer using the verbs below and the correct preposition. Use an English dictionary if you need help.

EXAMPLE: apply
 – *What did he apply for?*
   He applied for a grant.
 – *Who did he apply to?*
   He applied to the manager.

a rely	**f** interfere
b take pride	**g** admire
c look forward	**h** apologise
d prohibit	**i** accuse
e consist	**j** believe

Word formation

5 Look at the following words from the text in 14.1. What part of speech is each word? What other forms of the word are possible?

EXAMPLE: abilities *(plural noun)*
 able, disability, disabled, unable, inability, ably

Section A	abilities	agreeable	imaginary
Section B	expectations	reality	enthusiasm
Section C	measure	dismissive	clearly
Section D	transform	introductory	excuses

6 Use an appropriate form of one of your answers to 5 to complete each sentence below.

EXAMPLE: His complete *inability* to grasp the essentials of the exercise left him feeling downhearted.

a The departure of the gym manager was totally .... – he never said a word about leaving.

b The committee .... their complaints as having no basis in fact.

c We are very .... about going on biking holidays.

d I think your worries about your weight are all in your ....

e Steve's behaviour was .... last night for some reason – I can't believe he was so rude.

f The football manager is well known for his .... of vision – he can see how certain players will fit well with the team.

7 For questions 1–4, complete the second sentence so that it has a similar meaning to the first sentence, using the word given. **Do not change the word given.** You must use between **three** and **eight** words, including the word given. These all include some type of word formation.

1 Helen's running style seems to be improving now she has lessons.
   signs
   Helen's running style .... now she has lessons.

2 I really admire the changes you have made to your diet.
   full
   I .... the changes you have made to your diet.

3 Sam is reputed to inspire young athletes.
   has
   Sam .... young athletes.

4 I would have arrived even later at the meeting, if Professor McDougal hadn't kindly assisted me.
   kind
   But .... , I would have arrived even later at the meeting.

14.3 Listening and Speaking

1 Do you know of any health scares in your country about any of these products?

Do they make you anxious or are you complacent and take no notice of them?

2 **2 02** You will hear Alice Brown interviewing Professor Robert Atkins about health scares. For questions 1–5, choose the answer (A, B, C or D) which fits best according to what you hear.

1 How does Professor Atkins feel about the frequency of health scares in the media?
   A irritated that the media print nonsense
   B reconciled to health scares being a necessary evil
   C resigned to the media misunderstanding science
   D worried that the health scares might be real

2 What is Alice's attitude to the threat of lethal diseases?
   A She worries that new ones will occur.
   B She is doubtful that they can be contained.
   C She is concerned that they are spread more easily today.
   D She believes they pose less of a danger today.

3 Professor Atkins believes that the concerns people have today arise from
   A a lack of spiritual belief.
   B being misled by scientists and doctors.
   C bewilderment when their assumptions are challenged.
   D worry about how diseases are communicated.

4 What do Alice and Professor Atkins agree about when it comes to health scares?
   A some businesses have a vested interest in promoting them
   B some manufacturers see them as the best form of publicity
   C some doctors are at fault for not criticising them sufficiently
   D some researchers are looking for publicity

5 What worries Professor Atkins about health scares?
   A They could lead to people taking too many pills.
   B They are more damaging than real diseases.
   C They might make people disregard potential risks.
   D They are difficult to disprove.

Pronunciation

3 In the recorded interview, Alice and Robert used the following words.

> object   frequent   discount

2 **02** Listen to the interview again. How were those words pronounced?

Underline the part of the word which was stressed. Which part of speech are they?

> Certain words have a variable stress pattern, depending on whether they are used as a noun, adjective or verb, for example: *object.*
> *I don't ob**ject** to your opening the window.*
> *The boy tripped up over some **ob**ject in his path.*

4 Work with a partner and make up sentences which show the difference between the way the words below are pronounced, depending on the part of speech.

alternate	discount	entrance	frequent
incense	invalid	present	produce

5 With a partner, look at the photos below. You will need to compare and contrast them. Think about:

- the lifestyles of the people represented
- the possible implications for their future
- how modern life has impacted on health

You have about a minute to do this.

6 Work in groups to make a joint presentation about the following topic.

Imagine that there is going to be an advertising campaign to persuade young people to keep fit and healthy. Decide what form the campaign should take in order to have the greatest impact, e.g. online/phone/posters/TV/cinema/magazines/talks in schools, colleges, etc.
Also think about what aspect of health and fitness should be highlighted – should it be cigarettes/diet/exercise/drugs, etc?
You will need to give opinions, make decisions and evaluate the potential impact of the advertising campaign.

Writing folder 7

Part 2 Letter

In Part 2 of Writing, you may be asked to write a letter. This will be formal in register and the target reader may be the editor of a newspaper or magazine. You are not expected to include postal addresses but the letter should be paragraphed and have a suitable opening and close.

1 Read this exam task.

> You have read a critical article in the local newspaper about the sports provision at your college. As a member of the sports committee, you discover that substantial national funding is available for the upgrading and enlargement of facilities. You decide to write a letter to the editor of the newspaper, responding to the article and requesting suitable publicity for a grant application.

2 Look at the draft answer on page 125. An R or T to the right of a line means that the register or tone needs improving. Underline the parts to be edited and then suggest improvements to make the letter consistently formal in register and less aggressive in tone. An example is given.

3 The following expressions are useful when arguing for or against a course of action. Decide what each refers to, writing

  A do something positive without delay
  B deal with at some stage but low priority
  C stop working on.

  a give priority to **A**
  b take the initiative in
  c place less emphasis on
  d set in motion immediately
  e put on hold (temporarily)
  f allocate minimal resources to
  g back the establishment of
  h freeze the development of
  i sanction major investment in
  j pull out of

4 Now, using some of the expressions above, answer the task below in 280–320 words.

> An international student magazine has invited its readers to submit a letter arguing for immediate action on a key environmental issue. You decide to write a letter, briefly describing an environmental problem that concerns you, explaining why you are arguing for immediate action and recommending appropriate measures to rectify the situation.
>
> Write your **letter**.

Dear Sir or Madam

rather negative

Following your damning article on this college's current sports   T

provision, we demand that you think again and print an apology –   T

most of what you have written is garbage! We also want your   T

help regarding a funding application – please see below.

Your article claims that a lack of adequate facilities is hurting   R

our basketball and swimming teams, yet both have represented

the college at the highest levels of competition and done brilliantly   R

over the years. Indeed, your newspaper featured the recent success

of the basketball team in an article published in May. How ironic

is that?   T

Still, you're not wrong to say that the main sports hall requires   R

some work, especially the dodgy flooring and the pathetic lighting –   R

you can't even see the ball sometimes! In connection with this,   T

we've just spotted that funding is available nationally, which our   R

college would be in a good position to apply for. We reckon that   R

getting a grant would enable us to undertake the repairs alluded

to above, and also allow for an extension of the present changing

facilities, whereby separate 'wet' and 'dry' areas could be

introduced, to service the pool and hall respectively.

What do you think? Would you be willing to run an article in   T

support of our grant application? It would be in the public

interest, given that members of the public have daily access to our

sports facilities.

Hear from you soon, ok?   T

EXAM ADVICE

- Read the question carefully to understand the scenario.
- Think about the purpose of your letter – what should it achieve?
- Use a suitably polite tone for the target reader specified.
- Write in a consistently formal register.
- Use suitable paragraphing and a range of cohesive devices.
- State your reason for writing at the outset.
- Conclude your letter clearly and add a formal close, such as *Yours faithfully*.

The daily grind

1 Discuss these questions in pairs or groups.

- How likely are you to stay in the same field of work throughout your working life?
- Why are some people reluctant to switch career?
- How important is staff continuity in the workplace?
- What expectations do you have about job security in the long term?
- In what ways might the workplace change in the next ten years?

Listening

2 You will hear an interview with the head of an employment agency about job expectations. First read questions 1–5 and underline any unfamiliar vocabulary.

1 How does Diane Webber view 'jobs for life'?
   A She regrets the fact that this situation is no longer the norm.
   B She feels that many long-serving employees failed to make a useful contribution.
   C She believes that people should have challenged their employers' motives more.
   D She wishes the workplace had been more secure in the past.

2 According to Diane, younger workers in today's workplace
   A learn all the skills they need early on.
   B accept lateral moves if they are attractive.
   C expect to receive benefits right from the start.
   D change jobs regularly to achieve a higher level.

3 What does Diane say about staff continuity in companies?
   A It is desirable in both junior and senior management.
   B It is impossible to achieve in today's more competitive environment.
   C It is unimportant, due to the greater emphasis on teamwork.
   D It is necessary, but only up to a point.

4 According to Diane, what is the actual benefit of higher levels of personnel movement?
   A higher levels of output
   B better problem-solving
   C more creativity
   D greater efficiency

5 Diane considers that nowadays, companies are at most risk from
   A run-of-the-mill employees who play safe.
   B successful high-fliers who quickly move on.
   C unreliable staff who lack commitment.
   D external advisors who have undue power.

2 03 Now listen to the recording and, for questions 1–5, choose the answer (A, B, C or D) which fits best according to what you hear.

3 2 03 Listen again and then explain what Diane meant by the following expressions.

a a golden handshake
b cut their teeth
c progress up the rungs
d a mixed blessing
e dog-eat-dog
f the slightest whiff of
g snapped up
h a track record
i mindset
j the jury's still out
k a quantum leap
l quick fixes
m keep their heads down

Vocabulary

Collocations

4 The expressions *quick fix* and *quick exit* were used in the recording. Many other nouns collocate with adjectives describing speed. Explain the meanings of the underlined phrases in a–h.

a Let's get a <u>quick bite</u> before the play starts.

b Life in the <u>fast lane</u> was proving even more hectic than Henry had imagined.

c Benson had a reputation for trying to make <u>a quick buck</u>.

d Travellers in business or first class may use our <u>fast track</u> channel.

e With only a <u>brisk nod</u> in our direction, the man carried on with his presentation.

f Both parties issued a <u>swift denial</u>, but most of the tabloids ran the story in any case.

g The team pride themselves on their <u>rapid response</u>, generally one to two days maximum.

h After a <u>quick catnap</u>, he was ready to face the press.

5 Conversely, the adjective *slow* collocates with several nouns in the business context. Choose nouns from the box to complete these sentences from the Cambridge English Corpus. There are three nouns which you do not need to use.

decline	growth	lane	motion	pace
process	signs	speeds	tempo	

a With 40% unemployment, extremely slow .... , and a massive trade deficit, the economy remains dependent on foreign aid.

b Although sales nearly tripled that year, they grew at a slower .... than in the previous 12 months.

c The retail industry is showing slow .... of recovery.

d Overcoming the legacy of low-trust industrial relations is necessarily a slow ....

e The recession has turned the long, slow .... of newspapers into a brisk fall.

f Rural residents are too often stuck in the slow .... of the information highway, shut off from education and employment opportunities.

Idiom spot

Neologisms

Many of the expressions in 3 have only entered the language recently and are used particularly in business and in journalism. Complete these examples with one of the idioms or expressions (a–m) in the correct form.

1 It appears that .... on the question of the newspaper's survival.

2 The spin-off from his success is .... in attendance and greater commitment all round.

3 It only takes .... lower interest rates for the retail industry to get excited.

4 We live in a solution-hungry time, where people are confused, busy, and anxious to latch on to any .... they can.

5 The applicant who was chosen for the post had an excellent .... in hedge fund trading.

6 The arrival of the so-called independent advisors was .... for staff, who were asked to produce fresh data almost overnight.

The term *golden handshake* now has its opposite in business, referring to someone's entry into a company. Match the colours to the nouns given (one colour is used twice). Then use the expressions in sentences a–f.

blue	goods
golden	ink
green	chip
red	knight
white	hello
	shoots

a In spite of substantial investment, the company is still bleeding .... and drastic action is likely before the year end.

b Although we cannot report much that is positive, some encouraging .... are starting to appear, particularly in certain export markets.

c Typically, ... companies have been in business for a long time and are dominant in their particular markets.

d Sales volumes of .... such as dishwashers and freezers are virtually static.

e It is thought that top executive James Eagleton received a .... of around $2 million on joining the corporation.

f Rumours that a .... was about to step in proved unfounded and the company was taken over within a matter of weeks.

1 Read this article on internships. Do you think interns receive fair treatment in the workplace? Why? / Why not?

LANDMARK VICTORY SEES JOURNALISM INTERN AWARDED OVER £2,000 IN PAY AND DAMAGES

In the current period of austerity, employers are becoming more and more attracted to the creation of internships, as a cheap way of extending their workforce – and young people are usually more than willing to work unpaid or for minimal wages, in order to gain valuable experience and get them closer to the first rung on the career ladder. Unpaid interns are in a vulnerable position, often afraid to take action against their employers for fear that they might be shown the door.

However, a journalism intern has scored a victory for interns everywhere by successfully suing her publishing company employer, for whom she interned unpaid for several weeks. Keri Hudson, 21, proved in an employment tribunal that she had the right to be paid for two months' work she carried out last year, despite having no written contract with her employer.

The tribunal heard that Keri had received no pay from her employer, despite working 10am to 6pm every day, being responsible for a team of writers – and even for hiring new interns. Apparently, "the company had told her she was not eligible for any pay because they considered her an intern".

But the judge was having none of it. After hearing a description of the work she had carried out, he ruled that she was a "worker" by law – and was therefore entitled to the National Minimum Wage and holiday pay.

2 Suggest alternative linking words or phrases that could replace the two highlighted phrases in the first paragraph without changing the grammar of the clause that follows. What type of clause do they introduce?

G → page 185

3 What does the title of the article opposite suggest to you in terms of gender differences at work? Read the article to see if your ideas are covered. Ignore spaces 1–8 for the moment.

4 Now fill in spaces 1–8 with one word only.

THE SECRETARIAL GENDER DIVIDE

Male PAs are **(0)** ...on... a fast track to the top. Or **(1)** .... their female counterparts think, according to a new survey by a leading recruitment consultancy. In **(2)** .... is a female-dominated profession, these concerns clearly deserved to be investigated, yet in reality, there is absolutely **(3)** .... truth in them whatsoever.

It seems that men are increasingly applying for support roles in **(4)** .... to get on the career ladder. With nigh **(5)** .... double the number of students in higher education compared to a decade ago, graduates have had to find new ways into over-subscribed professions. And, **(6)** .... it appears that men are indeed mega-quick in getting promotion, this is fully explained by **(7)** .... active seeking out of higher-status roles, **(8)** .... than by anything more sinister.

5 Join the following clauses with suitable linking phrases from the box, paying attention to the register of the sentences. In some cases, more than one answer is possible. Be careful with negatives!

| for fear that | in case | in order (not) to |
| so as (not) to | so that | lest |

a Ambrose Greene checked everything at least three times .... he should fail to notice an error.

b Buy the relevant magazines every week .... miss any job advertisements.

c The company took up both references .... satisfy themselves that he was the right man for the new position.

d Always dispatch vital documents by registered mail .... they go astray and you need to trace them.

e It is worth allowing extra time if travelling on public transport .... you won't be in a rush at the other end.

f I used to commute into the office at the crack of dawn .... have to travel in overcrowded trains.

g The clients are being sent a map .... they don't know their way around.

h Elzevir paid great attention to his feet, ... he should slip on the ferns and mosses with which the steps were overgrown.

6 Finish these statements so that they are true for you, including an appropriate linking phrase of your choice. Use each phrase once only.

EXAMPLE: I would like to work abroad at some point, …

in order to learn another language.

a I would like to work abroad at some point, …

b When I'm older, I won't stay in the same job for more than two years, …

c I want to continue my English studies, …

d It would be useful for me to have my own website, …

e I want to find work that I can do from home, …

Corpus spot

The Cambridge Learner Corpus shows that even at C2 level, learners continue to make mistakes with linking words and phrases.

Choose one of the phrases in brackets to correct the underlined mistakes that exam candidates have made, making any punctuation changes necessary.

a I'm giving you the address of the school here <u>if</u> you want further information. (so that / in case)

b Everybody will agree that a bad product is only bought once. Therefore, <u>provided that</u> the advertising is dishonest and misleading, it will only cheat us once when we buy the advertised product for the first time. (even if / for all)

c Tourism will increase <u>on the grounds that</u> air travel will develop. (in the same way as / along the lines of)

d On the other hand, living longer could lead to some everyday difficulties. <u>Likewise</u> not being able to look after ourselves. (lest /such as)

e Even so, people ought to be more careful <u>as not to</u> damage the good things we have. (in case / so as not to)

f <u>After all</u>, I hope you are now persuaded to spend the money on a computer room. (Otherwise / In conclusion)

Style extra

In English, some words to do with people refer only to men *or* women, either because they are gender-specific, e.g. *maid*, or because usage is just like that. (Corpus evidence suggests that *taciturn* is only used of men.)

Group the nouns and adjectives below under these three headings. Decide also whether they are formal, informal or unmarked in terms of register, and whether there are any further restrictions on their use, e.g. offensive, old-fashioned.

used of men   used of women   used of both

nouns			adjectives
actor	bag	bimbo	bullish
bounder	chairman	charmer	chivalrous
chav	duchess	freshman	doting
geek	lout	mate	effeminate
neanderthal	nerd	partner	laddish
patriarch	sibling	spouse	lanky
thug	vamp	whizz kid	prickly
			wimpy

Now combine each adjective with a noun of your choice and produce an example sentence to illustrate usage and meaning. Use a dictionary if necessary.

EXAMPLE: *The bullish whizz kid had a reputation for making wild predictions about the futures market.*

1 Which of these leadership qualities are the three most important for each of the following people? What are the other characteristics of a successful leader?

   a a company chairman
   b a college principal
   c a military commander

decisiveness	intuition
vision	assertiveness
flexibility	fairness
good humour	openness
determination	humility
specialist knowledge	stamina

2 Read the texts on two contrasting leadership styles, ignoring the highlighting for the moment. Which style appears to be the more effective? Do you agree with what is said?

Text 1

The 'Affiliative Style' revolves around people – its proponents value individuals and their emotions more than tasks and goals. The affiliative leader strives to keep employees happy and to create harmony among them, building strong emotional bonds and then reaping the benefits of such an approach, commanding fierce loyalty.

There is a markedly positive effect on communication, and flexibility also rises because the affiliative leader gives people the freedom to do their job in the way they think is most effective. However, this style can allow poor performance to go uncorrected and, since affiliative leaders rarely offer advice, employees can be left in a quandary.

Text 2

The 'Pacesetting Style' focuses on tasks and goals, with the leader setting extremely high performance standards and exemplifying them personally. Underachievers are swiftly identified and more demanded of them – if they don't rise to the occasion, they are replaced. Employees tend to feel overwhelmed by the pacesetter's demands for excellence, and morale drops. Guidelines for working may be clear in the leader's head, but are often not stated clearly. People feel that the pacesetter doesn't trust them to take any initiative. Flexibility and responsibility evaporate; commitment dwindles because people have no sense of how their personal efforts fit into the big picture.

3 It is important to use your own words in the Part 1 essay. Find words or phrases in the texts that have a similar meaning to a–h.

   Text 1
   a advocates
   b ties
   c profiting from
   d predicament

   Text 2
   e deliver the goods
   f motivation and confidence
   g resourcefulness
   h the operation as a whole

4 Text 2 contains three verbs describing downward movement or decline. What are they? Suggest three more verbs you could use in their place. Then find the verb that describes an upward trend in Text 1 and think of two others to replace it.

5 Tick the linkers that can be used to contrast information.

Be that as it may	Even so	Nonetheless
By the same token	In contrast	On the other hand
Conversely	In other words	Similarly
Despite this	Likewise	Whereas

6 Read the paragraph below about effective leadership and complete linking phrases 1–5 with one or two words. Which phrases are used to contrast information?

To be an effective leader in business, it is essential to have vision, with a steady grasp of the bigger picture. **1** *What is* .... , senior management figures need to show determination and a firm belief in their ideas for change. **2** *That* .... , assertiveness can sometimes go too far and this will only serve to alienate staff. To avoid this **3** .... *the case*, any major shift in direction must be fully explained to all members of the company. **4** *In much* .... *way*, organisational change needs to be handled carefully, within an adequate timeframe that allows for some downward consultation. **5** .... *that*, strong leadership requires decisiveness and hasty U-turns should be avoided at all costs.

---

7 Choose linkers from 5 and 6 to contrast the colour-coded information in the two texts, using your own words as far as possible – you can include the words and phrases from 3 and 4. Write one or two sentences for each point.

   EXAMPLE: *Within the Affiliative Style of leadership, individuals count, and appropriate concern is shown for their welfare, whereas under the Pacesetting Style, the primary focus is on the achievement of objectives according to ambitious targets.*

8 Now evaluate these four ideas in turn, making notes of your own views. Combine this evaluation with your sentences from 7.

9 Write an essay in 240–280 words, summarising, contrasting and evaluating the ideas in the two texts. Start by introducing the two management styles in general terms (see the example in 7 for ideas, but use your own words). Then include your ideas from 8, suitably paragraphed. Finish off the essay with an appropriate conclusion.

Exam folder 8

Listening, Part 2 Sentence completion

In Part 2 of the Listening paper, you will hear a monologue or prompted monologue (that is someone introducing the main speaker). You will need to listen for specific information and stated opinion in order to complete spaces in sentences. There are nine spaces altogether. You will hear the piece twice and you must write your answer – in the form of a word or short phrase – on an answer sheet. You must spell the word or short phrase correctly.

1 Read through questions 1–9 and try to predict what the answers might be.

2 **2 04** You will hear a man called John Farrant talking about his job working for a car hire company. For question **1**, listen to the first part of the recording as far as '... a plastic wallet'. Then, with a partner, decide which is the word you heard which fits in the space.

John Farrant says that people doing his job have to act in a **(1)** .... way.

3 Underline the adjectives in the recording script below which describe the way people act. Why is there only one possible answer?

John Farrant: Good morning. My name is John Farrant and I have the job of reservations manager at a large, international car hire company, based in London. Dealing with the public can be a tricky business. You get to meet all types from the arrogant and rude to the downright abusive. We aren't expected to reply in kind, of course, or come over all ingratiating and deferential either. It's down to us to be respectful and remember the customer is always right. Sometimes it can be difficult, especially with a real joker. For example, when taking a booking, we have to ask certain questions, one of which is: 'Do you possess a clean driving licence?' To which one man snapped at me, 'Of course I do. I keep it in a plastic wallet!'

EXAM ADVICE

● You have 45 seconds to read through the questions before you hear the piece. Make good use of this time.

● Make sure you read ahead or else you will get lost and begin to panic. Always know the topic of the next question.

● You should write what you hear; there is no need to change the words into a different form. Make sure the word or short phrase you write fits the sense of the sentence to be completed.

● Look out for clues – e.g. *an* before the space; the use of a particular preposition, *in, on*, etc; the use of *many* rather than *much* to show a countable noun is needed.

● You shouldn't write a whole sentence.

4 **2** **05** Now, listen to the rest of the recording and then do the task below.

For questions **2–9**, complete the sentences with a word or short phrase.

John was asked by an older customer to talk him through a
(2) .... on the phone.

One tourist from the USA was worried about driving in the UK because he had little
or no experience of **(3)** ....

John says that car hire companies like customers who require
(4) .... because they make more profit from it.

A car which had been taken to Spain was covered in **(5)** ....
when it was returned.

One customer with a medical condition was given a **(6)** .... near
a car depot office.

The depot manager needed to use a car **(7)** .... to avoid being
in a collision.

John thinks that many customers don't believe that reservations clerks look after
their **(8)** ....

One customer needed a car which had **(9)** .... in order to travel
to Oxford.

Reading

1 What are the challenges and constraints of writing a short story, as opposed to a novel? Think about characters, chronology, detail and so on.

2 Read the text below, taken from *An old-fashioned story*, a short story by American writer Laurie Colwin, that was published in 1981. What is the significance of the title, in your opinion?

Nelson Rodker was two years Elizabeth's senior, and was a model child in every way. Elizabeth, on the other hand, began her life as a rebellious, spunky and passionate child, but was extraordinarily pretty, and such children are never
5 called difficult; they are called original. It was their parents' ardent hope that their children might be friends and, when they grew up, like each other well enough to marry.

In order to ensure this, the children were brought together. If Elizabeth looked about to misbehave, her mother placed her
10 hand on Elizabeth's forearm and, with a little squeeze Elizabeth learned to dread, would say in tones of determined sweetness: 'Darling, don't you want to see Nelson's chemistry set?' Elizabeth did not want to see it – or his stamp collection. As she grew older, she did not want to dance
15 with Nelson or go to his school reception. But she did these things. That warm pressure on her forearm was as effective as a slap, although her compliance was not gained only by squeezes and horrified looks. Elizabeth had begun to have a secret life: she hated Nelson and the Rodkers with secret
20 fury. While she was too young to wonder if this loathing included her parents, she felt that if they forced Nelson upon her and chose the Rodkers for their dearest friends, they must in some way be against her. At the same time she realised that they were foolable. If she smiled at Nelson, they
25 were happy and considered her behaviour impeccable. If rude, she spent weeks in the pain of constant lectures. Thus, she learned to turn a cheerful face while keeping the fires of her dislike properly banked. The fact of the matter was that an afternoon of Nelson's stamp collection was good for two
30 afternoons hanging around the park with her real friends.

The beautiful daughters of the nervous well-to-do are tended like orchids, especially in New York. Elizabeth's friends were carefully picked over. The little O'Connor girl was common; that her father had won a Pulitzer prize was of no matter. The
35 one friend her mother approved of was Holly Lukas, whose mother was an old friend. Elizabeth never brought her real friends home, since, with the exception of Holly, they were all wrong: the children of broken homes, of people with odd political or religious preferences or of blacklisted movie
40 producers. Elizabeth learned the hard way that these children would not be made comfortable in her house. This might have put a crimp in Elizabeth's social life except that none of her friends wanted to entertain at home. They knew early on that the best place to conduct a private life was in public.

Like most girls her age, Elizabeth became horse crazy. She
45 did not want to share this passion with her parents, who felt riding once a week was quite enough, so she made a deal with the stable that, in exchange for a free lesson, she would clean out the stalls on Tuesdays. This, however, was not known by her mother, who had her expensively outfitted. These riding
50 clothes Elizabeth carried in a rucksack along with her real riding clothes – an old pair of blue jeans and a ratty sweater. It was soon discovered that Elizabeth was coming home late one extra afternoon a week stinking of horse. She was made to remove her jodhpurs at the service entrance and, when
55 these garments were found to be relatively horseless, a search was made and the offending jeans rooted out. Elizabeth was mute. One word about manure, and her riding days were over. But manure was not on her mother's mind and, in fact, when she learned that Elizabeth spent one day a week in the
60 company of a pitchfork, she was much relieved.

At college, Elizabeth had her first taste of freedom. While similarly restrained girls went wild, she reveled in being left alone and staying up late reading anything she liked. Her parents were not against reading, but Elizabeth's reading
65 habits contributed to eyestrain and bad posture and, besides, all that reading made one lopsided. At home on holidays she was correctness itself. In the middle of her first love affair, she was grown up enough to restrain herself from calling her beloved in Vermont, lest her parents find him on the
70 telephone bill. Elizabeth's parents set great store on adult behavior. Had they known what sort of adult Elizabeth had become, great would have been their dismay.

After graduation, her decision to live in New York was not easily come by, but she loved New York and wanted to enjoy
75 it finally on her own terms. Using as collateral a diamond-and-sapphire bracelet left to her by her grandmother, she borrowed enough money to rent an apartment in Greenwich Village. Through a friend of the O'Connor girl's father, she found a job at a publishing company and went to work. Her
80 parents were puzzled by this. The daughters of their friends were announcing their engagements in the Times. Elizabeth further puzzled them by refusing to take a cent of their money, although her mother knew the truth: what you dole out to the young binds them to you. To have Elizabeth owing
85 nothing was disconcerting to say the least.

3 For questions 1–6, choose the answer (A, B, C or D) which you think fits best according to the text.

1 What characterised Elizabeth's treatment as a young child?

A She was surrounded with children who were older than her.

B She was regarded by adults as being exceptionally intelligent.

C She was excused any bad behaviour due to her good looks.

D She was painstakingly prepared for future relationships.

2 What is implied about Elizabeth's childhood in the second paragraph?

A She complied with her parents' wishes from a sense of duty.

B She tolerated her mother's plans in order to achieve her own ends.

C She spent time with Nelson despite his parents being set against her.

D She disliked having to hide her true feelings from those around her.

3 What do we learn about Elizabeth's school friends in the third paragraph?

A They were embarrassed that their parents had successful careers.

B They were reluctant to invite friends back to their houses.

C They felt uncomfortable in the presence of Elizabeth's mother.

D They caused Elizabeth to come into conflict with her parents.

4 When Elizabeth's mother found out about her daughter's work at the riding school, she

A calmed down, as she had been expecting something else.

B was angry about the unnecessary purchase she had made.

C was uninterested in anything to do with the riding school.

D forced Elizabeth to throw away the old pair of jeans.

5 Why would Elizabeth's parents have been disappointed in her during her college days?

A Her excessive reading went against how they had brought her up.

B Her changed appearance would not have been as they wished it.

C Her wild social life meant she could not be studying hard.

D Her clandestine relationship would have shocked them.

6 Once she moved back to New York, Elizabeth resolved to

A sell her grandmother's valuable bracelet.

B stay a single working woman.

C exist unsupported by her parents.

D try to be more positive about the city.

4 What is the main implication of this text, in your opinion? Choose one of the four options below, justifying your choice with reference to the text.

A It is inevitable that people make friends within their own social class.

B It is unnecessary to spend time gaining a good education in life.

C It is worthwhile for parents to talk to their children's friends.

D It is unrealistic of parents to expect to influence their children.

5 Explain the meaning of a–e in terms of the characters they relate to.

a in tones of determined sweetness (lines 11–12)

b turn a cheerful face (line 27)

c tended like orchids (lines 31–32)

d put a crimp in (line 42)

e set great store on (line 71)

6 Elizabeth is said to have been a *rebellious*, *spunky* and *passionate* child. Find suitable opposites of these adjectives in the list below to describe Nelson. Then suggest opposites for the remaining words.

apathetic	articulate	brazen
callous	conventional	fickle
flawed	garrulous	spineless
trustworthy	unflappable	

Use some of these adjectives when describing characters in Writing folder 8.

1 Look at these poems. What images do they create in your mind?

2 Can poetry be successfully translated? How much freedom should a translator have? Which poem would be easiest to translate into your language? Think of these aspects:

- rhyme
- rhythm
- idiom
- nuance

3 Read this review of a collection of poetry in translation. Use the word given in capitals at the end of some of the lines to form a word that fits in the space in the same line. There is an example at the beginning (0).

> *Pull the blinds*
> *on your emotions*
> *Switch off your face.*
> *Put your love into neutral*
> *This way to the human race.*
>
> Spike Milligan

> I rue the day
> She went away
> And left me here
> To sip cold beer.
>
> **Bud Weiser**

> Once at Cold Mountain, troubles cease –
> No more tangled, hung-up mind.
> I idly scribble poems on the rock cliff
> Taking whatever comes, like a drifting boat.
>
> **Gary Snyder**

It's hard to issue (0) __PREDICTIONS__ on exactly what impact **PREDICT**

Jonathan Galassi's superb translation and (1) .... of the **ANALYSE**

Italian writer Eugenio Montale's *Collected Poems: 1920–1954* will have

on English-speaking (2) .... and, more importantly, on **SCHOOL**

poets. Translations of poetry are often (3) .... today, not **TRUST**

because, as the poet Robert Frost once claimed, 'Poetry is what gets lost

in translation,' but because, (4) ...., the act of turning **SUPPOSE**

writing in another language into writing in 'ours' is part of a larger

(5) .... project. As a result, instead of attempting to **EMPIRE**

feel and think beyond the boundaries of any single nation-state, much

academic work (6) .... itself within a restrictively pure **PRISON**

nationalist framework of literatures – 'American', 'English', 'French'.

(7) .... as I already was with Montale's poetry, my own **FAMILY**

reaction has been an unexpected one. After consuming his three main

books in a two-day gulp, I felt stunned by the concentrated power of

his language. Without my particularly wanting them to, the poetry's

cadences have infiltrated my memory, and its (8) .... **ENIGMA**

images have invaded my dreams. As remote as Montale's poetry may be

from one's own world view in the twenty-first century, it nevertheless

has to be accommodated.

Style extra

Find the five occurrences of *as* in the text in 3. In which one could *though* be substituted?

What effect does the change in word order have in this example?

Though it is unlikely, } an original manuscript
Unlikely though it is, } may still be found.

Complete these sentences, using *as* or *though*.
a Although greatly acclaimed, I find this novel rather disappointing.
   Greatly acclaimed ...
b Despite being entertaining, the play is lightweight in comparison with earlier works.
   As ...
c Romano was a painter in addition to being a writer.
   As ...
d 'A poem begins in delight and ends in wisdom.' *Robert Frost*
   As ...
e Although the novel undoubtedly has a gripping storyline, its characters lack development.
   Gripping ...
f I have tried to get into the book, but it remains impenetrable.
   Much ...

Which of the sentences above contain concessive clauses? What other conjunctions are used in such clauses? Which are the most formal?

G → page 186

 Corpus spot

Even at Proficiency level, conjunctions are often confused or inaccurately used. Correct the errors in a–h.
a Although the nice atmosphere, it's a little bit noisy.
b We got on really well, despite that I only knew a little English.
c However it is not easy, I'm making progress day by day.
d Despite of what she felt towards him, making him wait was a game she truly enjoyed.
e Whereas one could see he was eager to talk, nothing came out of his mouth.
f Although that, I know that I will be a good mother.
g Even I was wrong, it didn't make any difference.
h He never achieved a similar success, in spite of he wrote fourteen more novels.

4 For questions 1–6, complete the second sentence so that it has a similar meaning to the first sentence, using the word given. **Do not change the word given.** You must use between **three** and **eight** words, including the word given.

1 It is permissible to lose rhyme in translation, but it is vital to preserve the cadences of a poem.
   even
   A translator must preserve a poem's cadences, ... in translation.

2 I've never attempted to write poetry, though I have had a go at short stories.
   hand
   Despite trying .... something I've never attempted.

3 Although poetry readings are fun, the way in which poems are read sometimes annoys me.
   exception
   Much as I .... how poems are read.

4 The biographer continued to make progress, albeit more slowly than at the beginning of the project.
   initially
   Good .... , work was now proceeding more slowly.

5 While most writers earn only modest royalties, a lucky few create a bestseller.
   strike
   A few writers .... earning only modest royalties is the norm.

6 The editor refrained from commenting on the author's lack of progress in case it prompted him to stop writing altogether.
   fear
   The editor refrained from commenting on the author's lack of progress .... prompt him to stop writing altogether.

1 Identify the different genres shown in the pictures. What are the ingredients in a good book? What makes a book hard to put down?

2 **2 06** You are going to hear two people talking about books that have impressed them. In each case, name the book, explain what genre it is and summarise its qualities according to the speaker.

3 **2 06** Listen again to note down the words which mean the same as a–h.

   a engrossed
   b overpowering
   c take for granted
   d conjectures
   e classic
   f perceptions
   g painstaking
   h bravery

Pronunciation

4 The first speaker spoke about the *subtleties* of the plot. Which consonant is silent in this word?

> Silent consonants occur for different reasons. Often it is because pronunciation has changed over time without a corresponding change in spelling. Some words have come to English from another language, where they are pronounced differently.

2 07 Look at these words and underline any consonants you think are silent. Then listen to the recording to check the pronunciation.

knowledge	heir	denouement	condemn
wretched	coup	pseudonym	apropos
rustle	indebted	doubt	penchant
rhythm	exhilarating	mnemonic	

5 Check your understanding of the words in 4 by completing the word puzzle. What silent letter is contained in the vertical word that is revealed?

1 _ _ _ _ _ _|_| with regard to
2 _ _|_|_   a brilliant achievement
3 _ _ _ _ _ _ _|_| a memory aid often using rhyme
4 _ _ _|_|_ _ _ _   a particular liking for
5 _ _ _|_|_ _ _ _ _   not a real name
6 _ _ _ _ _ _|_|_ _   events at the end of a novel
7 _ _ _ _|_|_ _ _   very grateful

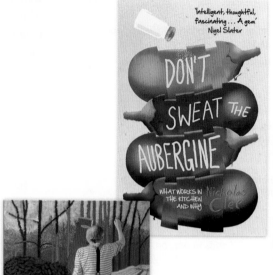

'Intelligent, thoughtful, fascinating... A gem'
Nigel Slater
DON'T SWEAT THE AUBERGINE
WHAT WORKS IN THE KITCHEN AND WHY
Nicholas Clee

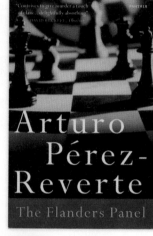

'Contrives to give murder a touch of class...delightfully absorbing'
DAVID HOCKNEY
Arturo Pérez-Reverte
The Flanders Panel

A Bigger Message
Conversations with David Hockney
Martin Gayford
Thames & Hudson

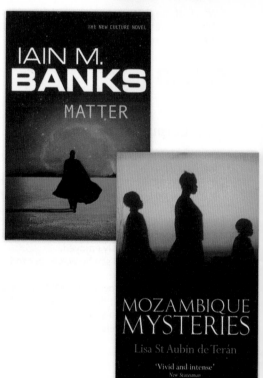

THE NEW CULTURE NOVEL
IAIN M. BANKS
MATTER

MOZAMBIQUE MYSTERIES
Lisa St Aubin de Terán
'Vivid and intense'
New Statesman

6 Look at the following Part 3 Speaking task.

> How important is the printed book in the twenty-first century?
>
> - technological alternatives
> - practical advantages
> - educational issues

Decide which prompt on the card above each of these statements refers to. Give your own opinion on each one.

a Although there are several benefits to downloading ebooks and being able to access them anywhere on a pocket-sized device, I would never contemplate giving away the hard copies of my favourite novels.

b Powerful though the arguments for the electronic book may be, I don't believe it will ever replace the physical object completely.

c Much as I enjoy sitting down with a good paperback, I'm excited by the availability of downloadable books, not least being able to track down obscure works that have been out of print for fifty years.

d While there is an initial cost implication in terms of classroom hardware, it cannot be denied that the electronic medium of instruction is far more engaging for students than battered old textbooks.

e Even though I love holding a real book in my hands, its manufacture is a waste of natural resources, which can no longer be justified given the existence of cheap electronic alternatives.

7 Plan your own talk on the importance of the book in the twenty-first century, working through the checklist below.

Planning stage

- Which ideas will you concentrate on, or will you touch on all three prompts?
- What other ideas do you intend to bring in?
- How will you introduce the talk?
- How will you move from one idea to another?
- What will your final point be?

Now record your talk. Stop after exactly two minutes and then analyse your talk, working through the checklist below.

Rehearsal analysis

- Did you cover all your ideas in the time?
- Were the ideas logically organised?
- In which part of the recording were you strongest? Why?
- Was there any repetition of ideas to cut out?
- Where could you have elaborated further?
- Were there any long pauses? How can you minimise these?
- Did you lack any specialist vocabulary? If so, how did you get round this?
- How large a variety of structures did you use? For example, did you remember to use concessive clauses?

8 In groups of three, listen to each talk in turn. While Student A talks, Students B and C should listen. Student C should stop the talk after exactly two minutes and ask Student B one of these questions.

- What are the advantages of using tablets for educational purposes?
- To what extent do you think the printed book will remain in widespread use?
- If you had to read all text in an electronic form, would there be any drawbacks?

9 After 30 seconds, Student C should ask Student A one of the questions below.

- What do you think?
- Do you agree?
- How about you?

Writing folder 8

Part 2 Set text question: Review

Question 5 of Writing, Part 2 offers two options, a) and b) – one on each of the specified set texts. You may be asked to write a review, article, report, essay or formal letter. It is essential that you refer clearly to the text you have studied, including appropriate detail and possibly brief quotations. Make sure you answer the question: don't just narrate the plot. Every set text question will demand more than narration – for example, description, comparison or evaluation.

1   Read this exam task.

A magazine is producing a special collection of readers' reviews entitled 'The importance of distinct characters in novels'. You decide to send in a review of the set text you have read, in which you give relevant information on the main characters and evaluate how successfully the author differentiates these characters.

Write your **review** in 280–320 words.

2   Now read the answer opposite and choose a suitable sentence opener (A–G) to fit the spaces (1–6). There is one extra opener that does not belong anywhere.

A	However, it has to be said that
B	The author achieves this
C	Last but not least
D	Similarly
E	Much as Kneale has tried
F	Throughout the novel
G	At the same time, the book

'English Passengers' is a meticulously-researched historical novel chronicling an expedition to Tasmania in 1857, where the theories of Darwinian evolution are juxtaposed with the religious beliefs of the day, often in a comical way. **1** [   ] deals sensitively with the bigger historical picture of the tragic destruction of the Aboriginal islanders' way of life at the hands of white settlers, ex-convicts and religious 'do-gooders', who all in their separate ways contributed to the Aborigines' demise.

2 [   ], events are narrated by a cast of some twenty characters, whose 'first-hand' accounts span fifty years and combine to give the reader a truly epic novel, that is rich in detail and variety.

3 [   ] largely through the varied use of language itself – from the formality of documents written by the island's governor, where official policy is revealed, to the base and harsh language used by convict Jack Harp. Shifty Captain Kewley incorporates words from his native Manx dialect into his vivid snapshots of the outward voyage, while the Reverend Geoffrey Wilson, the expedition's leader, has a predictably stiff style of narrating.

The pieces contributed by the expedition's doctor are written in scientific note-form, with judicious use of underlining to indicate his sinister concerns. This stylistic device, though hard to process at times, is most effective and develops as we learn more about Dr Potter's nefarious deeds. In the denouement, the notes become more truncated and you can almost see him underlining in rage. **4** [   ], when Wilson goes mad, the author is able to use subtle changes in language to reflect his sorry state.

Perhaps the most difficult character to portray credibly through language is Peevay, the Aboriginal hero. **5** [   ] even here the author successfully adopts a distinct style, incorporating paradoxical expressions learned from settlers, such as 'tidings of joy'. **6** [   ], the third expedition member Timothy Renshaw matures in the course of the novel and becomes the voice of reason and common sense. Helped by Peevay when abandoned in the wilderness, his awakening to the beauty of the land and decision to stay on the island could be seen as a final reconciliation.

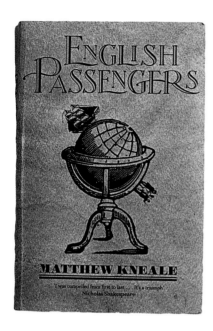

3 In the review, the book is referred to in different ways:

The pieces contributed by
In the denouement,

Read these sentence openers and decide on their function, writing

B for reference to the book
E for evaluation
C for comparison.

a Up to this point,   *B*
b In much the same way,
c Eventually,
d By and large,
e By the same token,
f Subsequent to this,
g To a certain extent,
h Within a matter of hours,
i On balance,
j As it turns out,
k For the most part,

Now write six sentences about the set text you are studying, choosing some of these openers.

EXAMPLE: *Up to this point, very little is known about the main character.*

4 The review refers to the book as a *meticulously researched historical novel*. Using adverb–adjective compounds like this will demonstrate your range of language. Make further adverb–adjective collocations from lists A and B and combine them with a suitable noun from list C. Only the adverbs should be used more than once.

EXAMPLE: *annoyingly paradoxical individual*
annoyingly trivial interpretation

A	B	C
annoyingly	accurate	characterisation
exquisitely	compelling	chronicle
hauntingly	detailed	depiction
ingeniously	enigmatic	hero
intensely	impressive	images
painstakingly	intricate	individual
subtly	moving	interpretation
utterly	paradoxical	narrative
zealously	pompous	plot
	realistic	portrayal
	trivial	protagonist
	woven	storyline

EXAM ADVICE

- When answering a set text question, decide what language functions the question requires.
- List ideas for each paragraph.
- Decide on key information to include about the book.
- Note down brief quotations (only if they are relevant!).
- Vary your linking devices.
- Introduce the book in different ways.
- Use as wide a range of language as you can.

5 Using the advice above, write the review outlined in 1, referring to the set text you are studying. As a general rule, you should start a new paragraph for each character you introduce, but this will depend on the number of characters and level of detail you go into (see the review in 2 for guidance).

Units 13–16 Revision

Use of English

1 For questions 1–8, read the text below. Use the word given in capitals at the end of some of the lines to form a word that fits in the space in the same line. There is an example at the beginning (0).

MAPPING BIODIVERSITY

Preserving (0) __ORGANISMS__ in museums is one way of retaining them for posterity, but most people agree that it would be nice to keep a few of them alive in the wild, too. At the moment, which species survive, which decline to threatened or even (1) .... status and which succumb to extinction is something of a lottery.

ORGAN

DANGER

WORLDMAP is easy-to-use software that identifies geographical patterns in diversity, (2) .... and conservation priorities.

RARE

It can perform a range of specialist biological (3) .... for countless numbers of species, in order to provide biodiversity data for research purposes.

ANALYSE

The program divides the surface area of the world into cells, usually arranged in a (4) .... grid. WORLDMAP can also predict the (5) .... of a hitherto unobserved species being found in an area on the basis of its known distribution. Given the (6) .... of most records, that is a useful trick. Furthermore, it can select (7) .... areas for preservation. These are not necessarily the cells with the highest individual biodiversity, but rather those which, together, (8) .... what is preserved by picking places with the least overlapping species.

RECTANGLE

LIKE

PATCH

COMPLEMENT

MAXIMUM

2 For questions 1–6, complete the second sentence so that it has a similar meaning to the first sentence, using the word given. **Do not change the word given.** You must use between **three** and **eight** words, including the word given.

1 'I always said I didn't do anything wrong!' the man said.
   outset
   From .... doing anything wrong.

2 Luisa and I never agreed on anything to do with the children's education.
   eye
   Luisa and I .... came to the children's education.

3 Although I am generally sympathetic towards them, I don't usually vote for the Green Party.
   line
   Much .... taken by the Green Party, I don't usually vote for them.

4 I know you'll find it hard to believe, but I've never read any of Shakespeare's works.
   seem
   Unlikely .... , I've never read any of Shakespeare's works.

5 Susie believes this job interview is really important.
   store
   Susie .... this job interview.

6 We were surprised when Daphne made such a rapid recovery.
   came
   It .... when Daphne made such a rapid recovery.

3 For questions 1–8, read the text below and decide which answer (A, B, C or D) best fits each gap.

GENETIC CLUE TO LONGEVITY UNCOVERED

The life-lengthening properties of reducing calorie (1) .... were first discovered in the 1930s, when laboratory rodents fed a severely reduced diet were found to outlive their well-fed (2) .... Since then, this effect has been observed on organisms as (3) .... as yeast, flies, worms and dogs.

A recent study using nematode worms (4) .... that a gene called pha-4 plays a key role and the (5) .... could be important for other species. Mammals, including humans, possess genes that are very similar to the pha-4 gene. Should the longevity link also (6) .... to human beings, it could well (7) .... to the development of drugs that mimic the effects of calorie (8) .... while allowing people to maintain their normal diet.

1 **A** induction	**B** intake	**C** input	**D** influx
2 **A** twins	**B** spouses	**C** peers	**D** fellows
3 **A** mixed	**B** various	**C** diverse	**D** assorted
4 **A** revealed	**B** betrayed	**C** disclosed	**D** exhibited
5 **A** verdict	**B** ruling	**C** decree	**D** finding
6 **A** imply	**B** assign	**C** direct	**D** apply
7 **A** lead	**B** steer	**C** draw	**D** prompt
8 **A** constraint	**B** restriction	**C** prevention	**D** restraint

Writing

4 Improve the register and tone in this letter, in an attempt to persuade the managing director to take action.

To Andy, our esteemed MD   April 1

We, the hard-working nerds in the IT Department, want to propose some changes to the daily grind. As you know, we're really whizz at sorting out the company's computing problems and, let's face it, you couldn't survive without us. To guarantee a rapid response, we've always been willing to burn the midnight oil when the need arises. But no more, mate! If you want us to slave away like this, you're gonna have to provide us with better conditions, which we demand herewith.

Firstly, it is totally out of order to expect any of us to struggle to work on the bus. Lots of us hit our desks by 6.00 in the morning and most of the guys are still hanging around after the pubs have shut. We therefore insist that you cough up for five stretch limos to provide us with adequate door-to-door transport. The pay-off for you is obvious: increased productivity and goodwill.

And another thing, we are fed up with the rubbish served up in your so-called restaurant downstairs and want our own top-class chef and eatery, to be located on this floor. Give us two hours minimum for lunch, or else – we need a quick catnap before going back to our screens.

Thirdly, to be brutally honest, the money you pay round here is peanuts. How come you've just landed a fat bonus and we've got the big 'O'? Put your money where your mouth is! We're warning you, if you don't do something about it pronto, you won't see us for dust.

We look forward to hearing from you before midday. Get the message, you April fool?

Frank

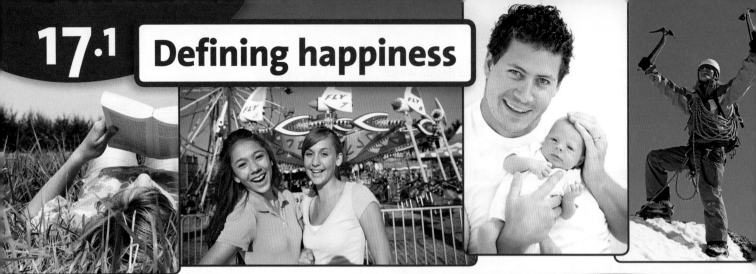

17.1 Defining happiness

1 What makes you happy? Explain the meaning of these quotes and say which comes closest to your own views.

'Happiness is not being pained in body or troubled in mind.'
'A person is never happy except at the price of some ignorance.'
'The happiness of your life depends upon the quality of your thoughts.'
'Happiness resides not in possessions, and not in gold – happiness dwells in the soul.'
'You're happiest while you're making the greatest contribution.'

Listening

2 Before listening, check your understanding of these words by putting them into three meaning groups.

bliss	contagious	elation	ephemeral
euphoria	fleeting	infectious	invasive
momentary	rapture	transient	virulent

Idiom spot

2 08 Listen again for the following idioms and expressions and explain their meaning.
a be on cloud nine (Speaker 1)
b through rose-tinted spectacles (Speaker 2)
c beyond my wildest dreams (Speaker 2)
d in my book (Speaker 3)
e put yourself on the line (Speaker 4)
f feel under the weather (Speaker 4)
g tip the balance (Speaker 5)

Choose four of the expressions above to use of situations 1–4.
1 In a roomful of people, Jack was the only one to stand up and challenge the speaker.
2 Fiona chooses to remember only the good things about her teenage years.
3 I think children should show respect for their elders.
4 They were undecided whether to take the day off, but then they saw the sun was shining.

3 2 08 You will hear five short extracts in which different people are talking about the nature of happiness.

TASK ONE
For questions **1–5**, choose from the list (**A–H**) which ingredient each speaker sees as contributing to happiness.

TASK TWO
For questions **6–10**, choose from the list (**A–H**) which happy memory each speaker mentions.

While you listen, you must complete both tasks.

A intellectual stimulation
B domestic harmony
C spectacular surroundings
D financial security
E success at work
F physical fitness
G close friendships
H mental well-being

Speaker 1 | 1
Speaker 2 | 2
Speaker 3 | 3
Speaker 4 | 4
Speaker 5 | 5

A enjoying a cosy environment
B feeling at one with nature
C making a contribution to society
D achieving a goal as a team
E discovering a secret place
F receiving a valuable gift
G experiencing something new
H winning a tournament

Speaker 1 | 6
Speaker 2 | 7
Speaker 3 | 8
Speaker 4 | 9
Speaker 5 | 10

Vocabulary

Metaphor

> ### ◎ Style extra
>
> In the recording, one speaker talks about *infectious* laughter, using the adjective metaphorically. The *Cambridge English Corpus* shows that many words to do with illness and health are used in this way.

4 Form collocates from the adjectives (list A) and nouns / noun phrases (list B) below. There may be more than one possible match.

A	B
bruised	bank balance
contagious	criticism
fatal	dose of scepticism
feverish	egos
healthy	flaw in the argument
jaundiced	loser
sick	sense of humour
sore	state of activity
	turnout of voters

5 Here are some sets of verbs that are often used metaphorically. Give each set a heading to reflect meaning and add any similar verbs.

EXAMPLE: break out, erupt, hurt, wound *medical/health*
similar verb: ache

a bloom, flourish, mushroom, spring up
b flow, ooze, ripple out, trickle
c burn out, flare up, ignite, smoulder
d blow up, break, rage, sweep
e dazzle, light up, shine, sparkle
f boil, bubble, simmer, stew

6 Make a noun phrase by combining an expression from list A at the top of the page with one from list B. Then use the phrase in your own sentence, continuing the theme with a suitable verb from 5.

EXAMPLE: *A flash of wild inspiration sparkled in her eyes.*

But a word of warning – don't mix your metaphors! For example, it would sound odd to talk about *a wave of sympathy igniting*, because waves are not associated with fire.

A	B
a crop of	critical reviews
an epidemic of	feverish activity
a flash of	minor complaints
a glut of	public sympathy
an outbreak of	pure joy
a plague of	scandalous stories
a storm of	spontaneous laughter
a surge of	unfair publicity
a wave of	violent protests
a whirlwind of	wild inspiration

7 In this extract from *My family and other animals*, the writer and naturalist Gerald Durrell recalls his idyllic childhood on the island of Corfu. For questions 1–8, read the text and decide which answer (A, B, C or D) best fits each gap.

Gradually the magic of the island settled over us as gently and clingingly as pollen. Those days were (1) .... , each with a tranquility, a timelessness, about it, so that you (2) .... it would never end. But then the dark skin of night would (3) .... and there would be a fresh day waiting for us, glossy and colourful as a child's transfer, and with the same (4) .... of unreality. In the morning, when I woke, the bedroom shutters were luminous and barred with gold from the rising sun. The (5) .... morning air was full of the scent of charcoal from the kitchen fire, full of eager cock-crows, the distant (6) .... of dogs, and the unsteady, melancholy (7) .... of the goat-bells as the flocks were driven out to pasture. We ate breakfast, a leisurely and silent (8) .... , out in the garden, under the small tangerine trees.

1 **A** compatible	**B** idyllic	**C** spotless	**D** picturesque
2 **A** wanted	**B** yearned	**C** wished	**D** aspired
3 **A** hang back	**B** draw in	**C** peel off	**D** spring up
4 **A** stain	**B** shield	**C** fleck	**D** tinge
5 **A** heady	**B** strong	**C** infectious	**D** robust
6 **A** bleat	**B** yap	**C** screech	**D** purr
7 **A** song	**B** hum	**C** tune	**D** buzz
8 **A** contest	**B** incident	**C** episode	**D** affair

8 Where in the text does Durrell use similes and metaphor?

Think of a particular moment when you were utterly content. Where were you? What was happening around you? Describe the scene and explain how you felt, making use of metaphor.

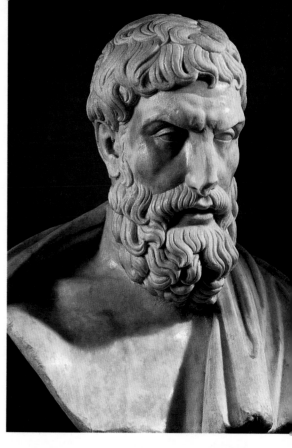

1 The following lists relating to happiness summarise the views of the Greek philosopher Epicurus. How far do they still hold true today, in your opinion? Would you add anything in each column?

WHAT IS AND IS NOT ESSENTIAL FOR HAPPINESS		
Natural and necessary	**Natural but unnecessary**	**Neither natural nor necessary**
Friends	Grand house	Fame
Freedom	Private baths	Power
Thought	Banquets	
Food	Servants	
Shelter	Fish, meat	
Clothes		

2 Read this text about Epicurus. For questions 1–8, think of the word which best fits each space. Use only one word in each space.

Life of Epicurus

E picurus, who was born on the verdant island of Samos, took early **(0)** ....**TO**........ philosophy. When only 14, he started travelling, to learn from the likes of the Platonist Pamphilus. Finding himself at **(1)** .... with much of this teaching, he decided to define his own philosophy of life. **(2)** .... immediately set this philosophy apart from other lines of thought was its emphasis on sensual pleasure. **(3)** .... , if any, philosophers had ever made admissions of this kind and Epicurus shocked many, not **(4)** .... when he set up a school **(5)** .... very aim was to promote happiness. Nevertheless, despite outrage and criticism, his teachings attracted support and spread **(6)** .... afield, from Syria to Gaul. Even today, Epicurus's name lives **(7)** .... in many languages in adjectival form – in English, 'Epicurean' signifies being dedicated to the pursuit of pleasure.

In fact, Epicurus drank water rather than wine, and usually restricted his diet to bread, vegetables and a palmful of olives. **(8)** .... were the tastes of the man who, after rational analysis, had reached the striking conclusion that the essential ingredients of happiness were the most inexpensive, however elusive they might be.

3 Comment on the following statements, which illustrate various ways of making comparisons. You don't have to agree!

a I'm as happy now as I was at the age of 10.

b I'd far rather spend time with close friends at home than be wined and dined at expensive restaurants.

c I'd much sooner be a penniless student than a lonely millionaire.

d Possessing wealth is nowhere near as important as being in good health.

e Listening to recordings of live concerts is nothing like as exhilarating as taking part in an actual live event.

f Watching a football match is not nearly as much fun as playing in one.

g Going on holiday is by far the best remedy for a broken heart.

h Relaxing by a warm fire is a good deal better than being out in a snowstorm.

G→page 186

4 Read sentences a and b. Then complete sentences c–h using similar comparative structures with your own ideas.

   a *The sooner the country clears its debts, the better things will be.*
   b *The later we hold the party, the more people will be able to come.*
   c The more possessions you own, the
   ....
   d The wider the gap between rich and poor, the
   ....
   e The .... , the less easy it will be to give them up.
   f The later .... , the worse ....
   g The higher .... , the harder ....
   h The more anxious
   .... , the
   ....

Vocabulary

Synonyms

5 The word *happy* has different meanings. Match the guidewords in capitals to sentences a–d. Then say which meaning the two dictionary entries for synonyms of *happy* are closest to.

   PLEASED   WILLING   NOT WORRIED   LUCKY

   a I'd be more than happy to help you get ready for the party.
   b Mum would be happier if I didn't have to travel alone overnight.
   c Meeting Mike at the concert like that was a happy accident.
   d People are generally at their happiest when the sun is shining.

   fortunate /ˈfɔː.tʃən.ət/ ⓤ /ˈfɔːr-/ *adj* APPROVING lucky: [+ *to* infinitive] *You're very fortunate* **to** *have found such a lovely house.* ○ *He was fortunate* **in** *his choice of assistant.* ○ [+ *that*] *It was fortunate* **that** *they had left in plenty of time.* ➲ The opposite is **unfortunate**.

   ecstatic /ɪkˈstæt·ɪk, ⓤ /-ˈstæt̬-/ *adj* extremely happy: *The new president was greeted by an ecstatic crowd.*

6 List all the synonyms you know for *happy* and decide which meaning from 5 is closest in each case. Then write an example sentence for each synonym, using the comparative or superlative form where possible.

   EXAMPLE: *exhilarated*   PLEASED
   The more exhilarated you feel, the less you want to sleep!

7 For questions 1–6, complete the second sentence so that it has a similar meaning to the first sentence, using the word given. **Do not change the word given.** You must use between **three** and **eight** words, including the word given.

   1 Their mother was determined to visit Paris and nothing would stop her.
   set
   Their mother had .... Paris and nothing would stop her.

   2 Graham took back his words on noticing there were fresh strawberries on the menu.
   tune
   Graham .... noticed fresh strawberries were on the menu.

   3 We found it difficult not to laugh because the situation was so funny.
   keep
   We found it difficult to .... such a funny situation.

   4 Jenny felt elated when she won the regional skating competition.
   cloud
   Jenny was .... place in the regional skating competition.

   5 Reading a thriller is far more enjoyable if you don't know the ending.
   nowhere
   Reading a thriller is .... fun if you already know the ending.

   6 Ralph needs to move out quickly in order to get on with his life.
   sooner
   The .... as to get on with his life.

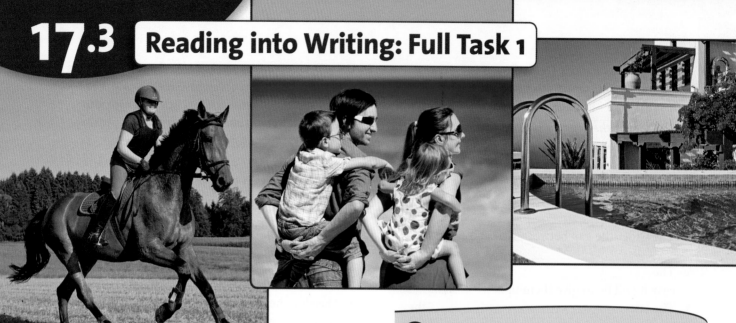

1 Use the pictures to help you define the term 'quality of life'.

What other factors are involved besides the ones illustrated? Discuss your ideas with a partner.

2 These factors are often used to measure quality of life. Which did your discussion in 1 include?

climate	gender equality
life expectancy	political freedom
stability in relationships	job security

3 Look at this exam task.

Exam spot

Remember the importance of reformulation – you will lose marks if you use words that occur in the texts. Think of synonyms you can use instead.

4 Read the Exam spot and then read the sample answer on page 149. Underline any words and phrases that have been 'lifted' from the texts and rewrite them. Quoted terms do not need to be replaced. For example, it would be better to change the underlined parts of the first paragraph as follows.

In both cases, healthiness is seen as a crucial attribute, since it dictates whether someone can hold down a job, and therefore influences other 'quality of life' indicators.

Write an essay summarising and evaluating the key points from both texts. Use your own words throughout as far as possible, and include your own ideas in your answer.

The phrase 'quality of life' embraces a number of different aspects, including physical health, emotional well-being, material wealth, community life, political stability, job satisfaction, and even geography and climate. Only the most fortunate of individuals will have access to 'perfect' conditions in all categories, and the various quality-of-life index calculations are averaged-out statistics. Yet it could be argued that a person's state of health determines their ability to work and benefit from community life, so is of prime importance. On the other hand, certain aspects are outside the individual's control – political freedom, for example, or the local climate.

Every year, much media attention is given to 'quality of life', usually following the publication of reports indicating the best cities to live in, the most temperate world climates, the country with the safest economy, and so on. Such analyses are interesting, but how much use can the individual make of them? In spite of advances in mobility, it is unrealistic for most of us to emigrate to this year's top country, nor should we have to take such a radical step. Everything starts at home – even those who struggle to make ends meet can enjoy a good quality of life providing they are healthy and supported by friends and family.

Both texts deal with the concept of 'quality of life' and consider which factors within this umbrella term are the most important in reality. In both cases, <u>physical health</u> is seen as <u>being of prime importance</u>, since <u>it determines an individual's ability to work</u> and <u>will determine many of the other aspects too</u>.

The first text gives an overview of the factors that go to make up a person's quality of life, mentioning health and well-being, social involvement, work, the political status quo and the local climate. Not only does it underline the fact that without good health, job satisfaction and an active and fulfilling role in the community are impossible, but also, it argues that some aspects cannot be changed – political background and freedom, for example.

The second text focuses on the annual phenomenon of quality-of-life indexes and, while viewing them as informative, questions the value of their having such prominence in the media. For most of us, it is academic which city in the world has the best quality of life, as we have no real opportunity to uproot our existence and rush to start a new life there. Nor is it necessary, argues the writer, as a good quality of life is still possible, provided that the individual is healthy and supported by friends and family.

While this may be true up to a point, it is nevertheless going to be far more difficult for people trapped in poverty to gain a quality of life equal to that of people at the other end of the wealth spectrum – especially in our materialist society, where possessions seem to count for so much and we are constantly encouraged to wish for more.

Idiom spot

In the second text, the idiom *make ends meet* is used. What does it mean?

Choose suitable idioms to match the cartoons below and then explain the meaning of all eight.

cut corners
down and out
keep your head above water
feel the pinch
in the red
on a shoestring
tighten your belt
a rough ride

Exam folder 9

Listening, Part 1
Multiple-choice questions

In Part 1 of the Listening paper you will hear three short extracts. There will be a mixture of monologues – only one person speaking – or a conversation between two, or possibly more, speakers. There are two questions for each extract with a choice of three answers for each question. You will hear each extract twice.

Here are some examples of the types of questions.

What does the speaker say about …?

What do the speakers agree on?

What is the speaker comparing X to?

Why does the speaker say …?

What is the speaker's opinion of …?

How did the speaker feel about …?

Normally in Part 1 there are three different extracts. Only two extracts are included here to give you an idea of what you might expect in the examination.

EXAM ADVICE

- You have 15 seconds to read the questions before you hear each extract. Make good use of this time.

- Use the first hearing to get a general idea of what the extract is about. The questions are in the order in which you will hear the answer on the recording. However, you sometimes need to hear the whole extract to answer some questions.

- Always keep the questions in mind when you answer. Some of the choices for each question may look correct, but not answer the question.

- The second time you hear the extract, mark your answer on your answer sheet.

- Always put an answer, even if you aren't sure. You have a 33% chance of getting it right.

- Points aren't deducted for wrong answers.

1 **2** 09 Read the Exam advice and then do the task below.

You will hear two different extracts. For questions **1–4**, choose the answer (**A**, **B** or **C**) which fits best according to what you hear. There are two questions for each extract.

Extract One

You hear two people talking about a new album by a singer called Lisa Gray.

1   What does the man say about Lisa Gray?

   A She's known to be unconventional.
   B She's uninterested in fame and success.
   C She's had to struggle throughout her career.

2   What do the speakers agree about?

   A The album will be too commercial for some of her fans.
   B The album is a radical departure from previous work.
   C The album contains a mixture of musical genres.

Extract Two

You will hear a woman talking about a book of photographs by artist, Dorota Kowalska.

3   What does the speaker say about Dorota Kowalska?

   A She's at her best portraying American working-class people.
   B She insists she prefers working in Europe to the USA.
   C She clearly feels little warmth for the USA.

4   What is the speaker's opinion of the photographs?

   A The artist is mocking her subjects.
   B The subject matter is in poor taste.
   C The photos evoke apathy in the viewer.

Listening, Part 3 Multiple-choice questions

In Part 3 of the Listening paper, you will hear a conversation between two or more speakers. There are five questions, all in the order in which you hear the information you need to answer them. The five questions each have a choice of four answers. The questions are testing whether you can understand the speaker's opinion, what the speaker is saying generally or in detail and also what you can infer from the conversation. You will hear the conversation twice.

EXAM ADVICE

- You have one minute to read the questions and possible answers.
- Don't get stuck on one question. Make sure you are always reading ahead so that you don't get lost.
- For more advice on how to answer the questions, see the Exam advice box for Part 1.

2 **2 10** Read the Exam advice and then do the task below.

You will hear two people, Darren and Helena, talking about Darren's new career. For questions **1–5**, choose the answer (**A**, **B**, **C**, or **D**) which fits best according to what you hear.

1   When she first heard Darren had given up his job in the City of London, Helena

    A thought it was just a temporary arrangement.
    B worried about how he would manage financially.
    C believed it would be easy for him to follow a new career.
    D claimed she knew that this might happen.

2   Helena and Darren both agree that the voluntary sector

    A shouldn't be seen as an easy option.
    B is not as well organised as other sectors.
    C employs fewer graduates than banking.
    D prefers to take people on long-term contracts.

3   How did Darren react when he got his new job?

    A He felt very pessimistic about his abilities.
    B He felt able to tell ex-colleagues his true feelings.
    C He suddenly got cold feet.
    D He decided to accept the challenge.

4   How did Darren get on in his new environment?

    A The slow pace got on his nerves at first.
    B He felt rather patronised by some of his workmates.
    C He fitted into the routine of things quite quickly.
    D It made him less cynical about people's motives.

5   Darren is planning to continue in the voluntary sector because he believes

    A he is temperamentally more suited to the work.
    B he likes the slower pace.
    C he feels he is making a difference.
    D he prefers the shorter hours.

1 The statements below form part of the Universal Declaration of Human Rights, adopted by the United Nations in 1948. How far are these statements adhered to in today's world?

- No one shall be held in slavery or servitude.
- No one shall be subjected to arbitrary arrest, detention or exile.
- Everyone has the right to a nationality.
- Everyone has the right to freedom of thought, conscience and religion.

Reading

2 You are going to read an extract from a book on human rights. Seven paragraphs have been removed from the extract. Choose from the paragraphs A–H the one which fits each gap (1–7). There is one extra paragraph which you do not need to use.

Values for a godless age

When the Berlin Wall came tumbling down in 1989 so did the plaster cast which had kept the idea of human rights in limbo. It was now free to evolve in response to the changing conditions of the late twentieth century.

| 1 |

Of course, in one sense, the quest for universal human rights standards after the Second World War was an early attempt to communicate across national boundaries, albeit a rather faltering endeavour, with its claims to universality challenged both in terms of authorship and content. More recently, a loosening of the reins of the human rights dialogue has ushered in wider debate.

| 2 |

Perhaps the best known of these is Amnesty International, established in 1961. Before Amnesty, there were very few organizations like it, yet now there are thousands operating all over the world. Whether campaigning for the protection of the environment or third-world debt relief, any such organization is engaged in the debate about

fundamental human rights. And it is no longer just a soft sideshow.

| 3 |

The fact that strangers from different countries can communicate with each other through the worldwide web is having a similar effect in dealing a blow to misinformation. During one recent major human rights trial over sixty websites sprang up to cover the proceedings, while sales of the government-controlled newspaper in that country plummeted.

| 4 |

The effect of increased responsibility at this highest level has been to continually extend the consideration of who is legally liable, directly or indirectly, under international human rights law. In part, this is an acknowledgement that even individuals need to be held responsible for flagrant breaches of others' rights, whether these are preventing protesters from peacefully demonstrating or abusing the rights of children.

| 5 |

It has been noted that paradoxically, in such circumstances, it may be

in the interests of human rights organizations to seek to reinforce the legitimacy and authority of the state, within a regulated global framework.

| 6 |

Part of the new trend in human rights thinking is therefore to include powerful private bodies within its remit. The International Commission of Jurists has recently explored ways in which international human rights standards could be directly applied to transnational corporations.

| 7 |

Whatever the way ahead, the lessons of the past must be learnt. Any world view or set of values which is presented as self-evident is ultimately doomed to failure. The case for human rights always needs to be made and remade. In a world where globalization too often seems like a modernized version of old-fashioned cultural imperialism, it is important to query the claim that human rights are universally accepted.

A

The problem is that the growth of globalization makes the protection of nation states a pointless goal in certain circumstances. Transnational corporations with multiple subsidiaries operating in a number of countries simultaneously wield significant economic and political power and it is often extremely difficult for the state – both home and host governments – to exercise effective legal control over them.

B

If the proliferation of pressure groups has raised the profile of the human rights debate, satellite television has reinforced much of the content of their campaigns. The fact that from our armchairs we can all see live what is happening to others around the world has had an enormous impact on the way the struggle for human rights is viewed. It would not be remotely believable to plead ignorance nowadays, for 24-hour news coverage from the world's hotspots reaches us all.

C

This is, after all, a uniquely propitious time, as the values and language of human rights are becoming familiar to more and more people, who judge the merits or otherwise of political and economic decisions increasingly in human rights terms. Arguments seem fresh and appealing in many quarters where once they sounded weak and stale.

D

On a global scale, it is not strong states that are the problem here but weak ones, as they fail to protect their citizens from private power – whether it is paramilitaries committing murder and torture or transnational corporations spreading contamination and pollution.

E

One of the most significant of these is what has come to be called 'globalization', the collapsing of national boundaries in economic, political and cultural life. From the expanding role of the world's financial markets and the spread of transnational corporations to the revolution in communications and information technology, more and more areas of people's lives are affected by regional, international or transnational developments, whether they are aware of this or not.

F

Not only must states not infringe rights, and enforce those rights which fall within their direct sphere (like providing a criminal justice system or holding fair elections), but they also have 'positive obligations' to uphold rights enshrined in human rights treaties, even when it is private parties which have violated them.

G

The results of its investigations were published in 1999 in a unique pamphlet on *Globalization, Human Rights and the Rule of Law*. The issue to be faced is whether to treat these and other corporations as 'large para-state entities to be held accountable under the same sort of regime as states', or whether to look for different approaches to accountability 'that are promulgated by consumer groups and the corporations themselves'.

H

No longer the preserve of representatives of nation states meeting under the auspices of the United Nations, a developing conversation is taking place on a global scale and involving a growing cast of people – for an increasing range of pressure groups now frame their aspirations in human rights terms.

3 How do you view the future for universal human rights? What role does the Internet play in social and political change? Will increasing globalisation lead to more or less freedom for the individual? Why?

4 Look back at the extract and find words or phrases which mean the same as a–f.

   a caught between two stages of development
   b a relatively weak attempt
   c a relaxing of the rules
   d a less important event
   e causing something or someone great difficulties
   f brief or scope

5 Replace these words and phrases in paragraphs A–H with suitable synonyms or phrases.

   a wield … power (A)
   b proliferation (B)
   c raised the profile (B)
   d propitious (C)
   e infringe (F)
   f enshrined in (F)
   g promulgated by (G)
   h under the auspices of (H)

1 Should animals enjoy the same rights as humans? Outline your views with reference to the animal welfare campaigns shown.

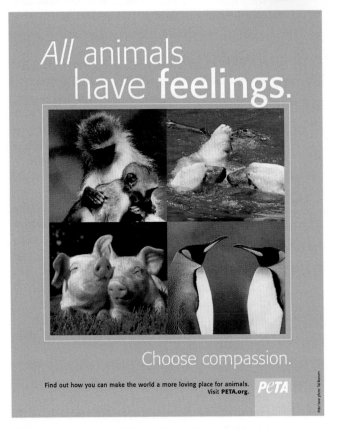

All animals have **feelings.**

Choose compassion.

Find out how you can make the world a more loving place for animals.
Visit PETA.org. **PeTA**

2 **2 11** Listen to this extract about the use of animals in medical research. Is the speaker for or against animal testing? Why?

The speaker used various modal verbs to express different functions. Here are two examples.
Animals must be used in order to trial new drugs and treatments safely. (obligation)
It could in fact be damaging to human health. (speculation)

Before you do the exercises in the Corpus spot, turn to the Grammar folder to review the different functions modal verbs have.

G→pages 186–187

Corpus spot

As the *Cambridge Learner Corpus* shows, modal verbs often cause problems, even at Proficiency level. Correct any errors in these sentences. One sentence is correct.

a Animals could be kept in zoos, but they must to have a comfortable place to live in.
b I've written a few notes about things that may be changed if the campaign is to succeed.
c His dog ought to be registered because then they might have been able to trace it.
d Much more should have been done to bring this epidemic under control.
e You mustn't have been here last summer – the café only opened a month ago.
f I needn't have bought these batteries if I had known you were going to buy some too.
g If only we should live our lives again, knowing what we know now!
h It can't be possible for you to phone back later?

3 Choose the correct modal form in each of these sentences.

a I *needn't have / shouldn't have* gone out last night as I had so much work to do.
b You *might have / needed to have* rung me to say you'd missed the bus – I was worried sick.
c It *must have / could have* been a full three hours later when the ship finally docked.
d Legally, people *mustn't / needn't* vote in a general election if they don't want to.
e I'm sure I *don't have to / mustn't* remind you of the need for confidentiality.
f You really *shouldn't / needn't* cover up for him every time – you'll get yourself into trouble one day.
g *Need / Ought* I to have let someone know about this earlier?
h *Would / Might* you mind if I didn't give you a lift all the way home tonight?

4   For questions 1–6, complete the second sentence so that it has a similar meaning to the first sentence, using the word given. **Do not change the word given.** You must use between **three** and **eight** words, including the word given.

1   You didn't spend enough time on this project.
    put
    You ought ....
    hours on this project.

2   Factory farming was surely less humane before these guidelines were established.
    prior
    Factory farming must
    .... of these guidelines.

3   I really admire people who are prepared to risk their job for the sake of their principles.
    line
    I really admire people who are prepared to
    .... for the sake of their principles.

4   You should have spilled the beans about Lisa before now.
    let
    If only you could
    .... secret before now.

5   It's time the organisation told the truth about the misuse of its funds.
    straight
    The organisation should set
    .... its funds were misused.

6   Would you mind if I asked you to sign this petition?
    raise
    Would you ....
    asking you to sign this petition?

5   For questions 1–8, read the text below. Use the word given in capitals at the end of some of the lines to form a word that fits in the space in the same line. There is an example at the beginning (0).

Mankind's intuition of freedom, and our **(0)** ...IDENTIFICATION... of freedom with knowledge, sets us apart from animals. The	**IDENTIFY**
animal's grasp of freedom is **(1)** .... in comparison, being only the freedom to respond to external stimuli. The	**SIGNIFY**
nearest creature to us on the **(2)** .... tree of life, the chimpanzee, cannot retain an image for a sufficient length of time to be able to reflect on it. So animal life is largely a matter of	**EVOLVE**
conditioned reflexes, performed in an **(3)** .... present; in short, animals are little more than machines with consciousness.	**TERMINATE**
While the animal is carried along **(4)** .... on the stream	**SUBMIT**
of time, mankind has certain capacities that **(5)**	**POWER**
us to resist the current or look into the future. Our **(6)**	**RESOURCE**
in developing language was the first step towards this 'conquest of time'. Language 'fixes' experiences, and places the experience of	
the past on an equal **(7)** .... with that of the present.	**FOOT**
Imagination was bound to follow, as a **(8)**	**NATURE**
progression from 'labelling' a past experience to conjuring up its mental image.	

1 Identify what aspect of freedom – or the lack
   of it – is shown in the three pictures A–C,
   using some of these words and phrases.

civil disobedience	political regime
free speech	sweatshop
child labour	

2 **2 12** Now listen to the first stage of a Speaking Test,
   Part 2, based on these pictures. Do both candidates
   do what is required? Could the discussion have been
   more balanced? If so, how?

3 **2 13** Listen to the second stage of the same task.
   What two additional aspects of 'freedom' do the
   candidates decide to include?

Pronunciation

4 **2 14** Read the Exam spot and then listen to utterances a–f taken from the recording. Notice how the speakers stress certain words and vary their intonation.

a Anyway, what about picture A?

b I didn't say they succeeded.

c Looking at picture B, I suppose it's illustrating the rights of the individual, isn't it?

d Yes, that's an important point – you don't have that freedom of choice everywhere.

e Speaking purely for myself, I'd want to include something on education.

f I'm not sure that's strictly about freedom, though.

5 Now read this task, which is based on the same set of photos.

> Imagine that all these photographs have been entered for an award: *Most powerful image in journalism*. Talk about the message that each picture conveys and decide which one should win the award. You have three minutes for this.

Think quickly of one or two points to make about each picture. When you are both ready to start, note the time. Speak for the full three minutes. Remember to give your partner a chance to speak!

6 For questions 1–8, read the text below and decide which answer (A, B, C or D) best fits each gap.

Social media – a toolkit for greater freedom?

In the 21st century, the revolution may not be televised – but recent experience suggests it is likely to be tweeted, blogged, texted and organised on Facebook. After **(1)** .... more than 3 million tweets, gigabytes of YouTube content and thousands of blogs, a new study finds that social media played a **(2)** .... role in shaping political debates during the Arab Spring. Conversations about revolution often **(3)** .... major events, and social media carried inspiring stories of protest across international borders **(4)** ....

During the week before former Egyptian president Hosni Mubarak's resignation, for example, the total **(5)** .... of tweets from Egypt – and around the world – about political change in that country ballooned from 2,300 a day to 230,000 a day. Videos **(6)** .... protest and political commentary went viral – the top 23 videos received nearly 5.5 million **(7)** .... And the amount of content **(8)** .... online by opposition groups increased dramatically.

	A	B	C	D
1	testing	analysing	judging	estimating
2	premium	firm	decisive	heavy
3	preceded	dated	backed	unfolded
4	visibly	instantly	firstly	directly
5	toll	ratio	equation	rate
6	issuing	starring	featuring	turning
7	looks	regards	sights	views
8	posted	mailed	fixed	joined

Writing folder 9

Part 2 Article

Writing folder 5 also dealt with the article task, considering aspects of style and ways of holding the reader's attention. This Writing folder focuses on sophistication of language and writing an article for a specific audience.

1 Read the exam task below. What is the intended readership of the article? What style would you expect as a result?

An academic journal has invited its readers to contribute to a series of articles on new technology and personal freedom. You decide to submit an article describing the effects that new technology, such as the Internet, social networking sites and mobile phones, has had on people's lives and explaining whether these changes have led to more or less freedom. You should also evaluate how positive the changes are for society.

Write your **article**.

2 Read this sample answer and decide whether the content is relevant to the task. Then underline any inconsistencies in style that you notice.

3 Tick the boxes that apply to the sample answer.

- ☐ Complex ideas are communicated convincingly.
- ☐ Style is consistently appropriate for the readership.
- ☐ Text is a well-organised, coherent whole.
- ☐ Errors only occur in less common words and may be slips.
- ☐ Grammatical forms lack control and complexity.
- ☐ Choice of vocabulary generally shows sophistication and precision.

HANG ON TO YOUR RIGHTS!

The prevalence of mobile communication devices together with the widespread use of social networking and the Internet have altered our way of life fundamentally. This article weighs up their impact on individual freedom and assesses whether the outcomes are really that great.

I think the big plus with Smartphones and tablets is that friends and family are always contactable. Parents need not be concerned for the welfare of their teenage children, as they can keep track of them. This may be beneficial to the older generation, but I think it imposes unfair limits on the liberty of their kids.

The downside of mobile devices from the working adult's standpoint is that they can be reached 24/7 and the distinction between work and home life becomes blurred. This again places constraints upon the individual, who has fewer opportunities to shut out the stress of everyday life.

At the same time, the Internet gives us the ability to control our lives, right? From booking a holiday to selecting a new home, everything can be done direct, without any middleman restricting what is on offer. So that is an example of greater freedom — the freedom of choice.

As for social networking, the chance to share ideas and communicate more effectively means that nobody need feel alone in the modern world. Furthermore, the role played by social media in disseminating information under less tolerant political regimes shows how networking sites can be used to help us out, contributing to profound social change.

However, I think the big snag of all this is an inevitable erosion of privacy. People seem happy to display their innermost thoughts and aspirations in a way that would have been unheard of in the previous century, but at what cost? It is impossible to turn the clock back, yet it must be acknowledged that through social media, restrictions have been placed on individual freedom, which society at large may come to regret.

4 Rewrite the parts of the answer you underlined in 2, using these words and phrases to help you. Correct any slips and decide on a more suitable title.

unequivocally advantageous (paragraph 1)
the main asset of; offspring (paragraph 2)
one drawback; at all times (paragraph 3)
it is undeniable that (paragraph 4)
for the greater good (paragraph 5)
the adverse impact (paragraph 6)

5 A good way of demonstrating sophistication in vocabulary selection is to draw on your knowledge of word families. Find words in the article that are related to the verbs in a–h. These occur in text order.

a prevail	**d** constrain	**g** aspire
b contact	**e** tolerate	**h** restrict
c benefit	**f** erode	

6 Look at the word family for the verb *tolerate*, which is taken from the English Vocabulary Profile. All of these words are within the level of C2 learners. Check your understanding of the five words in italics by using them to complete sentences a–e.

> **Word family**
>
> **Nouns:** *intolerance, tolerance*
>
> **Verbs:** tolerate
>
> **Adjectives:** *intolerable, intolerant, tolerant*

a Canada has a very .... and inclusive attitude to incomers and a great track record of entrepreneurship.

b The issue of same-sex marriage still has the power to polarise views and what is remarkable in this battle is how deeply each side feels itself a victim of the other's ....

c Sometimes, if a situation is .... , walking away is the only way to cool things down.

d The researchers give some possible reasons for the decline in juvenile violence, such as the growth of community policing, less cultural .... of violence, and more aggressive policies to regulate firearms.

e The nation is somewhat unfairly portrayed as an inward-looking society that is manifestly .... of minorities.

7 Read the exam task and use the mind map to help you plan your ideas. Then write an article of 280–320 words, following the Exam advice and using vocabulary from this Writing folder and Unit 18.

> An international research body is publishing a book entitled *Freedom in modern society* and has asked for contributions from around the world. You decide to submit an article for the book. You should describe the current situation in your country with regard to education, employment and family life and explain what aspects of freedom an individual has the right to expect. You should also evaluate whether there are too many limits on personal freedom nowadays.
>
> Write your **article**.

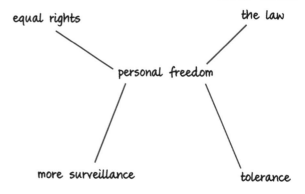

equal rights the law
personal freedom
more surveillance tolerance

Speaking

1 Why do you think the topic of ghosts, vampires and werewolves has been popular in fiction for many years, and more recently, in films? What evidence is there for the existence of the paranormal?

Vocabulary

2 Work with a partner and look at the adjectives below. Decide which word is the odd one out in each group. Justify your decision.

a	naïve	sceptical	ingenuous	simple
b	gullible	derisive	credulous	trusting
c	cynical	scornful	apathetic	contemptuous
d	sensitive	sensible	susceptible	suggestible
e	nosy	curious	inquisitive	humble
f	upright	immature	irresponsible	disrespectful
g	pushy	eccentric	persistent	assertive
h	pragmatic	resourceful	ingenious	inventive
i	tactful	diplomatic	impulsive	discreet

Which of the words above might you use to describe someone who believes in ghosts? Use an English–English dictionary to help you.

Listening

3 **2 15** You will hear a radio programme about ghosts. For questions 1–9, complete the sentences with a word or short phrase.

Athenodorus was disturbed by the noise made by (1) .... knocking against each other.

Athenodorus was no longer bothered by the ghost after a new (2) .... took place.

The ghost of a loved one in trouble is referred to by the speaker as a ' (3) .... '.

It has often been the case that people mistake a (4) .... for a ghost.

Harry Martindale was a (5) .... by trade.

Harry had placed his (6) .... on the spot where a Roman road used to be.

The soldier's head was level with Harry's (7) ....

Harry said that the soldiers badly needed a (8) ....

Harry described the soldiers' weapons as looking like a (9) ....

4   What do you think about Harry's experience? Do you think it has the ring of truth about it or not? Why? / Why not?

◎ Style extra

In the listening passage, what was described as 'rattling' and 'murmuring'?

Words like these are called onomatopoeic words because they seem to sound like their meaning.

Below are verbs connected with types of sound. Using an English–English dictionary, decide what you would use these words to describe.

EXAMPLE: *howl*
            the noise made by an unhappy dog, also by the wind

creak	rumble	slap	hiss	drip
tinkle	crunch	slam	growl	peal
squelch	slash	click	screech	slither

Complete the sentences below with one of the verbs above.
a The stairs .... as she tiptoed up to her room.
b The farmer's shoe .... as he pulled it out of the mud.
c Hooligans have .... my car tyres with a knife.
d The snake .... across the floor.
e You always know when the postman comes because he .... across the gravel.
f I was kept awake last night by the tap ....
g The glass .... as it broke on the floor.
h Steam .... as it came out of the pipe.

Write a paragraph about one of the following, using some of the verbs above to give a suitable atmosphere.
• Alone in a haunted house
• The Titanic sinking
• Home alone in a storm

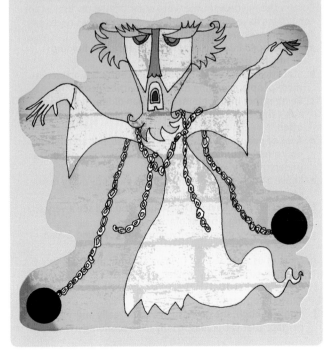

5   For questions 1–8, read the text below and decide which answer (A, B, C or D) best fits each gap.

POLTERGEISTS

Poltergeists have always been with us; there are (1)............... cases as far back as AD 530, and from all parts of the world. The German word poltergeist means (2)............... 'noisy spirit', and that describes the behaviour of this phenomenon very well. Among its manifestations are banging noises, things being thrown around, furniture being (3)............... and other destructive behaviour; but it also (4)............... itself in other, quieter ways, such as hiding things or writing messages. It is seen as a mischievous spirit because that is what the behaviour suggests; a disembodied spirit that enjoys upsetting people.

It is clear that many poltergeist activities do not follow the rules (5)............... by science; things move without being touched, objects move slowly through the air, solid objects pass through other solid objects, (6)............... fires occur, water appears from nowhere, and so on. It is possible that these paranormal events are (7)............... by powers and energies we have not yet recognised, but which everyone has the (8)............... to use.

1 A inscribed   **B** recorded   **C** minuted
   D registered
2 A literally   **B** exactly   **C** accurately
   D plainly
3 A loaded up   **B** set in   **C** turned over
   D stood out
4 A intimates   **B** divulges   **C** signifies
   D reveals
5 A brought out   **B** laid down   **C** carried out
   D put down
6 A spontaneous   **B** instinctive   **C** impulsive
   D voluntary
7 A triggered   **B** derived   **C** evolved
   D extorted
8 A proficiency   **B** competency   **C** accomplishment
   D potential

19.2 Word order and adverbs

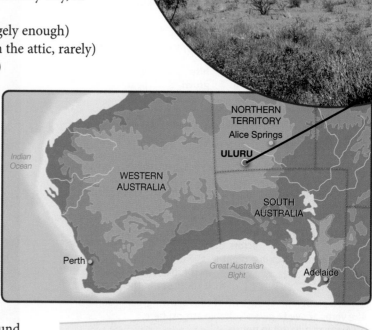

1 Work in a group. Decide where to put the adverbs or adverbial phrases in the following sentences.

a I went home. (yesterday, on foot)

b She walked to where another coach was waiting. (up the hill, briskly, later, luckily)

c I was in the mood to go swimming. (hardly, last night)

d He is lying. (of course, still)

e Stephen spoke to me. (the other day, in a friendly way, in fact)

f It rained. (non-stop, all day, heavily, strangely enough)

g People hide things of value. (apparently, in the attic, rarely)

h She performed the dance. (far, slowly, too)

i I think you should get out of the house. (to be honest, more often)

j I saw the comet. (only, in the sky, yesterday)

G → pages 187–188

2 Put the sentences, or parts of sentences, in order. The last word of each sentence is given in bold and capital letters are given. Then put the sentences in order to make an extract from an article about how Uluru, or Ayers Rock, in Australia came to be created. You will also need to add punctuation.

EXAMPLE: central a or Ayers huge Uluru mound sandstone Rock is in **Australia** …

Uluru, or Ayers Rock, is a huge sandstone mound in central Australia …

a tells a Another terrible after how **battle** …

b originally One Uluru legend that a was states **lake**.

c … that been to the for Aboriginal sacred has hundreds people of **years**.

d tell Earth paintings Many Aboriginal important **stories**.

e … world when the was the time **created**.

f … at to Earth rose up the blood-coloured revolt the form the great bloodshed in **rock**.

g in that was made They by it spirits the believe **'Dreamtime'** …

Corpus spot

Correct the mistakes in the word order of adverbs that exam candidates have made, making any other changes necessary. Two sentences are correct.

a He slumped into the nearby velvet armchair, holding tightly his briefcase in his hands.

b Statistically looked at, however, the centre has attracted more people, spending more money than before.

c Being rather into contemporary than old-fashioned art I don't find the good old Tate Britain a place I would visit too often.

d A lot of people actually do travel abroad, but apparently only a few return home with more knowledge and better understanding.

e I have always wanted to remember perfectly every movie I see and every book I read.

f It goes without saying that seldom you will see a very shy person wearing a bright orange shirt.

g Kerry is a very green county: you hardly can find a road where two cars pass each other.

h Most of us are aware of the fact that not always is this solution economically viable.

i Before he appeared on the music scene, there hardly existed 'Pop' music.

j Oddly enough, she never seems to be really angry and perhaps that is the reason why I like confiding in her.

- It is possible to change most adjectives into an adverb with the addition of *-ly*, for example *happy* to *happily*.

- Some adjectives do not have an adverb, for example *friendly*, *lonely*, *silly*. In this case you need to use an adverb phrase, for example *He looked at her in a friendly way*.

- Some adverbs have the same form as the adjective, for example *hard*. *He works hard. He's a hard worker.*

- Some adverbs may have two forms – one which looks like an adjective and the other with *-ly*. There is usually a difference in meaning.

3 Use one of the words from the box to complete each sentence below.

hard	hardly	short	shortly	right	rightly
high	highly	late	lately	wrong	wrongly

a I .... ever see her nowadays – she's so busy.
b Sally thought very .... indeed of the gypsy's fortune-telling powers.
c The interviewer .... claimed that the house was haunted.
d Sue thought long and .... about whether to take part in the experiment.
e Tell Marje I'll see her ....
f You've done this calculation ....
g They were just saying that they hadn't seen you ....
h The car turned .... round and went back the way it came.
i The article stopped .... of accusing anyone of a hoax.

4 For questions 1–8, read the text below and think of the word which best fits each space. Use only one word in each space. There is an example at the beginning (0).

Carrying out a ghost hunt

(0) ...SHOULD... a visit to a house convince you that there may be something worth investigating, follow these simple steps. There is much you can do in the way of preliminary research before you (1) .... any serious attempt to (2) .... out any practical investigation. Documents devoted to the area can often be (3) .... interest and a visit to the local museum will be invaluable. Maps can also provide information on the whereabouts of underground water. Water running underground through streams, old sewers and so (4) .... beneath or close to the foundations of a house may subject it to spasmodic thrusts. (5) .... the water builds up, such jolts cause objects in the house to move, increasing the general strain on the house, (6) .... produce noises that sound eerie at night. Such possibilities have to be (7) .... into account, depending on the reported paranormal activity. In (8) .... event, knowledge of previous buildings in the area may produce a clue to any apparitions seen.

1 Read these facts about two former American presidents, Abraham Lincoln and John F. Kennedy.

Abraham Lincoln was elected to Congress in 1846. John F. Kennedy was elected to Congress in 1946.

Abraham Lincoln was elected President in 1860. John F. Kennedy was elected President in 1960.

Both were particularly concerned with civil rights.

Both Presidents were shot on a Friday. Both were shot in the head with one bullet.

Both were rumoured to be killed in a conspiracy. Neither was confirmed to be a conspiracy.

Both successors were named Johnson. Andrew Johnson, who succeeded Lincoln, was born in 1808. Lyndon Johnson, who succeeded Kennedy, was born in 1908.

Some sceptics say that you could take any two famous people and find a number of similar-type coincidences between them. The only problem with that theory is that there really haven't been any listings of such comparisons. And certainly none has been as extensive as the Lincoln–Kennedy similarities.

Do you think this is pure coincidence or do you think there is more to it than that?

2 Can you explain the following expressions? Have you any experience of the situations they would be used for?

- Talk of the devil!
- To have a guardian angel
- It's a small world
- To have second sight
- Female intuition
- A feeling of déjà vu
- A sixth sense

3 Read the texts below.

Text 1

Coincidence
or evidence of
the paranormal?

An investigation of coincidences should be primarily designed to get at the truth, or at least make progress towards it. The moment that chance ceases to be a convincing explanation, uneasiness sets in. Most people are embarrassed to speak out in case they are thought of as eccentrics. Their experiences may be commonplace enough – the occasional precognitive dream; a feeling of déjà vu or thinking of somebody a moment before they ring up – but they still feel the need for anonymity.

But a surprising number of people who clearly regard themselves as free from irrational fears are ready to admit that even mundane coincidences can be disturbing.

Text 2

a reasonable EXPLANATION?

It is in the imagery of sight, hearing, touch, smell or temperature that paranormal cognition often emerges into the conscious mind. There may be no more than a sudden impression that something has happened, even no more than an unaccountable impulse to act; to cancel a seat on a flight which will shortly crash, for example. Even now, of course, such happenings are often dismissed as superstitious nonsense. In the same way, the report that the inhabitants of the island of St Kilda only got colds when a ship came in was said to be contrary to all common sense by critics in the seventeenth century, only to be accepted as a statement of fact when the germ theory of disease was established in the nineteenth.

4 Look at the following words from the texts. What part of speech is each word in the text? What other forms of the word are possible?

Text 1   **Text 2**
speak out   conscious
anonymity   impression
disturbing   dismissed

5 Use an appropriate form of the words in capitals to complete the sentences.

a He is a very .... critic of what he calls 'paranormal geeks'.   **SPEAK**

b The newspaper article was .... of the possibility of ESP (Extra-Sensory Perception).   **DISMISSED**

c Her one wish after her experience was to remain ....   **ANONYMITY**

d There was a rumour of some sort of a .... at the cemetery last night.   **DISTURBING**

e Children of primary school age are very .... and tend to believe what they are told.   **IMPRESSION**

f You may not be aware of things happening but your .... probably registers events.   **CONSCIOUS**

6 Look at the essay below, which is an attempt at the following exam task.

> Write an essay summarising and evaluating the key points from both texts. Use your own words throughout as far as possible, and include your own ideas in your answers. Write your answer in 240–280 words.

The essay is a poor attempt. With a partner, decide what you think needs to be improved and then rewrite it so that it fully answers the question.

> The two texts contrast the pros and cons of coincidences, whether they are evidence of the paranormal or can be explained on a purely rational level. Text 1 argues that people are often embarrassed by unusual happenings and prefer not to tell anyone about it. If they think of a person just before that person rings up then they don't tell them because they are worried that that person will think they are stupid.
>
> My feeling is that it is wrong to feel embarrassed as, in fact, there is always a rational explanation for nearly everything that happens.
>
> Text 2 says that we shouldn't believe in superstition because most things can be explained by science. Everyone thought that the people on St Kilda got colds for some paranormal reason when a ship came in. In fact, it was easily explained once the theory of germs was discovered.
>
> I totally agree with this as I think that science is showing us new things all the time. During my short life many things have been discovered which we would never have dreamt of in the past — e.g. the mobile phone, etc.

Exam folder 10

Speaking

The standard format for the Speaking paper is for there to be two candidates and two examiners. It is also possible to have three candidates and two examiners.

One examiner, called the interlocutor, asks the questions while the other only listens. Both examiners will assess you. They are looking for accuracy of grammar, a wide and appropriate range of vocabulary and the ability to express opinions and abstract ideas. Your pronunciation should be clear and you should be able to interact well with your partner(s).

There are three parts to the test and it lasts for 16 minutes (24 minutes for groups of three). Part 1 is two minutes (three minutes for groups of three), Part 2 is four minutes (six minutes for groups of three) and Part 3 lasts for 10 minutes (15 minutes for groups of three).

In Part 1 you will be encouraged by the interlocutor to talk about yourself and give some personal opinions. In Part 2 you and the other candidate have a decision-making task consisting of visuals (up to seven pictures or photos) and/or a written prompt. In Part 3 you will have the chance to speak for about two minutes on a topic given to you and then have a discussion with the other candidate, developing the topic you have been given.

EXAM ADVICE

- Don't worry if you think you do badly in one part of the test. You are assessed on the complete test.
- If the other candidate is better than you, or not as good, you shouldn't worry. You are assessed on what you do, not in relation to the other candidate.
- It's important to show sensitivity to the other candidate during the test. This means allowing the other candidate to speak and responding to what they say.
- Remember this is your opportunity to show you can speak English – use it!
- Do ask if you are unclear about what you have to do.

Do this complete Speaking test with a partner, taking it in turns to ask and answer the following typical questions. (Remember that in the exam the interlocutor will be asking the questions.)

Part 1

Ask each other these questions.

Questions for Student A to ask Student B

- *Are you working or studying at the moment?*
- *How do you spend your leisure time?*
- *What would be your ideal job?*

Questions for Student B to ask Student A

- *How do you travel to work/college every day?*
- *What are your plans for the future?*
- *How important are computers in your life at the moment?*

Part 2

Here are some photos of useful inventions. Look at pictures A and E and talk together about whether you could live without them. You have about one minute to do this.

A

B

C

D

E

Now look at *all* the pictures. Imagine that an exhibition is going to take place on the theme of 'Essential Inventions'. All these objects are to be included. Talk together about the importance of the inventions shown in the pictures. Then suggest two other inventions you would like to see included in the exhibition.

You have about three minutes to do this.

Part 3

In this part of the test you have to speak by yourself for about two minutes. You should listen carefully while your partner is speaking because you will need to comment afterwards.

Both students should look at Student A's card. There is a question written on it and Student A has to give his/her opinion on it. There are some ideas on the card for you to use if you like.

Student A

> How has life changed in the past hundred years?
> - work
> - education
> - family life

Student B is now asked a question. *Do you think marriage is as important today as in the past?*

Student A is then asked what they think about this topic.

Now the roles are reversed and Student B has the chance to speak, using the prompts below if he or she wishes.

Student B

> What changes do you foresee in the future?
> - accommodation
> - fashion
> - transport

Student A is now asked a question. *Does the future worry you at all?*

Student B is now asked to comment on this topic.

To finish the test both candidates have to talk about changes to our lives in general. This section lasts about four minutes.

Discuss together the following questions.

- *What can we do to make the world a better place to live in?*
- *Are we losing touch with the natural world?*
- *Are people becoming less important than machines?*

Speaking

1 What do you think about these types of comedy?

- slapstick
- political satire
- stand-up
- farce
- black comedy

Reading

2 Read this extract from a book by the American writer Bill Bryson, who is renowned for his dry sense of humour. It was written after the writer and his family moved back to the USA after living in the UK. His wife is English.

What impression does he give you of life in the USA?

How to have fun at home

My wife thinks nearly everything about American life is wonderful. She loves having her groceries bagged for her. She adores free iced water and book-matches. She thinks home-delivered pizza is a central hallmark of civilization.
5 I haven't the heart to tell her that waitresses in the States urge everyone to have a nice day.

Personally, while I am fond of America and grateful for its many conveniences, I am not quite so slavishly uncritical. Take the matter of having your groceries bagged
10 for you. I appreciate the gesture, but when you come down to it what does it actually achieve except give you an opportunity to stand there and watch your groceries being bagged? It's not as if it buys you some quality time. I don't want to get heavy here, but given the choice between free
15 iced water at restaurants and, let us say, a national health service, I have to say my instinct is to go with the latter.

However, there are certain things that are so wonderful in American life that I can hardly stand it myself. Chief among these, without any doubt, is the garbage disposal.
20 A garbage disposal is everything a labour-saving device should be and so seldom is – noisy, fun, extremely hazardous, and so dazzlingly good at what it does that you cannot imagine how you ever managed without one. If you had asked me eighteen months ago what the prospects
25 were that shortly my chief hobby would be placing assorted objects down a hole in the kitchen sink, I believe I would have laughed in your face, but in fact it is so.

I have never had a garbage disposal before, so I have been learning its tolerances through a process of trial and
30 error. Chopsticks give perhaps the liveliest response (this is not recommended, of course, but there comes a time with every piece of machinery when you just have to see what it can do), but cantaloupe rinds make the richest, throatiest sound and result in less 'down time'. Coffee grounds
35 in quantity are the most likely to provide a satisfying

'Vesuvius effect', though for obvious reasons it is best not to attempt this difficult feat until your wife has gone out for the day, and to have a mop and stepladder standing by. The most exciting event with a garbage disposal, of course, is when it jams and you have to reach in and unclog 40 it, knowing that at any moment it might spring to life and abruptly convert your arm from a useful grasping tool into a dibber. Don't try to tell me about living life on the edge.

Now basements I know because I grew up with one. Every American basement is the same. They all have a 45 funny smell – a combination of old magazines, camping gear that should have been aired and wasn't, and something to do with a guinea pig named Mr Fluffy that escaped down a central heating grate six months ago and has not been seen since (and presumably would now be better called 50 Mr Bones).

Occasionally, especially in starter homes, you will find that some young gung-ho dad has converted the basement into a playroom for the children, but this is always a mistake, as no child will play in a basement. This is because 55 no matter how loving your parents, no matter how much you would like to trust them, there is always the thought that they will quietly lock the door at the top of the stairs and move to Florida. No, basements are simply and inescapably scary; that's why they always feature in spooky 60 movies, usually with a shadow of Joan Crawford carrying an axe thrown on the far wall. That may be why even dads don't go down there very often.

I could go on and on cataloguing other small, unsung glories of American household life – refrigerators that 65 dispense iced water and make their own ice-cubes, walk-in closets, electrical sockets in bathrooms, but I won't. I'm out of space and anyway Mrs B has just gone out to do some shopping and it has occurred to me that I have not yet seen what the disposal can do with a juice carton. I'll get back to 70 you on this one.

3 For questions 1–6, choose the answer (A, B, C or D) which you think fits best according to the text.

1 In the first paragraph, what does Bill Bryson imply about his wife?

   A She has very poor taste in food.

   B She is only happy so long as she can get things for nothing.

   C She is only pretending to be uncritical of the American way of life.

   D She is relatively unsophisticated.

2 What is Bill's reaction to having his groceries bagged and getting iced water?

   A He feels that the country hasn't quite got its priorities right.

   B He would prefer to pay less and pack his own groceries.

   C He thinks that service could be even better in American shops and restaurants.

   D He is of the opinion that Americans waste a lot of time unnecessarily.

3 Why does Bill enjoy using the garbage disposal?

   A It fulfils his notion of what a household gadget should b

   B He has plenty of free time to experiment now he has moved back to the States.

   C He is finding it much easier to use than he thought he would.

   D It devours anything you put in it without any fuss.

4 What impression do you get of Bill when he talks about th garbage disposal unit?

   A He is irritated that the unit is so potentially dangerous.

   B He is keen to help around the house and will happily mend the disposal unit for his wife.

   C He likes to experiment with it without fear of interruption.

   D He thinks the garbage disposal unit should take a wider variety of garbage.

5 According to Bill, basements often

   A make people feel intimidated.

   B remind people of frightening incidents from their childhood.

   C make people want to start competing to see who can make the best conversion.

   D are a source of argument in families.

6 In describing his current home in the USA, Bill seems

   A quite critical.

   B fairly effusive.

   C sometimes nostalgic.

   D quietly indignant.

4 Find these expressions in the text. In your own words, explain what the writer means by each of them. (Sometimes you will need to explain the writer's choice of words.)

   a I don't want to get heavy here (lines 13–14)

   b a satisfying 'Vesuvius effect' (lines 35–36)

   c and presumably would now be better called Mr Bones (lines 50–51)

   d some young gung-ho dad (line 53)

   e other small, unsung glories of American household life (lines 64–65)

   f I'll get back to you on this one (lines 70–71)

5 Did you find the extract funny? Why? / Why not?

20.2 Uses of *have*, *get* and *go*

A man's car had broken down, so he stopped the next car that came down the street.
'What's the problem?' asked the driver of the second car.
'I need some help,' said the driver of the first car. 'My car has broken down and I must get it looked at.'
'I can't help you,' said the driver of the second car. 'I'm not a mechanic. I'm a chiropodist.'
'In that case,' said the first driver, 'you can give me a tow.'

1   The joke above is a play on words. Can you explain it?

   The first driver wants to have his car looked at. What does this imply?

2   Read the information about *have* and *get* in the Grammar folder and complete the following sentences.

   a Aunt Paula won't .... her son criticised by anyone.
   b I'll .... the dinner made if you set the table.
   c Trevor .... his clothes covered in oil when he tried to mend his bike.
   d We .... the TV and video stolen in the burglary last month.
   e Mr Johnson always .... his windows cleaned by Jack.
   f I couldn't .... the door unlocked with my key this morning.

G → page 188

3   In his book, Bill Bryson says he 'could go on and on', meaning he could continue indefinitely. The sentences below all contain a phrasal verb with *go*.

   Fill in the missing particle or particles in each sentence.

   a Last winter everyone in the house went .... flu.
   b Sue didn't normally go .... competitions but thought she might win this time.
   c At least £500 went .... museum entry fees last time we had a holiday.
   d The police went .... the evidence very carefully.
   e Would you mind going .... some eggs?
   f The boys sat on the beach and watched the tide go ....
   g They timed the fireworks to go .... at midnight.
   h Tamsin's shoes didn't really go .... her jeans.
   i Not many people go .... basic necessities in this country any more.
   j The milk went .... because Tim forgot to put it back in the fridge.

   Now match each phrasal verb above with its meaning below.

be spent on =	explode =
ebb =	match =
fetch =	go sour =
enter =	examine =
become ill with =	manage without =

4   For questions 1–6, complete the second sentence so that it has a similar meaning to the first sentence, using the word given (as part of an expression with *go*). **Do not change the word given.** You must use between **three** and **eight** words, including the word given.

   1 Penny Stone has become really self-important since she was promoted.
   gone
   Getting a .... head.

2 Paul couldn't stop thinking about the argument he had had with his brother.

over

Paul .... mind the argument he had had with his brother.

3 The manager told the press that his team had played very badly.

record

The manager .... that his team had played very badly.

4 My grandmother would always make us eat everything on our plates when we visited her.

waste

Nothing we were given to eat

.... at my grandmother's house.

5 I can never follow what he's saying – he's always changing the subject.

tangent

If he .... I would know what he was talking about.

6 Although Theresa was a hard worker, she was unable to get her business to succeed.

go

Theresa was unable to

.... of working hard.

 Corpus spot

With a partner, correct the mistakes in the following sentences. One sentence is correct. The rest all contain a variety of different common student errors.

a Being a wet evening, I stayed at home.
b We would like to know all what has happened.
c He already is here.
d Only by listening intently, you will hear it singing.
e It would be easier to decide if my son would be here.
f I have past my exam this summer.
g It's worth to be alive on such a lovely day.
h My family consists in six people.
i That is a mistake I do often.
j Your hair needs cutting badly.
k I suggest to do it immediately.
l This team is the best of the two.
m He is too honest a man to take that.
n My informations aren't up to date.
o I am wanting to meet you for a long time.
p I congratulate you to have got married.
q I wish it stopped raining.
r You can eat as soon as the dinner will be ready.
s It's a five miles journey.
t A man came into the compartment to control the tickets.

---

5 For questions 1–8, read the text below and think of the word which best fits each space. Use only one word in each space. There is an example at the beginning (0).

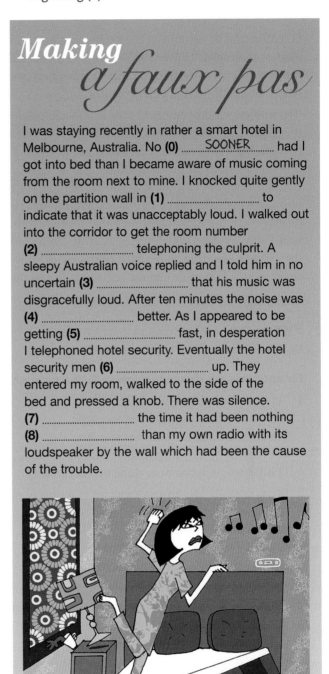

Making *a faux pas*

I was staying recently in rather a smart hotel in Melbourne, Australia. No **(0)** .....SOONER..... had I got into bed than I became aware of music coming from the room next to mine. I knocked quite gently on the partition wall in **(1)** .... to indicate that it was unacceptably loud. I walked out into the corridor to get the room number **(2)** .... telephoning the culprit. A sleepy Australian voice replied and I told him in no uncertain **(3)** .... that his music was disgracefully loud. After ten minutes the noise was **(4)** .... better. As I appeared to be getting **(5)** .... fast, in desperation I telephoned hotel security. Eventually the hotel security men **(6)** .... up. They entered my room, walked to the side of the bed and pressed a knob. There was silence. **(7)** .... the time it had been nothing **(8)** .... than my own radio with its loudspeaker by the wall which had been the cause of the trouble.

6 Have you ever had an embarrassing moment when you made a faux pas or put your foot in it? Talk about it with a partner.

1   How would you describe someone who is eccentric? Do you know anyone who could be called eccentric?

Eccentrics can be extreme in the exuberance with which they express their sense of humour. The way normal people regard the eccentric often depends upon what they find funny. Read this description of the antics of an eccentric.

'His mildest kind of practical joke is to push a dish of meringue trifle into the face of a lady guest at a smart dinner party in his home, having first asked her to smell it to see if it is 'off'. There is an oubliette under one of his dining room chairs, and any boring guest is seated over it and dropped into the wine cellar when he can stand no more. His coup de grâce was the miniature bomb that he planted inside his son's birthday cake, which the boy detonated by blowing on the candles, covering all his little friends with icing. The man's long-suffering wife had to clean them all up, then explain and apologise to their parents after the party.'

Would you find someone like this funny or irritating?

2   **2** **16** You will hear a discussion in which a student, Terry, is talking to his psychology lecturer, Dr Morris, about a new book on eccentricity.

For questions 1–5, choose the answer (A, B, C or D) which fits best according to what you hear.

1   Terry was surprised to read that
   A many famous people were eccentric.
   B eccentrics live longer than average.
   C eccentricity isn't a mental illness.
   D little research has been done on eccentricity.

2   What does Dr Morris say about a definition of eccentricity?
   A It is still a debated issue.
   B It was formulated for western societies.
   C It has recently been reassessed.
   D It is generally agreed to be outdated.

3   According to Dr Morris, what is most people's attitude to eccentrics?
   A They dismiss them as having mental problems.
   B They are irritated by their lack of conformity.
   C They regard them as being outside of society.
   D They have mixed feelings about them.

4   Dr Morris and Terry agree that the defining trait of an eccentric is
   A an interest in other people's hobbies.
   B a need to be the centre of attention.
   C a lack of regard for conventional behaviour.
   D a desire to change society.

5   Dr Morris says that new research has found that eccentrics tend to
   A remember their dreams clearly.
   B respond well to external stimuli.
   C score highly in belief in the paranormal.
   D be good at looking after themselves.

Pronunciation

3 **2 17** The woman in the interview talked about a *bizarre or risqué* habit. English has borrowed many words and phrases from other languages. Use a dictionary to find out the English meanings of these words and phrases, listen to the recording and then say them aloud.

in lieu of	protégé
ad infinitum	fracas
ad nauseam	cul-de-sac
par excellence	clique
quid pro quo	nom de plume
faux pas	bête noire
prima facie	tête à tête
niche	hoi polloi
risqué	coup de grâce

4 Using the expressions in 3, complete the following sentences.

a It was such an embarrassing .... when I asked the girl to introduce me to her father and I found out it was her husband!

b It's possible to give works of art to the government .... of tax.

c Female writers in the past often used a ....

d Some of Uncle Thomas's jokes tend to be a bit ....

e Rosalie and I decided to go to a café for a .... about the office.

f The boy next door talks about trainspotting ....

g You are apparently more likely to be burgled in a .... than on a main road.

h My .... is people who talk during a film at the cinema.

5 With a partner, look at the Part 3 Speaking tasks below. The prompts are to give you some ideas on the subject. You can use all, one or two or none of the ideas. Student A should look at Task A and then speak about it for about two minutes.

Task A

Is it better to conform or be different from your peers?

- fashion
- relationships
- leisure pursuits

Student A should now ask Student B the following question.

Generally speaking, do you feel pressurised to conform?

Student A should then give their opinion on this topic.

Student B now talks for about two minutes on the following topic.

Task B

How much are people's ideas affected by what they see on the TV?

- popular comedians
- documentaries
- politicians and other famous people

Student B should ask Student A the following question.

Which type of media influences you most?

Student B should then also try to answer this question.

Remember it is fine to hesitate in order to gather your thoughts – as long as you don't pause for too long! You can also repeat the question or use phrases such as:

Umm …	*Let me see …*	*As I see it …*
Well …	*I mean …*	

You might also want to add something you'd forgotten to mention or return to a previous subject. For this you can use phrases like:

By the way, …	*As I was saying, …*
Incidentally, …	*I forgot to say/mention that …*

It's very likely you will need to generalise during your talk. Use phrases such as:

Broadly speaking …	*In general …*
To a great extent …	*On the whole …*

Writing folder 10

Part 2 Articles and Letters

1   Read the Part 2 tasks below and decide what is involved in each
    one, choosing relevant aspects from the following list.

    comparison   narrative
    evaluation   opinion
    factual description   speculation

A

An in-flight magazine has asked its readers to
submit a light-hearted article with the title *Space
transport in 2050.* Write an article describing
possible future forms of transport and saying how
you would take advantage of them.

B

An international ecology magazine has invited
readers to contribute an article to a special edition
entitled *Ways to save our planet.* Write an article
outlining the environmental measures you think
should be taken by individuals and by governments
and evaluating their chances of success.

C

You see a reader's letter in a general interest
magazine, which claims that family life is no
different nowadays to how it was twenty years
ago. You decide to write a letter to the magazine,
giving your opinions on the changes in family roles
and relationships and suggesting likely future
developments.

D

Your school magazine is running a special feature
on books students have read, which is entitled
Every good book has a message about life. Write
an article about the set book you are studying,
explaining what you feel it has taught you that you
can apply to life in general.

E

The publisher of the book you have studied is
planning a new edition with pictures and has asked
you to suggest which parts of the book would
benefit from being illustrated. Write a letter to the
publisher, giving your suggestions and justifying
them with detailed reference to the book.

What should the style and tone of each task be?
Could all three articles (A, B and D) be written in
either a light-hearted or more serious tone?
Why? / Why not?

2 Select vocabulary from the pools below
   that could be used in each task. Some
   words can be used in more than one.

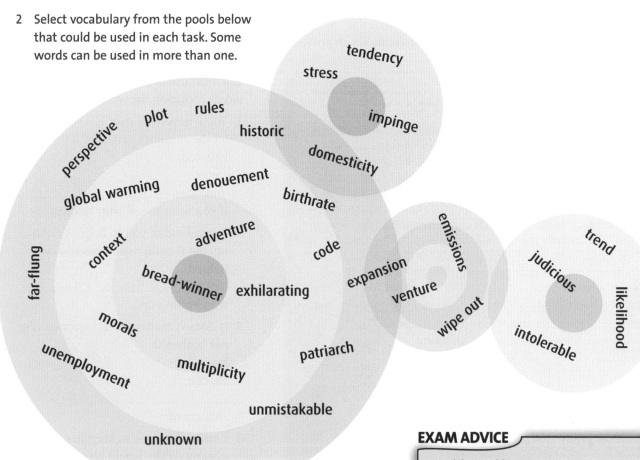

tendency
stress
impinge
historic
domesticity

perspective
plot
rules
global warming
denouement
birthrate
context
adventure
code
far-flung
bread-winner exhilarating
expansion
venture
emissions
wipe out
morals
multiplicity
patriarch
unemployment
unmistakable
unknown

trend
judicious
likelihood
intolerable

3 Don't waste time counting every word of your answer. Work out
   how many words you write on average per line and then count
   the number of lines you have written. There are 24 lines per page
   on the exam question paper.

4 Now answer one of the Part 2 tasks on the opposite page. Allow
   yourself 35 minutes and then stop writing. Estimate how many
   words you have produced, check what you have written and
   make any improvements within the next 10 minutes.

EXAM ADVICE

Articles and letters
● Decide on an appropriate style and tone
  for your letter or article.
● Spend a few minutes thinking about the
  angle to take.
● Make a list of possible ideas.
● Order these ideas logically and to best
  effect.
● Note down relevant vocabulary and
  expressions.
● Include rhetorical questions to preface
  opinions.

General advice for Writing
● Spend time planning each question.
● Allow equal time for each question (up
  to 45 minutes).
● Calculate approximately how many
  words you produce.
● Leave time to check your answer for
  spelling and grammar.

Units 17–20 Revision

Use of English

1 For questions 1–8, read the text below and decide which answer (A, B, C or D) best fits each gap.

Laughter's geography

Wherever you go, you meet people who think that foreigners have either no sense of humour or at best, a **(1)** .... one. They are wrong. Humour is universal. But language is not, and neither are **(2)** .... of reference. Puns that **(3)** .... on Chinese pictograms and their homophones are hard to **(4)** .... in English. Punchlines that assume an intimate knowledge of Italian politics **(5)** .... few laughs outside Rome. The comedy that travels easily is often the most obvious: Mr Bean and Beavis and Butt-head. Domestic humour is subtler and, generally speaking, more revealing. Take this example from Africa:

A poor beggar is sitting by the side of the road. Suddenly the President's gleaming motorcade **(6)** .... past. **(7)** .... afterwards, a plump and ragged man runs sweating by, **(8)** .... an obviously stolen goat under his arm. A minute later, two policemen come rushing up in pursuit. 'Did you see a fat thief come this way?' they ask. 'Yes', replies the beggar, 'but you'll never catch him on foot.'

1 A crude	**B** raw	**C** rude	**D** clumsy
2 A frames	**B** structures	**C** figures	**D** shells
3 A take	**B** work	**C** impose	**D** play
4 A furnish	**B** render	**C** supply	**D** submit
5 A acquire	**B** raise	**C** bring	**D** make
6 A sweeps	**B** slides	**C** tiptoes	**D** flounces
7 A Promptly	**B** Instantly	**C** Shortly	**D** Closely
8 A clutching	**B** retaining	**C** clinging	**D** possessing

2 For questions 1–6, complete the second sentence so that it has a similar meaning to the first sentence, using the word given. **Do not change the word given.** You must use between **three** and **eight** words, including the word given.

1 You'll never sell your house if you let the rumours persist of it being haunted.
carry
You ....
if you want to sell your house.

2 It was kind of you to help us clean up, but it really wasn't necessary.
helped
You ....
the cleaning up.

3 It doesn't matter when he comes: I'm not bothered.
far
He can
....
concerned.

4 I asked the press to keep her name a secret so she would remain anonymous.
had
In order
....
keep her name a secret.

5 Eliza did better than usual at her debut performance, even though she had a sore throat.
excelled
Despite
.... at
her debut performance.

6 She is unlikely to accept anything except a full apology.
would
It is unlikely that anything
.... to
her.

3 For questions 1–8, read the text below and think of the word which best fits each space. Use only one word in each space.

A recent report, entitled *Surveillance: Citizens and the State*, says Britain leads the world in the use of CCTV, with an estimated 4 million cameras. The report warns that "pervasive and routine" electronic surveillance, together **(1)** .... the collection and processing of personal information, is almost taken **(2)** .... granted nowadays.

Despite many surveillance practices and data collection processes **(3)** .... unknown to most people, the expansion in **(4)** .... use represents "one of the most significant changes in the life of the nation since the end of the second world war". The report challenges the claim that CCTV cuts crime, and questions **(5)** .... local authorities should actually be allowed to use surveillance powers **(6)** .... all. In **(7)** .... view, privacy is an "essential prerequisite to the exercise of individual freedom" and the growing use of surveillance and data collection **(8)** .... to be regulated by executive and legislative restraint.

Vocabulary

4 For sentences a–j decide which word is correct.

 a The lock opened with a sharp *click/knock*.
 b I woke up to the *rumble/peal* of bells from the town clock.
 c The dog *growled/hissed* when it heard the garden gate open.
 d I think it was my sister's *trusting/tactful* manner that made her vulnerable to pushy sales people.
 e Todd gave a *naive/derisive* laugh when he found out who had won the election.
 f Becoming a government adviser has gone to Trina's *heart/head*.
 g My mother wouldn't allow any food in the house to go to *waste/rubbish*.
 h Please stop going off at a *tangent/path* – keep to the subject.
 i Thomas committed a *coup de grace/faux pas* when he told his grandmother what he'd been up to.
 j There was a bit of a *fracas/bête noire* last night outside the town hall.

Writing

5 Read this Part 2 letter, written to a magazine on the subject of the supernatural. Add about 100 words to complete the missing narrative, using suitable words and phrases from Unit 19.

Dear Sir

I read the article entitled *Inexplicable Events* in your magazine this month with great interest. As you have asked for anecdotal evidence from your readers, I am writing to share my own story with you.

Before I tell you my own experience, I should stress that, up until last January, I had not been in the least superstitious. Indeed, I have always been very sceptical about the whole area of the supernatural. What I am about to relate has changed my views for good!

I was driving home from a meeting one winter's afternoon and took a country road across the hills to avoid the motorway traffic. As the car snaked its way up the narrow road, the sky darkened around me and it felt quite spooky. I turned up the radio and sang along, in an attempt to raise my flagging spirits. Round the next bend, however, was a sight I never wish to witness again …

Can any of your readers explain my ordeal?

Yours faithfully

Jessica Langley

Grammar folder

Unit 1
Perfect tenses

The perfect tenses are used in English in a number of ways.

Present perfect simple tense

- when talking about events or situations that started in the past and are still true
  Amelia Kenton has lived in the same house all her life.

- when thinking about the present effects of something that happened in the past
  I've lost my purse so I need some money for the bus.

- when talking about a recent event or situation
  Jack has just phoned to wish you good luck.

- when referring to something that will happen at some time in the future
  As soon as I have settled in, come and stay!

Present perfect continuous tense

This can sometimes be used instead of the present perfect simple tense. So, in the first example above, you could also say *Amelia Kenton has been living in the same house all her life.*

Main uses of the present perfect continuous tense are:

- to stress the period of time involved
  I've been sitting at this computer all day!

- to refer to a situation that continues
  Membership numbers at this club have been falling year by year.

- to focus on the present effects of a recent event
  You can tell it's been raining – the seats are still damp.

- to refer to something that has recently stopped
  Have you been crying?

Note that stative verbs such as *be, know, seem* are not usually used in continuous tenses. For example, you would not say *I've been knowing Jim since he was 15*, but *I've known Jim since he was 15.*

Past perfect simple tense

This tense is generally used to clarify the timing of an event. It is used

- to refer to an event which took place before something else
  Sailing towards the harbour, I remembered how it had looked on my first visit, ten years earlier.
  Sometimes this involves using words like *already* or *just*.
  I had just stepped into the bath when the phone rang.

Past perfect continuous tense

This tense is used

- to stress the continuity of an event at an earlier point in time
  Their cat had been missing for over a week when a neighbour spotted it in the local park.

  See also information regarding stative verbs.

Future perfect simple tense

This tense is used

- to refer to events which have not yet happened but will definitely do so at a given time in the future
  By the end of September, I will have started that course in London.

Future perfect continuous tense

This tense is used

- to indicate duration at a specified time in the future
  Come next Saturday, we'll have been going out together for a whole year!

Other modal verbs

To express regret about the past, *should* or *ought to* is combined with a perfect tense form.
We should never have bought Alex that drum kit!

I'm sorry, I ought to have remembered that you can't eat strawberries.

Unit 2
Aspects of the future

There are many ways of expressing the future in English depending on meaning. We can use:

Will + infinitive

- to predict what is going to happen based on past experience or opinion
  You must go to India – you'll enjoy it.

- in more formal contexts for arrangements which have been made in some detail
  The tour will begin at 9.30 and all visitors to the site will need to wear good walking shoes.

- for decisions which are made on the spur of the moment
  I think I'll go to Paris next weekend.

Going to + infinitive

- to predict something that you have evidence for
  Look at those clouds – I'm sure it's going to rain.

- to express intentions or decisions
  I'm going to see the Museum of Modern Art when I get to New York.

Shall + infinitive

- to talk about the future instead of *will* with *I* and *we*, although it is used less nowadays than previously
  I shall certainly travel first class next time I go abroad.

- for offers
  Shall I carry your bags?

Present continuous

- to talk about activities or events which have already been arranged or are definite. The future continuous can also be used in this context. It is a little more formal.
  I'm travelling on the Orient Express to Venice.
  I'll be travelling on the Orient Express to Venice.

- to avoid *going to + go* we can use the present continuous form of *go* instead
  He's going climbing in the Alps next summer.

- for surprising or unexpected events
  Paula is taking her mother on her honeymoon!

Present simple

- to talk about future events such as a timetable or programme
  The train for Burnley leaves at 5.00 sharp every Friday evening.

- in temporal clauses after a time conjunction
  When you arrive in Beijing, go directly to the hotel and I'll meet you in the lobby.

Future continuous

- to talk about something that is going on at a particular time or over a particular period in the future
  The ship will be travelling at 20 knots as it cruises in the Caribbean.

- for something that has been arranged previously
  Luisa will be visiting us again in the fall.

- when you want to appear very polite
  Will you be needing anything to drink, Sir?

be + infinitive

- for official notices, newspaper reports, formal instructions and to give orders
  Passengers are to leave by the rear door of the aircraft.

Future perfect

- to say when something will be completed by
  I hope they will have finished the building work on the hotel before we go on holiday.

Future perfect continuous

- to emphasise how long something has been going on for by a particular point in the future
  The airline will have been carrying passengers for fifty years at the end of March.

Note that this tense isn't used with stative verbs, e.g. *see, believe, hear, know, become,* etc.

Expressions

- There are various expressions in English which are used to express future meaning. These include:

  to be about to
  to be on the verge/point of
  to be bound/certain/likely/unlikely to
  to be on the brink of

Unit 3
Conditional clauses

There are four main types of conditional clauses.

- **Zero conditional** – to express real situations
  If/When + present tense | present tense
  If I eat too much in the evening, I can't sleep at night.

- **First conditional** – to express real situations
  If + present tense | future tense *will*
  If you don't apologise, you'll regret it later.

- **Second conditional** – to express unreal situations
  If + past tense | *would/could/might*
  If I had some money, I would live somewhere warmer.
  If I were you, I'd go now before it rains.

- **Third conditional** – to express unreal situations
  If + past perfect | *would/could/might + have +* past participle
  If she hadn't had the chocolate chip ice cream, she would have been in a worse mood.

- **Mixed conditionals**
  If + past tense | *might/could/should/would* – for situations in the present which affect the past
  If I weren't so untidy, I wouldn't have lost your keys.
  If + past perfect | *would/might/could* + infinitive – for situations in the past which affect the present
  If I had moved to California, I would be much richer today.

Inversion and conditionals

Sentences with inversion are more formal than those with 'if'.

- **First conditional**
  This often expresses a tentative idea/request/offer, etc.
  If you should require more assistance, please telephone.
  Should you require more assistance, please telephone.

- **Second conditional**

  If you went out in this weather, you'd be thoroughly soaked.

  Were you to go out in this weather, you'd be thoroughly soaked.

- **Third conditional**

  If I had known there was going to be a storm, I would have stayed indoors.

  Had I known there was going to be a storm, I would have stayed indoors.

Other conditional clauses

- If + would | will: *If you would take a seat, the doctor will see you shortly.*
- If + will | will: *I'll clean the house, if you'll mow the lawn.*
- Other words and phrases can be used to introduce conditional clauses:

  Providing, provided that, as/so long as are similar to *if*. They are all emphatic forms emphasising a condition.

  Even if introduces an extreme condition.

  Well, it's true, even if you refuse to believe me.

  Unless can be replaced by *if ... not* or *providing ... not* but sometimes works better with **except when**.

  I won't give a waiter a tip except when / unless I get excellent service.

  Supposing should be used at the beginning of the sentence and is often not used as a linking word, but rather in the sentence setting up the condition.

  Supposing/suppose it rains tomorrow. What will we do?

  Given that is used when some fact is already known.

  Given that this area is liable to flood, it would be unwise in the extreme to consider buying a house here.

  But for and **without** are often used with third conditional sentences.

  But for his help, I would never have managed to survive the ferry crossing.

Unit 4

Talking about the past

There are a number of ways of talking about the past in English.

- To talk about completed actions, the past simple is used.
  Novak Djokovic won his first Grand Slam singles title in 2008, at the age of 20.
- To talk about events which occurred regularly or habitually in the past, *would* or *used to* can also be used.
  It was our little ritual. I would nod, she would smile and he would look longingly.

I used to go swimming four or five times a week.
Every spring, Grant visited his elderly aunts in Maine.

- To talk about something which continued to happen before and after a given event, the past continuous is used.
  While Kevin was away visiting friends in Italy, his flat was burgled.
- To talk about a temporary situation in the past, the past continuous is used.
  The two families were eating a meal together for the first time.

For information about the past perfect, see also the section on Perfect tenses on page 178.

Speculating about the past

- To express certainty or near-certainty about something in the past, the modal verb *must* is used with *have* and a past participle.
  Those early settlers must have had access to fresh water.
  You must have seen that Johnny Depp film at least five times!
- To express uncertainty about something in the past, the modal verbs *could, may, might* are used with *have* and a past participle.
  I suppose it could have been my mistake, though I labelled everything clearly.
  Experts are suggesting that the virus may have been carried long distances on the wind.
  We might have met at that party in 2010?
- To express impossibility about something in the past, the modal verbs *can't* or *couldn't* are used with *have* and a past participle.
  You can't have got to Leeds yet – it's a four-hour drive at least!
  James couldn't have played cricket last week as he was away.

Using the passive in the past

- The passive is formed with the verb *be* and a past participle.
  The telephone was invented by Alexander Graham Bell.
  Repairs were being made to the bridge at first light this morning.
  Fork-like implements have been used for over 2,000 years.
  Both sides had been advised to seek fresh legal representation before the trial.
- There are only two passive infinitives that are commonly used in English, the present and the perfect forms.
  This yoghurt needs to be eaten before the 25th.
  Radical cuts to the budget seem to have been made by the Managing Director.

Note that passive infinitives are often used after the verbs *appear, prove* and *seem*, as in the second example above.

Unit 5
Nouns

Nouns can be countable or uncountable.

- **Countable** nouns can:
  use *a/an* or *the* or *some*
  be used in the plural
  take the following determiners: *many, a large number of, several, a few, few, a lot of*

- **Uncountable nouns**:
  can use *the* or *some* or nothing
  are used only in a singular form
  can take the following determiners: *much, a great deal of, a large amount of, little, a little, a lot of*

- Common uncountable nouns include:
  most substances – *coal, china, flour*, etc.
  abstract nouns – *happiness, admiration, freedom*
  all sports
  most nouns ending in *-ing* – *shopping, sightseeing*
  accommodation, information, traffic, advice, luggage, luck, weather, work, homework, furniture, evidence

- Some nouns can be countable and uncountable with a slight change of meaning.
  She has grey hair. There are hairs on your jumper.
  The bridge is built of stone. I've got a stone in my shoe.

- Some nouns can be countable and uncountable but completely change their meaning.
  What's the capital of your country?
  The company has very little capital to work with.

- The majority of uncountable nouns can be made singular or plural by adding a *bit/piece* of or *bits/pieces* of. However, there are sometimes specific words which should be used instead.
  a lump of sugar
  a shaft of sunlight

- Some nouns with a singular form can be treated as singular or plural, depending on whether the noun is seen as a unit or a collection of people.
  The class is/are doing exams at present.
  The committee is/are looking into the matter of vandalism.

- Some nouns look plural but take a singular verb.
  The news is on at 8.00 pm.
  Athletics is an important part of the Olympics.

- Some nouns like *police* look singular but take a plural verb.
  The police are involved in trying to catch the thief.

Possessive forms

Possession can be signalled in English in three different ways – using an apostrophe, using *of* and using a noun as an adjective.

- For people and expressions concerning time and distance an apostrophe is generally used.
  my uncle's sister
  the boy's shoes
  a year's salary

- For objects *of* is generally used.
  the back of the room
  the cover of the book

- A noun is often used as an adjective to indicate kind, use or place.
  a table leg
  a night flight
  a shop window

Unit 6
Degrees of likelihood

- **Can** is used to express possibility without reference to past, present or future.
  He can sound off-key at times when he sings.

- **Could**, **may** and **might** express present possibility with reference to the future, present or past.
  It may/might/could be a good concert/ have been a good concert.

- **May not** and **might not** express possibility negatively.
  Get your ticket for the concert today; there may/might not be many left.
  He may/might not have bought the album you wanted.

- Deduction is expressed by **must be / must have been**, **will be / will have been** and **should be / should have been**.
  You must be tired after your performance.
  That'll be my guitar teacher; I heard him ring the door bell.
  She should have been able to sing at the concert, her sore throat was much better.

- Impossibility is expressed by **cannot/can't** and **could not**.
  It can't be a flute; it sounds more like a clarinet.
  You couldn't have seen the new film – it hasn't been released yet.

- **Could** and **might** can be used to imply criticism or irritation. Intonation is very important in carrying meaning with these modals.
  You might have told me you'd be coming late.
  You could practise a bit more.

- Various expressions can be used to express likelihood:
  it's a foregone conclusion
  the chances are
  there's every likelihood
  he's bound to
  there's a slim/faint chance
  it's doubtful

Unit 7
Participle clauses

Participle clauses give more information about someone or something. In many ways, their function in a sentence is similar to defining relative clauses.

The man dancing over there is my brother. (The man *who is dancing over there* is my brother.)

The painting sold at auction yesterday has already been shipped to New York. (The painting *that was sold at auction yesterday* has already been shipped to New York.)

- The position of the clause can affect meaning.
  Standing at the top of the hill, I could just see the village. (refers to the subject, 'I')
  I could just see the village standing at the top of the hill. (refers to the object, 'the village')

- **Having** + past participle refers to previous action.
  Having reached the top of the hill, I could just see the village.

- **Being** + past participle is used to express a passive.
  The report being published today will force local governments back to the drawing board.

- Past participle *-ed* clauses are used in a similar way.
  The images provided by the Hubble Space Telescope have given astronomers fresh insights.

Unit 8
Inversion

In the normal word order of a sentence, a subject is followed by a verb.
Madrid offers its visitors an excellent choice of restaurants and some wonderful bars too.

However, sometimes this word order is changed, or inverted. This is usually done to give emphasis within the sentence. For example, the sentence above could be rewritten as:
Not only does Madrid offer its visitors an excellent choice of restaurants, but there are also some wonderful bars.

- The broad negative adverbs **barely**, **hardly**, **rarely**, **scarcely**, **seldom** can be used like this.
  Barely were we into our costumes when it was time to go on stage.
  Seldom does a day go by without someone ringing up to complain about the product.

- **Never** and **nowhere** are used in a similar way.
  Never had I felt more relaxed than that first week on Corsica.
  Nowhere could we find fresh vegetables, and some dairy products were in short supply too.

- Other negative words and expressions like this are **little**, **no sooner**, **not**.
  Little did we realise what we were letting ourselves in for.
  No sooner had Phoebe arrived than she helped herself to a drink without asking.
  Not a single word of thanks did they hear from her.

- The fixed expression **Had it not been for …** is used to talk about the reasons for changed results.
  Had it not been for supportive friends and family, she could not have handled the constant intrusion of the media.

- Inversion also occurs at the end of sentences with **neither**, **nor** and **so**.
  Tim didn't feel like facing the press and neither did Lucy.
  Students haven't welcomed the new syllabus and nor have their teachers.
  Karl will be pleased to finish work and so will I.

- Sometimes a time clause precedes inversion.
  Not until two days later did we remember to call the school.
  Only once before have I felt like this about a project.

- Sometimes an adjunct of place precedes inversion.
  At the end of the path lay the meadows.
  In the distance stood the foothills of the Himalayas.

- Inversion occurs with certain prepositional phrases.
  On no account are you to leave this room!
  Under no circumstances can a replacement card be issued.
  In no way does that imply defeat.
  At no time did you give me an accurate picture of what was going on.

- Inversion can occur with **so** + an adjective.
  So loud was the music that we couldn't attempt to chat.
  So consistent has John's performance been that he has earned the nickname 'Strongman'.

- **Such** is used in a similar way to emphasise the extent of something.
  Such is the demand for tickets that they are selling at double their face value.

See also Unit 3 on page 179 for information about inversion in conditional clauses.

Unit 9
Gerunds and infinitives

Verb + object + *to*-infinitive
- Some verbs include an object before a *to*-infinitive: *consider, warn, allow, believe, encourage,* etc.
  I encouraged her to wear her school uniform.

- Some verbs don't require an object: *decide, refuse, hope, fail, agree, start,* etc.
  I decided to throw out all the clothes I hadn't worn for a year.

- Some verbs sometimes take an object and sometimes don't: *hate, help, like, love, want, prefer, need.*
  I like to swim every morning.
  I like you to swim so that you get some exercise.

Verb + (object) + bare infinitive
- Some verbs are followed by a bare infinitive after an object: *hear, feel, make, notice, see, watch, let,* etc.
  I made him shave his beard off.
  Her parents let her choose the shoes she wanted.

Verb + *to*-infinitive or *-ing*?
- Some verbs are followed by a *to*-infinitive: *agree, aim, ask, demand, prepare, hope, manage, wish,* etc.
  I agreed to wear the uniform.

- Some verbs are followed by *-ing*: *consider, avoid, envisage, miss, imagine,* etc. and all phrasal verbs.
  Liz couldn't imagine wearing an evening dress.

- Some verbs take either a *to*-infinitive or *-ing* with little or no change in meaning: *begin, start, cease, continue.*
  They began singing/to sing early in the programme.

- Some verbs take a *to*-infinitive or *-ing* but change their meaning: *go on, stop, try, remember, forget, regret, mean, come, hear,* etc.
  They came to accept her opinions. (gradual change)
  He came running into the room. (way of moving)
  He went on to talk about the dress code. (next topic)
  He went on talking even when everyone started yawning. (continue)
  I mean to wear jeans to the barbecue. (intend)
  It means buying a new pair of shoes. (involves)
  I regret to say that you are not properly attired. (present/future)
  I regret telling her that she looked scruffy. (past)
  I remember visiting the Costume Museum when I was young. (remember – second action)
  I remembered to post the parcel to her this morning. (remember – first action)

They stopped dancing when she came into the room. (ceased)
They stopped to have a cup of coffee halfway through the morning. (reason)
Try to stand up straight. (attempt)
If you can't get the car going, try ringing the garage. (experiment)
I heard Adele sing in London. (once)
I hear the birds singing every morning. (repeated action)

Verb + *-ing*
- Some verbs must have an object before an *-ing* when they are in the active: *catch, discover, observe, see, watch,* etc.
  I overheard them talking about the new manager.
  but
  They were overheard talking about the new manager.

- Some verbs don't have an object before *-ing*: *admit, advise, consider, deny, face, finish, suggest,* etc.
  I suggested going to the party early.

Unit 10
Expressing wishes and preferences

Wish and *if only*
- To talk about the present a past tense is used.
  I wish I could speak Spanish.

- To talk about the past a past perfect is used.
  If only they had listened to their teacher.

- To express irritation or criticism of something happening now *would* is used.
  I wish he would stop answering me in English when I want to practise French.

Note: *would* isn't used if the object and subject are the same.

- *If only* is perhaps slightly stronger than *I wish*.

Would rather / It's time, etc.
- are followed by a past tense to express a present idea with an object.
  It's time the government invested in language training.
  I'd rather you learned Spanish at school.

- are followed by an infinitive when making a general statement.
  It's time to leave.
  I'd rather learn Chinese than Russian.

Unit 11
Gradability

A gradable adjective can be combined with an adverb like *reasonably* or *extremely* to quantify that adjective. So, for example, you can be *fairly happy* or *very happy*. This cannot happen with an ungradable adjective, as the adjective itself already holds some notion of quantity or degree. These adjectives can be combined with adverbs like *absolutely* or *totally* to add emphasis.

We all feel slightly frustrated by the lack of communication on this project.

Charlotte was absolutely furious when she heard the decision.

adverbs	gradable adjectives
deeply	angry
extremely	cheerful
fairly	happy
immensely	hurt
rather	irritable
very	upset

adverbs	ungradable adjectives
absolutely	awful
completely	broken-hearted
entirely	impossible
totally	terrible
utterly	wonderful

- **Pretty** can be combined with both gradable and ungradable adjectives in informal English.
  Tom finds it pretty quiet around here in the evenings, so he often shoots off to town on his motorbike.
  It's pretty amazing that someone who was at death's door three months ago has just run the London marathon!

- **Really** can also be combined with both types of adjective, though with ungradable adjectives, the use can only be informal.
  For a really comfortable night's sleep, choose Maxton's mattresses every time.
  I've just had a really awful run-in with Duncan over his marketing plan.

- **Quite** can be combined with both gradable and ungradable adjectives, but there is a change of meaning.
  I'm quite busy at work at the moment, but I've known it much worse. (= fairly)
  You're quite impossible at times – sweet wrappers go in the bin not on the floor! (= completely)

Some adjectives can be both gradable and ungradable, and this is often accompanied by a change in meaning from literal to more figurative use.

Jake has been blind since an accident in childhood.
Our consumer society is fairly blind to the issue of poverty.

Unit 12
Passive structures

Formation

The passive is formed with the verb *be* and a past participle. For modals it is formed with the modal + *be* + past participle.

An unmanned submarine has been developed to automatically track down and follow whales and tuna, alarming many conservationists.

Miniature versions can now be produced at minimal cost.

This table shows the formation of all passive tenses. Those crossed through do not normally occur in English.

Simple present	*It is made.*
Present continuous	*It is being made.*
Present perfect	*It has been made.*
Present perfect continuous	~~*It has been being made.*~~
Simple past	*It was made.*
Past continuous	*It was being made.*
Past perfect	*It had been made.*
Past perfect continuous	~~*It had been being made.*~~
Future	*It will be made.*
Future continuous	~~*It will be being made.*~~
Future perfect	*It will have been made.*
Future perfect continuous	~~*It will have been being made.*~~

Use

The choice of active or passive voice often defines the focus of the sentence. Compare:

Massive waves destroyed the harbour wall. (Active voice, the focus is on the waves and what they did.)

The harbour wall was destroyed by massive waves. (Passive voice, the focus is on the harbour wall and what happened to it.)

In the second sentence, the waves are the agent. The agent is typically introduced with the preposition *by*.

The passive is used without an agent:

- when the action is more important than the person doing it
  It's going to be quite some time before car body panels are cast from titanium.

- when the person or thing that performed the action is not known
  In separate incidents across the city, shop windows were smashed and goods taken.
  The oily stain had been hidden from view until now.

The passive voice can be used to produce an official or impersonal tone.

Visitors must be accompanied by a member of staff at all times.
Each solution was heated to boiling point prior to lab analysis.

Unit 13
Reported speech

- As reported speech is used to tell someone else of what happened, all pronouns change, almost all verb tenses, except second and third conditionals and past perfects, change and all words referring to a particular time or place change.
  'I saw this film two weeks ago.'
  → *She said she had seen that film two weeks before.*

- Some changes are not quite so straightforward. *Must* changes to *had to* and *mustn't* becomes *was not to* for obligation. If *must* is used to talk about laws or general truths then it doesn't change.
  'I must buy a new bicycle.'
  → *She said she had to buy a new bicycle.*

  'You mustn't tell my mother.'
  → *She said I was not to tell her mother.*

  'You must not go more than 40 kph.'
  → *He said you mustn't go more than 40 kph.*

- With the first conditional, the verb tenses in the *If* clause backshift in the usual way and *will* changes to *would* in the main clause.
  'If you don't hurry up, you'll miss your flight.'
  → *She said that if we didn't hurry up, we would miss our flight.*

- As a general rule, the second conditional doesn't change.
  'He would be pleased if you visited him.'
  → *She said he would be pleased if she visited him.*

- Often a verb or a verb and adverb are used which contain many of the elements of what is being reported.
  'What about picking up the litter?' she said.
  → *She suggested picking up the litter.*

  'Goodness! Look at that rubbish tip!' he said.
  → *He exclaimed in horror when he saw the rubbish tip.*

  'I had absolutely nothing to do with it,' he said.
  → *He categorically denied having anything to do with it.*

Unit 14
Articles

- Plural, abstract and uncountable nouns do not need an article if they are used to talk about things in general. To limit these nouns a definite article is required.
  Sport is good for you.
  The sport played the most is football.

- Singular, concrete nouns require an article, except for some idioms. The definite article is precise and refers to something, while the indefinite article is vague and more general, or is used when something is mentioned for the first time.
  The runner in first place came from Kenya.
  Steve is going to be a runner in the New York marathon.

- No article is used with: certain countries; names of mountains; meals, unless they are formal ones; *bed, school, hospital, prison* if they are being used for their intended purpose.
  I intend to visit Australia.
  She's in prison for stealing.
  Come down for breakfast!

- The definite article is used with: rivers, seas, oceans, chains of mountains, gulfs and bays; newspapers; before musical instruments; before a superlative adjective; when we know there is only one of something.
  Tessa plays the violin.
  I read The Times.
  The Sierra Nevada is a beautiful mountain range.
  The sky is very blue.

- The indefinite article is used when we mean 'one' of something unless we want to emphasise the amount.
  I'd like a cup of coffee.
  Just one cup, not two.

Unit 15
Purpose and reason clauses

- A purpose clause normally comes after a main clause.
  I keep my mobile switched off when I'm working, so as not to be distracted.

- Purpose clauses are introduced by the following conjunctions:
  for fear that (formal)
  lest (formal)
  in order to
  in order not to
  so as to
  so as not to
  so that

- A reason clause can come before or after the main clause.
  As it was late, Jenny went straight to bed.
  I'd shut the window in case it rains.

- Reason clauses are introduced by:
  as
  because
  in case
  since

Unit 16
Concessive clauses

These are used to give contrasting information to that given in the rest of the sentence. A concessive clause can come before or after the main clause.

Although Moravia had more than thirty books published in his lifetime, his first novel is undoubtedly the best.

Shakespeare remains on the syllabus, even though many British teenagers find his plays inaccessible.

- Concessive clauses are introduced by the following conjunctions:
  although
  despite
  even if
  even though
  in spite of
  much as
  though
  whereas
  while

- *Much as* and *whereas* are less commonly used and occur mainly in formal written English.

- With *though* and *although*, it is possible to omit the verb in the concessive clause.
  Although (we were) exhausted, we stayed up to watch the end of the film.

- *Despite* and *in spite of* cannot be followed by a verb, but take a gerund or noun.
  Despite running all the way to the station, we missed the train.
  In spite of the weather, we had a good time.

- It is possible to add *the fact that* to these conjunctions and then include a verb.
  Despite the fact that Jess had very little money, her trip to Lisbon was a great success.

Unit 17
Comparison

There are various ways of making comparisons in English.

- Using a comparative or superlative adjective
  I'm happier now than I've ever been.
  That is the most outrageous suggestion you've made today!

- Using the structure *not as ... as*
  Holly is not as fast on the tennis court as she used to be.
  Note that the variant *not so ... as* is less common nowadays.

- Other related expressions are *nowhere near as ... as, not nearly as ... as* and *nothing like as ... as.*
  The new sports commentator is nowhere near as good as John Motson.
  This album is not nearly as good as their last one.

- Including an adverb of degree gives added emphasis. The nouns *a bit, a good deal, a great deal, a little, a lot* are also used in this way.
  You're by far the cleverest person in this class, you know.
  Sally is a great deal younger than her brother.

- Using a sentence with two comparatives shows that as one thing changes, another thing also changes:
  The sooner we get home, the happier I'll be.
  The more you practise the violin, the easier it will become.

Unit 18
Modals review

Here are further examples of the many different functions of modal verbs. See also Unit 3 Conditional clauses and Unit 6 Degrees of likelihood.

Strong obligation
All passengers must observe the no smoking policy on board.

You'll have to wait in line like everyone else, I'm afraid.

I had to walk to school when I was young.

Weak obligation
I ought to save a bit more money each month.

You really should try to keep on top of your homework.

Unfulfilled obligation (past)
George should have gone to visit his parents more often than he did.

We ought to have done more to this house.

Prohibition
Students must not bring any personal belongings into the examination room.

I don't care what you say, you can't stay out later than midnight.

No necessity
We don't need to buy the cinema tickets in advance.

You needn't have bothered to come and see me off at the station.

Speculation
Could it have been the right answer after all?

There might be some money in it for you.

Deduction

That must be the turning just beyond the garage.
It must have been Mike's girlfriend you met.

Ability

I can get by on my forehand, but I can't play a backhand shot to save my life.
Everyone in the class could understand sign language perfectly.

Impossibility

Andrew can't play squash tonight.
There couldn't have been a power failure – the computer's still on.

Advice

You should cut down on chocolate if you want to lose weight.
Jerry really ought to see a doctor about his back problem.

Permission

You can have a break now.
You may leave if you wish. (formal)

Unit 19
Word order and adverbs

There are three normal positions for adverbs:

- at the beginning of a sentence – **Last night** *I saw a ghost.*
- in the mid-position – *I have* **never** *had a paranormal experience.*
- at the end – *She left work* **in a hurry**.

It is important to remember that there are exceptions to the following general rules regarding the position of adverbs, usually depending on what the speaker is emphasising or sees as most important. Note that some types of adverb can go in more than one position.

Initial position adverbs

- Connecting adverbs – *However, Then*
- Adverbs of time – *Last night, Tomorrow*
- Some adverbs of frequency – *Usually, Once a year, Occasionally*
- Some adverbs of certainty – *Maybe, Perhaps, Naturally*
- Negative adverbials with inversion – *Seldom, Rarely*
  Seldom have I seen him so angry.
- Adverbs of manner, for emphasis – *carefully, terribly, easily*
  Carefully he placed the slide under the microscope.

Mid-position adverbs

The rule here is that these go before a main verb, between an auxiliary and main verb and after the verb *to be*.

- Adverbs of certainty – *definitely, certainly*
  He will definitely win the cup.
- Adverbs of indefinite frequency – *often, seldom, rarely, never, usually, occasionally*
  She often loses her keys.
- Adverbs of manner – *quickly, slowly, carefully*
  He quickly dived into the water.
- Adverbs of completeness – *almost, partly, nearly*
  I have nearly finished the washing.
- Adverbs of degree – *completely, quite*
  She was quite convinced that she was right.
- Focus adverbs – *just, even*
  He didn't even apologise for forgetting my birthday.
  They just appeared out of nowhere.

End position adverbs

- Adverbs of manner – *quickly, slowly, carefully*
  She crossed the lane slowly. He dived into the water quickly.
- Adverbs of place
  She walked into the park.
- Adverbs of time – *last night, tomorrow, yesterday*
  We saw her only last week.
- Adverbs of definite frequency – *yearly, every hour*
  I go to the gym twice a week.

If there is more than one end position adverb in a sentence or clause, the general rule is to put them in the following order: manner – place – time, though this order can vary for reasons of emphasis.

We were walking peacefully along the beach yesterday, when we got a terrible fright.
She walked hurriedly out of the room.
She ran out of the room in a frenzy.
I met him for the first time at a concert last week.

Any position adverbs

- Comment adverbs – *personally, in theory, foolishly, in my opinion, undoubtedly*
  Personally, I'm very annoyed with him.
  I'm personally very annoyed with him.
  I'm very annoyed with him, personally.
- *Sometimes*
  I'm sometimes late with work.
  Sometimes I'm late with work.
  I'm late with work sometimes.

hard/hardly, etc.

In some cases there is a difference in the meaning of an adverb which sometimes uses *-ly* and sometimes doesn't. Adverbs that change meanings include: *hard, direct, short, wide, late, free, wrong, right.*

I saw the UFO high over the mountains.
He thinks highly of the research done on Aboriginal beliefs.

Unit 20

Uses of *have, get* and *go*

- We use the structure of *have* + object + past participle when we talk about other people doing things for us, for example *I have my hair cut every three weeks.*

- Another use of *have* + object + participle is of 'experience', for example *I had my car stolen last night.* This is something that happened to me. I didn't organise it. The following are similar examples.
  It's good to have the birds singing in the morning now it's spring.
  I had a dog follow me home yesterday.

- *Have* + object + infinitive or *-ing* form is also quite common.
  I won't have you coming home late every night!
  Have Mrs Jones sit down and wait please.
  The teacher had us all running round the field in the rain.

- Look at the following uses of *get* + object + participle.
  I got the car repaired. – This is a more informal way of saying *I had the car repaired. She got herself lost on the underground.* – It was her own fault.
  I'll get the washing done if you do the ironing. – This implies I'll do it myself.
  I'll never get this done by tomorrow. – I'll never be able to finish it.

Revision crosswords

These crosswords include some of the idioms, phrasal verbs and other vocabulary you have learned so far in the units. The number of letters required is given in brackets.

Units 1–4

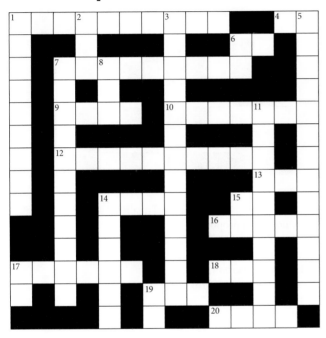

ACROSS

1 do what is expected of you (3,3,4)
4 (and 8, 2 down) .... easy as .... , ... , three (2,3,3)
6 see 19 across
7 cannot go wrong (9)
9 take .... a business (phrasal verb) (4)
10 verb related to 'prevalent' (7)
12 uncertain of a successful outcome (5,3,2)
13 not tell the truth (3)
14 .... chalk and cheese (4)
15 have no objection .... something (2)
16 see 17 down
17 (and 6 down) instead of (2,4,2)
18 see 19 across
19 (and 18, 6 across) manage to avoid (3,3,2)
20 see 19 down

DOWN

1 find with some effort (phrasal verb) (5,4)
2 see 4 across
3 impossible to get another (13)
5 tell a secret (5,3,5)
6 see 17 across
7 pay (4,3,4)
8 see 4 across
11 sorry (10)
14 (and 15 down) be as good as expected (phrasal verb) (4,2,2)
15 see 14 down
17 (and 16 across) fashionable (2,5)
19 (and 20 across) return or retreat (phrasal verb) (2,4)

Units 5–8

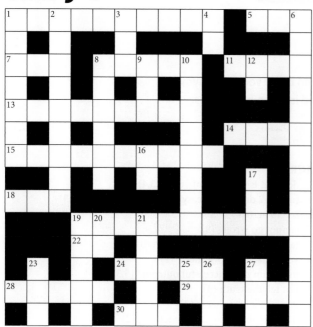

ACROSS

1 ostentatious, stylish (often used of clothes) (10)
5 a .... hate (3)
7 .... close to call; .... hot to handle (3)
8 very bad weather: the eye of the .... (5)
11 very cheap: going for a .... (4)
13 not as good as believed to be (9)
14 a grain of .... (4)
15 someone who can't stop making purchases (10)
18 having respect for: in .... of (3)
19 briefly (2,1,8)
22 on .... account (2)
24 inflexible (5)
28 see 19 down
29 origin (6)
30 (and 3 down) leave (phrasal verb) (3,3)

DOWN

1 moronic, stupid (7)
2 certain to happen: .... conclusion (1,8)
3 see 30 across (3)
4 compare: liken .... (2)
6 little time to complete tasks or projects (5,9)
8 a .... of abuse (6)
9 (and 16 down) .... the blue (3,2)
10 (and 23 down) stay up late working: burn the .... (8,3)
12 a stroke .... luck (2)
16 see 9 down
17 turn a blind .... to someone's faults (3)
19 (and 28 across) morally justified (2,3,5)
20 under ...... circumstances (2)
21 a loud or unpleasant sound (5)
23 see 10 down
25 the grass ...... always greener (2)
26 promptly: on the ...... (3)
27 leave someone high and .... (3)

Units 9–12

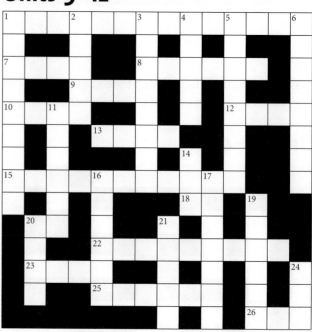

ACROSS

1 able to recognise things of good quality (14)
7 say no: .... a proposal (4)
8 a .... of hair, thread, DNA, etc. (6)
9 ready money (4)
10 danger; also verb (4)
12 calm .... (phrasal verb) (4)
13 spick and .... (4)
15 not sleep properly (4,3,4)
18 Thanks! (informal) (2)
20 bit .... bit; minute .... minute (2)
22 not definite (9)
23 between two states: on the .... (4)
25 puzzle, such as a crossword: brain .... (6)
26 eat humble .... (3)

DOWN

1 variety (used especially of species) (9)
2 see 24 down
3 didn't catch exactly what was said (8)
4 standard ways of behaving in society (5)
5 make a piece of writing less offensive (phrasal verb) (4,4)
6 enormous (8)
11 sentimental; also used of weather conditions (6)
14 see 21 down
16 rather rude or short with someone (6)
17 ecstasy or extreme joy – a literary word (7)
19 deliberately incite an emotion (phrasal verb) (4,2)
20 see 24 down
21 (and 14 down) .... a solution; extract (phrasal verb) (5,3)
24 (and 2, 20 down) return to the past: turn .... (3,5,4)

Units 13–16

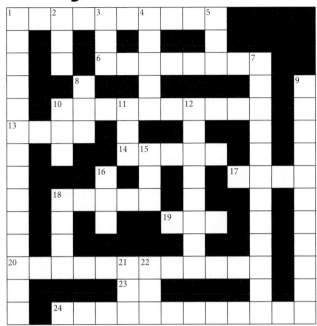

Units 17–20

ACROSS

1 gripping; urgent (10)
6 regular; with a beat (8)
10 describes heavy traffic (4,2,4)
13 successor (starts with a silent letter) (4)
14 fast .... ; .... record (5)
17 close down: .... up shop (4)
18 desire; want very much (5)
19 the .... of the problem (3)
20 forgetful (6-6)
23 exclamation (2)
24 become unable to deal with things (4,4,4)

DOWN

1 opt for something unsuitable, in desperation (6,2,6)
2 large and unruly crowd (3)
3 deal with things as they happen : play it by .... (3)
4 blame: .... someone's door (3,2)
5 good to chew (3)
7 ignore: give someone the .... (4,8)
8 neither… .... (3)
9 huge advance or improvement (7,4)
10 zero; the big 'O' (3)
11 .... your heart out! (3)
12 quiet or monosyllabic (8)
15 (and 21, 16 down) regret (a literary phrase) (3,3,3)
16 see 15 down
18 losses or reductions (4)
21 see 15 down
22 polite modal verb (3)

ACROSS

1 something to think about (4,3,7)
6 supporting a cause or ideal passionately (7)
7 an advantage or benefit; the opposite of 'minus' (4)
9 keep body and .... together (4)
10 see 29 down
12 be on cloud .... (4)
13 fate; what will happen (7)
14 mistake: a .... in the argument: (4)
15 good at noticing or realising things (10)
19 word used in similes (2)
22 scornful (12)
27 noise made by a contented cat (4)
28 have a debt (3)
30 cause to happen; also noun: pull the .... (7)
31 call a .... a .... (5)
32 the very last clue: the .... (3)

DOWN

1 not have as much money as you used to (4,3,5)
2 verb used to describe the movement of mud, oil, etc. (4)
3 noisy quarrel or fight: originally a French word (6)
4 make a sound like a snake; also noun (4)
5 naïve (8)
7 play on words: noun and verb (3)
8 take legal action for damages (3)
11 clenched hand (4)
13 Never .... my door again! (6)
16 on time; without delay (6)
17 set the wheels .... motion (2)
18 see 29 down
20 cunning; astute (6)
21 a .... of joy; also verb: increase suddenly (5)
23 dull sound; also verb (4)
24 unadulterated, not mixed with anything (4)
25 prefix meaning 'three' (3)
26 a ...... loser (4)
29 (and 10 across, 18 down) It's your decision: It's ....
   (2,2,3)

Answers and recording scripts

The following pages contain all the answers to the exercises, sample answers for the writing tasks, the recording scripts, and lots of additional notes, including useful background information on the texts and topics. The *Map of Objective Proficiency Student's Book* on pages 3–5 gives full details of the language and exam skills covered in each unit. The *Content of the Proficiency Examination* on pages 6–7 provides information about the exam, with links to the relevant Exam folder, Writing folder or Unit.

Unit 1

1.1 pages 8–9

Speaking

1   The two idioms are *a change for the better* and *a change of heart*. *Ring the changes*, the unit title, is also an idiom. Note that you can also say *a change for the worse*.

> **Possible answers**
> When my family moved to a new house, it was definitely a change for the better. That is also the earliest change I can remember. I had my own large bedroom for the first time, instead of having to share with my sister, and there was a much bigger garden too.
> When I left home and went to university, I moved to the opposite side of the country, which was very different from where I had grown up.
> I used to have a stressful job in investment banking, but two months ago I resigned and went off travelling. This new experience made me think seriously about my future and when I came back, I decided to retrain as a teacher.
> I found some old letters the other day, which I had kept for more than twenty years – but I had a sudden change of heart and burnt the lot!

Idiom spot

Idioms are an important area of vocabulary at Proficiency level. Try to record new ones you come across in a vocabulary notebook, and use them in your writing. However, use them sparingly! Too many idioms in a text will sound unnatural.

> 1 b   2 a   3 b   4 b

Listening

2   The underlined parts of the recording script confirm the answers. The phrasal verbs are highlighted.

> 1   gaining media attention
> 2   stepping in for someone
> 3   heading the wrong way
> 4   being made redundant
> 5   meeting 'Mr Right'

Recording script 1 02

Speaker 1: I've had a really fantastic year. It all started last November, when I was dragged along to a party by a friend. I was in a terrible mood, I remember, and nearly didn't go. Anyway, I was wearing an outfit I'd made myself – in soft black leather and antique lace, quite an unusual combination! Kelly Johns, the presenter of a big daytime TV show, was there and my little number caught her eye. We got chatting and she asked whether I could come up with something original for her to wear on the show. I jumped at the opportunity. That was a real turning point for me and I was soon able to quit my day job and concentrate on the clothes side full time. Through Kelly's show, I've had lots of orders. I've just finished an exclusive range for a top designer and I've even taken on an assistant to help me. Just think if I'd stayed at home that night!

Speaker 2: People often ask me how I got to be where I am today, with sell-out concerts in big stadiums around the world, thinking that I've spent years playing in local clubs, but the truth is, I'm literally an overnight sensation! I don't mean that arrogantly. It was just one lucky break, all down to being in the right place at the right time. There I was, an absolute nobody, hanging around backstage with Arrowhead, when their lead guitarist tripped over a pile of speakers and broke his arm, five minutes before they were due on. I'd been telling them about my awesome guitar style, so naturally, they all turned to me and said 'Kid, help us out here …' and I did. The place was packed and I can still feel my hands shaking as I played that very first solo. It went OK though, and the rest is … history.

Speaker 3: I was in Milan visiting friends, trying to cheer myself up after a dismal few months – my long-term boyfriend and I had broken up, plus I'd left a job without another to go to. My money was running out and I was planning to leave a few days later. Anyway, my friends suggested that I should take a look at Verona before going back home and told me what time train I could get from Milan. Well, for some reason, I ended up on a slow train going south, without realising my mistake – both trains had left at the same time. I fell asleep in the compartment and woke just as the train arrived in Bologna! I had a wander round and fell in love with the place, and knew it was where I wanted to be. Everything just fell into place – I found a teaching job, took a room in a beautiful flat and settled in immediately. I lived there for six years and I go back regularly.

Speaker 4: It's funny how you can hit a run of bad luck: one moment, things are moving along quite normally in your life and then, bam, something comes out of the blue and knocks you sideways and then, wham, something else. I'm OK now, but I've had a difficult couple of years. My problem was quite simply that I'd been living beyond my means for a long time and some debts finally caught up with me. Even then, I thought I'd be OK; I arranged to pay them off little by little from my salary, monthly, you know. But then, the place where I was working cut back on its workforce, and they let me go. Well, that was it, I suppose I panicked, I wasn't thinking straight, you know. So I just packed a bag, got on a coach and left town for London, where my life went downhill fast. I got in with a bad crowd, and one thing led to another. It's a miracle my brother ever tracked me down, but he's got me back and sorted, with a roof over my head and a new job on the cards.

Speaker 5: It could be a story in *True Romance*, but it really happened just like this. Almost twenty years ago to the day, I was waiting for a bus after another mind-numbingly awful day at work, no bus in sight, of course. I was in a rut, my job was going nowhere. Anyway, there I was, staring gloomily at my reflection in a puddle, feeling utterly sorry for myself and thinking: is this really all there is to life? Then I saw two things in that puddle, one imperceptibly after the other. The first was no surprise, huge splashes of rain, as the heavens opened yet again, but then, this enormous red umbrella, appearing behind my head as if by magic! A gorgeous gravelly voice to my left said did I mind, it was big enough for two and he didn't want my hair to get wet. Very fortunately, it was another fifteen minutes before the bus finally turned up and hooray, it didn't stop raining! His name was Terence, though he's been Terry to me ever since – and Dad to our three wonderful children.

Vocabulary: Phrasal verbs

4 Keep a list of new phrasal verbs in a vocabulary notebook. You can record them by main verb, by particle or by topic.

Be careful with word order when using phrasal verbs. The verb and particle cannot be separated:

- when it is a three-part phrasal verb
  I caught up with Jack further down the road.
- if the phrasal verb is used intransitively (without an object)
  All my hard work paid off.
- when the particle is a preposition
  Sally jumped at the chance of visiting Rome.

---

break up (Speaker 3)
catch up with (Speaker 4)
cheer sb up (Speaker 3)
come up with (Speaker 1)
cut back on (Speaker 4)
end up (Speaker 3)
get in with (Speaker 4)
hang around (Speaker 2)
help out (Speaker 2)
jump at (Speaker 1)
pay off (debts) (Speaker 4)
run out (Speaker 3)
settle in (Speaker 3)
take on (staff) (Speaker 1)
track (somebody) down (Speaker 4)
turn up (Speaker 5)

5
a was / had been paid off
b tracked (me) down
c jumped at
d cut back on; were / have been taken on
e broke up
f getting in with
g turned up
h help (me) out

6 This Part of Reading and Use of English tests different aspects of vocabulary, including phrasal verbs (see questions 4 and 8).

1 A   2 D   3 C   4 B   5 A   6 B   7 C   8 D

1.2 pages 10–11

Grammar clinic

1 Think about areas of grammar that remain problematic for you. This lesson concentrates on perfect tenses.

Yellow = Perfect tenses
Blue = Passive forms
Pink = Relative clauses
Green = Reported speech

2 Refer to the Grammar folder on pages 178–188 if you are unsure of a point covered in any unit. Even at Proficiency level, you need to spend time studying grammar and you should check your written work for grammatical accuracy. Here is a checklist of things to watch out for:

- subject–verb agreement
- choice of modal verb
- tense in conditional structures
- choice of past/present/future tense
- choice of preposition
- punctuation in relative clauses
- structure with reporting verbs, e.g. *insist on doing, urge someone to*

Corpus spot

These sentences were written by past *Cambridge English: Proficiency* candidates and show typical errors with perfect tenses at this level.

a went to **b** has been used **c** had never seen **d** were measured **e** I've been practising, (I've been) trying / I've tried **f** you have bought **g** they had got married **h** people care

3

a *has gone* = he is still there
went = he is no longer there
b *has been suffering* = ongoing situation, i.e. unemployment is still high
was suffering = continuous situation at unspecified time in the past
c *were given* = one specific instance in the past
have been given = task is ongoing
d *have been dealing* = continuous action that is not yet completed
have dealt = action completed, i.e. problem successfully handled
e No difference in meaning
f *I've thought* = focus is on the result, implies that a decision has been taken
I've been thinking = focus is on the activity, implies that person is still thinking
g *could have done* = past speculation
will have done = future forecast, e.g. 'I'm writing up our annual report – is there anything else we will have done (by the end of the year)?'
h No difference in meaning, though the future perfect continuous tense is more common, as 'living here' is continuous and ongoing.

4

Possible answers
a I've been learning English for ten years.
b I've never done a course in deep-sea diving, though I would really like to.
c One particular street in the centre has been closed to private cars, which has made traffic in other parts of the town much worse.
d My quality of life would be improved by the purchase of a dishwasher because then I wouldn't have to wash everything up by hand.
e I may have moved to another city for work.

5

1 have been continually transformed
2 being improved / improving / having improved / having been improved
3 was further stimulated / was stimulated further
4 would have been able to
5 even have thought / have even thought
6 be being used constantly / constantly be being used
7 have embraced / be embracing
8 have been depleted / be depleted

1.3 pages 12–13

Reading into Writing: Summarising ideas

1 The pictures on the left show the same location in New Orleans during and after Hurricane Katrina in 2005 and the ones on the right show school children working in an IT suite and school children using tablets in a class.

Background information

Hurricane Katrina is the costliest natural disaster to take place in the USA to date. New Orleans suffered huge devastation and most of its major roads were damaged. A 2007 report found design flaws in its flood protection levees.

Suggested answers
The pictures on the left show a natural disaster that has caused a change in the environment. The road is flooded in one picture and people are using small boats to get around, so they may have lost their homes. In the other picture, things are back to normal although the road is still wet so the weather conditions must be bad. Other environmental changes include the effects of global warming – flooding again, or dry river valleys – and the results of deforestation, although that could also come under the commercial category?
The pictures on the right show technological change, in the space of only a few years I suspect? The children in the computer room are working with clunky big machines, whereas the kids using tablets are working in their normal classroom. There are countless other recent technological changes in the world around us, for example wind turbines and solar panels for generating electricity would not have been prevalent twenty years ago.

Vocabulary: Word formation

Using the *English Vocabulary Profile* you can run an advanced search for words containing individual prefixes and suffixes at each level of the Common European framework. The Word family panels within *English Vocabulary Profile* entries also indicate the level at which members of a word family are likely to be known – anything in italics is probably restricted to learners at C1 and C2 level. Visit www.englishprofile.org to sign up to the resource.

2

commerce – ial (drop the 'e' and add 'ial')
technology – ical (drop the 'y' and add 'ical')
create – ive (drop the 'e' and add 'ive')
vary – iable (change 'y' to 'i' and add 'able')
Examples of *-ous*: ambitious, luxurious, monotonous, nutritious, rebellious, suspicious
Examples of *-ful*: doubtful, eventful, fruitful, pitiful, resourceful, thoughtful
Examples of *-less*: countless, faultless, helpless, priceless, tactless, tasteless

3

a predictable   b alternative   c hopeful   d philosophical
e experimental   f speechless   g noticeable   h flawless
i disposable   j disastrous
Adjectives formed from four remaining words: adventurous, identifiable, massive, understandable

4   Underlining important information is an important first step in planning a summary, as it shows which ideas must be included.

Extract 3
Rather than burgers and fries being a <u>product</u> of the <u>social changes</u> seen over the <u>last fifty years in America</u>, the author suggests that <u>fast food brands</u> were to a large extent <u>responsible for these changes</u>, as they profoundly <u>affected both lifestyle and diet</u>.
Extract 4
<u>Tiny holes</u> found <u>in human teeth</u> estimated to be <u>over 8,000 years old</u> are now believed to be the <u>earliest evidence of dentistry</u>, for when these holes were examined with an electron microscope, researchers found their <u>sides were too perfectly rounded</u> to be caused by bacteria and have therefore proposed that they were <u>drilled by prehistoric dentists</u>.

1   The sentence summarises the general idea that people pick up on things through facial features, but it omits any reference to health and social status, which means it is less clear than the original text.

2   The word *judge* could be replaced with *assess* or *evaluate*.

3   The underlined words in text 2 that could be replaced are: *produced* (developed, concocted, made); *chance* (accident); *revolutionised* (changed, updated, modernised); *innovations* (new techniques/inventions); *significantly* (notably, importantly). A word like *mauve* or *aspirin* cannot be paraphrased, as it is something very specific.

5

c   is the best choice, as it captures all the important information, uses new words not in the text where possible, is written in a suitably neutral register and is concise (13 words).
Comments on the other sentences:
a   Omits reference to Perkin and does not highlight the fact that aspirin was the most significant innovation.
b   Unduly informal, with use of phrasal verbs; quite wordy.
d   Unnecessary reformulation of *mauve* leads to lack of clarity and wordiness; other words are lifted from the text, e.g. *revolutionary*, *innovation*; too long a sentence.
e   Wrong focus of information (aspirin); incomplete.
f   Good attempt at reformulating, but lacks precision due to omission of *mauve*; register slightly too informal – better if sentence started 'Commercially' rather than 'Commercially-speaking'.

6

Suggested answers
3   According to the author, fast food has caused social change recently, by influencing how Americans live and changing their diet. (20 words)
4   Research has uncovered evidence of prehistoric dentistry, as minute, round holes in 8,000-year-old teeth cannot have been caused by bacteria. (20 words)

Exam folder 1 pages 14–15

Reading and Use of English, Part 3 Word formation

Affixes

1   This exercise gives practice in the range of different affixes that are commonly tested. You should take particular care to note plural forms.

a extracurricular   b beneficial   c opinionated
d kingdom   e compulsive   f apparent   g innovators
h constraints   i consumption   j Domesticity
k strengthened   l misfortune   m irreplaceable
n disapproval   o occupants

Compounds

2   Compounds are often tested at this level. More than one answer is possible for some of the examples.

framework; update/upturn; outfall/outbreak; windfall/
windbreak/windproof; rainfall/rainproof; creditworthy;
downfall/downturn

3 The photos are of:
  • a young woman with tattoos and piercings
  • a man with traditional designs on his body and face

1 antiquity 2 dominant 3 customising/izing 4 kinship
5 apparently 6 underline 7 Arguably 8 infinitely

Unit 2

2.1 pages 16–17

Speaking

1 The photos are of:
  • a campsite
  • an expensive hotel
  • Barbados – Bottom Bay
  • Machu Picchu

Background information

Barbados is an island in the Caribbean.

Machu Picchu is a 15th-century Inca site located in a
mountainous region in Peru, South America. It is often referred
to as the 'Lost City of the Incas'.

Possible answers
Beach scene: be able to chill out; end up spending a
fortune; be in the lap of luxury
Machu Picchu: possibly have to rough it; get by on a
shoestring budget; enjoy being a culture vulture; get back
to nature
Campsite: get off the beaten track; possibly have to rough it;
get by on a shoestring budget; get back to nature
Expensive hotel: end up spending a fortune; be in the lap
of luxury

Reading

2 Read through the Exam spot. For more advice look at the
   Exam folder on pages 64–65.

The writer thinks that holidays away from home are
overrated and that thinking about them is probably better
than actually going on one.

3 Do the example question and read the guidance that
   goes with it. Then read the questions and try to find the
   paragraphs that contain the information. Underline the
   word or phrase that contains the information.

1 B 2 D 3 B 4 C 5 A 6 D 7 B 8 A

Vocabulary: Collocations with *traveller*

4 Use an English–English dictionary to help you. Decide
   which of the two options collocates with *traveller/
   travellers*.

a frequent b independent c Seasoned d intrepid
e weary f discerning g an armchair h inveterate
i unwary

5

Possible answers
I don't totally agree with the writer. I really enjoy my
holidays and I think you can get more out of meeting
people and being immersed in a different culture, than
from just reading a book. I do understand what he means
though, especially, when I've arrived at a resort, only to
find that the hotel is a building site.

2.2 pages 18–19

Aspects of the future

1 Refer to the Grammar folder on pages 178–179 if you are
   unsure about which tense is used to express a particular
   aspect.

Possible answers
a To talk about arranged plans for this evening; things
   you have already organised or booked, e.g. a cinema or
   theatre visit or friends for dinner.
b To talk about plans which are not organised and maybe
   are just ideas or spur of the moment plans. These
   could include plans which might change depending on
   circumstances, e.g. If it rains, I'll watch TV instead of
   playing tennis.
c To talk about your intentions this evening; something
   which you are thinking of doing but haven't quite got
   around to booking/planning in detail.
d Usually used to talk about a specific time in the future,
   e.g. What will you be doing at 8.00 this evening? I'll be
   washing my hair.
e To talk about what will have happened by a certain
   time in the future. You are looking into the future and
   saying 'this will have happened', e.g. I will have finished
   all my homework by 10 tonight.
f To talk about plans which have been abandoned for
   one reason or another, e.g. I was going to play tennis
   tonight, but now I have to stay in to babysit my little
   sister.

2

a he's going to get b will be c leaves d is going to get
e I'll go f I'm not going g will you be doing h will have
travelled i is not allowing j will do k will have been
painting l will have finished m he'll feel n will you do
o is p am having q arrive r will be arriving s Shall

3

Possible answers
a I'm going to clean my car tomorrow.
b It's going to rain.
c It will rain next week.
d I'm having salmon and salad for dinner tonight.
e My government will have found a solution to pollution by the year 2050.
f I'll be a doctor in 10 years' time. / I'm going to be a doctor in 10 years' time. Note that you can't say *I'll be being a doctor in 10 years' time.*
g The flight to Singapore leaves at 6.00 on Fridays.

4 *To be bound to* expresses a strong feeling of certainty. It is often tested at Proficiency level.

Possible answers
a I expect that we will be able to travel to the USA in less than a couple of hours and to the other side of the world in a maximum of four hours. Travel within a country will be very rapid, which will mean that you will be able to live quite a distance away from your work.
b I am unlikely to have become a millionaire by the middle of the century, but I hope I will be reasonably comfortable. I am bound to have been to university and trained to become a doctor. I am also likely to have married and had three children.
c I think you can expect to have a good time in my town. There's quite a bit to see and there are many cafés and restaurants to have a coffee or a snack in. The people will be quite friendly, especially if the sun is shining. There's a good bus service and lots of taxis but they are quite expensive. In the afternoon, you'll be able to walk alongside the river or even go out on a boat.

5

Possible answers
Lack of rain will leave Africa on the verge/brink of a disaster.
I'm about to go to bed.
Some animals are on the verge/brink of extinction.
The country is on the brink of revolution.
She was on the verge of leaving home when she received the news.
I am about to leave home to get the bus.
I'm about to get married.
Scientists are on the brink/verge of a scientific breakthrough.

Vocabulary: Prepositional phrases

6

These are paraphrases of the prepositional phrases:

in the region of – about
on the brink of – to say when something good or bad is about to happen
to some extent – partly
in conjunction with – together with
on behalf of – instead of
in vain – without success
on the verge of – to say when something good or bad is about to happen
on the grounds (that) – because
with the exception of – not including

a on the grounds   **b** on behalf of   **c** to some extent
d on the verge of   **e** on the brink of   **f** in the region of
g in vain   **h** in conjunction with   **i** with the exception of

Have no ...

7 You should learn the construction *have no* + noun as it is often used and frequently appears in key word transformations.
a I have no interest in going somewhere like Las Vegas. ...
b I have no regrets about spending too much money on my last holiday. ...
c I have no recollection/memory of childhood holidays. ...
d I would have no hesitation in booking a cruise. ...
e I have no alternative/choice/option but to stay at home this year rather than go away. ...
f I have no intention of ever going to Disneyland. ...
g I have no time to look at lots of travel brochures. ...

2.3 pages 20–21
Listening and Speaking

1

The subject of the listening extracts is expectation.

Try to work out what the words in italics mean from the context they are in. The words are in the extracts you will hear and it is helpful to know what they mean before you listen.

Suggested answers
a annoy me   **b** overexcited   **c** pay   **d** large   **e** limited
f be unrestrained / go unchecked   **g** determined to
h similar to

2

Answers
Extract One B   **Extract Two** C   **Extract Three** B

Recording script 1 03
Extract One
There was a mad excitement about standing in front of a world map and tracing a circumnavigation with my fingertip. Everything seemed possible and my family's nagging doubts really got my goat. I'd say you can't really go *wrong* when choosing the stops on a round-the-world trip, but I found that some routes worked out better than others. You need a good variety of destinations. You might love the beach, but a trip that stops in California, Australia and

Thailand, all for the sun and sand, does get a bit repetitive. At the same time, I didn't want to get carried away trying to see the whole world.

Next, I knew I would have to fork out a pretty hefty sum for the plane ticket as I didn't intend to be thumbing lifts. My budget was tight so I had to play around with my route to get the best value for money. I also had to research my destinations to see what the average daily costs would be and figure out a budget (adding a good 10 or 20 per cent buffer to be on the safe side). I decided to spend longer in cheaper countries and have a relatively short stay in more expensive places, which was sometimes quite a difficult decision as there were so many things I wanted to see. In fact, planning the trip was just as much fun as the actual travelling. I really let my imagination run wild and the trip itself was everything I'd expected.

Extract Two

I really hope to make it as an entrepreneur and I guess the person who's influenced me most has been a well-known British businessman. I was given a copy of his autobiography for my fourteenth birthday and it really made a huge impression on me. He had an amazing childhood. Apparently, when he was just four years old his mother stopped the car a few kilometres from their house and made him find his own way home. Then when he was eleven or twelve his mum decided that he should cycle seventy kilometres to another town to teach him the importance of stamina and to learn a sense of direction! He said he felt great when he'd done it but his mum wasn't worried or relieved or anything – just acted calm as you like and told him to go and help someone in the village chop some logs. His family seemed to thrive on challenges – physical ones rather than educational, which I think's quite unusual. I know my family are dead set on my getting a degree but quite a few entrepreneurs start out without one and look at them!

Anyway, there was another occasion he mentions when his aunt had promised him some money if he learnt to swim. He spent a holiday trying desperately, but just couldn't do it. Then, on the way home in the car, he spotted a river. He made his father stop the car and just dived into the river in his underpants. The river was quite fast-flowing and it seemed like he was going to drown, but then he pushed really hard and actually managed to swim. My childhood was nothing like that, but I guess what I read has made me realise I need to take on challenges and try to fulfil my hopes and aspirations.

Extract Three

According to the latest survey, commissioned by one of our leading banks, over three-quarters of 12- to 19-year-olds said they kept track of their money, up from twelve months ago. Half of young people said they were content that they had enough money, something only 46 per cent said a year

earlier, while the amount that those who were unhappy said they would need to be happy has fallen. However, the 9,000 young people questioned continued to have unrealistic salary expectations. The average teenager said they thought they would be earning double what is actually the current average salary for a 35-year-old. Not only this, but nearly three-quarters of those interviewed thought they would have a car by the time they were 21, while more than half hoped to own their own home by the age of 25. Overall, the bank calculates that the average expectation gap between where people thought they would be financially, and where they would actually be, was around £72,133, a small drop compared with last year's figure. Interestingly, although the figures differ somewhat, the findings are very much in line with previous surveys done over the past twenty years.

Phrase spot

Many nouns for parts of the body also have a related verb, as in the example *thumb*. Sometimes the verb takes on a figurative or idiomatic meaning. Use an English–English dictionary to help you match the verbs with the words or phrases.

> **1** f   **2** e/c   **3** b   **4** a   **5** c   **6** d
> **a** shoulder the burden   **b** foot the bill   **c** faced the music
> **d** toed the line   **e** stomach/face the idea   **f** elbowed people aside

3   Try to use some of the phrases in the Exam spot in your answer.

Possible answers
a   On the whole, I don't have a great deal of opportunity to get away for a while from my desk. At my level in the company, I get very little holiday. However, given the chance and the choice, I'd go to Tahiti.
b   Speaking personally, a round-the-world trip would be incredibly stimulating – just think of all the cultures and landscapes you would be able to sample.
c   My main objective in life is to join the police force and become a super sleuth, a detective like my hero Sherlock Holmes. I think the salary is now much higher than it used to be and people generally have more respect for the police in my country than for many other professions.
d   Given the problems that abound with recession, in my view your best chance is to get as well qualified as you possibly can.
e   It's my belief I'm not cut out to become an entrepreneur but I admire people who are. They seem to have some sort of inner drive which pushes them on to obtain their objectives.
f   Personally, I guess my main priority would be to make sure they were safe and happy, but also that they were able to mix socially with people from different backgrounds.

Pronunciation

4

Possible answers

a	way	How much do you weigh, now you've been on your diet?
b	pairs	I love pears, but I can't stand apples.
c	meet	Meat and two veg is still the standard English meal in some parts of the country.
d	heir	The air is wonderfully clear in Majorca.
e	aisle	I have never visited the Isle of Skye in Scotland.
f	principal	Some people put their principles before common sense.
g	Grate	The new band that played last night were really great.
h	mane	We took what looked like the main road through the town, but still got lost.
i	plaice	This place is great for real Spanish tapas.

Writing folder 1 pages 22–23

Part 1 Essay

The compulsory task in Writing, Part 1 involves reading two short texts in order to summarise and evaluate the ideas they contain. *Objective Proficiency* develops the language and skills needed for this task in the Reading into Writing lessons, which occur in alternate Student's Book units. In this Writing folder, there is specific advice on how to answer Part 1.

1

> The texts contain opposing points of view with regard to the use of technology: Text 1 sees this as an appropriate way of widening the audience, while Text 2 suggests that it undermines a museum's primary role, that of educating its visitors.

2   In the exam, there will be four main points covered across the two texts. If you underline the key ideas in the texts, this will help you to plan your answer. The relevant parts of the texts are given below and in the next column.

Text 1
b '... museums have become more community-orientated ...'; '... museum curators have looked to modern technology to breathe more life into exhibits, ...'
e 'Over the last decade in particular, ... the majority seek to be inclusive rather than elitist, reaching out to everyone.'

Text 2
c 'The dumbing down of exhibitions is widespread – in short, the medium has become more important than the message'; 'Learning is all too often compromised by technological wizardry, which may impress on a superficial level but essentially trivialises, and provides a content-lite "experience"'.
f 'The purpose of a museum is to stimulate learning and broaden the horizons of its visitors, yet many museums nowadays appear to neglect this responsibility ...'; 'Whether this is in response to government cuts or merely reflects a trend among museum directors, it is undoubtedly a change for the worse.'

3   Try to vary the beginning of sentences to demonstrate your language knowledge and remember to use your own words where possible – if you copy words and phrases from the texts, you may be penalised in the exam. You can include occasional quotes from a text but make sure this is limited to a short phrase.

Suggested answers
Text 1
b The first text suggests that the policy of introducing new technology into museum displays has been of benefit to visitors because it is more meaningful and 'hands-on'.
e The writer is of the opinion that in the last ten years in particular, museums have tried to engage a broader cross-section of the public.

Text 2
c The second text raises the issue of 'dumbing down', claiming that insufficient content is conveyed in 'modern' museums, due to the implementation of these creative effects.
f Additionally, it is argued that many museums are ignoring their original function, to educate and inform, which the writer sees as regrettable.

4

> All four points from the texts are summarised.
> Only the points in Text 1 are evaluated.
> The writer has copied a considerable amount of input from Text 2 rather than using their own words.
> The writer has not included any of their own ideas.

5   Think of how you could represent the ideas in the second text in your own words. Use a dictionary if necessary.

Suggested answer
Many museum curators seem to have forgotten that their institutions exist in order to promote the transfer of knowledge and the writer sees the introduction of new technology as a bad thing, because the actual subject matter has become subservient to the method of delivery.

6 In the exam, it will not matter if you go a little beyond the upper word limit – it is much more important to bring your piece of writing to a suitable close. However, you should not exceed 300 words on the Part 1 task – if an answer is substantially longer than this, it is likely to include some repetition or irrelevance.

Suggested answer
These texts present different reactions to what museums are offering in the 21st century. To my mind, their curators have acted appropriately in embracing the new technology at their disposal. The current reality where I live is that many more people are going to museums than before and the majority of them benefit from this experience. Any transfer of knowledge is a positive outcome and museums definitely contribute to a better-educated society. (72 words)

Note on assessment

The Cambridge English Language Assessment C2 assessment criteria that are used for *Cambridge English: Proficiency* operate across five bands of performance and there are four distinct assessment scales. These are Content, Communicative Achievement, Organisation and Language. Further information about the marking of Writing with sample answers and examiner comments can be found in the *Cambridge English: Proficiency* Handbook, downloadable from the Cambridge English Language Assessment website.

Unit 3

3.1 pages 24–25

Speaking

1   The photograph is of a sunset to show 'red sky at night'.

Possible answer
I think the one about *red sky at night, shepherd's delight* is true. I've often noticed that if there is a red sky at night the weather the following day is good. It's something to do with the refraction of ice crystals in the atmosphere I think.

Listening

2   Read through the questions carefully before you listen. A rain goose is a type of bird. Play the recording twice – first to get an idea of what it is about and secondly to write your answers. The underlined parts of the recording script confirm the answers.

| a T | b F | c F | d T | e F | f T | g F | h T | i T | j T |

Recording script 1 04

Sue: Good morning. Now, the huge growth of interest in environmental issues has led to a careful re-examination of all kinds of traditional lore. With me today, I have Peter Watkins. He's written a best-selling book *The History of Weather Folklore*, which explains country sayings and the role of animals and birds in forecasting the weather. Sayings my granny used to come out with, like *Birds flying low, expect rain and a blow*, which I've always felt rather sceptical about.

Peter: Well, Sue, the way in which animals and birds can apparently predict changes in the weather before we can has always fascinated people and, for that matter, still does. If it didn't, the sayings wouldn't still be in current use, and of course, nowadays the weather is anxiously studied because of climate change.

Sue: But is there any truth in these old sayings? Given that there are so many, apparently 500 at the last count, and they've been around a while, presumably they should be fairly accurate?

Peter: Mm, well generally, there's a better chance of their being right for short-term weather forecasting rather than long-term. Of course, the most interesting natural weather forecasters are the birds, which is why there are so many sayings relating to them. Birds depend on the right weather conditions for flying and, in particular, birds that fly very high, like swifts and swallows, stand very little chance of survival if they get caught in a bad storm. They are also insect feeders and when the weather is fine the insects are high and the birds will follow them. Insects have good reason to dive for cover if rain is imminent as they are covered with water-repellent hairs. It actually doesn't take much for them to get completely soaked, so they respond quite rapidly if there's a drop in temperature or a rise in humidity.

Sue: Oh, so there's an element of truth in that one. Now, I used to live off the coast of Scotland and they had a saying on the islands about a bird called the red-throated diver. They used to call this bird the rain goose, and the saying went pretty much like this: *If the rain goose flies to the hill, you can put your boat where you will, but if she flies to the sea, you must draw your boat and flee.* I must say that I used to be rather puzzled by this saying, as I didn't understand why it would fly out to sea when the weather was getting worse. Anyway, one time when I was out in a boat the wind started to get up. We tuned into the radio and it said a gale was due from the north. We saw the geese everywhere flying around and heading out to sea. Despite common sense telling you otherwise, the saying of the local people seemed to be true.

Peter: Yes, and we still don't know the reasons for its strange behaviour. But you know, not all weather lore is about misery. Some birds can predict when things are about to brighten up. Certain geese set off for their breeding grounds in Iceland when the weather is fine – you just have to wait and watch and then plan your harvesting or house painting!

Sue: Not very practical! However, if there is some truth behind these weather sayings, do they ever have any practical use?

Peter: Obviously, weather lore had a very important application in the farmer's world. Farming and weather are intrinsically linked and the ability to predict, or at least think you could predict, was very important to them, <u>although of course, they weren't the only ones with a vested interest in weather forecasting</u>. One of the things about human beings is that we do not like to feel that things are happening with no purpose whatsoever. Weather lore makes a connection between something that is happening and something that is going to happen – <u>we need to feel we're not simply the victims of chance and circumstance</u>. Although it's very difficult to put dates on these sayings, many of them probably go back thousands of years. Some of them work and some of them don't, and some of them don't even make sense. Many actually negate each other.

Sue: <u>Quite</u>. So, how reliable are sayings which predict the year ahead, if we can't even rely on ones predicting the weather the next day?

Peter: Mm, well, I find it very difficult to believe that you can tell the rest of the winter from the way birds are flying or how your cat behaves in the autumn. By putting our own interpretations on how nature works we can get it completely wrong. For our ancestors the weather was a life and death situation – not just an inconvenience – and I think that had they had anything more reliable, they wouldn't have had to base their predictions on this kind of thing. <u>They were really clutching at straws when they observed animal and bird behaviour and linked it to the weather</u>, but they really had no other choice.

Sue: My thanks to Peter Watkins. Next week we'll …

Phrase spot

These were the phrases that needed correcting: time and again; fame and fortune; flesh and blood; touch and go; life and soul
a thick and thin   **b** fame and fortune   **c** touch and go
d First and foremost   **e** Time and again   **f** give and take
g life and soul   **h** flesh and blood   **i** high and dry   **j** black and white

Vocabulary: Modifiers

3 *Quite, fairly* and *rather* are often confused. Check in the Grammar folder on page 184 if you need more help.

Read the note about gradable and ungradable adjectives before you listen to the recording.

> **1** a   **2** b   **3** a   **4** b   **5** a

Recording script 1 05

1 You're quite wrong in what you say about her!
2 It's quite a nice dress, but I can't make up my mind whether to buy it or not.
3 Quite!
4 She's quite happy in her new house, but she does still miss her friends.
5 This cake is quite delicious.

4

> **Possible answer**
> I'm fairly certain that 'Early to bed, early to rise, makes a man healthy, wealthy and wise' – and women too, of course. Going to bed early would mean that you would avoid the temptations of late-night clubbing and so would be able to get up fresh and keen to get on with the day's business. The harder you work, the more you earn and therefore you would end up healthier and wealthier.

5 The article is about animal behaviour and how it may be possible to use it to predict major earthquakes.

You are given the answers here, but in the examination you have to think of them yourself.

6

> **1** far   **2** date   **3** given   **4** turn   **5** make   **6** put
> **7** whatever   **8** as

3.2 pages 26–27
Review of conditional clauses

1

> **Possible answer**
> I'm not sure that the personality of people in a country is influenced by the type of weather they have. They say the British are reserved because it's so cold and rainy, but there are many British people who are quite jolly! Again, not all Latin types are easy-going and lazy. People from hot countries work equally hard and I'm sure worry just as much about life as people from cold countries. I don't agree with reinforcing stereotypes.

2 The sentences are all conditional.

Suggested answers
a there are 50% more traffic accidents and 20% more industrial injuries.
b the air will make you feel invigorated.
c the number of murders would rise.
d if there hadn't been a Santa Ana blowing.
e you leave Switzerland during a Föhn.
f I would go to California if I wanted to murder my husband.

3 You should be able to explain what kind of conditional sentence each is. They are all examples of basic forms. Check in the Grammar folder on pages 179–180 if you have any problems with this.

a Zero conditional used for general truths.
b First conditional used when something is possible.
c Second conditional used to talk about something that is unreal and is improbable.
d Third conditional to talk about something impossible.
e Zero conditional to talk about a general truth.
f Second conditional to talk about something which is unreal or improbable.

Corpus spot

Making the verb following *unless* negative – should be *unless he succumbs to …* .

If someone treats these two things equally, he can easily succeed in both, unless he succumbs/if he does not succumb to the temptation of laziness.

4 This exercise gives examples of other forms of conditional sentences.

a inverted first conditional to express tentative statements = *If you should happen to …*
b polite use of *would* = first conditional
c parallel conditional – first conditional = *I'll do something if you do something.*
d disguised conditional – *as long as* = *if*
e inverted third conditional = *If I had known about the weather conditions …*
f disguised first conditional – *provided that* = *if*
g mixed conditional – second + third using *now* to show past effect on present
h inverted second conditional to express tentative statements = *If the Prime Minister were to announce …*
i zero conditional with *unless* = *if not*

5 This exercise is also an awareness exercise to check that you realise that other words and phrases are possible in a conditional sentence besides *if*.

a Given that   b Unless   c As long as / Provided that
d But for / Without   e Even if   f on condition that
g Suppose / Supposing

6 Many of the forms used here, especially the inversions, are quite formal.

Suggested answers
a Should you see her, could you tell her my address? OR Should you happen to see her, could you tell her my address?
b Given that people were dependent on farming for their livelihood, it's not surprising that they used animal behaviour to predict the weather.
c Provided that you take care of it, you can borrow my bike.
d If you'd (like to) take a seat, I'm sure Mr Johnson won't be long.
e If I were you, I'd get another job.
f If I had worked harder to pass my diploma, I would be earning more money now.
g But for my grandmother leaving me some money, I wouldn't have been able to afford to go to university.
h Were climatic changes to occur / Were there to be climatic changes, weather lore would be rendered obsolete.

Speaking

7

Possible answers
a I'll book into a hotel.
b I'll just have to do it!
c I'll ring up my service provider.
d I'll grab my things and rush out.
e I'd have a year-long holiday.
f I'd report it to the police.
g I'd try to keep a low profile.
h I'd just take off wherever I felt like it.
i I would / I'd have been delighted and studied hard to make the most of it.
j I would / I'd have tried to get into one of the Ivy League universities.
k I would / I'd have done my best to make money.

3.3 pages 28–29
Reading into Writing: Reformulation 1

1

Possible answer
The thing that makes me cross the most is when computers keep crashing. As I work from home, I really need my computer and any little problem with it makes me go beserk!

2

a rage, fury   b dread, terror   c bliss, delight   d sorrow, dejection   e incredulity, astonishment   f tedium, apathy

3

1 **A** in a magazine or newspaper (style, language, vocabulary – not specialised, neutral register)
2 On the surface there seems to be no reason for it.
3 **inward:** feeling annoyed/tense/anxious; raised blood pressure
outward: sweating; averting gaze; hiding; making yourself immobile; hair-pulling; foot-tapping; getting red in the face; leaving

Vocabulary: Word formation

4 Refer to the Exam spot. Students often find it difficult to find different ways of saying the same thing. Here you are introduced to the use of negative prefixes. You will gain marks if you can show you can manipulate language, either to make a sentence shorter or to show you can paraphrase a sentence.

a unpredictable **b** undeniable **c** unconscious
d insignificant **e** irreplaceable **f** inexhaustible
g unassertive / non-assertive **h** inconclusive

5

Suggested answer
Human beings are often quite unconscious of reacting to an invasion of their personal space with anger.
OR
Human beings are often quite unconscious that their reaction to an invasion of their personal space is anger.

Exam folder 2 pages 30–31

Reading and Use of English, Part 2
Open cloze

You will need to write your answers in CAPITAL LETTERS on your answer sheet in the examination.

Read through the information and Exam advice before you attempt question 1.

1 The photos are of Henri Cartier-Bresson.

Read through the text very carefully before you fill in the spaces.

1 would/should/could **2** wherever **3** which **4** itself
5 did **6** nothing/little **7** by **8** rate

Reading and Use of English, Part 4
Key word transformations

2 Read through the information and the Exam advice before you attempt the questions. Remember that only between three and eight words are required. A contraction counts as two words. Don't forget to use the key word.

1 was put in jeopardy / was put at risk
2 friendship with Paula dates back
3 (any) responsibility for breaking / having broken
4 has finally come to terms with
5 no expectation of/for an upturn
6 were given / had no choice/alternative/option but to

Unit 4

4.1 pages 32–33

1 The pictures show:
- a Japanese Tea Ceremony
- a bride and groom cutting their tiered wedding cake.

Another example of ritual behaviour in eating and drinking is making a toast at an official dinner, where everyone raises a glass and drinks to something or someone.

2 The underlined parts of the recording script confirm the answers.

Before the meal: phone calls to relations, preparation of lots of food
On the day itself: eating, praising the food, criticism of family members, family disputes, more general arguments about politics, coffee, senior member leaves, end of event

Recording script 1 06

Unlike many modern families, mine still holds to the tradition of large family meals at times of celebration or crisis. I use the word 'large' of both the group and the amount of food on offer. The pattern is always the same: endless phone calls weeks ahead of the occasion to mobilise distant cousins and elderly aunts; on the eve of the event, the preparation of excessive amounts of food by the host family member, which never fails to be stress-inducing for all concerned; and then, on the day itself, we slip into our well-established roles, devouring all that is set before us and expressing the joy and contentment that convention demands. Once the wine has started to flow, the praise of succulent dishes gives way to another, more sinister part of the ritual: snide comments on family members not present, the surfacing of ancient grudges and petty family rivalries. This in turn leads to the more general but equally predictable debates on politics and the world at large.

Manners always prevent us from actual bodily assault, but the verbal gloves are certainly off at this late stage in the proceedings. As the insults start to fly, the host hurries away to prepare coffee, hunting out chocolates and jugs of ice-cold water, in a valiant attempt to restore calm. Ritual behaviour dictates that all hostilities cease at this point and so, finally, peace prevails. After his second cup of coffee, handing down a final blessing to the assembled group, the most senior member takes his leave, signalling that it is time for others to do the same. Another memorable family occasion draws to a close.

Possible answer

In Melbourne last Christmas, I was invited to Christmas lunch with my brother-in-law's Armenian family by marriage. There were over thirty people present, ranging from young children to grandparents. We started off in the garden, eating appetisers and toasting everyone's good health – including the health of the entire Liverpool football team. Eventually we all went inside and sat down together, at the longest table I have ever seen! There were so many succulent things to eat, including huge trays of sliced roast lamb and pork, different types of potato dishes, vegetarian salads and roasted vegetables. The meal was a leisurely affair, punctuated every so often by fresh supplies of warm bread. A tempting selection of desserts was then wheeled out and we were allowed to help ourselves and adjourn once more to the garden, where the sun was shining. Later still we came inside again, for the children to be given their presents. It was a truly splendid day.

Reading

3   The narrator, Triton, is Mister Salgado's cook.

Background information

Romesh Gunesekera has been favourably compared to Chekhov and Graham Greene. Much of his writing portrays the dilemma of living in Sri Lanka during the long period of civil war (1983–2009), where violence and political unrest were a part of daily life. *Reef*, his first novel, was shortlisted for the Booker prize in 1994 and won the Italian Premio Mondello in 1997. His other books include *Monkfish Moon*, a set of short stories, and other novels, *The Sandglass* and *The Match*.

4

1 B	2 C	3 A	4 D	5 A	6 C

Detailed explanation:

1   The answer, B, can be found in the sentence *He was concerned to make sure there was plenty of time to prepare, even though he acted so nonchalant.* A is ruled out because the narrator says *it had never happened before in his life.* C is wrong as Mr Salgado did give his cook advance warning. D is plausible though the first paragraph shows that Triton has plenty of culinary experience.

2   The answer, C, is supported by the references Triton makes to Miss Nili's manner of eating in the second half of the first paragraph: *she ate like a horse, so hungry-looking* and *I expected her to bulge out as she ate ... .* A, though plausible, is not stated in the text. B is falsely suggested by the words *I don't know where she put it.* As with A, Triton does not pass judgement on Miss Nili, so D is ruled out.

3   The answer, A, is rooted in the whole paragraph that begins *Triton made it*, where Triton talks of his 'coming of age'. B is wrong, as it was *the one phrase Mister Salgado would say ... again and again.* C is ruled out by Miss Nili's words in the next paragraph, where she says that Triton *makes a lovely cake.* D is not suggested by the text, apart from Triton's general comment on *the petrified morass of all our lives*, which is beyond the scope of the tea party.

4   The answer, D, lies in the words *I rode in it like a prince.* A is wrong, as although Triton implies that the taxi is slow, *a black tortoise*, there is no suggestion that he is annoyed by this. B is not suggested by the text and it would be inappropriate for Triton, a servant, to have such feelings. C is wrong, as it is Miss Nili who is helped into the taxi by Mister Salgado.

5   The penultimate paragraph (the one before the final paragraph) shows that Triton feels positive about life when his work goes well: *Suddenly everything becomes possible and the whole world ... pulls together*, so the answer is A. B is the opposite of Triton's view, for he *felt stupid* to need the praise. C is not suggested by the text; in fact Triton appears to prefer being the sole owner of the kitchen. D is not suggested by the paragraph.

6   The answer, C, is rooted in the sentence *It was as if he couldn't believe his eyes, seeing Nili sitting there in front of him.* A is wrong, as, although Mister Salgado drank lots of tea, he ate nothing. There is no evidence in the paragraph for B, as it was Nili who *would murmur her approval.* D, though plausible in view of Mister Salgado's nervousness before her arrival, is not suggested in the paragraph and Triton is the one who orchestrates the delivery of each part of the meal, with the exception of Mister Salgado's words *No, bring the cake now.*

Style extra

Using similes sparingly in your own writing will demonstrate your range. Another useful device is to replace a standard colour adjective with a noun phrase – for example, instead of 'brown', you could say *coffee-coloured* or *the colour of mud*. You can also supplement the adjective with a noun, to give a more vivid description – for example *mint green, ice blue*.

> The animals associated with Miss Nili are:
> a horse *she ate like a horse*
> a snake *like a snake swallowing a bird … one leg coiled under her*
> a cow *She made a lowing sound between bites.*
> The effect is to accentuate her appetite and unconventional behaviour.
> By referring to the taxi as having a *butter-coloured* top, the author brings his own writing to life and also skilfully reminds us that Triton the narrator is also Triton the cook, who sees life through his cooking (see the answer 5A in the multiple-choice questions above).

Vocabulary: Collocations

5 The *Cambridge English Corpus* is a large collection of texts held electronically. The texts come from novels and non-fiction books, journalism, academic writing, everyday speech and other forms of written and spoken English. These examples of 'savour' and the examples in the exercise 6 answers below have been chosen from the corpus to show typically modern uses.

> *savour the aftertaste* – enjoy the sensation of flavour left in her mouth
> The noun collocates are: *success, freedom, memories, past, word, wine*

6

> **Possible answers**
> a consume + equivalent, quantity, time
> *A typical teenager consumes a staggering quantity of commercial media online.*
> b devour + books, news
> *People in Redwood City, California, eagerly devoured news of the jury's decision.*
> c relish + challenge, thought
> *Montoya relishes the high expectations and says he loves pressure.*
> d swallow + pill, pride, news
> There has been less retail activity over the last two weeks, perhaps as people swallow news of job cuts and a worsening economic outlook.

4.2 pages 34–35
Review of past tenses

1 The picture shows a selection of old and new forks. The top fork is the oldest and is around 500 years old. Some plastic 'sporks' are shown at the end of the text.

> **Possible answers**
> People would certainly have been using some form of knife to cut up meat and other foodstuffs 2,000 years ago – not metal knives of course, but some kind of sharp cutting implement. People could have been using basic forks, too, though metal ones must be a more recent phenomenon, probably only dating back a thousand years or so. The ancient Egyptians used spoons made of ivory, wood and other materials.
> The design of the spork is very clever, as it gives you a spoon, a fork and a serrated 'knife' all in the one implement. Produced in bright colours, it looks very attractive too – just the thing for a picnic or camping trip.

2

> **Suggested answer**
> Appearance: three longer prongs became four shorter ones in the nineteenth century.
> Use: 'shared' forks became less common in the nineteenth century; one-handed eating in the nineteenth century gave way to holding the fork in the left hand and the knife in the right, introduced by the English towards the end of the nineteenth century.

3 Read the section in the Grammar folder on page 180 if you are unsure about these tenses.

> a past perfect (*the knife was put down once the food had been cut up*)
> b used to; would (*used to use special spoons; people would more often share forks with others*)
> c modal verbs (*as well they might have done; scooping with them must have been impossible*)
> d present perfect (*have been used for over 2,000 years*)
> e *is thought* **to have been used** (past passive infinitive)
> f **was being carved** at table (past continuous passive)
> **were satirised** / these **were** now **shortened** … / the fork **was then used** / the knife **was kept** (simple past passives)
> g **had been making** forks (past perfect continuous); **were** successfully **introducing** (past continuous); *as we* **have been doing** ever since (present perfect continuous)
> h spread (spread); strove (strive); done (do); bore (bear); seen (see); sought (seek).

4 A *tine* is the technical term for the prong of a fork.

> **a** tools **b** list **c** female-like behaviour: used to show disapproval **d** picking up **e** fussy or ultra-careful **f** sin **g** still / without moving **h** spread (widely) **i** changing **j** fashionable

5

a was thought; had mastered
b have carved; was carried out
c have always insisted; should be torn; arose; is/was dressed; may/might/can/could react
d had murdered; was given; ate; drank
e continued; had started / had been starting
f have been supported; have been chosen

6

Suggested answers
1 a an orphan baby lamb b an undergraduate c junior staff
2 a about to be impeached b hyper-inflation c risking disqualification
3 a a company plaque b a bathroom tap c a pen
4 a to hold it together b to prevent it smelling c to keep them hot
5 a ice cream b oranges c some types of yogurt
6 a a tiger b a football hooligan c a vampire
7 a a dish b a recipe c a jar of baby food (to prevent criminal activity)
8 a silly, not serious b with perfect features and immaculate clothes c wise, bright-eyed

4.3 pages 36–37
Listening and Speaking

1 The fruit shown, from top left, includes grapes, a lime, a grapefruit, an apple, a mango, a pineapple, a lemon, a nectarine, redcurrants, bananas, pomegranates, passion fruit, a kiwi fruit, a melon, a watermelon, a coconut, a peach and oranges.

Suggested answers
A mango is fleshy, juicy when ripe, and rather sensuous. Redcurrants are quite sharp but they are appetising, and look exquisite as a garnish – like bright, red beads. Lemons can be quite fibrous and their juice is sour.

2 The main points below are also underlined in the recording script. Play the recording twice.

Ideal temperature for ripening: over 40 °C
Chief mango-growing area: to the north of Calcutta (Eastern India)
Facts about the mango tree: up to 60 feet (about 18 metres) tall, has a massive trunk, shiny green leaves
History of mango-growing in India: established by the Moghuls in the seventeenth century and taken up by the Nawabs, who diversified the varieties grown

Recording script 1 07

For the last two months, across much of India, temperatures have soared daily to over 40 degrees Celsius – perfect ripening weather for the mango, perfect wilting weather for humans. The thing about India, and Calcutta in particular, is that everyone here eats seasonally and mangoes are everywhere – in every home, on every hotel menu, and sold on every street corner. In the markets, they're beautifully arranged, stacked up according to variety on big wide wicker baskets.

The main mango-growing areas are situated to the north of the city. I headed out to an old family estate where they still have a number of the original orchards. This estate, laid out around an old indigo-planter's house, is wonderfully peaceful and the air so clean – a million miles from Calcutta. Against the exotic foliage of the coconut palm and the banana plant, the mango tree looks like a shiny-leaved evergreen oak. It has a massive, gnarled trunk and can easily grow to a height of sixty feet. Many trees were planted over a hundred years ago.

Indians today have the Moghul dynasties of the seventeenth and eighteenth centuries to thank for the amazing diversity of mangoes available now. They established large plantations across the northern states of Uttar Pradesh and Bihar. It was the Muslim leaders – the Nawabs – who cultivated the fruit in Bengal. They were great fruit-loving people and they missed their apricots and their melons. They cross-pollinated the mango, they got 101 varieties, and these are the sophisticated mangoes that grow mainly in eastern India. When the Moghul empire was in its decline, the Nawabs moved southward and here they cultivated their mangoes, planting them according to their different varieties in orchards – they gave them the most romantic and poetic names, names like 'passari', the loved one, 'begum pasan', the Nawab's wife's favourite …

3

a The speaker uses the word 'perfect' ironically: although the high temperature is perfect for ripening the mango, it causes people to 'wilt', that is, become tired and without energy.
b The mangoes are arranged in piles according to their varieties.
c leaves that grow in the tropics or another faraway place from the speaker's point of view
d the Moghul Empire or royal families
e incredible variety (101 different types)

4 Remember that the adverb *seasonally* comes from the noun *season*. There is also a related adjective *seasonal*. Note that the verb *season* and the noun *seasoning* belong to a different word family within the topic of food:

season (verb) = add salt, pepper or other spices to food to improve the taste

seasoning (noun) = the spices that you use to add flavour

Suggested answer
Buying produce out of season appears to offer maximum choice and flexibility, but can be very disappointing in terms of flavour because the fruit in question has been flown halfway around the world in chilled conditions. Fresh soft fruit like strawberries and raspberries, or vegetables such as asparagus, taste so delicious when they have been freshly picked. Also, because they are only available at a set time of year, you look forward to eating them and savour them during their short season.

Idiom spot

a icing; cake **b** lot; plate **c** eggs; basket **d** fish **e** pill
f pinch; salt **g** beans **h** hot cakes **i** egg; face **j** pie

There are many English idioms to do with food. A few more examples are given below.

Suggested answers
a This government is sweetening the pill of higher taxation by introducing new benefits for employees at the same time.
b I've put all my eggs in one basket work-wise.
c Harry got egg on his face when Professor Samuels confronted him in the canteen queue.
d Valentina isn't staying on here as a student as she has bigger fish to fry in the US, with a Harvard scholarship.
e After the rugby team's outstanding performance, journalists will have to eat humble pie.
f I finally got Simon to spill the beans about his wedding.
g Sharon has a lot on her plate at the moment.
h Maria's earrings are selling like hot cakes on the market stall.

More idioms to do with food:

the best thing since sliced bread (referring to something new and exciting, though often used ironically)

know which side your bread is buttered (understand how you can benefit from something or someone)

bread and butter (the main part of your income)

that's the way the cookie crumbles (that's life)

a tough cookie (a brave or independent person)

chew the fat (chat with someone)

have sour grapes (be jealous of someone else's success)

a/the gravy train (a secure and easy way of making money)

keen as mustard (very eager)

doesn't cut the mustard (is not up to the job)

talk turkey (have a frank discussion: used mainly in American English)

5 As the Exam spot explains, Part 2 of the Speaking Test has two stages: an introductory task followed by a discussion. Read the Suggested answer aloud and time yourself doing this – it should last for approximately one minute.

Suggested answer
The two photos illustrate different aspects of food consumption that are somewhat problematic. The green beans in Picture A have been grown in Egypt but are being sold in the UK, so the supermarket concerned has incurred air miles. The buying power of large supermarkets is such that they can afford to pay these transport costs and they know that people will buy them when they are not in season in the UK. It would be much better for the environment if shoppers restricted their buying of fruit and vegetables to local seasonal produce.
All the bananas for sale in Picture B have been shrink-wrapped, which is just so unnecessary! Excessive packaging like this causes so many issues, including rubbish disposal – the landfill sites cannot cope with the quantity of rubbish that is generated. Some shrink-wrapping has health implications too – take the way meat is packaged for example, with chemical treatment to extend the sell-by dates.

6 The discussion stage in Part 2 involves all the visual material. In the exam, you should give the other candidate opportunities to speak and comment on his/her ideas. You have read about Pictures A and B above. Now read the Suggested answer below about Pictures C and D. Then think about how you would comment on the topic in relation to all four pictures – you may not agree with the views expressed here!

Suggested answer
Picture C shows appalling waste – a rubbish skip being inundated with loaves of bread that cannot be sold by the supermarket because they are a day beyond their 'best before' date! For me that picture suggests something totally unacceptable. We need to seriously rethink our food consumption and it has to start with the supermarkets. Maybe they should restrict the choice on offer? Or perhaps it is down to us – we should begin to make our own bread alongside growing our own vegetables like the lady in Picture D? That big, fat leek she has just pulled out of the ground looks fantastic, plus it has been grown in season and so hasn't created any air miles. We all need to do what she is doing, even if it is just tending a window box on a balcony.

Writing folder 2 pages 38–39

Part 2 Review

If you decide to write a review in Part 2, remember to address the question rather than merely describe what happens in the book or film you are reviewing. Make early reference to the title for clarity.

1   The picture is a 'still' from the film *The Perfect Storm*, showing the fishing boat amidst massive waves.

Possible answers
The steel grey sea looks bitterly cold and very sinister. The huge waves tower menacingly over the fishing boat. Such a vast amount of heaving water threatens the lives of everyone on board the vessel.

2   The paragraph plan covers all parts of the exam task, including the general aspect at the end.

3

Suggested answers
The review is not very successful. There is only a minimal lead-in. The film is not named. The third paragraph is all plot, most of which should have been omitted. There is insufficient description of the special effects in the fourth paragraph. The evaluation is barely attempted.
To improve the review, the balance of the content needs to be addressed: there should be less plot, more reference to the special effects used, and some expansion of the general evaluation at the end.

4   The exercise focuses on how you can extend your range of vocabulary and expression.

See also the corrected and improved answer at the top of the next column.

a   Hollywood blockbuster (film)
b   the budget (money spent)
c   an interesting sub-plot (part)
d   portrayed (acted) by George Clooney
e   he heads out (goes) to sea
f   the safety of his crew (men)
g   through the eye of the storm (worst weather)
h   the special effects kick in (start)
i   really outstanding (very good)
j   clever use of digital imaging (computers)
k   those gigantic (big) waves
l   the film also stars (has) Mark Wahlberg
m   the film cuts to (shows)
n   the girlfriend, scanning the horizon (looking out to sea)
o   a prerequisite (essential part) of all films
p   its best feature (thing)

5

Corrected and improved answer
As part of the feature on special effects, the film *The Perfect Storm* is a very good example to consider. In one way, it is not a typical Hollywood *blockbuster*, as there is no happy ending, but in other ways – the actors used, *the budget*, the special effects – it is.
Why is it 'perfect'? It is actually a weatherman who uses this word. As he tracks the worsening weather out at sea, we see him getting genuinely excited about the unique set of weather conditions. This was *an interesting sub-plot* for me.
The captain of the fishing boat, *portrayed* by George Clooney, does not care about *the safety of his crew* and only wants to find more fish and make money. His irresponsible risk-taking eventually leads the tiny boat into the very *eye of the storm*, which is brought vividly to the screen by *really outstanding* use of special effects, including some *clever use of digital imaging*. When *the special effects kick in*, you feel as though you are in the boat with the crew, facing *those gigantic waves*. At the end, the ship goes down and we see one of the sailors – *the film also stars* Mark Wahlberg – drifting on an empty sea. The huge waves tower menacingly over the poor fisherman. Somewhat unbelievably, he is shown thinking beautiful thoughts about his girlfriend. Then *the film cuts to the girlfriend, scanning the horizon* with an anxious look on her face.
Are special effects *a prerequisite* of all films today? In my own opinion, it depends on the type of film – a psychological drama has no need of special effects to heighten the tension between characters. However, most of today's younger cinema-goers choose action films and they do expect special effects to be an integral part of the entertainment. In *The Perfect Storm*, they were probably *its best feature*. (309 words)

6   Follow the sample paragraph plan below when writing your review.

Sample plan
Para 1   Introduction to review/advert chosen
Para 2   Brief description of the advert
Para 3   Visual effects
Para 4   Other features – music, actors, voice-over, etc.
Para 5   Assessment of influence adverts have on us

Sample answer

It is true that advertising has become an art form in its own right. Nowadays, some of the very best film directors are employed to produce a visually impressive fifty or sixty seconds of footage that we will remember and associate ever afterwards with the product being sold. My own favourite is a recent Guinness advert, which lives up to the high standards set by earlier adverts for this dark beer from Ireland.

The product becomes part of a visual extravaganza, set somewhere in South America or the Caribbean. At the outset, you are unsure what you are witnessing. Tension is in the air and you realise that a race is about to start – incredibly, a snails' race! Each snail lines up in its own lane, with a number on its shell, and bets are taken on which one will be the winner. Snails being what they are, the race gets off to a slow start, but then, one snail finds its way into an almost-empty glass of Guinness, takes in the necessary sustenance and streaks home, to the wild cheers of the crowd.

One striking image follows another and special effects are judiciously used to accentuate the snail's speed. The film is also shot from unusual angles – a snail's eye view, you might say, where human faces become slightly distorted and more unusual. At the end, we are almost participants in the vibrant celebration, which is fuelled by Guinness and exudes only good humour and love of life. Characteristically of a Guinness advert, loud music alternates with silence, busy scenes with stillness. There is no need for a voice-over, which would only labour the point. The overwhelming impression created is that you are watching something utterly unique, a message that you will then associate with the product itself.

In general, I believe adverts have a huge effect on our lifestyle and aspirations. If they didn't, far less money would be spent on them. (324 words)

Units 1–4 Revision

pages 40–41

The aim of this revision unit is to focus on the language covered in Units 1–4, as well as extending the work done on reviews in Writing folder 2. Specific exam practice is provided for Reading and Use of English, Parts 1, 3 and 4. This section could be done as a timed test of 30 minutes.

Use of English

1 The photo shows a side canal in Venice. You should read through the text carefully before attempting to do the task.

1 undertook 2 glorious 3 encircled 4 uninviting
5 antiquity 6 inhabitants 7 perpetually 8 gratitude

2

1 have no alternative but to ask
2 known there was going to / would be a delay OR known about the delay
3 was made to / had to shoulder the financial burden of
4 he was on the verge of tears/crying
5 you find it necessary / it be necessary to contact me urgently
6 hotel is bound to be good as/because/since Pablo

3 The saying *Waste not, want not* that appears in the title of the text means if you make good use of what you have, you won't need anything more. Like the similar expression *Make do and mend* it is associated with times of austerity and hardship, such as wartime.

1 C 2 B 3 B 4 D 5 A 6 C 7 D 8 A

Writing

4

The review originally appeared in the *Guardian* newspaper, in a slightly longer version. The writer is fairly negative about the book, dismissing it as 'publishing froth'.

Punctuated and paragraphed review

No one has yet written 'Froth: the Trend that Changed History' but Universal Foam comes pretty close to being the definitive example of publishing froth. The book blends two recent publishing trends, the newer of which is the wacky science subject. If there is a market for books on cryptography, chronometry or cod – /, and books on all these subjects have sold well in the last decade – /, then there is no reason why any subject should seem boring.

Once you have discovered a subject so obscure that no other publisher has come across it before, all that remains is to prove that it holds the key to universal understanding. 'Cod: / – a Biography of the Fish that Changed the World' / "Cod: / – a Biography of the Fish that Changed the World" / Cod: / – a Biography of the Fish that Changed the World is a pretty good example, but 'Universal Foam: / – the Story of Bubbles from Cappuccino to the Cosmos' / "Universal Foam: / – the Story of Bubbles from Cappuccino to the Cosmos" / Universal Foam: / – the Story of Bubbles from Cappuccino to the Cosmos outdoes it, since it permeates the universe from the smallest to the largest scale. After all, there aren't any galaxies stretched on the skin of unimaginably vast cod ; /, nor do physicists speak of the world arising from fluctuations in the quantum codfish. So 'The Boys' Bumper Book of Froth' / "The Boys' Bumper Book of Froth" / The Boys' Bumper Book of Froth might contain – /, / (as every bestseller should – /, /) everything you need to know about the universe. Then again, / [no punctuation] it might contain everything else. That's pretty frothy too.

In fact, 'Universal Foam' / "Universal Foam" / Universal Foam runs into another current publishing style: / – the book of lists. Among the subjects covered here are: / [**no punctuation**] volcanoes, shaving-foam, champagne, fire-fighting / **firefighting** equipment and meringues. Then you list everything you know about everything in the first list: / – 101 important facts about galaxies ; / – then 20 things you never knew about the cappuccino, / [**no punctuation**] and so on.

Finally, all this is wrapped up in the academic style, / – / (as old as exams, / – /) where you simply cram in all the knowledge that you can possibly get hold of and regurgitate it, / [**no punctuation**] with the echoing solemnity of a **TV** anchorman on 'The Simpsons' / "The Simpsons" / The Simpsons, suggesting a rhetorical question: / – 'Can everyday foams like milk foam ever be fully understood and controlled**?'** / "Can everyday foams like milk foam ever be fully understood and controlled**?**" At which point, / [**no punctuation**] there is foam flecking this reviewer's lips.

You can't really blame the author, / [**no punctuation**] / (Sidney Perkowitz, /) who has worked hard and writes clearly. It is not his fault that he has nothing particular to say after he has got through the bits that particularly interest him: / – the fairly technical discussions of how to measure foams and describe them mathematically. However, the fact is there is no sound reason for this book to have been written in the first place.

Crossword

This includes some of the idioms, phrasal verbs and other vocabulary from Units 1–4.

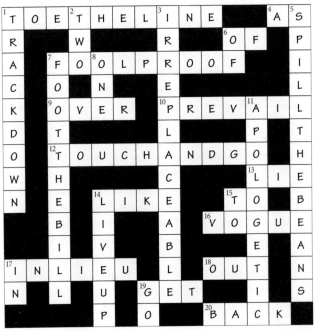

Unit 5

5.1 pages 42–43

Speaking

1

> **Possible answer**
> I would probably be a shopaholic if I had enough money. As it is, I do tend to buy too many shoes. I hardly ever wear some of them, so I guess I am wasting my money. Designer labels are important to me as well. I really adore Armani, but it's a little expensive. I think it's important to keep in fashion. I always make a point of complaining if I buy something which has a fault. I take it right back to the manager and ask for my money back. I never want an exchange. I know my rights and if I had a real problem I would have no hesitation in getting a lawyer in to plead my case.

Listening

2 Read the Exam spot carefully before listening to the recording. If you need more information on this part of the exam, refer to Exam folder 8 on page 132. Play the recording twice, as in the exam.

> **1** consumer slot **2** database **3** lawyers **4** title
> **5** kitchen (door) **6** online **7** hairspray/hair-spray
> **8** squeaked **9** publicity

Recording script 1 08

Paula: Good morning. On the programme today we have Mike James, a familiar face on television as the champion of consumers' rights. Mike, you've been doing *Pricewise* a long time now, is it something you set out to do?

Mike: Far from it Paula. It all began in 2002, when I was a reporter on a nightly news programme. They wanted a consumer slot, so I took it on. It wasn't until nearly ten years later that it became a programme in its own right. Now, we regularly get more than ten million viewers.

Paula: Where do the stories you look into come from?

Mike: Well, from you, the public. We get thousands of letters, phone calls and emails that tell us about poor service, ridiculous small print, malpractice and the need for information. We actually read all the correspondence and we follow up some stories immediately but most are filed for future use on our database.

Paula: What happens when you get a particularly juicy story?

Mike: We check it out thoroughly of course, and then we contact everyone involved, write the script and arrange filming. Sometimes we use actors and sometimes real people. Of course, it's essential that our lawyers check the script over. It's all done to very tight deadlines.

Paula: Do any particular stories stand out in your memory?

Mike: Oh, yes, many. There was one about an advert which promised to give you a title for anything up to £1,000. So, Bob and Trace became Lord Robert and Lady Tracy de Vere. You also get a piece of land but that only measures 20 cm by 20 cm. One of our researchers handed over the cash and tried to find out if being a lord would help him out in London.

Paula: And did it?

Mike: He went to Harrods, the department store, and they were very nice to him, but then they're nice to everyone. He then tried to book a table in a trendy restaurant and he got one – but not in a prime position next to the window – but by the kitchen door! So, really, it won't do you a lot of good being a lord nowadays.

Paula: Any other interesting stories?

Mike: Well, we did a programme not long ago about shopping on the Internet. The big supermarkets will deliver to your door if you order online, as you know.

Paula: Yes, it's a great idea, but I've not actually tried it out.

Mike: Well, it does usually work well. However, we did find that some customers hadn't received quite what they'd ordered. One poor man had asked for apples and got hairspray! The supermarket was very apologetic when we pointed out these problems and sent the customer some shopping vouchers.

Paula: Do you think consumers are more ready to complain these days?

Mike: Oh, yes. Research has been done that shows that attitudes have changed remarkably in the last forty years. Take a well-known brand of trainer. You could understand if they leaked, but actually these particular ones squeaked. Now, as they cost upwards of £100, people weren't prepared to put up with this, but when they returned them to the shop, the shop didn't want to know.

Paula: So they wrote to you for help.

Mike: Yes. We bought a pair of the trainers and sent them to be inspected by an expert who said that some of the glue inside the shoe had come unstuck. We contacted the manufacturer with evidence of the problem and they were more than happy to back down and refund the money paid by the purchasers.

Paula: Another success then.

Mike: Yes, it's funny how quickly manufacturers and retailers react when they think they might attract bad publicity.

Paula: Indeed! It just shows what a good job you're doing. Now next week …

Vocabulary: Phrasal verbs

3 The aim of this exercise is to learn phrasal verbs in context, rather than in a list. Write down the whole sentence in your vocabulary notebook.

a to set out **b** to take on **c** to look into / to check out **d** to follow up **e** to stand out **f** to find out **g** to try out **h** to point out **i** to put up with **j** to back down

Phrase spot

Use an English–English dictionary to help you with this exercise.

a By rights **b** as right as rain **c** in the right **d** right under their noses **e** the film rights **f** right on time **g** within your rights **h** makes all the right noises **i** the right way round **j** serve (Michelle) right

4

1 D **2** A **3** C **4** B **5** A **6** D **7** B **8** C

5

Possible answer

I prefer to shop in a town centre because there are more independent stores. I hate out-of-town shopping centres or malls because they are just full of the big chain stores, all selling similar things.

I think it's terrible that there are so few small independent shops in my town. I can quite understand why people go out of town to do their shopping – after all, it's probably more convenient and possibly the prices are lower – but I prefer the variety that small independent shops provide.

Parking provision is probably the main reason why shopping centres or malls are so popular. Added to that is the fact that, in some cold, rainy climates, it is more comfortable to shop in a warm, indoor mall rather than having to battle against the elements on the High Street.

5.2 pages 44–45

Nouns review

Corpus spot

Most of the sentences in this exercise contain the type of errors that students make when they write. The importance of knowing whether a noun is countable or uncountable cannot be stressed too highly as it affects the whole grammar of a sentence.

a correct
b How <u>much luggage</u> did you bring with you?
c Doctors and scientists, with their <u>research</u>, have managed to give us a better life.
d The news this morning <u>was</u> terrible – more price rises and a teachers' strike.
e Thanks to the revolution in <u>transport</u>, travelling has become easier.
f correct
g correct
h <u>Equipment</u> such as the tape recorder and stereo are very outdated.
i correct
j The future <u>behaviour</u> of our children will depend on a good upbringing.
k I live on the <u>outskirts</u> of the city.
l The fishmonger weighed out three kilos of <u>fish</u>.
m correct
n The <u>scenery</u> in New Zealand <u>is</u> spectacular.
o correct
p The police <u>are</u> aware of the break-in.
q My father is a Professor of <u>Economics</u>.

1

a **work** – job; **works** – factory/of art/literature/road
b **iron** – material; **an iron** – machine for smoothing garments
c **a disorder** – an illness; **disorder** – untidiness
d **a speech** – a talk; **speech** – language/noise
e **a room** – a place; **room** – space
f **a language** – German, Greek, etc; **language** – the method of communication
g **home comforts** – a comfortable bed, central heating, etc; **a comfort** – someone or something that gives you sympathy
h **an experience** – something that happened to you; **experience** – what you have learned doing something
i **a capital** – chief city; **capital** – money
j **a coffee** – a cup of coffee; **coffee** – the plant or beans

Suggested answers

a The work I do is confidential.
There are road works on the motorway.
I've never read the *Complete Works of Shakespeare*.
The Tate Modern has some wonderful works of art.
b The box was made of iron.
I used an iron to make the dress look more presentable.
c He is supposed to be suffering from a heart disorder.
Her room is in a terrible state of disorder.
d The Minister made a brilliant election speech.
Her speech was affected by the accident.
e Go to your room at once!
There is no room in our house now we have four children.
f What languages do you speak?
Language is one of the features that sets human beings apart from other animals.
g I love my home comforts like the microwave and Jacuzzi.
It is a comfort to know that someone cares about me.
h I had a terrible experience on a train once.
Does she have enough experience for the job?
i The capital of Italy is Rome.
The company had depleted its reserves of capital.
j Would you like a coffee?
Coffee grows in certain places in Brazil.

2 In some cases, for example for *glass*, it is not wrong to use *a bit of* or *a piece of*. However, for other cases it is essential that the right word is used and a higher mark would be gained if the best word was used with *glass*.

a a burst of applause b a pane of glass c a stroke of luck d a grain of sand e a gust of wind f a speck of dust g a stream of abuse h a ray of sunshine
i a source of amusement j an item of clothing/news
k a rumble of thunder l a puff of smoke m a state of emergency

3 Spelling is important in all the papers in the examination, but particularly in Reading and Use of English and Writing.

Look around. You're in the midst of a global maelstrom. A swirling mass of converging technologies and new business <u>opportunities</u> unleashed by the Internet. All waiting to be harnessed by large IT service <u>providers</u>. As one has said: 'We've focused our energy and <u>resources</u> on creating technology to solve the unique problems of <u>thousands</u> of individual businesses. Last year alone we invested $2.5 <u>billion</u> of our global IT and <u>telecommunications</u> <u>revenues</u> on R & D. <u>Innovations</u> that keep your company one step ahead of the Internet. And light years ahead of the <u>competition</u>.'

4   Students are often confused as to how to use the apostrophe s in English. As a result they tend to use *of*, which is often not correct. Use the notes in your book to justify your answers.

a back seat   **b** boss's wife / wife's boss – depending on whether the boss is male or female   **c** corner of a/ the room   **d** pay day   **e** week's holiday   **f** wine glass   **g** moment's delay   **h** Anne's best friend   **i** door handle   **j** sports field

Vocabulary: Prepositions

5   Prepositions are often a problem in English for students of all levels. Make sure that you learn which preposition goes with a word when you put it in your vocabulary notebook.

1 in   **2** with   **3** of   **4** by/into   **5** in   **6** of   **7** with/in   **8** to   **9** in/at   **10** of   **11** into/on   **12** with   **13** towards/to   **14** on   **15** without   **16** at

5.3 pages 46–47

Reading into Writing: Working with two texts

1

Possible answer
I have really liked an advertisement that uses model animals to advertise car insurance. It is clever because the animals are cute and cuddly and have nothing to do with car insurance at all. The advertisement is like a soap opera and is worth watching for itself.
I think children are more vulnerable than adults to advertising because they lack judgement when it comes to what they are presented with. I think that junk food, for example, should never be advertised during children's TV programmes.

2   Spend about five minutes reading the two texts and then answer the questions.

Text 1 is possibly from a newspaper. The style is fairly informal, e.g. *shell out, dawn on, nagging, even down to*
Text 2 is possibly from a research paper. The style is academic, e.g. *cognitive ability, embedded within, inherently*

3

Text 1: occur to – dawn on; pester – nagging; including – down to; whim – impulse, evaluate – weigh up
Text 2: assess – evaluate; extent – scope; claim – contention; essentially – inherently; exaggerated – overstated

4   You will need to find the two main points in each text in the examination.

Text 1: b, d
Text 2: a, c

5

Suggested answer
The two texts discuss the pros and cons of advertising to young people. Text 1 claims that young people have an enormous impact on what the people around them, friends and family, decide to spend their money on, even affecting decisions normally made by adults. Not only this, but young people, unlike older ones, do not spend time carefully considering their purchases or asking around to get advice.
Text 2 argues that, even though there is some unease about targeting young people with advertising, in fact, this group have some immunity to it as they have been subjected to it over a long period of time. There is also the point that advertising can enable young people to make sensible decisions about their purchases by giving them the facts they need about the goods advertised. (135 words)

Vocabulary: Abstract nouns

6   As you have seen in Unit 3, it is important to be able to manipulate words, both for the word formation task in Reading and Use of English and in answering Writing tasks.

a boredom   **b** obsolescence   **c** awareness   **d** pride   **e** confidence   **f** austerity   **g** generosity   **h** independence   **i** inefficiency   **j** insecurity   **k** meanness   **l** Individualism, responsibility   **m** aspirations   **n** scepticism

Exam folder 3 pages 48–49

Reading and Use of English Part 1 Multiple-choice cloze

The photograph is of a fresco by Giovanni Stradano (1523–1603) of the Piazza del Mercato Vecchio in Florence.

You need to get used to organising your vocabulary systematically. This will help when you come to do this type of exercise. It's important to read through the text from beginning to end to get a good idea of what it is about and also the register it is in. Some answers may depend on register rather than meaning.

1 B   **2** B   **3** A   **4** A   **5** D   **6** B   **7** A   **8** C

Unit 6

6.1 pages 50–51

Speaking

1 The photos are of:
- a young woman student listening to an MP3 player and studying
- a teenage boy playing an electric guitar

Possible answers
I'm afraid I find it very hard to concentrate if music is playing – it doesn't matter what type it is, I still find it very distracting.
It's quite true that every child should learn to play an instrument, although getting them to practise may be a problem. Learning how to read music is very good.
I think the piano is much easier to learn than the violin. Your playing can sound fairly reasonable much faster on the piano than on the violin.
Pop music can improve my mood, but it depends – sometimes it just makes it worse!
I don't believe that classical music is superior to pop music. They both have their positive aspects.

Reading

2 This part of the Reading and Use of English paper is the one students often have the most trouble with. Read all of the base text and then all the extra paragraphs before doing the exercise. Some of the important references have been highlighted in bold as this is the first example of this type of task. They are not in bold in the examination. Read both sides of the gap to make sure you have the right answer. Just reading the paragraph before the gap will not always help.

1 F	2 D	3 B	4 G	5 A	6 E	7 H

Links to underline:

3 'statistical connection' (para 2); 'truly convincing study' (para B); 'musical ability enhances mathematical ability' (para B); 'the two are interestingly related' (para 3)

4 'piano' (para 3); 'are mathematicians more drawn to this rather than to other instruments' (para G); 'can we at least argue' (para G); 'Indeed, yes, we can' (para 4)

5 'not the kind of obscure connection' (para 4); 'the straightforward link' (para A);

6 ' we don't … mysterious connection between mathematical ability and linguistic ability' (para 5); 'because the link exists but not the uncertainty: grammar feels mathematical' (para E); 'paradoxical' (para E); 'contradiction' (para 6)

7 'solve problems of the "A is to B as C is to D" kind' (para 6); 'Music is full of little puzzles like this' (para H)

Phrase spot

Phrases with *take* are often tested in the examination.

> **a** exception to   **b** notice   **c** place   **d** part   **e** the view
> **f** account of   **g** issue   **h** advantage   **i** by surprise
> **j** second place   **k** into account/consideration
> **l** for granted   **m** a stand

6.2 pages 52–53

Modals: Degrees of likelihood

Refer to the Grammar folder on page 181 if you are not clear about the uses of these modal verbs.

1 Take about ten minutes to do this exercise. There may be more than one answer to some questions.

A c, f, h, l	**C** m
B a, b, d, e, g, i, j	**D** k

2

Possible answers
a There is every likelihood that another Mozart will be born. I can't believe that only one musical genius will ever exist.
b I guess an asteroid could hit the Earth, but the government is bound to do all in its power to prevent it.
c People may well have brain transplants in the future – after all, we have transplants for most parts of the body, don't we?
d I think there's only a faint chance that English will be the language of the Internet in the future. I think Chinese will take over.
e There's no chance of New Zealand winning the football World Cup – not when there are teams from France, Spain, Italy and Brazil.
f It's a foregone conclusion that electric cars are the cars of the future. It stands to reason that oil reserves won't last forever.

3 Try to work out who or what is being talked about in this exercise. You may have different answers to the ones suggested below.

Possible answers
a landing on the Moon
b a royal wedding
c possibly Madonna
d possibly Federer – anyone who is a sports champion who is about to retire
e possibly polio, AIDS or smallpox

4 Refer to the Exam spot for advice before doing the exercise.

1 chances are (good/excellent) (that) Alan will be/get
2 's/is doubtful that Professor Potts will take
3 bound to get the Head's job if / providing (that) / provided (that)
4 all likelihood the cause
5 a foregone conclusion (that) a/the gold medal
6 likely (that) the audience will take no notice

5 The article is about how bands are often 'manufactured' by people in the music industry for profit.

a The writer is rather cynical.
b The comparison between groups in the past who got together themselves and what is happening now.
c That music bands are like any other product.

1 Not   2 as   3 out   4 in/to   5 may   6 With   7 who/what   8 far/much   9 Although/Though/Whereas/While/Whilst   10 before   11 having/likely   12 together   13 charge/control   14 fact/reality   15 any

6.3 pages 54–55
Listening and Speaking

1 Use an English–English dictionary to help you with this exercise if you are unsure of the answers.

brass: trumpet
electronic: synthesizer
keyboard: piano
percussion: triangle; drum; xylophone
string: violin; guitar; cello
woodwind: clarinet; flute; saxophone

2 Read through the questions before listening to the recording. Try to predict the answers. Write down what you think the answer is going to be and check whether you were right after you have heard the recording. Play the recording twice, as in the exam. The underlined parts of the recording script confirm the answers.

1 carved   2 cold   3 flexibility   4 wastage/waste   5 ribs
6 glue   7 neck   8 varnish   9 tone

Recording script ●1 09
Interviewer: Any string player will tell you that no instrument is identical to another. Thirty violins may look the same, but each has a characteristic, however subtle, all of its own. Middleton College runs a violin-making course for students of all ages. And I must say that to see a violin in its stages of development, and especially the intricately <u>carved</u> wood, really

fascinated me. The head of the violin school is one of its ex-students, Sue Pearson. I met her in the violin workshop. Sue, before you start to make a violin into the instrument we all know and love, where do you go to find your wood?

Sue: Various places. The pine really needs to come from places where the weather is <u>cold</u> enough for the tree to have grown fairly slowly, so that it grows straight and has close, uniform grain lines.

Interviewer: Why is that – that you need such finely grained wood?

Sue: It's all relating to <u>flexibility</u>, and it needs to be incredibly strong too, of course. We make the front of the violin from pine and the back from maple. These two woods have the qualities we're looking for.

Interviewer: What we've got here are basically just blocks of wood, aren't they? As with any great piece of woodwork, you can never believe for a moment that you could just produce something out of a boring block of wood.

Sue: This piece here is basically for just one part of the violin. In any operation in violin-making, I think you're looking at 80–85% <u>wastage</u>.

Interviewer: And you've got some other bits as well. Very thin pieces.

Sue: These are what we call the <u>ribs</u>. These are about one and a half to one and three-quarter millimetres wide, and before they can go onto the instrument, they'll be reduced in thickness.

Interviewer: We've got the *shape* of the body here. What happens next?

Sue: Basically we shape the top and bottom and then we use <u>glue</u> to stick them together. We don't use a nail or machine for this. We've still got the <u>neck</u> to do and this is easily the most elaborate part of the instrument. It's always quite difficult for a novice student to undertake. We're really dealing in three dimensions.

Interviewer: There's an instrument that looks finished over there, but it's an unusual colour. Why is that?

Sue: Well, it's not finished yet. It needs a good clean – it can get a bit grubby when it's being made. It needs to have <u>varnish</u> applied and this can affect the sound – makes it more mellow in my opinion.

Interviewer: Some of the greatest violins are fairly old. Are you expecting when you make these instruments that they might still be around a couple of hundred years hence?

Sue: That's one of the things that always interests us. We're all mortal and it would be nice to think one of your instruments was still being played in two to three hundred years and that it would even improve in <u>tone</u>. Obviously it will increase in value too, but that's not something that worries me too much.

Style extra

Collocations are often tested in the examination and you can gain more marks if you use them in your compositions.

Suggested answers
a A monster is widely believed to live in Loch Ness.
b She gave her boyfriend a carefully chosen birthday present.
c Designer clothes are more keenly priced in out-of-town retail outlets.
d The seats for the rock concert were staggeringly expensive.
e The new album has been singularly successful and has reached number one.

Idiom spot

The idioms here all derive from words to do with music. One word is used more than once.

a note   b tune   c song   d string   e score   f note
g chord

3   Refer to the Exam spot.

The photos are of:
- a classical concert
- a man and his grandchild listening to an MP3 player
- an outdoor music festival
- a rock concert

Possible answer
(These are ideas for one side of a conversation.)
I think that the person listening to music on an MP3 player is probably the most representative of the way people listen to music today. Since its introduction the iPod® and similar devices have really become popular as they mean that you can listen to whatever music you want, wherever you are, without annoying anyone else. At one time, it was possible to overhear a tinny noise when someone was using an MP3 player, but with the new types of earphone, this is no longer the case. I'm sure that even better devices will be invented very soon as well.

Pronunciation

4   This exercise looks at contrastive stress. This is particularly important for the modal auxiliaries you have seen in this unit as the meaning can change depending on how they are said.

Suggested answers
a irritated   b reproachful   c irritated   d suggesting
e worried   f angry

a   You could have rung me from the station.
b   You could have rung me from the station.
c   You might ask before you borrow the car.
d   You might ask Pete if you can borrow his car.
e   Liz should have got here an hour ago.
f   Liz should have got here an hour ago.

5

Recording script and answers 1 11

a   I <u>thought</u> you'd gone home.
    Yes, she/he has gone home.
b   I thought you'd gone <u>home</u>.
    No, he's/she's gone somewhere else.
c   She's an <u>English</u> teacher.
    Yes, she teaches English (not Spanish).
d   She's an English <u>teacher</u>.
    Yes, she teaches English; she's not a student.
e   I'm not buying a <u>car</u>.
    No, he's getting a bike, etc.
f   I'm not <u>buying</u> a car.
    No, he's hiring one.
g   She's not <u>pretty</u>.
    No, but she's intelligent/friendly, etc. or possibly she's ugly.
h   <u>She's</u> not pretty.
    No, but her friend is.
i   I <u>had</u> wanted to see the paintings.
    No, he didn't see them.
j   I had <u>wanted</u> to see the paintings.
    Yes, he saw them.

Writing folder 3 pages 56-57

Part 1 Essay

Look back at Writing folder 1 for basic facts about this compulsory question. This Writing folder helps you to express ideas from the texts in your own words, add variety to your sentences, and paragraph your ideas.

1   Try to write four sentences summarising the ideas in the texts.

Suggested answers
Text 1
Although music is all around us, it does not enjoy a high status in contemporary society.
It is challenging for talented musicians to survive in their chosen profession.

Text 2
Music is often cut from the school curriculum so that more resources can be given to mathematics and science. There are unforeseen benefits to children from the study of music in school.

2 Underline useful vocabulary in the sentences that conveys the ideas in the texts.

Sentences b and e do not reflect the content of the texts.

3 Remember that in the exam, you must use your own words wherever possible.

4 Notice that the sentence openers are all impersonal in tone.

5 Write around 50–60 words.

Suggested answer
Nobody can deny that music features in our lives and yet, as the texts point out, it is undervalued in society. The first text considers the plight of professional musicians, while the second focuses on the low prestige of music in schools. This essay argues that music is important and requires investment to secure its presence in education and culture. (60 words)

6 Follow the Exam advice given.

Sample answer
Nobody can deny that music features in our lives and yet, as the texts point out, it is undervalued in society. The first text considers the plight of professional musicians, while the second focuses on the low prestige of music in schools. This essay argues that music is important and requires investment to secure its presence in education and culture.

What then is the role of music today? Professional musicians are sometimes highly regarded yet earn a pittance. From the classical performer's point of view, the reality is that it is very hard to find orchestral positions nowadays. This must be disheartening after so many years of study. Perhaps more should be done by the state to support young musicians who are embarking on their working life?

Similarly, on the question of teaching music in school, not enough is done. People tend to regard music as a less essential part of the school curriculum than mathematics or science. At the same time, there are unforeseen advantages for children who learn music from a young age, as it encourages creativity and allows them to develop social skills through participation in a group event. This is not to say that everyone should be able to read music, but they should have access to it.

Music plays a fundamental role in both the educational and cultural spheres, and its beneficial contribution to shaping our lives needs to be better understood by all members of society. If more resources were made available to schools and young musicians were given adequate financial support through government subsidy or other means, society would profit significantly. (268 words)

Unit 7
7.1 pages 58–59
Listening

1 The pictures all have the word 'eye' in common. They show:
- a 'macrophoto' of the human eye, showing the dark central pupil surrounded by a blue iris
- the eye of a needle with thread
- a cat's eye, the device used on main roads to guide drivers at night

2 As the Exam spot mentions, there are three short extracts in Listening, Part 1. In the exam, you will have 15 seconds before each extract to read through the questions. In this time, try to predict what you might hear. Play each extract twice. The underlined parts of the recording script confirm the answers.

1 B 2 A 3 C 4 B 5 B 6 A

Recording script 1 12
Extract One
Interviewer: Dr Joanna Walters, your new book *The Complex Eye* has been featured in many newspapers this week. In it, you remind us that the eye is not only a passive receiver of information, but a great communicator too.

Joanna: Um, I should point out that I collaborated on the book with a leading zoologist – it's the human communication side that's my field.

Interviewer: Sorry. That's journalism for you. I've been misinformed. Anyway, we all remember being told by our mothers that it's rude to stare.

Joanna: Right. Staring is the most aggressive facial expression with which to threaten a rival and in the animal kingdom, those species that can't frighten off their would-be attackers in this way, from moths to fish to birds, have evolved false eye spots, which fulfil the same function.

Interviewer: And you draw parallels with human beings here.

Joanna: Absolutely. Because it's taboo for us to physically stare someone out, other, subtler, strategies are often in play. Look in your rear-view mirror late at night and you may see a pair of dazzling headlights eyeballing you. What do you do?

Interviewer: Let them overtake?

Joanna: That's right, avoid confrontation, especially in these days of road rage. Once we're behind the wheel, those headlights become an extension of our persona, whether aggressively so, or in self-defence.

Extract Two

Woman: When Sam was two and a bit, he began to use one of the living room walls, which was unfortunately white at the time, as a drawing surface. It was always the same wall and he appeared to be attempting pictures, as well as showing a definite sense of colour. I had no wish to stifle any artistic genius he might have, so I tended to turn a blind eye to what he was doing, making sure that he was armed with washable felt-tips and cleaning up after him without delay. But one weekend I was out and my husband caught him at it … a boat with two funnels, as I recall, and he hit the roof, both with Sam and with me. In the end we compromised: I bought some huge rolls of white paper and taped it to the wall, all the way along. As soon as Sam completed one *magnum opus* I would take it down and replace it with a fresh canvas, so to speak. It cost me a fortune, but I've never regretted it. In fact I feel proud of myself, as I believe it helped to make him the way he is. But Sam loves to wind me up about it. You see, he has absolutely no leanings towards art, being heavily into information technology!

Extract Three

Man: Percy Shaw always had an eye for practical solutions. Driving home through the unlit outskirts of Halifax at night, he found the perfect substitute for night vision, following the glint of his headlights in the metal tramlines. But he ran into a problem: no longer in use, these rails were soon taken up for good. With this serious setback, Shaw decided it was time to come up with something that would help him – and others – to steer in the dark. His now ubiquitous invention, modelled on the eye of a cat, consists of a mirror and a spherical lens mounted on a rubber pad. Each time a vehicle runs over it, the assembly is forced into its iron base and the lens is wiped clean by the rubber, which acts like an eyelid. Shaw patented his invention in 1934 when he was only 23 and, thanks to the cat's eye, became a very rich man.

3 Read the two extracts from the recording script and explain the meaning of the phrases in your own words.

> **Suggested answers**
> **Extract Two**
> *sense of colour* – a feeling for how colours work together
> *magnum opus* – major work (of art, here)
> *no leanings towards* – without any interest in
> **Extract Three**
> *the perfect substitute* – the ideal replacement
> *serious setback* – a problem that affects your ability to do something
> *ubiquitous invention* – an invention that is in use everywhere

Idiom spot

The idiom used in the recording was: *turn a blind eye to.*

Catch someone's eye means to be attractive or different enough to be noticed by people; there is a related compound adjective: *eye-catching.* (*Catch someone's eye* also means 'get someone's attention by looking at them'.)

Look someone in the eye/eyes means to look at someone in a direct way, without showing fear or shame.

Have an eye for means to be good at noticing a particular type of thing

See eye to eye (with) means that two people agree with each other.

Be in the public eye means to be famous and often featured in the media.

> **Possible answers**
> a … that pair of orange silk pyjamas hanging out of the school window.
> b … the child's petty stealing of sweets from the shop counter: he needed to be taught what was right and wrong.
> c … 'I'm afraid we're going to have to let you go.'
> d … my younger sister, but her decision to quit college is her stupidest yet.
> e … interesting accessories – I love those earrings.
> f … behave responsibly and always tell the truth.

4 Look back at Exam folder 1 on pages 14–15 before doing this word formation task.

Background information

Georges Seurat was a highly innovative artist, responsible for the whole Pointillist movement. He was not really appreciated by the Parisian art establishment during his lifetime. His most famous painting is *Un dimanche après-midi à l'île de la Grande Jatte* (Sunday afternoon on the island of Grande Jatte), shown on page 59. This painting took three years to complete (1884–1886) and is now on permanent exhibition in the Art Institute of Chicago, USA. The painting was the subject of a successful musical by Stephen Sondheim, *Sunday in the Park with George.*

> 1 essence   2 Hitherto   3 unpredictable   4 intuitively
> 5 stability   6 incomparable   7 influential   8 interaction

Using extended noun phrases is an effective way of varying the beginning of sentences. It would be particularly appropriate to use them in an article or review.

Possible answers
a A highly-regarded and ground-breaking film-maker, Werner Herzog has now produced a film in 3D about some ancient cave paintings in France.
b Best-known for their awe-inspiring poetry, Byron, Keats and Shelley formed part of the English Romantic movement in the early nineteenth century.
c The most significant political thinker of his generation, James Harrington recognised the fundamental link between economic distribution and political power.
d A leading innovator in her field of expertise, Amanda Wixted has developed some of the best-selling computer games of all time.

7.2 pages 60–61
Participles

1 a In the example, *dazzling* is an adjective; *eyeballing* is a participle.

b

i The participle *Driving* is active and refers to Percy Shaw.
ii The participle *modelled* is passive and refers to his invention (the cat's eye); the clause could be rewritten as a defining relative clause: *His invention, which is modelled on the eye of a cat, …*

c

i The cat is sitting on the roof.
ii The person is sitting on the roof.

2 The two pictures show:
• Fort Vimieux (oil on canvas) painted by Joseph Mallord William Turner (1775–1851)
• an image taken by the Hubble Space Telescope of gas pillars in the Eagle Nebula, which is about 7,000 light years from Earth.

Possible answer
The painting by Turner is a spectacular interpretation of sunset and is indeed beautiful. The space image also has beauty and the gas clouds are almost flamboyant in their towering grandeur. There is something very awe-inspiring about this image.

3 Read the article quickly to be able to answer the question about art and beauty.

Suggested answer
In the nineteenth century and earlier, the artistic tradition was to paint the beauty of nature, but modern artists rarely represent nature on canvas, so their works are not usually described as 'beautiful'. The writer refers to Ruskin's views on art and beauty in connection with images from the Hubble Space Telescope, seeing them as contemporary examples of beauty derived from nature.

4 Read the section in the Grammar folder on page 182 after doing this exercise.

having viewed: active; previous action
taken: passive; previous action
having been launched: passive; previous action
sending: active; simultaneous action
being (successfully) **repaired:** passive; simultaneous action
seeing: active; simultaneous action
imitated: passive; previous action

5

Possible answers
1c Receiving mixed reactions from members of the public, the exhibition includes some rather shocking images.
2f Often occurring in open landscape, Andy Goldsworthy's sculptures are particularly effective during dramatic weather conditions.
3b Wanting to create order from chaos, physicists are constantly trying to reduce the universe to a set of basic principles.
4e Having taken quite a few warm-up shots, the photographer then caught the model unawares in a more relaxed pose.
5a Coming in from the street for an hour's rest, people don't realise that the beds – and they themselves – are part of an installation.
6d Having bought two previous works by this artist, I am now looking out for a third.

6

a (being) chosen b shown c sold d made
e being searched f announced g damaged

7.3 pages 62–63
Reading into Writing: Exemplifying your ideas

1 The pictures show:
• a twee picture of a kitten
• a clichéd image of two people dressed as punks
• a hackneyed picture of the global business handshake

Possible answer
I find the kitten all in pink to be the most clichéd image. You see the same thing all the time in magazines and on cards. It's so posed too – when would a kitten sit like that of its own accord?

2 This Reading into Writing lesson focuses on how to include relevant examples of your own ideas in response to the points made in the two input texts in Writing, Part 1.

Suggested answer
The two texts are complementary in their ideas, both focusing on when and how original images become clichéd.

3

Suggested answer
The second text includes specific examples – squat greetings card, popular poster, radiant sunset over a tranquil sea – in order to support the argument and make the contrast between originality and cliché more understandable.

4

Reference to specific examples underlined:

'... such as those by Irving Penn and Diane Arbus among others'

'Take for instance the cliché-ridden use of visuals like the business handshake or the world as a globe'

5 Look back at Exam folder 1 (pages 14–15) on the testing of compounds in Reading and Use of English, Part 3.

1 experimentation 2 landmark 3 inspirational
4 dismissively 5 countless 6 persuasive 7 devalues
8 commonplace

6

1 b 2 d 3 a 4 c

Exam folder 4 pages 64–65

Reading and Use of English, Part 7 Multiple matching

Read through the Exam advice carefully before doing the exercise.

1 D 2 B 3 E 4 A 5 C 6 B 7 C 8 D 9 A 10 C

Unit 8
8.1 pages 66–67

1 The pictures show the cities of:
- **Sydney** – the Opera House and harbour
- **Rome** – a square with open-air restaurants
- **Delhi** – a hectic street scene

Possible answer
Factors ranked 1–5:
1 effortless access to amenities
2 sufficient open spaces
3 diverse employment opportunities
4 low levels of pollution
5 spacious living accommodation

For me, the best thing about city living is the easy access to entertainment and culture – having a choice of concerts and galleries on your doorstep is a real plus, which makes up for possibly having to live in a small high-rise apartment.

Think about the advantages and disadvantages of city living as opposed to living in a small town or village. Use the five phrases to contrast these two lifestyles.

Possible answer
Obviously a big city has diverse employment opportunities, not to mention good access to many cultural amenities, such as an opera house, and plenty of nightlife. Cities often have historical buildings too. There is usually a lively atmosphere, with so many people. On the other hand, big cities are noisy and polluted, usually without many green areas for recreational use, and it often takes a long time to travel from one district to another. Smaller towns and villages have lower levels of pollution and can offer more spacious living accommodation, together with sufficient open spaces.

Reading

2 In Reading and Use of English, Part 7 of the exam you will have to process a text or set of texts at speed to find specific information. Look back at the advice given in Exam folder 4 on pages 64–65 before you do the task here.

This text is taken from an academic journal article, and evaluates a particular approach to city architecture in the USA called the New Urbanism.

3 Underline the parts of the texts where you find the answers to 1–10 (see answers below).

Possible answer

1 B *They give some priority to <u>accessible public spaces, community institutions and a variety of parks and other green spaces</u>, in order to <u>foster exemplary civic behaviour</u>.*

2 A *However, during <u>the grim California recession</u> of the 1990s, the original developer for this scheme <u>went bankrupt</u> and the entire project was taken over by <u>a less sympathetic developer, who contravened virtually all of CNU's principles. Had Laguna West been completed</u> as Calthorpe planned it, <u>it would have been</u> one of the great visionary new towns of the late 20th century.*

3 D *The US government-sponsored company Fannie Mae's research into housing preferences shows that <u>up to 80% of US households would prefer</u> to live in a single-family dwelling with a garden, regardless of income, race or current tenure status.*

4 A *As things have turned out, it is just another conventional, <u>car-dependent suburb</u>.*

5 B *They have <u>a strong preference for 'infill' development</u> – that is, the use of land within a built-up area, especially as part of a community redevelopment project – <u>rather than the endless expansion of cities sometimes referred to as 'urban sprawl'</u>.*

6 E *Most NU communities <u>are being built on green field sites some distance away from the central city</u>...*

7 C *<u>The same idea of 'self-containment'</u> was one of the principles behind <u>the creation of the British new towns of the 1960s</u>, such as Milton Keynes and Telford.*

8 E *... and <u>infill development has been limited</u> – probably <u>of necessity because of land scarcity – to tiny pockets</u>.*

9 D *Urban capital stock is already largely in place and remains a constant, while <u>much of the residential housing in the US has been built in the last 40 years</u>, so <u>innovation through renewal is off the agenda for the time being</u>.*

10 C *The overwhelming tendency was for residents to work elsewhere, with the jobs available in the new towns filled by commuters from outside, with <u>the net result being more use of fossil fuels rather than less</u>.*

Vocabulary: Compound adjectives and their collocations

4 The compound adjectives *mixed-use* and *car-dependent* are hyphenated forms that are only used before a noun, as in *mixed-use neighbourhoods*.

Suggested answers

quick-thinking (politician)
long-running (TV series)
short-sighted (policy)
well thought-through / well thought-out (argument)
far-sighted, far-thinking (planner)
poorly-constructed (building), poorly-fitting (cupboards), poorly thought-through / poorly thought-out (plan)
smashed-up (car)
blown-down (trees), blown-out (windows), blown-up (buildings)

8.2 pages 68–69
Inversion

1 Read the section in the Grammar folder on page 182.

2

Possible answers

a Never before have I felt as contented as I do now.
b Only once in my life have I regretted taking a trip.
c Scarcely had the clock struck midnight when the lights went out.
d No sooner had I put my raincoat on than the sun came out again.
e Hardly had I sat down before someone else hammered on the door.
f Not until last month did I feel in control of my workload.
g Seldom do any birds visit the garden, due to the number of cats around.
h Rarely will there be an opportunity for proper discussion.
i Had it not been for the fact that my cousin was coming to the party, I would have stayed at home.

3 See the Grammar folder for further examples of prepositional phrases.

1 stood   2 sat   3 hung   4 had   5 stretched   6 were
7 did

4

1 once did the train run on time / on/to schedule
2 had Brian and Sue met when/before/than
3 no circumstances are you to
4 sooner had they left their car than/before/when
5 one postcard did Kerry send us while
6 had the bus company put their prices up
7 high has the demand for tickets been that
8 only are the buildings beautiful / only are there beautiful buildings but the climate

8.3 pages 70–71
Listening and Speaking

1 The meaning of *The grass is always greener …* is that there always appears to be a better situation than your own.

2

Possible answer
Sally is Meg's daughter and they currently live in Wales. Kevin works in London but is disenchanted with the rat race and plans to swap living accommodation with Meg and Sally temporarily.
It does sound very unusual. I suppose the success of the lifeplan will depend on how well the three of them get on – and on how well they look after each other's properties. It does give Kevin an escape from city living and gives Sally and Meg more flexibility. The downside is that they will all lack a permanent base and it might be difficult to make long-term plans.

Recording script 1 13

Interviewer: OK, well there are three people sitting in the studio with me now – Sally, Meg and Kevin – who are about to embark on a rather unusual 'lifeplan' as they call it, something that will bring about a change of gear for all three of them. By way of introduction, we need to go through some recent history, and I'm going to start with you, Sally, because it's your discontent about where you're living now that has played a large part in all this. Sally, tell us where you and Meg call home at the moment.

Sally: It's a tiny village in the Welsh hills, which no one will have heard of. Last November we quit London and headed for the border. Mum and Dad decided to go their separate ways, you see – I think Mum took this literally, she wanted to get as far away as possible from Dad at the time.

Meg: It wasn't quite like that, but yes, the divorce had a lot to do with needing to get out of the city and start again.

Interviewer: So out of the blue you chose a remote Welsh village?

Meg: Not quite, I had good friends there …

Sally: Who have since left.

Meg: Yes, but, well, anyway, as Sally will tell you, it hasn't quite worked out for her, though for me at the beginning, winding down was a godsend, it gave me the chance to rethink my life and decide on priorities.

Interviewer: Mm, so, Sally, why has it been less than perfect for you?

Sally: I'm 15 now and I left really good friends behind me, some I'd known my whole life. Plus, I've had to learn Welsh to even function at school and that's been hard. And as you can imagine, there isn't exactly a lot to do where we are – most people of my age just hang around the village green or go to each others' houses. It's not that great. Fortunately, I've been staying some weekends at my Dad's place – so I can meet up with some of my old friends, go to clubs, you know.

Interviewer: Mmm … so the country idyll, not such good news for you, but for you, Meg, you're content with your life there?

Meg: Yes and no-o. I have to confess that once the honeymoon period was over (a rather unfortunate term in my case) well, you know after a while I woke up and realised that this wasn't right for me either. It's hard to pin down exactly why – I don't suffer from boredom, and I still get a rush out of the sheer beauty and calm that surrounds us, but I … I feel that I'm missing out too, that I should be working, socialising more, going to exhibitions, all those things I used to take for granted, but which are totally out of the frame at the moment.

Interviewer: And that's where Kevin comes in …

Kevin: One lucky break all round …

Sally: Well, it's pretty flukey. Basically Mum and I sat down one night and agreed we had to get back somehow … but we realised that there was no way we could expect to move back to London as easily as we'd left.

Meg: Selling the cottage wouldn't be easy, and nor would finding somewhere in our price range in London.

Sally: Mum had this real brainwave. She decided to look for anyone who might be interested in changing places, house swaps, that sort of thing.

Kevin: And thanks to the power of the Internet, they tracked me down.

Interviewer: And everything's fallen into place. But what's in it for you, Kevin? You've already told me you have a large flat in a very desirable part of London, a good job, …

Kevin: What I've got is a nice flat I hardly ever see, a high-profile, high-stress job in share-dealing, no girlfriend, 'cos she dumped me a month ago, so life's not exactly a bed of roses. But I've been very successful and can afford to negotiate my future. Well, I want to get out for a while but not burn my boats completely, so Meg's proposal is perfect.

Interviewer: And how is this lifeplan going to unfold now?

Meg: In a nutshell, we've agreed to change places for three months initially, swapping everything – we leave the car, the furniture, the tins of soup in the kitchen …

Kevin: Not the clothes though!

Meg: If we're all happy, then we'll extend to a year, which will give Sally and I a wonderful base in London and Kevin some peace and quiet to realise his dream.

Interviewer: Which is?

Kevin: I've got an idea for the next bestseller, a racy paperback on city slickers.

Interviewer: Ah, plenty of first-hand experience to draw on – sounds promising! And Sally, you'll get back your social life, but isn't it potentially disruptive, to your schooling and so on?

Sally: We're going to be moving at the start of a new school year, so there's a natural break anyway. And if things don't pan out, I can always move in with Dad.

Meg: But I think we're all quietly confident that it *will* work out.

Kevin: Yeah, 'cos it's what we all want deep down. And if I make it as a writer, well it might end up a permanent arrangement, you know, six months on, six off, the best of both worlds.

Interviewer: Well, they say *the grass is always greener*, but you seem to have things pretty much sorted out. Meg, Sally, Kevin, the very best of luck.

All: Thank you.

3

The idioms are underlined in the recording script in 2 above.

a 5	b 4	c 6	d 3	e 2	f 1

Idiom spot

The key word is *burn*.

a burn a hole in your pocket – have money that you want to spend
b burn the midnight oil – work late into the night
c get your fingers burned/burnt – have something go wrong
d fiddling while Rome burns – focusing on something trivial during a crisis
e have money to burn – have lots of money
f burn your bridges – take action which you cannot reverse

Vocabulary: Phrases with *place*

4 The word *place* has a number of meanings in English and is a very common word, so it is worth reviewing your knowledge of this word. The gaps require one or two words to complete the phrases.

a taking	b in	c all over	d first	e out of

5 There are two extra words that you don't need to use.

1 acronym 2 network 3 spaces 4 sector
5 regeneration 6 neighbourhood 7 demolition
8 consultation

6 Remember that the three ideas on the Part 3 prompt card are there to help you, but you don't have to cover them if you don't want to.

7 The phrases in a–l will help you to organise your ideas in a logical way. Use them to plan what you are going to say.

a B b B c D d E e B f D g E h D i E j D k B
l E

8 Time your long turn, which should take approximately two minutes. If you can record yourself, do this and then play it back to see where you could improve your performance.

9 Read the Exam spot. It is important that you listen carefully to the other candidate, so that you can respond appropriately to the interlocutor's question and contribute relevant ideas to the subsequent discussion.

Writing folder 4 pages 72–73

Part 2 Set text question: Film tie-in

1 Try some of the online suggestions in relation to the set text you are studying.

2 *The Secret Life of Bees* has been a set text on *Cambridge English: Proficiency* and a film tie-in is available on DVD. Further background information to the historical period is given below.

Background information

Key dates: African-American Civil Rights Movement

1955 Rosa Parks refused to give up her seat on a public bus for a white passenger and was arrested. The ensuing protest made Martin Luther King a national figure.

1957 Nine African-American students won the legal right to attend Little Rock Central High School, but were harassed by white students all year. The local school system then closed public schools rather than continue to integrate.

1961 Freedom rides organised by activists on interstate buses travelling to the American South tested an earlier Supreme Court decision that had supposedly ended segregation on buses. By the end of summer, more than 300 freedom riders had been arrested in Jackson, Mississippi, held in tiny cells and beaten. Public sympathy and support for the freedom riders led President John F. Kennedy's administration to issue a new desegregation order.

1964 Almost 1,000 activists, most of them white college students, travelled to Mississippi to help register voters and teach in 'Freedom Schools'. Through this action, some 17,000 black people attempted to register to vote, though less than 10% succeeded. More than 80,000 African-Americans joined the Mississippi Freedom Democratic Party at this time, to show their desire to vote. On 2 July, President Johnson signed the Civil Rights Act into US law.

3   If you have seen the film, make some notes in answer to questions 1–5.

Possible answers

1   Having been brought up in Georgia, Dakota Fanning would have been very familiar with the accents and dialect of the Deep South, as well as with the agricultural setting in which the events of the film take place. In the film, Lily 'comes of age' – that is, she begins her journey from childhood to adulthood – leaving home and experiencing her first love. As a 'real' fourteen-year-old, Dakota Fanning embodies that transitory period between childhood and adulthood.

2   In the film, Rosaleen does not appear to be much older than Lily. We see how differently the young black woman and the young white woman are treated by society, even though they are both victims of abuse. When Rosaleen and Lily escape, it is Lily who is in charge and this is credible, given their proximity in age in the film. As a younger woman, it also seems natural for Rosaleen to take May's place in the Pink House after May's death. It would have seemed less plausible for an older woman to have been accepted so easily by May's older sisters.

3   The bee theme provides a narrative framework for the story. It is auspicious that Lily is visited by bees at the beginning of the film and that her father does not see them. When she conquers her fear of them and keeps one as a pet in her father's house, we know that bees will be important symbolically for her in her story. It is the honey label that she finds in her mother's possessions which leads Lily to Tiburon and ultimately to the Pink House. While she is there, August teaches Lily how to care for the bees and this is a metaphor for the nurturing which Lily has lacked since her mother's death. The community of industrious bees is a reflection of the ordered and successful community in which the sisters live.

4   August is the most maternal of the three sisters, and in addition to being the bee-keeper, she makes all the big decisions in the household, such as deciding that Rosaleen and Lily can stay for a while, even though June is suspicious. June is more 'cold' than August – she is wary of the unexpected visitors and nervous of committing to marriage with her long-term boyfriend – although she can express herself more freely through her music. May is the most emotional and sensitive of the three. She is very prone to tears and extreme feelings, due in large part to the death of her twin sister, April, during childhood. Eventually, she feels unable to continue bearing the weight of the world on her shoulders.

5   Objects in the Pink House look as though they have come directly from 1964, even down to the smallest piece of kitchen equipment. The same is true of the clothing – whether it is the immaculately-turned-out attire that the three sisters and their friends wear, or the shabby clothes in which Rosaleen and Lily arrive. In Tiburon, the cars, the shops and the movie theater all look convincingly like they belong in the early 1960s.

4

Suggested answer
The Secret Life of Bees gives a vivid picture of the rise of the American Civil Rights movement in the late 1950s and 1960s and is well-researched in terms of period detail. The various examples cited above indicate how successfully the film represents the book and brings the characters and action to life.

5   The words and phrases in the box may be useful for an essay relating to a film tie-in.

1 scene setting   **2** crew   **3** cinematography   **4** action
5 props department   **6** wardrobe manager   **7** script writer   **8** screenplay

Units 5–8 Revision

pages 74–75

The aim of this revision unit is to focus on the language covered in Units 5–8 and to support Writing folder 3 on essays. Specific exam practice is provided on Reading and Use of English, Parts 1 and 4. These tasks could be done as a timed test of 30 minutes.

Use of English

1 The picture shows someone wearing a Lacoste jacket.

> **1** B **2** C **3** A **4** C **5** D **6** B **7** D **8** C

2

> 1 a widespread belief that having your/a photo
> 2 can't have set off yet
> 3 takes great pride in
> 4 did we know at the time what a
> 5 had I returned from the supermarket than
> 6 the time you've come to mind

Vocabulary

3

> **a** nose **b** burst **c** singularly **d** stroke **e** for granted
> **f** eye **g** exception **h** chord **i** widely **j** thunder
> **k** tune **l** view **m** seen **n** childish **o** note

Writing

4 The picture shows a sculpture by Andy Goldsworthy.

> **1** C **2** A **3** E **4** B **5** D

Crossword

This includes some of the idioms, phrasal verbs and other vocabulary from Units 5–8.

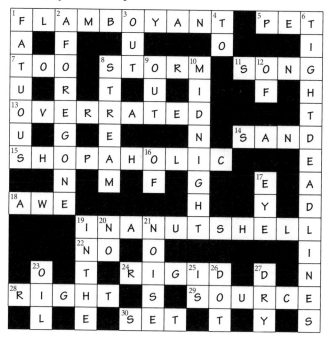

Unit 9

9.1 pages 76–77

Speaking

1 The photos show:
- a female Goth
- a man in overalls and a hard hat
- a woman in a sari
- a man in a business suit
- three UN peacekeepers

Possible answer
These people are in clothes which identify them as part of a certain group. The girl in black wants to be accepted by Goths. The man wears his overalls to protect his clothing from damage and also possibly to protect himself from being injured by machinery. The woman in a sari wishes to conform to Indian traditions. The man in a business suit is presumably expected to conform to office policy. The UN peacekeepers wear their uniforms so that they are easily identified by members of the public.

2

Possible answer
I would wear whatever I fancied to a classical concert. I don't think people bother too much about formality these days.
For a rock festival I would wear comfortable clothes – jeans and a T-shirt.
On a long-distance plane trip I would wear a tracksuit as you really need to be as comfortable as possible on a plane.
On a first date it's really difficult. Perhaps something that reflects what your date was wearing when you first met? At a club, definitely not jeans. Possibly chinos and trainers. Ties are out generally – you get so hot in clubs.
At a job interview, a very smart suit, absolutely. Polished shoes, new haircut and briefcase.
I'd wear a hat and something stylish to a wedding. A summer dress or a good suit.
To the gym, I'd wear my trainers, shorts and a T-shirt.

Vocabulary

3 This exercise will help you to understand some of the vocabulary in the listening task. Use an English–English dictionary to help you with any words you have trouble with.

> **a** down **b** stuck **c** outlay **d** clear **e** hooked
> **f** eyebrows **g** nose **h** opt

Listening

4   Read the Exam spot before you listen.

| 1 C | 2 D | 3 A | 4 H | 5 F | 6 H | 7 C | 8 A | 9 B | 10 G |

Recording script ❶ 14

Speaker 1

When I left school, I was taken on by an environmental charity. I turned up in a suit, but instead of being stuck behind a desk, I was out on the streets, fundraising. My boss at that time was a bit of a rebel. She had quite a funky hairdo and tended to wear ethnic stuff she'd picked up on her travels. I guess she came across as something of a hippie. We got on really well and I thought I'd opt for the same kind of outfits – I can't remember anyone saying anything to make me do that but, to be honest, I think the others at work saw me more as one of them. But I do remember my mother not recognising me when she saw me in the street!

Speaker 2

I play in a metal band called Zandroid. I have a dragon tattoo on my face and wear a leather jacket with a dragon on it. It does mean that people can spot me immediately and I'm constantly getting asked for autographs when I'm out which is great! It makes me feel loved by the fans I guess! I had the tattoo done properly by this guy who I really respect and it wasn't cheap, I can tell you. It was funny how my look came about – I was on the train to a music festival and I picked up one of those free papers. There was a whole thing about dragons in it. I was hooked on the idea in a flash.

Speaker 3

The dress code at my school is fairly formal so I have to wear smart clothes, but I go for tops and trousers rather than suits and high heels. I wouldn't want to raise too many eyebrows among the other staff members so no jeans. Not that the school is super posh or anything, but very casual clothes wouldn't go down too well. What I wear is great really because I have to spend quite a bit of time delving into cupboards. I tend to go for high-end clothes which aren't skin tight – ones that move with me. And they should last – if they were cheap, they'd soon come apart.

Speaker 4

When I left university, I had long hair and wore old jeans. Job interviews were coming up and I didn't want to get up any interviewer's nose and lose out on a good job. There was this job advertised which seemed perfect as a designer at this factory making cars, so I got myself a suit and tie and landed the job. I realised later that I'd got hold of the wrong end of the stick as no one was the least bit bothered, but there you go, better safe than sorry. Anyway, one thing

I've found is that suits are good as there's only a minimum outlay and now we have dress-down Friday I can still wear my jeans then.

Speaker 5

I'm Indian, but I live in the US, doing research in a university. For years, I've worn western clothes, mainly skirts and blouses. I'd always steered clear of the sari as it seemed to me to be not quite right for the workplace, although some other colleagues wear them. Something changed for me last year when I went back to India to see my relatives. The women in saris looked so elegant and I realised that the only person who was stopping me wear one was myself. Now, when I put on my sari, I feel pride in my heritage and realise that what I wear is not going to come between me and promotion or being accepted by others.

Phrase spot

Expressions with *come* are often tested in the examination.

| **a** come round/over   **b** came over   **c** came out in sympathy with   **d** come easily   **e** come between   **f** first come, first served   **g** comes up with the goods   **h** coming along   **i** come to terms with   **j** came in for |

9.2 pages 78–79
Gerunds and infinitives

1   This first exercise aims to review some key points about verb patterns. Refer to the Grammar folder on page 183 if you have problems with this.

| **a** wearing   **b** to wear   **c** you to wear   **d** wearing / to wear   **e** him to shave   **f** her wear |

Corpus spot

This exercise looks at common mistakes which are made with gerunds and infinitives.

a I would have helped her find / to find the right wedding dress.

b We shouldn't spend so much time trying to find bargains in the sales.

c I suggest you use a plaster if you have a blister on your foot.

d The old uniforms in the museum are worth seeing.

e We enjoy ourselves laughing at the stars at the Oscars.

f My new glasses enable me to read more easily.

g We should let them enjoy themselves while they are young.

h I missed talking to my sister when I was away from home.

i I convinced him to apply to the Editor of the magazine.

j You aren't allowed to come into the hotel without wearing a tie.

2 These verbs often cause problems.

a I mean to = I intend to
b It will mean = It will involve
c We regret to inform you = We are sorry to have to tell you
d I regret wearing = I wish I hadn't worn
e The first thing that happened is the walk, now I remember it.
f First remember, then buy the milk.
g First not forget, then post the letter.
h First meeting boyfriend, then not forgetting.
i Try to = Make an attempt
j Try doing = Experiment with
k First he talks about one subject, then another
l goes on talking = continues talking
m After a period of time he accepted this
n A way of moving, describing the action
o I heard Muse once
p I heard them regularly

3 This exercise gives practice in the type of transformation found in Part 4 of the Reading and Use of English paper.

a I don't object to your leaving early.
b Do they allow you to smoke outside your office entrance?
c It's not worth asking her out, she's always busy.
d My father forbade my sister to go / from going to the club in town.
e Book early and you will avoid having to queue / to avoid having to queue.
f His doctor recommended that he do / doing more exercise.
g Don't worry, I promise to post that letter for you.
h I suggest we take our bikes with us. / I suggest taking our bikes with us.
i You had better move your car immediately or else I'll call the police.
j Peter denied causing / having caused the accident.
k His mother made him apologise.

4 The woman is talking about the uniform she had to wear when she was at school and how she felt about it.

Suggested answer
The uniform was bottle green for the girls with a shirt and tie. The rules were very strict. The English teacher was inspirational and wore interesting clothes.

Recording script 1 15

Woman: What do I remember about being at school? Well, it was some time ago now – in the 1990s in fact. I was at a posh private school. I do remember the uniform – it was bottle green, rather dingy, and all the girls had to wear a shirt and tie, which was a pain, I can tell you. The uniform was really uncomfortable and I often felt self-conscious, especially when I was walking down the street.

The girls' skirts had to be the right length. If one of the teachers thought you were wearing a skirt which was too short, then they'd make you kneel down and measure the length from the hem of the skirt to your knees. You had to go home and change if it was too short. Some teachers were worse than others of course. I remember my English teacher, in particular. She used to wear the most amazing clothes – red swirly skirts and purple and silver shoes. She had blonde hair tied back in a ponytail and large glasses with a range of different coloured frames, over which she could peer. I guess she brought a bit of colour into our lives. I thought she was undervalued though by the rest of the staff. I guess they thought she was a bit flashy.

She really inspired me though. She gave us a book list once and said: 'Read these.' The books were brilliant, not fuddy-duddy at all. I used to go to the library every Saturday and hunt them out.

Possible answer
I didn't have to wear a uniform at school, but I suppose wearing jeans and a T-shirt was some sort of uniform. Many of the girls wore dresses but I never did. We only had school in the morning – we started at 7.00 and finished at 1.00 because in the afternoon it got too hot for class. I remember going home and spending about an hour doing homework and then going to the swimming pool to meet my friends. Once a week I had dance class and also my piano lessons.

Vocabulary: Prefixes

5

a refers to person talking – conscious of themselves
b wrongly heard
c going against something, not productive
d for something, in favour
e too much of something
f under/below
g more than – here it is more than human
h against something
i before – arranged before
j to do more in the sense of competition here
k less – the idea that something isn't given its true worth

6 It is important to know how prefixes are used, although you will never be asked to form a word in the Reading and Use of English paper which has a hyphen. Take care, as dictionaries often do not agree on the use of hyphens. Use the prefixes you looked at in exercise 5 to complete this exercise.

> **a** self-contained   **b** sub-tropical   **c** has outlived
> **d** underestimate   **e** misunderstanding   **f** pre-packed
> **g** super-concentrated   **h** anti-lock   **i** overhear   **j** counter-argument   **k** pro-American

7

> We have become more informal and less rigid in both what we wear and when we wear it.
> **1** would/does   **2** intents   **3** time   **4** tell/see   **5** between
> **6** say   **7** our   **8** into   **9** come   **10** such   **11** ourselves
> **12** out   **13** being   **14** when   **15** do

8

> **Possible answer**
> I think clothes aren't as important as personality. Clothing is important but not to the extent that you wouldn't be friends with someone who was, in your eyes, badly dressed. I think that people in the public eye should take more care with what they wear than ordinary people and that also applies to people who work in certain environments such as an office.

9.3 pages 80–81
Reading into Writing: Linking

Speaking

1 The photos are of:
- a boy with a pierced lip
- a makeover – when someone is either digitally enhanced or make-up/cosmetic surgery/botox is used to make someone look younger

> **Possible answers**
> I don't think it is important to look attractive, although society nowadays seems to think it is. An attractive face means having symmetrical features and good skin. I think cosmetic surgery is slightly weird unless it is done for really good reasons, like someone who has a cleft palate. Any facial piercing is dangerous in my opinion. Make-up is fine as long as it isn't too heavy and wigs are also acceptable.
> A politician should get a vote because of his or her policies not his or her looks.
> I would describe myself as fairly tidy and tending towards the casual when it comes to dress. I would never look scruffy or unkempt.

2

> In Text 1 the points made are:
> - people are unconsciously attracted by the way a candidate looks
> - people believe that looks equate with trustworthiness, intelligence, likeability and ability.
> In Text 2 the points made are:
> - it may be necessary to stop people using modern technology to make people look better in photos than they are
> - the tendency to make people look better is something that has always happened.

3

> **1** B   **2** A   **3** C   **4** B   **5** A

4 Refer to the Phrase spot. Use suitable phrases from here to link your sentences effectively. This exercise will also give you practice in giving your own opinion.

> **Possible answer**
> First of all, I believe that the use of modern technology to make politicians more attractive is just another way that politicians can bribe the public into voting for them. It does not seem sufficient for people in politics to have suitable policies to attract the voters; they additionally need to use psychological methods. However, I do think that the majority of people are able to see through these tricks and are able to come to their decisions independently. Moreover, it is highly unlikely that someone will vote for a 'pretty boy' or 'proto-Barbie doll' if they don't have a strategy for improving the economy or creating more jobs. To my mind, it would be incredible if the general public were that credulous.
> Personally, I believe that today people are much more aware of the use of digital enhancement than in the past. Consequently, people nowadays are more likely to take any picture of their favourite star of stage or screen looking amazingly thin or curvy, with a pinch of salt. Then again, we have actually been enhancing people's looks for longer than the advent of digital airbrushing. After all, didn't Henry VIII of England receive a painting of Anne of Cleves, only to find that, disappointingly, it bore little resemblance to the real woman? Portrait painters in the past knew that it was part of their job to make people look a bit better than they actually were and I believe that everyone was aware of this. (248 words)

5 It's a good idea to increase your range of vocabulary so that you don't repeat the same word when you write or speak.

a correct
b wrong – they have a lot to say on every subject, whether they know what they are talking about or not
c correct
d wrong – they are lively and excitable
e wrong – they hoard things
f correct
g wrong – they have good taste
h wrong – they see no need for change even if needed
i wrong – they like to remain in the background
j wrong – they try to control people
k correct

Exam folder 5 pages 82–83

Reading and Use of English, Part 6
Gapped text

This type of reading comprehension requires the reader to understand what is happening both in terms of content and also in terms of reference. Sometimes the links between the paragraphs are not obvious and it will require some skill to sort them out. Read the base text first and then the gapped paragraphs. Think about the scenario, i.e. what the passage is about. Are there any references, e.g. *it/she/they* or *moreover/ secondly/however* which might give a clue?

This text on lying has some clues to help you with the first few questions.

1 E 2 B 3 F 4 A this sort of background (i.e. university qualifications) – a smooth-talking lawyer and consummate liar – lying in corporate culture 5 C body language – visual clues – shifty eyes 6 H more reliable than body movements 7 D doesn't take too much mental planning ... make up a story about something they know well

Unit 10

10.1 pages 84–85

Speaking

1

The languages (from left to right) are:
Chinese, Hungarian, Bulgarian, Greek, Polish, Turkish.
There are about 6,000 languages in the world.
A language dies about every two weeks.
The language spoken more than any other is Chinese.

Possible answer
I think my language, Portuguese, is definitely worth learning. It really helps you to understand your own language if you learn another one. Also Portuguese is a beautiful language and is spoken in Brazil as well as Portugal.

Reading

2 Scan the text to find the answers to the questions.

a It is a pun (play on words). A 'death sentence' is the words used by a judge to condemn someone to death. The use of the word 'sentence', which is connected with language, also relates to the topic of the article, the death of languages.
b He seems ambivalent/undecided. (*Or so they think.*)

3 Ignore the words in italics when you read through the article at this stage.

4 Reference devices are often tested in the Reading and Use of English paper.

a the death of a language   b Kasabe   c the 6,000 languages   d the fact that half are going to die out   e languages   f language death   g language death   h what we learn from a language   i some people

5 These questions test understanding of points in the text.

a made an impact / been considered a matter of some importance
b People start out by being forced to speak the majority language. Then there is a period when both languages are spoken and finally the old language is totally forgotten and the majority language takes over.
c You need to have a wide range of species of animals for a healthy environment. The same is true of different cultures.
d If you lose a language you lose more than just a method of communication.
e medical treatments, early civilisations, new ideas about language itself
f One language is not enough to hold all human/world knowledge.

6 The cartoon is someone asking in Esperanto if the shop accepts credit cards.

Possible answer
I think Esperanto never became popular because it was based on European languages. It is quite an easy language to learn, but only if you already speak a romance language. People from Japan, for example, would have as much difficulty with it as they do with German or Spanish. My language, Hungarian, could never be a world language because so few people speak it.

Background information

Esperanto is the best known of the world's auxiliary languages and was invented by Ludwig Zamenhof in 1887. It was designed to overcome problems of international communication. Newspapers and journals are published in Esperanto, together with the Bible and the Koran. It is also taught as a school subject in many countries.

7 This text is taken from an encyclopaedia. It is written in an impersonal and informative style.

> **1** D is correct. A is used for a piece of guesswork; B is for a person who you only know slightly; C is also used with *between* but in the sense of two things having something in common.
> **2** D is correct. A, B and C all have the idea of *come from*. An idea can *stem from* or *spring from*. A declaration is *issued*.
> **3** A is correct. B takes the preposition *from* and C and D don't collocate with the idea of language.
> **4** A is correct. Only A takes the word *on* in this context.
> **5** D is correct as it collocates with *rely on*.
> **6** C is correct. *Once* here has the meaning of *when*.
> **7** B is correct. A language may *expand*, feet *swell* when they are hot, you can *enlarge* a photograph and *increase* is a general word which can't be used here.
> **8** A is correct as it takes the preposition *from*.

10.2 pages 86–87

Wish and *if only*

1 This extract is from an English newspaper and is a true story.

> **Suggested answers**
> I wish they wouldn't look so embarrassed.
> I wish I could speak to them.
> I wish the interpreter was/were here.
> I wish this meal would end.
> I wish someone would say something.

2 and 3

These exercises should act as a review of the structures. Refer to the Grammar folder on page 183 if you have problems with them.

> **a** the past simple
> **b** the past perfect
> **c** *would* – be careful with this, it can't be used when the subject is repeated, i.e. you can't say *I wish I would ...*
> *If only* and *I wish* have more or less the same meaning. Some people believe *If only* is slightly stronger / more formal in tone.

Corpus spot

> **a** I do hope ...
> **b** I wish I could suppress ...
> **c** She wishes she were / could be
> **d** I hope you like
> **e** I hope you have
> **f** they had allowed us
> **g** He wishes he were able to / could remember
> **h** hope
> **i** her children were
> **j** they would stop smoking
> **k** I wish there could always be / I hope there will always be
> **l** hoping

4

> **Possible answers**
> For my family, there is nothing more I could wish for – we are all quite happy as we are. However, for my studies, I wish I could concentrate in class more and also that I had a photographic memory. I wish my country had a better public transport system and also that everyone went to a state school and we had a fully socialist system. I wish the world were a happier place and that poverty had been eradicated, along with wars and disasters.

Would rather, *It's time*, etc.

5 *It's about time* and *It's high time* are slightly stronger than *It's time*. Note that *I'd rather* is never used with *prefer* as in *I'd rather prefer*.

> **a** to go **b** you went **c** spend **d** left / had left **e** had given **f** he did **g** she took

6 The sentence transformations practise the structures reviewed in this unit.

> **1** you stood up for your rights / for yourself
> **2** you stopped behaving as though you were
> **3** they carried out
> **4** would/'d rather all students wrote
> **5** I hadn't splashed out
> **6** he had/he'd let me know
> **7** she had been aware of the strength / she had known the strength
> **8** would/'d rather you took off / you didn't wear

Phrase spot

Some of these phrases are easy to guess, e.g. *turn as red as a beetroot*. Others are more difficult, e.g. *a turn-up for the books*. Use an English–English dictionary to help you.

> **a** Well, there's a turn-up for the books – I never thought he'd get a girlfriend.
> **b** He has a nice turn of phrase.
> **c** He turned as red as a beetroot when ...
> **d** From the turn of the (last) century, we see ...
> **e** I didn't know which way to turn when the airline ...
> **f** I tossed and turned all last night.
> **g** but he's suddenly taken a turn for the better and ...
> **h** Muriel didn't turn a hair when
> **i** Now, everyone must take it in turns to have a go ...

10.3 pages 88–89

Listening and Speaking

1 The photos are of:
- McDonald's in Marrakech
- a Mongolian yurt with satellite dish
- someone skyping

2 The photos are supposed to reinforce the idea that things are global and that everyone nowadays sees/eats/enjoys similar things.

> **Possible answer**
> I think the term 'global village' is very depressing in many ways. It would be better to highlight differences between people rather than to make everyone the same, with the same interests, culture and so on.
> I think that globalisation permeates all aspects of life in my country, from food to clothes to films. This is accelerating at an alarming rate, due, I believe, to the influence of the Internet.
> Global culture is making inroads into the generation gap. Old people are often the very people who are checking for the best deals on their car insurance on the Internet or booking their holidays with budget airlines online. They don't, perhaps, feel so much in need of a Smartphone as younger people though.

3 Play the recording twice, as in the exam. The parts underlined in the recording script confirm the answers.

    1 B   2 C   3 B   4 C   5 A   6 A

Recording script ●1 16

Extract One

F: There is much heated debate about the true effects of globalisation and if it is really such a good thing. Good or bad though, there isn't much debate about whether it's happening or not. Today we have Steven Bright, MP, in the studio. Mr Bright, what exactly are your objections to globalisation?

M: Well, on the one hand, there's greater access to foreign culture now which can't be bad, but then again some people think that we've ended up as one big superculture. And then there's that awful word, 'outsourcing', which *can* be detrimental to the economy, but not always. Fundamentally, however, I believe that <u>countries are becoming too dependent on each other to thrive. Governments are becoming less influential</u> in the face of an increasingly market-driven world.

F: But, surely, helping developing countries to succeed by giving them loans is a good thing, isn't it?

M: You'd think so, wouldn't you? It may look that way on the face of it, but actually if you get a large organisation handing out money, <u>it is usually with strings attached and those strings often want a particular path to be followed</u>. A solution to, for example, an African problem is often thought up in New York or London. It can be disastrous.

Extract Two

F: I've spent the last twenty years researching into how being bilingual sharpens the mind, but I didn't set out to find out whether bilingualism was good or bad. I did my doctorate in psychology, on how children acquire language. When I finished, there was a job shortage in the US. The only position I could find was with a research project studying second language acquisition in schoolchildren. It wasn't my area but it was close enough. As a psychologist, I brought neuroscience to the study, like 'How does the acquisition of a second language change thought?' <u>It was these types of questions that led me to the bilingualism research. The way research works is, it takes you down a road.</u> You then follow that road.

One interesting thing is that bilingualism helps with multitasking. <u>It was something I'd always had a sneaking suspicion about, but as a result of one experiment, there's now no question.</u> Now, I don't advise anyone to try this at home but we put monolinguals and bilinguals into a driving simulator. Through headphones, we gave them extra tasks to do – as if they were driving and talking on their cellphones. We then measured how much worse their driving got. Everyone's driving got worse, but with the bilinguals, their driving wasn't quite so bad. This is because the bilingual brain has had more practice at multitasking.

Extract Three

Bob: One summer my sister Elena talked me into spending ten weeks learning Chinese with her. I have to say I hadn't covered myself with glory during my previous forays into language learning at school, so I wasn't exactly chomping at the bit to go through it all again, especially with a language which is widely seen as difficult. But Elena convinced me to give it a go <u>and, as she'd previously studied Spanish very successfully, she had quite a few language learning techniques</u> I'd never thought of up her sleeve.

Of course we did the assigned homework, but we didn't spend any extra time quizzing each other on grammar points or vocabulary, which you may think was a bit rash. Instead, we used post-it notes to put a Chinese label on everything in our house we could think of.

The fridge, the bookshelves, the walls, the cooker, the doors, nothing escaped a post-it note naming the object in question in Chinese. Then, whenever we could, we'd make lame observations in Chinese. 'The chair's brown; I don't want to be old; Where's my favourite pencil?' <u>You might laugh, but that really worked</u>. We also rented as many Chinese movies with English subtitles as we could. Ten weeks later we finished the course and we got 'A's. I enjoyed it so much I decided to do Chinese at university.

Pronunciation

4 Noun + noun usually has the stress on the first word.

Adjective + noun usually has the stress on the second word.

Some extra words can be made with *red* and *old* but not all are included here.

red <u>carpet</u>	<u>horse</u> race	<u>race</u>horse	<u>sheep</u> dog	tea bag
<u>boat</u> house	<u>house</u> boat	<u>road</u> sign	back <u>seat</u>
<u>glass</u>house	old <u>woman</u>	red <u>wine</u>	

5 Prefixes might be tested here as well as suffixes. Always read the passage carefully before you do the exercise.

1 meaningful **2** scholarly **3** literary **4** obsession
5 response **6** conception **7** unsatisfactory **8** spectacle

Writing folder 5 pages 90–91

Part 2 Article

1

a Google **b** Coca-Cola **c** Apple iPod® **d** BMW

2 Remember to include a title when you write an article.

The best title is **c**.
Title **a** doesn't reflect the argument expressed; **b** is uninformative; **c** is catchy and in the spirit of the article.

3 Look back at Unit 10 for useful vocabulary. The sample answer in exercise 7 includes further ideas on globalisation.

4 Try to use some of these expressions in your writing, as they offer further ways of linking and reinforcing ideas. However, it would be inappropriate to use them in an essay, due to their journalistic style. They are best used in articles, reviews and letters (to newspapers).

a end **b** all **c** come **d** cold/clear **e** all

5 Rhetorical questions are appropriate to both articles and essays (they were used in the essay on art in Units 5–8 Revision on page 75).

Possible answers
a Don't American products impose a way of life on us that many regard as alien at the end of the day?
b All things considered, mightn't globalisation bring more equality to the world?
c When you come to think of it, isn't it rather depressing to find a McDonald's in every town?
All in all, is it so disastrous that everyone can link up to the Internet?
In the cold light of day, won't these transnational companies bring much-needed investment to poorer countries?
Do we all want to wear the same branded clothes, in the final analysis?

6

Sample 'balancing' paragraph
Although, when you come to think of it, isn't it rather depressing to find a McDonald's in every town? The 'invasion' of global fast food chains sometimes creates problems at the local level too, driving down the takings in established cafés and even forcing closure. That can't be good news for the community at large.

7 When you write your article, follow the advice given in the Exam advice on page 91.

Sample answer
Are we living in one big, happy global village? Or are we currently witnessing, as one journalist so neatly put it, 'global pillage'? Globalisation is a complex issue, but one thing is certain: it is irreversible. Many transnational corporations are now more powerful than national governments; they will not give up their dominance, as too much is at stake economically.
Yet at the same time, the decline of the centralised nation-state is allowing more independence at local level. Regions (which were often countries in their own right formerly) are re-asserting themselves, from Scotland and Wales to Catalunya. Far from mourning the loss of tradition, these parts of the world are strengthening their cultural identities. Take the speaking of Catalan in north-east Spain, for example. Banned for decades, it has resurfaced stronger than ever in the last 25 years, and is now the medium of instruction in schools, the language of local government and often of business too.
However, in the cold light of day, it cannot be denied that global pillage is going on. Doesn't every town boast a McDonald's? Isn't everyone dressed in Nike trainers and Tommy Hilfiger sweatshirts? Companies such as these have made huge profits from our desire to conform. Nevertheless, if people want to make those choices, that is their decision.

My own reaction to globalisation is to take it with a pinch of salt. I do not see any evidence of regional differences dying out and, as I have argued above, the opposite is actually true. There are many positive aspects to the new world order. Not least of these is the Internet, which has revolutionised communication and encourages a political openness that may serve to prevent world war rather than instigate it. All in all, we have much to look forward to in the 21st century, if we concentrate on dealing with the real threat to our individual survival: environmental change.
(319 words)

Unit 11

11.1 pages 92–93

Speaking

1

> **Possible answer**
> The couple on the left look as though they've been together for decades! They seem to have a good relationship, and are very close, whereas the couple on the right are clearly going through some sort of communication breakdown. I think you need to respect your partner and be willing to support them whenever necessary. There will be good times and bad, after all. The external factors that can impinge on a relationship are many: stress at work, lack of money, poor living conditions, or other family members' influence.

2   Think about the seven attributes in turn and decide which one is the most important in a relationship.

> **Possible answer**
> What counts above all in a relationship is the ability to compromise – both partners need to show some give and take, because otherwise there will inevitably be friction in the relationship and unpleasant arguments.

Listening

3   The Listening, Part 3 multiple-choice task requires careful listening 'between the lines' for inferred meaning, so spend some time working through this one – it is the first full-length Part 3 task in the course. Play the recording twice, as in the exam. The underlined parts of the recording script confirm the answers.

1 D   2 A   3 B   4 B   5 C

Recording script   1 17

Interviewer: Last week, Steve came into the studio to prove to us that life still has some happy endings. Here's his story … So, Steve, your relationship with Abby has been through some ups and downs but is definitely on a high now?

Steve: That's right, and we're finally tying the knot next month. Just over five years ago, I met this bubbly little lady – Abby. We went out, shared some laughs, and pretty soon, I knew she was the one for me.

Interviewer: And was it love at first sight for her too?

Steve: She was happy enough to spend lots of time with me, but treated me more like a big brother, if anything – she even told me about another guy she was hoping to get together with. At which point, realising I would get nowhere romantically, I decided I'd better cast my net elsewhere. I met a nice girl called Samantha, very down-to-earth – the opposite of Abby – and we started seeing each other once in a while. We had well-paid jobs and money to burn. After a good holiday in Spain, we decided to move in together. I think we both understood that it wasn't true love, but we rubbed along fairly well. Unfortunately, quite soon after that, Abby made up her mind that I was Mr Right after all, and made this very plain to me, though not to Samantha.

Interviewer: How did you take this bolt from the blue?

Steve: It was baffling. I actually wondered whether she was joking, she used to do that, but I knew deep down she wouldn't pull that trick any more. I rationalised it as her whipping up a fleeting fantasy – she had time on her hands, as she'd been fired from her job and was on her own a lot – her then current boyfriend worked long hours.

Interviewer: And there were displays of obvious jealousy, weren't there?

Steve: Yeah, we'd be at the same pubs and there would be anguished looks from Abby across the room, deep sighs if she was ever standing next to me at the bar, that sort of thing – I misread the situation for ages – she's always had a streak of theatricality.

Interviewer: What was your reaction once you realised it was genuine?

Steve: Well, it dawned on me that I was calling the tune now; if I wanted it, Abby and I would have a life together – otherwise, things would stay the same. It wasn't straightforward, there was Samantha to consider. She'd always been very supportive and loyal. For a while, I couldn't decide what to do. To fend off the problem, I threw myself into my job.

Interviewer: And did colleagues at work pick up on anything different about you?

Steve: Very much so – <u>I'd never been that keen and efficient before!</u> Although my daily routine was much the same, I was glad to get to work, because it distracted me – but I made sure I kept my private life out of our usual conversations. As time went on, there was growing pressure on me to do something – for all I knew, Abby might give up in disgust.

Interviewer: Then, one summer's day …

Steve: Yes, one beautiful morning last June, I couldn't keep up the pretence any longer. I sat Samantha down at the kitchen table and blurted everything out. She was terrific, far from holding back tears, she didn't even seem mildly phased by the revelation that I'd been carrying a torch for someone else and it was over. Just rolled up her sleeves and started sorting out my life for me: <u>phoned my office to say that I was at death's door</u> and wouldn't be coming in, then told me to get round to Abby's place pronto, preferably with a big bunch of flowers – she let me buy those myself.

Interviewer: And so Samantha walked out of your life and Abby walked in.

Steve: Yeah. Abby and I rented a cottage out in the country. Last summer was idyllic, and, well, it matched our mood. We got to know each other properly, spent every evening gazing into each other's eyes at sunset and … well, I'm sure you can picture the rest.

Interviewer: Absolute rapture, straight out of *True Romance* … how wonderfully slushy! So when did you finally pop the question, Steve?

Steve: I was at a big family wedding, one of my cousins, and Abby hadn't come, I think she had flu. Anyway everything seemed to fall into place at that event. I managed to sit down with my mother and talk about Abby – Mum'd been giving me the cold shoulder, as she'd really liked Samantha and, social norms being what they are, had seen her as a prospective daughter-in-law. Anyway, she came round after our heart-to-heart and I went off to offer a lift to my cousin's old schoolfriend, who lives in the States – <u>I hadn't seen him for five years. Well, he looked me between the eyes and said, 'You've always loved Abby, so how come you're not married yet – get a grip, Steve.'</u> So I did, leapt in the car without him, drove back and proposed. It's funny though, it had taken someone at one stage removed from my life to state the obvious.

Interviewer: Well, Steve, I wish you and Abby every happiness – you certainly deserve it.

Steve: Thank you.

4

> **Possible answer**
> It's got as good a chance as any marriage. At least Abby knows what she really wants now, and Steve seems pretty keen.

5

> Steve means that Abby sometimes likes to behave in a dramatic way.
> Some collocations with *streak* can be positive, e.g. *romantic*.
> **1** first sight **2** streak **3** slushy **4** displays **5** one
> **6** popped

Vocabulary: Phrasal verbs

6 Both examples contain phrasal verbs (with noun collocations).

> **Suggested answers**
> blurt out a problem, a secret
> bottle up a problem, emotions
> choke back tears, emotions
> fend off criticism, blows, accusations
> keep up appearances
> shoot down an argument, accusations
> sweep aside an argument, accusations, criticism
> tease out a problem, a secret
> tone down criticism, accusations
> whip up rage, emotions

The sentences should include:

a bottle up / blurt out a secret
b tone down criticism
c whip up emotions
d fend off blows
e choke back tears / bottle up emotions
f shoot down an argument

Idiom spot

If necessary, play the recording again or look at the recording script for 3.

> **a** tying the knot – getting married
> **b** cast my net – look around for someone else
> **c** bolt from the blue – a total surprise
> **d** time on her hands – plenty of free time
> **e** calling the tune – in charge
> **f** carrying a torch for – in love with
> **g** rolled up her sleeves – behaved very practically
> **h** at death's door – very ill
> **i** giving me the cold shoulder – ignoring me
> **j** get a grip – take charge, get in control
> **k** hands **l** grip **m** sleeve **n** clutching **o** grasp **p** grips
> **q** hands **r** grabs

11.2 pages 94–95

Gradability

1 The picture shows a girl using a social networking site.

Possible answer
Facebook is great. I couldn't plan my social life without it and it means I can keep in touch with people I don't get to see very often. I guess there are disadvantages to do with privacy and security, but it doesn't actually worry me that much.

2 Richard and Cindy met through an Internet chat room.

1 since/from **2** anything **3** hardly/barely/scarcely
4 Having **5** as **6** Within **7** most **8** sooner

3 Refer to the Grammar folder on page 184 if necessary.

You cannot say 'completely affectionate', as 'affectionate' is a gradable adjective; conversely, 'devastating' is an ungradable adjective, so you cannot say 'extremely devastating'.
The adverbs *deeply, fairly, immensely, rather, very* go with A (gradable adjectives) and the adverbs *absolutely, entirely, utterly* go with B (ungradable adjectives). The three adverbs that can go with both are *pretty, quite, really* but there are register restrictions.

4

a utterly miserable
b doubly disappointing
c slightly embarrassed
d highly suspicious
e absolutely staggering
f somewhat envious

Possible answers
(Two remaining phrases)
Helena seems **fairly laid-back** about tomorrow's interview, but I know she has spent ages preparing for it.
Your forecast about the weather was **remarkably accurate** – how on earth did you know it was going to be sunny today?

5

The first use is ungradable – nationality is an absolute. In the second use, the degree adverb *very* can be used – here, the adjective is gradable, as 'Britishness' exists on a scale from mild to very strong, or stereotypical.

6

a **First example:** used to describe food that keeps for a long time in a freezer (in a frozen state)
Second example: INFORMAL and non-literal, used when a person feels very cold
b **First example:** If something is empty, it does not contain anything.
Second example: having no meaning or value
c **First example:** used to mean very difficult to deal with – note that although this sentence is fairly informal, the meaning is not restricted in register – e.g. UNMARKED *Trapped in a war zone, the journalists are facing an impossible situation.*
Second example: If an action or event is impossible, it cannot happen or be done.
d **First example:** INFORMAL, non-literal, meaning very stupid or crazy
Second example: (old-fashioned use) seriously mentally ill
e **First example:** non-literal, used of a situation where there is little or no hope for the future
Second example: literal use – if a place is bleak, it is cold, empty and not attractive.
f **First example:** lacking in taste or flavour – note that although this sentence is quite informal, the meaning is not restricted in register – e.g. UNMARKED *The meat was dry and tasteless.*
Second example: offensive, likely to upset or anger people

7

a alternative b cautionary c collapsible d detestable
e honorary, honourable f laborious g loathsome
h hypocritical i philosophical j repulsive k tenacious
l theatrical m virtuous n voluntary

8

1 indeterminate
2 setting(s)
3 decidedly
4 disclose
5 alliances
6 crucial
7 outcomes
8 inroads

11.3 pages 96–97

Reading into Writing: Reformulation 2

1 The pictures show members of a street gang on a housing estate and team bonding at a business meeting.

Possible answers
People conform in society by wearing similar clothes, having similar tastes in entertainment and leisure activities and by behaving in the same way. Being part of a group offers security and the feeling of belonging, rather than being an outsider. People may join a sports club to play sport, but they often want to make new friendships too. Being accepted into a gang is also a form of conformism.

2 There is overlap in the discussion of belonging to a group, but the contexts are very different.

3 Statements 1 and 3 reflect ideas in the first text.

4 As said earlier in the course, it is extremely important that you use your own words in Writing, Part 1 as you will lose marks if you copy the wording of the texts.

Suggested answers
a people's biased attitudes and failings
b there is a trend of extreme behaviour
c members are inclined to inflate the group's worth / regard the group as better than it is
d the belief that the group is invincible
e a rigidity in outlook
f a desire for homogeneity
g the suppression of individual views
h any opposition is firmly dealt with

5 The answer has a strong introduction that puts the topic into context and includes own language. The remaining paragraphs concentrate on the second text – the first text is only summarised briefly and there is no evaluation of it. In the rewriting, most phrases can be used from exercise 4; 'disregarding' can be replaced by 'ignoring'.

Exam folder 6 pages 98–99

Listening, Part 4 Multiple matching

1 Look at the information and the Exam advice. You will always hear the recording twice.

2 Play the extract for Speaker 1 twice. Underline the information containing the answers and look for where the distraction is occurring.

Answers and Recording script 1 18

You are going to hear Speaker One. Look at both Task One and Task Two and decide which answers are true for the first speaker. You will hear the recording twice.

Speaker 1
I was at a twenty-first birthday 'do'. I'd just broken up with a beautiful girl who I'd been head over heels in love with and my loyal friends thought it was time to find me someone else. I'm quite shy but I was instantly taken with this girl they introduced me to, called Sarah. <u>She struck me as really fun and sparkling, ready to chat to anyone, even me!</u> Anyway, we were married a year later. She's a wonderful person – she must be to have stayed married to me all these years! <u>She's been there through thick and thin</u>, and I can tell you there have been times when money's been extremely tight.

3 Play the extract for Speaker 2 twice and follow the same procedure as for Speaker 1, above.

Answers and recording script 1 19

2 C   7 C

Now listen to Speaker Two and, with a partner, decide on the answers for Questions 2 and 7.

Speaker 2
I'm a bit of a workaholic and so actually finding someone to have a relationship with was always tricky. I'm at the top of my game, head of a large fashion house, and I've found that men find me a bit intimidating because I'm so determined to succeed. I guess that's why I've always liked older men – they're usually less insecure. My partner is great, <u>so shrewd about people</u>, much better than me, although when I first met him, even though he was as stylish as everyone around me, <u>it was his intellect that drew me to him</u>. I like to think we're really well matched.

4 Play the extracts for the other three speakers and complete the task.

3 G   4 B   5 A
8 F   9 D   10 G

Recording script 1 20

Now listen to the other three speakers and, for Questions 3 to 5 and 8 to 10, choose from the lists A to H. Use each letter only once. There are three extra letters which you do not need to use. You will hear the recordings twice.

Speaker 3
I'm a writer and I'd lived alone for years. Anyway, I went to a friend's party and there was this woman there surrounded by admiring men – someone told me they thought she was 'gorgeous' but I didn't think she was my type. Anyway, when I did get to talk to her we got on like a house on fire. <u>She just seemed to be so full of stamina, so dynamic.</u> We

married six weeks later – a whirlwind romance! Anyway, we've had our ups and downs obviously over the years but it's her warm personality that keeps me close. We do have rows, mainly about money, and I get very impatient with her, but we always soon make up.

Speaker 4

I started online dating when I moved to London. I didn't know anyone so I was determined to give it a go, and it was cheap! That's how I met my husband. We're kindred spirits really and I really like the fact that he's such a perfectionist – everything has to be just right – I guess I am too really. Some people say it would drive them mad but not me. Of course, I didn't notice that about him when we first met. Most people see the handsome face first but it was his attitude to people that attracted me. He was so broadminded and really opened my eyes to the problems some people have in society.

Speaker 5

I went on quite a few dates when I first moved to New York. My workmates fixed me up with people. One was this model with not a hair out of place who looked terrific, but was extremely dull. Not long after her, I met this wonderful girl on a plane to Tokyo. She wasn't conventionally pretty, I guess, but she just managed to see the funny side of everything. We got married soon after and we're still in love. What I love about her is that she's happy to spend ages reading to our kids and, not only that, she can find time to sit and chat to my elderly parents and that's not easy as my mother's beginning to forget things.

Unit 12

12.1 pages 100–101

1 The three questions are typical ways in which an examiner might ask you to extend topic discussion with the other candidate after the individual long turns in Speaking, Part 3.

Possible answers
Ordinary people have greater life expectancy due to improvements in medicine. DNA analysis has led to better crime detection and conviction of criminals.
This area of genetics and biotechnology is bound to give rise to new discoveries, as further work is done on the human genome.
Multinational companies are very powerful and the attempt to introduce GM (genetically modified) food illustrates that government ministers need to keep a close eye on what they are doing. Current legislation and governmental controls may be inadequate.

Reading

2 The photo shows the minuscule guitar from Cornell University that is referred to in the opening sentence of the text.

Suggested answer
The writer has tried to simplify the difficult subject matter by referring to things from the real world – parts of cells are likened to scissors, motors, pipes and so on, and the DNA helix is compared to a ladder. Atoms and molecules become busy commuters, rushing around the body. The A, T, C, G base pairings in DNA are 'just a string of four-letter words' (almost certainly included to raise a laugh from the reader, as 'four-letter words' is a common euphemism for swear words, and is rather appropriate to a discussion of life as these tend to refer to the sexual organs and the act of reproduction!).

3 You must spend enough time reading the text and missing paragraphs, in order to work out the links involved. In the exam, underline key phrases in both as you read.

The parts of the text which link to the underlined phrases in paragraphs A–H are given alongside the answers below. Notice that there isn't always a link both before and after a gap.

1 D before gap: *tweezers, scissors*, etc.;
      after gap: *collectively*
2 H after gap: *urban environment, commuting*
3 A before gap: *no overseer supervises their activities*;
      after gap: *nowadays, convincing explanation*
4 F before gap: *they say*
5 C before gap: *more than the sum of its parts, the job of explaining life*;
      after gap: *with the discovery of DNA, early 1950s*
6 G before gap: *handrails, rungs*
      after gap: *A, T, C, G*
7 B before gap: *slot together snugly, complementary projecting arms*;
      after gap: *this is guaranteed to be identical to the original*

4

a a pump   b valves   c (a pair of) scissors
d (some) tweezers   e a (padlock and) chain

Idiom spot

a nail – something that has finally caused failure
b spade (a) spade – to speak directly
c tubes – to fail
d chain – unreliable part of something, usually used of people
e fuse – to lose your temper
f strings – unconditional
g wires – to misunderstand
h bolt – to fail
i gear – to start to deal with something effectively
j knife – to deliberately make someone feel worse

12.2 pages 102–103

Passive structures

1

> **a** 1 **b** 3 **c** 5 **d** 4 **e** 2

2 Refer to the section in the Grammar folder on page 184 first if necessary.

  a Marie Curie was given the Nobel Prize for Chemistry for her discovery of radium.

  b Homes in and around the city have been affected by lengthy power cuts all this week.

  c The 'miracle' drug was found to have unpleasant side-effects.

  d Meteorites have been found in Antarctica which are believed to have come from the Moon.

  e Dark matter is said to exist in the universe, but (it) has not been detected as yet.

  f The car will no longer be manufactured in Europe, due to recent global restructuring.

  g The Truman Capote Award for Literary Criticism was won in 2011 by Mark McGurl / was won by Mark McGurl in 2011.

  h The latest version of Adobe Flash should be installed to get the best from this application.

3 Use of the passive will make your writing appropriately neutral and impersonal in tone.

> **Suggested answer**
> **a** Food and drink must not be brought into the lab.
> **b** No photographs may be taken inside this museum.
> **c** Infra-red equipment is being used to search for further survivors.
> **d** The award for best innovation will be shared by/ between three postgraduate students.
> **e** Thorough safety checks are to be / will be carried out immediately.

Corpus spot

> **a** be reminded **b** being delayed **c** being damaged
> **d** to have been invited **e** having been asked / being asked **f** be discovered

4

> **1** was discovered **2** could not have been caused
> **3** was detected / had been detected (specific to one research project) OR has been detected (traces of iridium continue to be found there) **4** must have been formed
> **5** would have been thrown **6** to be blotted out
> **7** were eaten **8** would have been killed

5

> **Possible answer**
> **a** Publication/The publication of these scientific papers will be delayed until next year.
> **b** An announcement of big job losses has just been made on the local news.
> **c** Consideration is being given to the planning application for a new sports centre.
> **d** A recommendation will be made for the immediate closure of the hospital.
> **e** An investigation of the case in more depth is to be carried out. OR A more in-depth investigation of the case is to be carried out.
> **f** No explanation was given as to how much the project would cost.

6

> **1** for a probe to be landed
> **2** will need/have to be worn for the duration
> **3** be seen by/with the naked eye OR be discernible/visible to the naked eye
> **4** increasing number of planets have been found
> **5** to be on the brink of
> **6** being / having been advised against physics / not to continue with physics

12.3 pages 104–105

Listening and Speaking

1 Remember that the prompt card is there to help you in the exam, rather than to restrict your ideas.

> **Possible answers**
> career opportunities – more now than ever before
> commercial interests – very strong, may go against government policy
> moral issues – tampering with nature

2 The recording lasts the full two minutes.

Recording script 1 ㉑

Interlocutor: Now, in this part of the test you're each going to talk on your own for about two minutes. You need to listen while your partner is speaking because you'll be asked to comment afterwards.

So Jana, I'm going to give you a card with a question written on it and I'd like you to tell us what you think. There are also some ideas on the card for you to use if you like.

All right? Here is your card.

Jana: Well, I don't have a scientific background, but I think science is something that affects us all nowadays. You can't afford to ignore what's going on in advanced science. There's a lot of media interest right now in the latest developments in, say, genetics and DNA profiling.

Er, I do think it's worrying how genetic testing can be used, actually. For example, if you have a genetic disorder of some kind, you may not be able to take out life insurance … or get a job even. But then, on the other hand, DNA analysis is helping to solve crimes, and that's good for society, so it's good and bad, I suppose. The main problem centres around information. Most people don't know the facts and so naturally they're worried. So what is needed is more information in simple language for ordinary people to understand – and perhaps this needs to come from the government. Because I think the biggest worry of all is that the whole area of genetics is being driven by the business world. Much of the research going on today is backed by big companies – drugs co…, pharma… pharmaceutical companies and so on – and they're going to want something back from their investment. Which means that the research is not being done just as research, it's not pure, not independent. … I think too, that they're not controlling this research.

The public needs to be properly informed. There are potential benefits, yes, but we must be told what's happening and why. You know, things are being pushed ahead at such an alarming rate and … mm, I don't know, it seems to me, it's maybe not always going to be helpful for society.

Interlocutor: Thank you. Erik, what is your view on current career opportunities in science?

Erik: I'm actually in the final year of a biology degree so I can comment on that personally. We're always being told by our lecturers that more progress will be made in biology in the next five to ten years than has occurred in the last fifty. It's a fast-moving field. As Jana said, there are many new companies … biotech companies springing up, so yes, job prospects are good for someone like me, I think, plenty of different directions to go in. So it's not all doom and gloom, far from it.

Interlocutor: What do you think, Jana?

Jana: Well, Erik is speaking from experience! It's good to hear his positive take on things.

Interlocutor: Thank you.

Pronunciation

3

a 3	b 4	c 5	d 1	e 2	f 6

Notice how Jana stresses important points (underlined in the recording script on the next page) and pauses for emphasis (shown by … in the recording script).

Recording script 1 22

a You can't <u>afford</u> to … <u>ignore</u> what's going on in the <u>vanguard</u> of science.

b So it's … a <u>double-edged sword</u>, I suppose.

c So what is needed … is more <u>information</u> in <u>simple</u> language … for the <u>lay</u> person to understand.

d Which means that the research is not being done for its <u>own sake</u> … it's not <u>pure</u> … not <u>independent</u>.

e I think too, that the research is … not subject to <u>enough regulations</u>.

f It's maybe <u>not</u> always going to be for … the <u>greater good</u>.

4 Practise building up these phrases, repeating aloud after the speaker.

Recording script 1 23

a concern
cause for concern
considerable cause for concern
There's considerable cause for concern in the whole area.

b duty
duty bound to
Governments are duty bound to regulate the industry.

c repercussions
possible repercussions
There are a number of possible repercussions.

d significance
the social significance
The social significance of biotechnology should not be underestimated.

e cusp
on the cusp of
We're on the cusp of completely new forms of treatment.

f reservations
extreme reservations
I have extreme reservations about the confidentiality of all this information.

Phrase spot

(clockwise)
set the wheels in motion, set the world on fire, set the scene, set out your stall, set your heart on, set the record straight, set a dangerous precedent, set in stone, set your sights on, set your teeth on edge
The other verbs are *pull* and *run*:
pull your weight – work as hard as other people in a group
pull your socks up – improve your behaviour or work
Pull the other one! – if you use this expression, it means you don't believe what someone has just said to you. Also:
Pull the other one, it's got bells on it.
pull the strings – control people or an organisation
pull a fast one – trick someone
run rings round – beat or do better than someone
run the risk of – do something although something bad might happen because of it
run counter to – have the opposite effect to something else
run a tight ship – manage something efficiently

5

a Jenny **set her heart on** having the new gadget.
b The consultant **set out her stall** to the whole department.
c Allowing her teenage son to stay out late has **set a dangerous precedent**.
d Nothing is **set in stone** as yet.
e The vivid description of the Martian landscape **sets the scene** at the beginning of the book.
f The sound of a young child attempting to play the violin really **sets my teeth on edge**.
g A leading biotech company immediately **set the wheels in motion** to recruit the young scientist.
h Carla's a good singer, but she's never going to **set the world on fire**.

6 Notice that two of the expressions with *run* are used in the text: *run the risk of* and *run counter to*.

1 B   2 C   3 A   4 C   5 D   6 B   7 A   8 D

Writing folder 6 pages 106–107

Part 2 Report

1 The work you have done on passive structures in Unit 12 can now be used in your writing. Notice how passives are used in the report.

Improved answer with sub-headings and bullets
This report summarises the current career opportunities for science graduates, drawing largely on the experiences of past and present students. Many final-year students have already been invited to interviews and some have even been offered jobs, conditional on graduation.
A broad scope of employment
The first point to stress is that interesting opportunities exist outside the specialist scientific fields. This is dealt with in the final section of the report.
Academic research
Returning to pure science, it has been estimated that there will be over a thousand post-graduate posts available for the next academic year, countrywide. Students should consult their tutor for advice in the first instance. High-achievers should contemplate applying for scholarships to the U.S.A., where so much research is at the cutting edge. Students wishing to follow up on specific research possibilities in the States are advised to consult Professor Grimbleton.
Exciting new opportunities
The fast-moving developments in biotechnology and genetics look set to provide good job opportunities, as many companies are being expanded in their bids to become market leader. Four local companies have specifically requested graduate trainees from this college. They are:
• Bio-futures   • PJF Seed Research
• Genotech   • Railton Systems.
Application forms can be obtained from the Administration Secretary.

Education as a career
Several past students have opted for jobs in teaching and it is recommended that anyone considering such a career should attend the information day planned by this department. At this event, it will not only be possible to meet Head Teachers and Science Coordinators from schools in the region, but also former college students who are now qualified and practising teachers.
A more unconventional path
As indicated above, any report on current opportunities would be incomplete without mentioning other non-scientific jobs that past students have taken up with relish. While none of these jobs can be said to demand the recall of actual science, the generic skills that students have been given through their undergraduate courses are directly relevant.
Here are some of the more unusual career moves:
• accountancy
• stockmarket brokering
• counselling
• air-traffic control
• casino management.
Next steps
More details can be found on the student website. A booklet is also in preparation. (360 words)

2

Other examples of signposting:
This report summarises
The first point
This is dealt with in the final section
Returning to pure science
Here are
Referring forward: c, e, g
Referring back: a, b, d, f, h, i, j

3

a high-achievers
b fast-moving, recently-formed
c un- (unconventional), post- (post-graduate), non- (non-scientific)
d -al (unconventional, conditional), -ally (specifically), -ist (specialist), -ship (scholarship)
e at the cutting edge, career move

4 Do you find spider diagrams helpful? There are many other ways of making notes, so use the one you prefer when planning your report.

5 Write your report, following the advice given on page 107.

Sample answer
KELVINGTON FILM CLUB ANNUAL REPORT
Following another successful year, the club is able to make ambitious plans for the coming twelve months. This report will summarise its current financial situation, review recent events, and outline future plans.

Financial affairs

The club has seen a slight rise in expenses: film rental costs were increased last July and mailing costs have also risen, due to a notable increase in membership: 32 new members have joined and their fees have contributed to the club's healthy bank balance. Moreover, in March, the club was awarded a grant of £500 from the Princefield Film Institute, due to the impressive bid submitted by the Chair.

Main events

The highlights of last year's programme are given below:

- Welcome for new members, February
- Short season of Bertolucci's films, March
- Talk by screenwriter Todd Grafton, April
- Visit to the Cannes Film Festival, June
- Summer barbecue and party, August
- Lecture series on animation techniques, October
- Annual club dinner, December

Of these, the Cannes visit was particularly popular and thanks must be given to Joy Wellman for organising everything so well. In contrast, the lecture series in October was poorly attended, and enrolments barely covered the costs of the venue and speaker. It would be appreciated if members could give the committee feedback about this event, so that the same mistakes are not repeated.

Future plans

As always, the film programme is defined largely by members' requests. While the booking secretary already has a potential list of screenings, it is not too late for further films to be proposed.

One exciting development is the imminent setting up of a DVD library, which has been requested by many members. The scheme will allow members to rent up to two films at a time, for periods of three to five days.

Finally, the club is proud to confirm that the Canadian director Brad Eastwood has accepted the invitation to give a talk to members, date to be confirmed. This event promises to be both informative and exciting, as Brad is known to be a lively and controversial speaker. (340 words)

Units 9–12 Revision

pages 108–109

This revision unit practises the language covered in Units 9–12 (and earlier units), as well as extending the work done on reports in Writing folder 6. Specific exam practice is provided for Reading and Use of English, Parts 2 and 4. This Use of English section could be done as a timed test of 30 minutes.

Use of English

1 This text comes from a magazine.

1 with	2 us/readers	3 Not	4 but	5 come	6 nothing
7 all	8 gives	9 among/perhaps/possibly	10 but/while/whilst/although	11 go/date	12 everyone	13 When/Once	14 might/could

2

1 agreed to take it in turns to tidy
2 went on to discuss
3 Peter had put on a suit for
4 is remembered for always having
5 not/never lose sight of the fact that luck
6 as friendship is concerned, I'd rather have

Vocabulary

3

a came in for b turn c vivacious d set e chain
f shoulder g choke back h pompous i sets j blue
k a spade a spade l coming along m nettle n blurting out

Writing

4 Using compound adjectives in your writing will show your range of language.

Here is my report on our club's recent exchange visit to Australia. Without exception, members who participated in this trip were highly appreciative of the **meticulously-planned** itinerary, not to mention the warm welcome extended by our **easy-going** Australian hosts. This **long-standing** relationship continues to flourish and we will be hosting a **record-breaking** number of visitors this summer (see below).

Travel

The **inter-continental** flights went smoothly and we arrived in Melbourne on schedule. A coach had been organised to transport us to the civic reception, where our individual hosts awaited us. Travel within Australia was mostly by plane – unfortunately, our visit coincided with industrial action, so our transfers were not entirely **trouble-free**.

Trips

The highpoint was the Great Barrier Reef, where two exhilarating days were spent **deep-sea** diving. Those members who chose not to dive were given the alternative of a **half-day** cruise in a **glass-bottomed** boat, which was said to be very enjoyable for all concerned. Some members have suggested that the visit to the Kakadu National Park could have been extended, as it was rather rushed. In subsequent years, it might also be more informative to visit during the dry season, which would allow **wider-ranging** access to the park.

Return visit

There will be 48 visitors to us in July, including six families with young children. In view of this, it will be necessary to find extra hosts. Strategies for achieving this should be agreed at the next club meeting. In anticipation, could the following suggestions be tabled:

- advertising in relevant journals
- feature in local newspaper
- posters in public places, e.g. library
- mailshot to schools and colleges
- interview on KJY radio
- club website?

Perhaps other members should be asked for further suggestions in advance of the meeting.
(288 words)

Crossword

This includes some of the idioms, phrasal verbs and other vocabulary from Units 9–12.

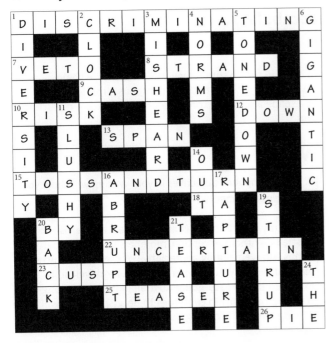

Unit 13

13.1 pages 110–111

Vocabulary: Environment collocations

1

fossil fuel
severe famine/shortages
pristine environment / ice cap
finite resources
greenhouse gases
water shortages/resources
climate change
solar energy
population density/change
melting ice cap
rising sea levels
life expectancy

Speaking

2

The photos are of:

- an overpopulated city
- smog from cars and scooters
- deforestation

Possible answers
I'm not sure we are doing enough to save the planet. The more trees we cut down, the worse soil erosion will get. This will lead to severe famine and food shortages. After all, we only have finite resources.

3

Possible answers
Recycle glass, paper and cans.
Don't carry shopping in plastic carrier bags.
Don't use disposable containers or cups.
Turn off lights, computers and TVs.
Turn down the thermostat in your room.
Plant a tree.
Ride a bike to work or college.
Use recycled stationery and toilet paper.
If you use a car, go electric and share car space.
Use energy-efficient light bulbs.
Volunteer to help in local environmental programmes.
Fix any dripping taps.
Always use biodegradable products.
Don't use herbicides or insecticides in your garden.
Use paper carefully.
Turn off the tap when you clean your teeth.
Use washing machines that use less water.

Listening

4 Read through the questions before you play the recording. Play each extract twice. The underlined parts of the recording script confirm the answers.

1 B   2 B   3 A   4 C   5 A   6 C

Recording script 1 24
Extract One
Kids love it when I say I talk rubbish for a living, but it's the truth. As a recycling officer, I'm pretty obsessed with cutting down on consumption and waste. People come into this field from a mix of backgrounds. Mine is teaching, which is ideal, and most days during term time I'll have some contact with schools. <u>Kids are very receptive to the 'save the planet' message and they're actually natural collectors of everything from bottle tops to newspapers, which is useful.</u> If it's a keen school, I'll ask questions and they'll bombard me with questions of their own, which is great. But if I ask, 'What's recycling?' and someone answers 'Riding your bike' I know I've got a long morning ahead of me. Usually they're completely spellbound, they've a rough idea of what the local 'dump' is, but with a video and descriptions and the occasional trip, I can really spell out what landfill means. The cost of burying rubbish is enormous. <u>Even taking into account the roller coaster changes in price for recycled plastics, glass and paper, it's still worth recycling, and children are receptive to that. What really gets me is the lack of local initiatives – there is often no direct link between policy and action.</u>

Extract Two

Interviewer: Now, Professor Dean, the greenhouse effect has made finding alternative sources of energy all the more urgent, hasn't it?

Professor: Indeed. If not for the greenhouse effect, we may have been able to postpone finding a replacement for fossil fuels for some time. Places like India and China, for example, have huge quantities of cheap coal at their disposal, but with the greenhouse effect we need to make the transition earlier. But renewables, such as solar and wind power, all tend to be very episodic and the power density is low. Investment and take-up of renewables has been variable.

Interviewer: And what about biomass energy?

Professor: Well, that brings you to the inevitable land-use issue. Say that by 2050 you wanted to supply ten terawatts of power, which equals the current total energy consumption of all humankind, and you wanted to do it with biomass energy, you would need an area equal approximately to ten per cent of the Earth's land surface area. Eventually you'd have people and you'd have wheat but nothing else. I'm not sure how popular that policy would make a government.

Extract Three

Presenter: With me to talk about environmental issues today is Dr Jane Dove, of the University of Melchester. Welcome, Jane.

Woman: Good morning.

Presenter: Today we're discussing the Gaia hypothesis, a theory about the Earth put forward in 1965 by James Lovelock. Now Lovelock was a scientist outside the British establishment. He took issue with the accepted view that the Earth was just a passive host to millions of species of plants and animals, and that these living organisms simply adapted to the environment they found themselves in. Jane, nowadays Lovelock's theory that denuding forests will ravage delicate ecosystems is generally accepted, isn't it?

Woman: Indeed, but you know, even in the 1960s he was thought of as a tree-hugger – someone who goes around hugging and worshipping trees. A bit of a weirdo really. Of course, it didn't help that he called his idea the Gaia hypothesis.

Presenter: Yes, in fact this name, after the Greek goddess of the Earth, pushed Lovelock even further away from his peers.

Woman: I guess to them it seemed to represent the very opposite of rigid scientific enquiry.

Presenter: True, more a 'holistic' view of the Earth – that's as a whole rather than its individual components. He wasn't an amateur though, and his ideas have since gained acceptance.

---

5 Play the recording again and decide which register each extract has.

You need to get some idea of register in English because you are often tested on it in different parts of the exam.

Extract 1: informal – 'to talk rubbish' is a play on words; quite a few words are informal: *pretty, kids, cutting down, spell out, a rough idea*; use of *bombard* – exaggeration for effect

Extract 2: the man uses formal speech; *postpone, at their disposal, the transition, humankind*

Extract 3: man uses fairly formal speech; woman more informal – *a bit of a weirdo, I guess*

6 These words are all taken from the *Cambridge Learner Corpus*.

a *people* is unmarked; *persons* is used in notices and government handouts
b *amelioration* is formal; *improvement* is unmarked
c *bloke* is informal; *man* is unmarked
d *stuff* is informal; *things* is unmarked
e *frequented* is formal; *went to* is unmarked
f *reckon* is informal; *think* is unmarked
g *boozing* is very informal/slang; *drinking* is unmarked
h *mates* is informal; *friends* is unmarked
i *fellow* is rather dated informal; *guy* is modern informal
j *snaps* is informal; *photographs* is unmarked
k *pluses* is informal; *advantages* is unmarked
l *lousy* is informal; *terrible* is unmarked
m *prudent* is formal; *careful* is unmarked
n *mad* is informal; *annoyed* is unmarked

7

a broke (*destitute* is a formal, literary word)
b skinny (*skinny* is more negative in tone than *slender*)
c enemies (*opponents* is mainly used in sport)
d sneaking into (*entering* is just unmarked; *sneaking* has the idea of doing something underhand)
e commence (*kick off* is used to talk about sport or informally to mean 'begin'; *commence* is more formal and suitable for the context)
f lost his cool (*became displeased* is formal; *lost his cool* is the same register as 'socked him in the jaw', i.e. informal)
g struck (this is much stronger than *touched*)
h trickling (*trickling* is for water that is moving slowly; *flooding* is more for a river)

8

1 D	2 A	3 C	4 B	5 A	6 A	7 C	8 B

13.2 pages 112–113

Reported speech

1 This listening task is aimed at introducing reported speech. Play the recording once or twice and make notes.

> 1 southern Africa 2 desert landscape 3 collect plants and paint 4 (rhino) footprint 5 geologists 6 (the) media 7 thriving / doing well

Recording script 1 ▸ 25

Presenter: Nowadays we're all aware of the need for biodiversity. Without a range of animals and plants our planet would be a poorer place. Well, I've recently been to <u>southern Africa</u>, which is the last truly wild home of endangered black rhinos. Here something is being done, albeit in a small way, to encourage biodiversity. In most other places black rhinos live either in fenced enclosures or under armed guard. But here in this out of the way <u>desert landscape</u> they are completely free to roam. And yet the fact that any rhinos survive in that part of the world at all is partly due to our guest today, Susan Newhall. Susan, how did you come to get involved?

Susan: I was in the desert <u>collecting plants and painting</u> and I came across <u>a rhino footprint</u>. That was how I first found out that there were rhinos in the area. I didn't realise that this was unusual until I met up <u>with geologists</u> who were working there, and they said there was a terrible slaughter going on and showed me places where dead rhinos were lying around. So I launched ahead and used <u>the media</u> to help me expose what was going on.

Presenter: It's amazing to think that if you hadn't found that footprint, things could've been different.

Susan: Yes, that's right. It's extraordinary you know. Thanks to one rhino which I didn't even see.

Presenter: That was back in 1980, and after her discovery Susan got together with a group of other people to help form an organisation to help the rhinos. At the time, poaching in the region was so rife it seemed unlikely the rhinos could be saved, but Susan and her dedicated supporters refused to admit defeat and today rhinos are not just surviving in their harsh desert home, <u>they're positively thriving</u>.

2 Use your notes to report what was said. Refer to the Grammar folder on page 185 if you are unclear about how sentences in reported speech are formed. The reporting doesn't have to be word for word as long as the gist of what is said is there.

Suggested answer

Southern Africa is the last truly wild home of endangered black rhinos. In most other places they live in either fenced enclosures or under armed guard. The man said that in the desert they are/were completely free to roam. He stated that rhinos were helped to survive in southern Africa because of Susan Newhall.

She said she had / 'd had no previous knowledge of rhinos being in the desert and that when she was looking / had been looking for plants and doing some painting she came / had come across a rhino footprint. She eventually met up with / had eventually met up with geologists who were working / had been working in the area and they told / had told her about the terrible slaughter and took / had taken her to see the dead bodies. As a result she used / had used the media to expose what was / had been going on.

The man congratulated her on finding the footprint, as things would have turned out differently if she hadn't found it. She agreed and said that it was an amazing story, especially as she hadn't actually seen a rhino.

The man went on to say that Susan had got together with some friends and started an organisation to protect the rhino. He said that poaching in the country had been rife and if it hadn't been for Susan there wouldn't be any rhinos today.

3 Refer to the notes on page 112 before you do the exercise, which contains some examples of unusual patterns. More information on these forms can be found in the Grammar folder.

Suggested answers

a She said that her grandmother had been able to walk / could walk to school without worrying about traffic.

b She said that it would be good if I came to tea sometime / that I must/should come to tea sometime.

c She said that I had to remember to recycle the rubbish.

d She said that I mustn't smoke in the restaurant.

e She said that companies which pollute rivers must be fined.

f She said that if she had been mayor, she would have made public transport free.

g She said that if the children picked up the rubbish regularly, she would pay them.

4 Read the notes on page 112 before you do this exercise.

Suggested answers
a Tina suggested going to Crete this year for their/our holiday.
b Fred declared that he would always love Daphne. / Fred declared his undying love for Daphne.
c Colin decided to take the job.
d My mother sighed and forgave me for breaking it.
e The old man objected to the window being opened.
f Rose claimed that I had her book in my school bag.
g My brother insisted on going out.
h Lucy refused to go by train.

5 This exercise shows how using an adverb can enliven a reported sentence.

Suggested answers
a Tina tentatively suggested …
b Fred declared passionately that …
c Colin reluctantly decided …
d My mother sighed resignedly …
e The old man peevishly objected …
f Rose confidently claimed …
g My brother stubbornly insisted …
h Lucy categorically refused …

6 Remember to write in direct speech for this exercise, not reported speech.

Possible answers
a 'You'll pay for that broken jar!' the shopkeeper exclaimed angrily.
b 'Well, you've blocked that exit very nicely with your car, sir,' the police officer said sarcastically.
c 'No, Patricia, a colon, not a dash,' the teacher stated pedantically.
d 'Now, where are my glasses?' my grandfather muttered absent-mindedly.
e 'I think I'll go shopping this afternoon,' Theresa said decisively.
f 'What did you say your name was?' the doctor murmured reassuringly.
g 'Then don't let your children near my house,' my neighbour retorted rudely.
h 'Well now, I'll have to think about a pay rise,' his boss said cautiously.

7 This text is about how man began to study nature.

1 as   2 having   3 turned/gave   4 way/style   5 up   6 not
7 sake   8 common   9 hardly/scarcely/barely NOT rarely
10 such   11 more/better   12 without/lacking   13 because/since   14 it   15 keep

8

Possible answer
I believe that animals shouldn't be kept in zoos. The best way to preserve endangered species is to have a sperm bank and then to try to organise national parks in the animal's country of origin with the aim of re-introducing native species back into their own habitat.

13.3 pages 114–115
Reading into Writing: Giving opinions

1 The illustration is of a blue whale, an Ascension frigate bird, a gorilla, an American bison and a giant panda. The bison is the only one which is no longer endangered, thanks to a special breeding programme carried out in the USA.

2

a prey   b to prey (on)   c predatory   d demographic
e sustainability   f sustainable/unsustainable
g domesticate   h coniferous   i diversity/diversification
j diversification/diversity   k diverse   l evolve
m evolutionary   n inevitability

3 Keep a note of nouns and their dependent prepositions as they are often tested.

a of   b to/towards   c into   d of   e of   f in   g of   h in/to   i on   j to

4

Suggested answer
Text 1
• Large animals are very important to the ecology of their habitat.
• Helping an animal to survive will, generally, have far-reaching effects on other animals and lead to greater recognition of dangers to the planet.
Text 2
• It is not worth trying to save certain types of animal.
• Trying to decide which animal to protect is often not practical, as the nature of the Earth's eco-system is so complex.

5

Possible answer
I think tigers and polar bears are very useful in the sense that they are very accessible symbols of what is happening to many animal species. However, we mustn't forget that other animals, which aren't so attractive, such as certain types of insect, are also endangered.

6

Suggested answer

The two texts contrast differing views of what to do about nature conservation. According to the first passage, which gives the example of the tiger, large species are of fundamental importance to the ecology of their habitat. Helping a species such as this to survive will, for the most part, have far-reaching effects on other species and lead to greater recognition of dangers to the planet.

Personally, I believe this argument to be correct. Even though it would appear that we are concentrating too many of our efforts on one 'flagship' species, as a rule, these species are at the top of the food chain and thus are vitally important for the survival of other species. Without them, the balance of nature would be in jeopardy.

The second text puts forward two contrasting ideas. One is that it is not worth trying to save certain types of animal. In the case of the panda, for example, its decline and eventual disappearance seems to be inevitable. The other line of argument is that assessments of this nature are not practical, given the elaborate nature of the Earth's ecology.

I believe that, if we accept the premise that the natural world as we know it today will disappear entirely and that we should do nothing to counter it, then we are also accepting an impoverished future for our own species. For this reason, I cannot agree with one of the ideas put forward in the second text. I do, however, feel that, with respect to certain species, for example the polar bear, perhaps too much effort has been spent highlighting its problems at the expense of smaller, equally endangered animals. In conclusion, I would say that everything should be done to help all species, as this can only help the planet. (299 words)

Exam folder 7 pages 116–117

Reading and Use of English, Part 5
Multiple-choice text

This text is an extract from an article in which two books are reviewed.

You need to try to guess the meaning from the context. Sometimes it is difficult to guess the meaning, but it is always worth a try. You are not allowed to take a dictionary into the examination. Don't forget to read the Exam advice.

1 C *Here is an uplifting array of thrift, vetch, yarrow and dozens more that toss and chatter, apparently immune to the salty south-westerlies.*

2 A *Only the dreariest Linnaean sergeant-major could want to dragoon all these into arum maculatum.*

3 D *Their champion is the naturalist Richard Mabey, whose Defence of Weeds must be the most eye-opening book I have read.*

4 C *Exotics arrive from round the globe, spilling from cargos on to roads and railway lines.*

5 B *Wild flowers have evolved a class system of their own: effete respect is shown to Raven's country cousins while war is declared on Mabey's 'vegetable guerrillas that have overcome the dereliction of the industrial age'.*

6 D *Despite the damage they do to other flora, that splendid weed, the daffodil, is planted out 'wild' by councils … When a friend of mine drove round … hurling poppy seeds from his car and delighting in the subsequent harvest of red, he found a year later that it had fallen foul of ministry herbicide.*

Unit 14

14.1 pages 118–119

Speaking

1 One photo is of a girl doing Pilates and the other is of people working out on exercise bikes in front of TV screens.

Suggested answers

a false – Depends on what your daily routine is. If you work on a building site then you probably don't need so much as someone who sits at a desk all day.

b false – You need to keep active to keep your bones and muscles healthy.

c true – They're carbohydrates, good sources of energy.

d true – It will be digested much more easily than a large evening meal.

e false – It is just one form of exercise. It is best in combination with other types of exercise.

f false – The only known way of living longer is to live on a very low calorie diet.

g false – Although having a personal trainer may make you more motivated.

Reading

2 Read the article and then read the questions and decide which section A–D contains the answer.

1	B (lines 14–17)
2	D (lines 16–18)
3	A (lines 16–18)
4	C (lines 12–15)
5	A (lines 7–9)
6	D (line 8)
7	B (lines 8–9)
8	D (lines 14–17)
9	C (lines 9–12)
10	A (lines 11–13)

3

Possible answer
I think I would much prefer to have a personal trainer who could tailor exercise to my particular needs. Knowing that someone would be coming to my house at a certain time every week would really motivate me to carry on exercising. I have tried Pilates and found it very difficult and some of the other types of exercise mentioned don't seem very effective.

4 This exercise gives practice in emphasis. Having a wide vocabulary that is used appropriately will create a better impression in Writing.

a harangued **b** resolved **c** swear **d** scrounge **e** craved
f was seething **g** yank **h** unearthed **i** flouted

Phrase spot

a lived it up
b learn to live with
c lived up to our expectations
d live down
e lived through
f lived by his wits

14.2 pages 120–121
Articles review

1 This exercise should throw up any problems you have with articles. Articles are a constant problem for students of English and you should regularly revise your knowledge of them. Refer to the Grammar folder on page 185 for greater clarification.

1 Indonesia, Berlin, Europe, Oxford University
2 European, university, one-day ticket, household, union, hotel
3 **a i** Ken's job is as a personal trainer. Article needed before jobs.
  b Both are correct. *The* gym – we all know which one.
  A gym – the first time it's been mentioned or one of many.
  c i
  d Both are correct. You use an article when you are referring to something in particular, no article if it is more general.
  e ii With nationality words of this type you need an article.
  f Both could be correct. Generally you don't use an article with meals. The exception is for public events, e.g. *the rugby club dinner*.
  g ii *I play violin* is American usage. British usage is an article before an instrument.
  h i No article with sports.
  i i *I want a drink of water* is more usual. *I want one drink of water* emphasises how many. You can say *I want one more drink of water*.
  j i You always use *the* with *weather* unless you are using an attributive adjective, e.g. *We won't go out if the weather's bad*. BUT *Fishing boats don't go out in bad weather*.
  k ii We use the possessive rather than an article for parts of the body unless they are referred to generally in a medical context.
  l Both are correct. No article if you are talking about the purpose for which the bed exists, i.e. to sleep in. You use *the* if you are talking about the piece of furniture. Similarly you use an article with *prison/hospital/school* if you are just referring to the building, but no article if you are referring to the building's purpose.

2 Read through the article quickly to find out what it is about. There may be more than one answer, depending on meaning.

1 The **2** the **3** the/– **4** the **5** the **6** the **7** the
8 the/– **9** – **10** a **11** a **12** – **13** – **14** a **15** a/the/–
16 the **17** – **18** the **19** the **20** – **21** the **22** –

3 These idioms can be grouped together as nouns which don't take an article when they are part of an idiom. This may help you to remember them. The meaning of the idioms is given in brackets.

Possible answers

a All the orders were given by word of mouth to avoid leaving written evidence which might be later discovered. (by speaking only)

b The child lay face downwards in the sand and screamed. (on its stomach)

c Man first set foot on the island in the nineteenth century. (landed)

d My mother took me aside and suggested we have a heart to heart about my new boyfriend. (a good chat)

e They walked down the street hand in hand. (holding hands)

f Phil and I strolled arm in arm along the beach. (with arms linked)

g Traffic is nose to tail every morning on the road into the city centre. (bumper to bumper)

h Liz came face to face with Roger at the party. (met unexpectedly someone she didn't want to meet)

i His family lived from hand to mouth while he was growing up because his father was unemployed. (they were very poor)

j All our pottery is made by hand. (not by machine)

k The MP fought tooth and nail to get the bill through Parliament. (to fight very hard)

l I'm finding it increasingly difficult to see eye to eye with my boss. (to agree with)

Vocabulary: Prepositions

Corpus spot

a in **b** to **c** at **d** to/at **e** about/of **f** at/near **g** to
h of **i** on/against/for **j** on **k** on **l** for **m** on

4 This exercise gives practice in using prepositions accurately. Some words in English – prepositions, pronouns, conjunctions, articles and auxiliary verbs – have two pronunciations: one is used when they are stressed, and the other when they are not. Prepositions are stressed when they come at the end of a question.

For example:

What did he apply for? *strong* for /fɔːʳ/

He applied for a grant. *weak* for /fəʳ/

Also remember that, when using a verb with a dependent preposition, the preposition will go at the end when in a question.

Possible answers

a Who did he rely on? He relied on his parents.

b What does she take pride in? She takes pride in her appearance.

c What are they looking forward to? They are looking forward to their holiday.

d What are they prohibited from? They are prohibited from smoking in the classroom.

e Who does the group consist of? It consists of three teachers and six students.

f What did he interfere in? He interfered in my plans for the party.

g What do you admire her for? I admire her for her strong opinions.

h Who did she apologise to? She apologised to my brother. What did she apologise for? She apologised for being rude.

i What are they accused of? They are accused of arson.

j What do you believe in? I believe in truth and justice.

Word formation

5 This exercise links word formation with the sections A–D of the article in 14.1. You need to be able to say exactly what part of speech a word is. The main forms are listed. There may be one or two which are not in this list.

Suggested answers

agreeable (adjective) – disagreeable, agree, disagree, agreement, agreeably

imaginary (adjective) – imagine, imagination, unimaginable, unimaginably, image, imaginable

expectations (plural noun) – expect, unexpected, expected, unexpectedly, expectant

reality (noun) – real, realise, realism, unreality, unreal, realistic, realistically, unrealistically, surreal, surrealism

enthusiasm (noun) – enthusiastic, enthusiastically, unenthusiastic, unenthusiastically, enthuse

measure (verb) – immeasurable, measurement, measurable, measureless, measured

dismissive (adjective) – dismiss, dismissal, dismissively

clearly (adverb) – clear, clarity, clarify, unclear, unclearly

transform (verb) – transformer, transformation, transformed, untransformed

introductory (adjective) – introduce, introduction

excuses (noun) – excusable, inexcusable

6

a unexpected **b** dismissed **c** enthusiastic
d imagination **e** inexcusable/disagreeable **f** clarity

7 Word formation is often tested in Reading and Use of English, Part 4.

1 is showing / shows signs of (some/an) improvement

2 am full of admiration for

3 has the reputation of inspiring / of being an inspiration to/has a reputation for inspiring

4 for Professor McDougal's kind assistance / for the kind assistance of Professor McDougal

14.3 pages 122–123

Listening and Speaking

The photos are of:
salt, tomatoes, meat/a chicken, eggs, a sausage, coffee, cheese, a burger, orange juice, a mobile phone, deodorant

1 A health scare is when the public is made aware of a possible health hazard. However, more often than not, there is no good basis for the story.

Possible answer
I take absolutely no notice whatsoever of all the health scares that appear in the headlines in my country. After all, they say that one day these things are good for you and the next day they will cause you harm.

2 Play the recording twice – once for general understanding and the second time to pick up on detail.

The underlined parts of the recording script confirm the answers.

1 B   2 D   3 C   4 A   5 C

Recording script   2 02

Alice: Health scares – don't they make you sick! Or do they challenge your complacency? Every few days a new story appears in the newspaper about, first of all, butter is bad for you, then butter is good for you. Salt is bad for us, salt is good for us. You just have to pick up a cup of coffee and you're engaged in a health debate. With me today to discuss this issue is Professor Robert Atkins. Robert, what do you think about all this?

Robert: Personally, <u>I'd rather have ten false health scares and one of them prove to be serious – then it leads to action, than the cynical sense that somehow all this is just a media confection. That's what I really object to.</u>

Alice: Mm, but how often do health scares come true?

Robert: There are random events in which microbes do emerge. They can be extraordinarily lethal and these account for massive epidemics that have occurred in the past in human history and I think we would be arrogant in the extreme to think that such things may not occur again in the future.

Alice: You're thinking of bubonic plague, of course. But nowadays it seems is the best of times and the worst of times if you want to be healthy. This is a paradox, because, on the one hand, we live in a relatively healthy society. Our longevity is unprecedented. <u>By historical standards communicable lethal disease is exceptionally controlled.</u> Yet we seem to be getting better, but feeling worse. Why, if we're so healthy, are we so easily spooked?

Robert: If you were living two or three hundred years ago, you were in the hands of God or Fate and if you were struck down by a mortal disease you thought you'd been sinful, but you also had your beliefs to console you – you'd go to paradise or heaven or whatever. Nowadays, we have tremendously high expectations about long healthy life continuing and some of us no longer have an expectation of an afterlife. <u>It's partly a matter of a crisis of rising expectations.</u>

Alice: Um, so our health anxiety is like a big eater's gluttony or a rich man's miserliness. Health excites expectations of perfection. <u>It's also an anxiety spread by commercial concerns, isn't it?</u>

Robert: Indeed. The <u>margarine industry,</u> for example, is actually now a very powerful instrument in pushing the line that butter is bad for you and actually there's a strong industrial lobby that has a stake in making sure that we are all anxious and worried about our health.

Alice: And they're not the only players. <u>If health scares sell pills they also sell papers.</u> And what about the research community which keeps the health scare industry supplied with stories?

Robert: Health is always in the news. Sometimes it's the doctors themselves who are maybe responsible. In every branch of life there are people who like a touch of publicity and enjoy the turbulence. Others are often so convinced by their findings that they ignore the critical views of other doctors and have this urge to promulgate their ideas when it may not be appropriate to do so. If I wanted to avoid heart disease, I'd be taking aspirins, reducing my weight, I would probably frequent my local gym a bit more. I would eat this, that and the other and so on. Then there might be another disease I might get. What do I do then?

Alice: Mm, how much difference would it make to you if you made all those changes? Should you just discount what you read and hear?

Robert: Who knows? Some health scares can actually seriously damage your health – they lead to stress, deprive us of the comfort of eating chocolate and clog up doctors' waiting rooms. There is clearly an information overload and unfortunately, <u>when the real thing comes along, people might have difficulty distinguishing it from all the background noise.</u>

Alice: And of course it's difficult to disprove something once a claim has been made, however fallacious that risk is. Thank you, Professor Robert Atkins.

Pronunciation

3. The general rule is that when the word is used as a verb the stress is on the last part of the word; when it is used as a noun then the stress is on the first part of the word.

    Alice and Robert
    say: obj**ect**   fre**quent**   dis**count**

    This is because these three words are being used as verbs in the listening extract.

4.

> **Possible answers**
> Not all the words here follow the general rule given in 3, eg *alternate*. The stressed syllable is shown in capitals.
> I freQUENted the same places as Hemingway did in the 50s.
> He's a FREquent visitor to the club.
> The ENtrance to the hall is via the side door.
> She was enTRANcing in the part of Ophelia.
> I was inCENsed to find my car had been vandalised.
> I can't stand the smell of INcense.
> Your visa is inVALid, I'm afraid.
> Her aunt has been an INvalid for over ten years.
> Is everyone PREsent?
> I bought a PREsent for my father.
> Can I preSENT Mr Delgado to you?
> Students receive a DIScount on entry prices.
> Don't disCOUNT everything she says just because she's a child.
> The stall was covered in local PROduce.
> The factory proDUCes 5,000 components every year.
> I can see you on alTERnate mornings only.
> You will have to ALternate with Fred over who uses the room.

5. This section gives more practice in Speaking, Part 2. You should remember not just to describe the photos but to talk about the lifestyles of the people and make comments or give opinions on them. Make sure you time this activity so you get used to being concise and not spending too much time thinking.

    The photos are of a group of teenagers slouched on a sofa eating pizza and watching TV and a teenage girl, running outside.

> **Possible answer**
> The young people in the photo are obviously very happy to just sit and watch TV. They probably watch far too many DVDs and get very little exercise.
> I think that the fit young woman probably gets up fairly early in the morning, doesn't drink, eats moderately healthily, but probably does eat junk food, and takes her training very seriously. She probably doesn't socialise as much as she would like and goes to bed early on nights before an athletics meeting. It's not a lifestyle I would consider personally.

6. It might be useful to go through the unit underlining vocabulary connected with health and fitness, and then try to incorporate it into your talk.

> **Possible answer**
> Possibly a poster campaign would have the greatest impact. I always remember the campaign for teenage pregnancy with a man looking pregnant. That had a great impact. The posters could be distributed around schools, youth clubs and even in bus shelters – anywhere where young people congregate. I think cigarette smoking and drinking alcohol should be highlighted because of the rising number of teenage girls who smoke and also the problem with under-age drinking in this country.

Writing folder 7 pages 124–125
Part 2 Letter

2

> **Improved answer**
> Dear Sir or Madam
> Following the **rather negative** article on this college's current sports provision, we **would like you to reconsider your views** and print an apology – **the lion's share of your article is inaccurate**. We **would also like to seek your support** regarding a funding application – please see below.
> Your article claims that a lack of adequate facilities is **affecting the performance of** our basketball and swimming teams, yet both have represented the college at the highest levels of competition and **excelled themselves** over the years. Indeed, your newspaper featured the recent success of the basketball team in an article published in May. **This would appear to contradict your claim.**
> **At the same time, there is some truth in your suggestion** that the main sports hall requires some work, especially **the substandard flooring and inadequate lighting, which occasionally makes it hard to play at one's best.** In connection with this, **it has come to our notice that** funding is available nationally, which our college would be in a good position to apply for. We **estimate that this** grant would enable us to undertake the repairs alluded to above, and also allow for an extension of the present changing facilities, whereby separate 'wet' and 'dry' areas could be introduced, to service the pool and hall respectively.
> What **would be your opinion on this**? Would you be willing to run an article in support of our grant application? It would be in the public interest, given that members of the public have daily access to our sports facilities.
> **We look forward to hearing from you in due course.**
> **Yours faithfully,**
> (273 words)

3

aA bA cB dA eC fB gA hC iA jC

4

Sample answer
To the editor,
I am writing in response to the invitation to readers that featured in the last issue of your magazine. What I am currently most concerned about with regard to the environment is the shipping of hazardous waste around the world, which is sometimes referred to as 'toxic colonialism'.
This practice seems to have grown alarmingly in recent years. The apparent reason for this is that environmental laws on waste disposal have been tightened up in the more developed countries, whereas the governments of many poorer developing countries are willing to accept hazardous material as a source of revenue. In reality, these 'host' countries may not be able to process or store toxic waste safely and there have been several cases of contamination on farms and other areas of land in Africa, for example.
Not only does this state of affairs threaten the health of ordinary people in the developing world but it also poses a serious threat to marine life while any toxic cargo is in transit. If a ship carrying radioactive waste were to run aground or be damaged in some way while on the high seas, the leakage of lethal material could pollute a huge expanse of ocean and cause widespread loss of wildlife.
To my mind, an international campaign to stop this unnecessary movement of harmful substances should be set in motion immediately. Governments worldwide should give priority to this environmental issue. Countries belonging to the G20 group of nations could back the establishment of a global investigation into the actual amount of transportation that is going on and would ideally sanction major investment in safe methods of disposal in the countries of origin.
We must take the initiative now to protect our planet. I urge your readers to join me in seeking an immediate end to toxic colonialism.
Yours faithfully,
(308 words)

Unit 15
15.1 pages 126–127

1   The pictures show a blacksmith working in his forge and office workers in a call centre – the office workers' jobs will have changed more due to modern technology. In contrast, a blacksmith crafts metal artefacts by hand and the skills needed will not have changed much in hundreds of years.

Possible answers
It depends – I'd like to stay in the same field, but I'm likely to have to move abroad to gain more responsibility.
Probably because the job market is so competitive – it's safer to stick with what you know.
It's crucial, as experienced people know so much more about how things work in an organisation.
I don't expect to stay with the same company, though I believe there will always be opportunities in my field.
Perhaps the workplace will become even more automated and computerised, with more mundane jobs being done by robots.

Listening

2   Before you listen to the recording, read through the questions and check anything you are unsure of. You will have one minute in Part 3 of the exam to look through the multiple-choice questions. Play the recording twice, as in the exam. The underlined parts of the recording script confirm the answers.

1 B   2 B   3 D   4 C   5 A

Recording script 2 03

Interviewer: Diane Webber, you've switched careers more than once during your own working life, and you now run a highly regarded employment agency for media high-fliers, where, above all, you advise your clients, both companies and applicants, to be fully flexible. You seem to see this as a fundamental principle, if your agency slogan – 'Keeping your options open' – is anything to go by. Is that a fair assessment of how you operate?

Diane Webber: Absolutely. I know that not so very long ago we used to see jobs for life as the norm, with unquestioning company loyalty, and a golden handshake at the end of it all – which, nine times out of ten, probably wasn't in actual fact deserved – but things are very different now. And yes, there does seem to be something positive in all this, despite the obvious question mark over security. Successful players in the current job market cut their teeth in one firm, and are willing to step sideways more than once to gain fresh experience. Unlike their predecessors, they may only progress up the rungs when they land their third or fourth job, or even later in their career. This increased movement brings benefits, not just for them, but for the companies they work for, too.

Interviewer: In spite of the instability? Surely it's important to have some continuity?

Diane Webber: Well actually, it's a mixed blessing. Individuals can get terribly stale if they stick in one place for too long, especially if they report to managers who fail to challenge them. That implies a hierarchy riddled with complacency and under-achievement, which can no longer be tolerated in today's fast-moving, dog-eat-dog world. Also, much of today's work consists of fixed-term projects, done in teams, and if one or two members drop out along the way, it really doesn't matter, provided that the team remains an entity. The one exception to this is the team leaders themselves, who are not only the driving force, but the guardians of the project, who hold important historical detail in their heads, so yes, continuity is important there. But even then it's a clearly defined cycle. We're frequently approached by highly-experienced team leaders who, having completed one project, decide they can't face even the slightest whiff of repetition and so come to us seeking fresh challenges.

Interviewer: And they manage to find work?

Diane Webber: Oh, they're snapped up! Because generally speaking, a project-based job can easily demonstrate a track record, it's there in the successful completion of the project.

Interviewer: And these people would have no problem getting references from the employers they're essentially walking out on? I would have thought that that could be an issue …

Diane Webber: Employers don't view it like that at all. Their mindset is different now, as I said earlier, and companies actually take steps to foster a more dynamic environment, as they feel this yields better productivity, though the jury's still out on this, in my view. Nevertheless, with a flow of people, there's a quantum leap in terms of the ideas generated, not to mention the chance of new ways of problem-solving imported from elsewhere. These effects are tangible and they're often very attractive because they're perceived as lean and efficient, instant solutions, even if they generally turn out to be only quick fixes which later have to be reversed.

Interviewer: Ah, but isn't that the nub of it all, that this shifting and fragmented approach leads to poor decisions? Of course, the perpetrators are never taken to task, as they've already made a quick exit and are knocking on your door for another job!

Diane Webber: That's a bit unfair! For one thing, there've always been bad decisions. No company can rely on its personnel to make the right choices one hundred per cent of the time – even with the help of highly-paid outside consultants, staff will continue to get it wrong from time to time. However, I'd argue that it's the mediocre employees, who just want to keep their heads down, who are far more likely to cause problems than the risk-takers, who, don't forget, are only as employable as their last success.

Interviewer: Ruthless …

Diane Webber: Pragmatic!

Interviewer: Which brings us neatly back to your slogan, doesn't it? Keeping your options open. How far do you encourage people to go in this?

Diane Webber: With new opportunities opening up all the time, the sky's the limit really. It's certainly never too late to contemplate a move, and so the maxim has to be, don't rule *anything* in or out.

Interviewer: We'll end on that positive note. Diane Webber, thank you.

Diane Webber: It's been a pleasure.

3

a financial reward for long service
b get experience
c climb the career ladder
d good and bad
e fiercely competitive
f a tiny bit of
g recruited immediately
h evidence of previous success
i way of thinking
j people haven't decided
k huge improvement
l apparently simple and instant solutions (which don't succeed)
m avoid trouble by behaving in a quiet way

Vocabulary: Collocations

4

a something quick to eat
b the quickest but most competitive route to success (original meaning: the outside overtaking lane of a motorway)
c (earn) money fast
d the quickest line in e.g. airport check-in
e a quick move of the head in acknowledgement
f a public announcement to say that something isn't true, given quickly to prevent media interest
g answering/reacting quickly
h brief sleep, usually during daytime

5

a growth b pace c signs d process e decline f lane

Idiom spot

Many new expressions are entering the language, particularly in the areas of business and journalism.

1 the jury's still out 2 a quantum leap 3 the slightest whiff of 4 quick fixes 5 track record 6 a mixed blessing

a red ink b green shoots c blue chip d white goods e golden hello f white knight

15.2 pages 128–129

Clauses 1

1 An *intern* is a student or other young person who works in a company for a short period in order to gain experience, generally earning little or no money. The picture is of Keri Hudson.

Possible answer
The judge's ruling makes sense in this case. If an intern is working long hours and genuinely contributing to the company, a fair wage should be paid. On the other hand, if an intern has no experience whatsoever and is merely there to learn from the company, then I don't believe they necessarily need to be paid for the work they do.

2 Note that according to the Cambridge English Corpus, *lest* appears to be more commonly used than the phrase *for fear that*. Both are fairly formal in use and less frequent than the phrase *in case*.

Suggested answers
in order to – so as to
for fear that – lest
Both phrases introduce a purpose clause.

3

Suggested answer
Although there are both male and female secretaries in an office environment, the men see themselves as more important, often spending time on the phone networking.

4

1 so 2 what 3 no 4 order 5 on 6 while/whilst/though/although/if 7 their 8 rather

5

a lest / for fear that b so as not to / in order not to c in order to / so as to d in case e so that f so as not to / in order not to g in case h lest/ for fear that

6

Possible answers
a I would like to work abroad at some point, in order to broaden my experience.
b When I'm older, I won't stay in the same job for more than two years, so as not to get stale.
c I want to continue my English studies, in order to get a better job.
d It would be useful for me to have my own website, so that I could promote my products.
e I want to find work that I can do from home, in order to be able to spend more time with the children.

Corpus spot

a in case b even if c in the same way as d (comma not full stop) such as e so as not to f In conclusion

Style extra

A good dictionary will give you information on usage restrictions.

Nouns
used of men
bounder (old-fashioned), charmer (slightly derogatory), geek (informal), lout, Neanderthal (informal and derogatory), nerd, patriarch (formal), thug
used of women
bag (informal and offensive), bimbo (informal and offensive), duchess (old-fashioned), vamp (old-fashioned)
used of both
actor, chairman (many people prefer to say chair or chairperson as a gender-neutral choice), chav (informal and offensive), freshman (US – the British equivalent is fresher), mate (informal), partner, sibling, spouse (formal), whizz kid
Adjectives
used of men
chivalrous, effeminate
used of both
bullish, doting (but see Possible answers below), laddish, lanky (but usually of men and boys), prickly (but see Possible answers below), wimpy.

In the **Possible answers** in the next column, the examples containing the eight adjectives are taken from the *Cambridge English Corpus* – the type of source is given in brackets. Additional usage notes reflect the corpus evidence.

Possible answers

I think you're the most chivalrous man I've ever met. (popular novel)

Beckham is such a doting dad that he's just had Brooklyn's name tattooed on his back. (tabloid newspaper – referring to the footballer David Beckham) *Note*: although the adjective can be used of men and women, there are notably more examples of *doting dad* and *doting father*.

A pale, delicate, effeminate boy, who might have been taken for my master's brother ... (novel: *Wuthering Heights* by Emily Brontë) *Note*: most corpus lines are from literary sources and the use appears to be slightly old-fashioned.

As Jon and I are the newest of new men, this insinuation of laddish sexism cuts very deeply. (student newspaper website) *Note*: the example contrasts a laddish attitude with the now slightly old-fashioned expression *new man* (a man who is sensitive and caring, and takes responsibility for childcare and traditionally female chores).

The lanky centre forward found himself rushing towards a head-on collision with the goalkeeper. (sports report) *Note*: there are many similar examples in the corpus relating to sports players.

He has a reputation as an efficient and decisive if somewhat prickly manager. (broadsheet newspaper) *Note*: the *Cambridge English Corpus* indicates that the adjective is more often used of men than women. The adjective is also used to describe things that cause anger or annoyance, e.g. *a prickly issue/matter/subject*.

Beautiful men are a bit vain and wimpy. (tabloid newspaper)

15.3 pages 130–131

Reading into Writing: Contrasting ideas

1

Suggested answers
a decisiveness, intuition, vision
b assertiveness, determination, fairness
c decisiveness, specialist knowledge, stamina
Other characteristics:
ambition, ability to articulate ideas, being a good public speaker, charisma

2

Suggested answer
For me, the Affiliative Style described in Text 1 is likely to be the more effective as it values staff, consequently promoting harmony and company loyalty. Conversely, the leadership style in Text 2 is bound to lose employees through its demotivating approach.

3

a proponents   b bonds   c reaping the benefits of
d quandary   e rise to the occasion   f morale   g initiative
h the big picture

4

The three verbs for downward movement or decline are *drop*, *evaporate* and *dwindle*. Other possible verbs are:
drops – plummets
evaporate – fade
dwindles – diminishes.
The verb that describes an upward trend is *rises*. Possible verbs to replace it are *soars/blossoms*.

5

Be that as it may   Conversely   Despite this   Even so
In contrast   Nonetheless   On the other hand   Whereas

6

1 more   2 said (contrastive)   3 being   4 the same
5 Notwithstanding / Having said (contrastive)

7

Possible answers
(Yellow highlighting) The 'Affiliative Style' of leadership treats employees as individuals and they therefore become very committed to the company, whereas the 'Pacesetting Style' doesn't engender any such allegiance and employees don't recognise their role within the organisation at large.

(Blue highlighting) Under the 'Pacesetting Style', employees can easily become demotivated as their targets are unrealistic. Conversely, the 'Affiliative Style' ensures that morale is kept high and the company is likely to get more out of its employees because of this.

(Pink highlighting) Affiliative leaders allow employees far greater independence and have faith that they will get the job done in the best way possible. Pacesetters, on the other hand, are reluctant to delegate responsibility and discourage individual creativity.

(Green highlighting) It seems to be the case that individuals who underperform within the 'Pacesetter Style' of leadership are rapidly detected and measures are taken to either increase their productivity or to get rid of them. In contrast, underachievement may not be addressed within the 'Affiliative Style'.

8 Draw a grid with two columns for the two styles of leadership. Think about your own views on each idea and record these in the two columns.

9

Sample answer

Leadership styles within companies often vary enormously. The texts provide two contrasting examples – the 'Affiliative Style' and the 'Pacesetting Style'. The former is probably the more appropriate, though it is not without its flaws. Let us consider both approaches here.

The Affiliative Style of leadership treats employees as individuals and they therefore become very committed to the company, whereas the Pacesetting Style doesn't engender any such allegiance and employees don't recognise their role within the organisation. This could be wasteful in terms of human resources.

Under the Pacesetting Style, employees can easily become demotivated as their targets are unrealistic. Conversely, the Affiliative Style ensures that morale is kept high and the company should get more out of its employees because of this.

Affiliative leaders allow employees far greater independence and have faith that they will get the job done in the best way possible. Pacesetters, on the other hand, are reluctant to delegate responsibility and discourage individual creativity. Personally, I would find it impossible to work under such a 'repressive' regime.

It seems to be the case that individuals who underperform within the Pacesetter Style of leadership are rapidly detected and measures are taken to either increase their productivity or to get rid of them. In contrast, underachievement may not be addressed within the Affiliative Style. Even so, this might not adversely affect the company performance at large, since the majority of employees would be 'achievers'.

In reality, the optimum leadership style may well be a blend of these approaches, since it cannot be denied that objectives have to be set by the leader and met by the workforce. However, if a company is to succeed in the longer term, it has to rely on its employees. The investment in people shown by the affiliative leader undoubtedly contributes to the greater good and should ensure that the company prospers, unless outside circumstances prevent this. (314 words)

Exam folder 8 pages 132–133

Listening, Part 2 Sentence completion

Read through the advice carefully, then look at the questions and try to predict what the answer will be. Time spent looking carefully at the question paper is never wasted, and you have 45 seconds to do this. It is important to read ahead when listening so that, if something is missed, there is no sense of disorientation. There is no need to panic, as the piece will be played again.

Play the recording twice to simulate exam conditions.

The underlined parts of the recording script confirm the key.

2

1 respectful

Recording script 2 04

You will hear a man called John Farrant talking about his job, working for a car hire company. For question 1, listen to the first part of the recording as far as '… a plastic wallet'. Then, with a partner, decide which is the word you heard which fits in the space.

John Farrant: Good morning. My name is John Farrant and I have the job of reservations manager at a large international car hire company based in London. Dealing with the public can be a tricky business. You get to meet all types from the arrogant and rude to the downright abusive. We aren't expected to reply in kind, of course, or come over all ingratiating and deferential either. It's down to us to be <u>respectful</u> and remember the customer is always right. Sometimes it can be difficult, especially with a real joker. For example, when taking a booking, we have to ask certain questions, one of which is: 'Do you possess a clean driving licence?' To which one man snapped at me, 'Of course I do. I keep it in a plastic wallet!'

3

You will hear 'rude' and 'deferential', but only 'respectful' is correct. The words 'arrogant' and 'ingratiating' do not fit grammatically.

4 Play the rest of the recording.

2 refresher course   3 roundabouts   4 long-term rental(s)
5 (thick) mud   6 test drive   7 handbrake   8 (best) interest(s)   9 hand controls

Recording script 2 05

Now listen to the rest of the recording and, for Questions 2 to 9, complete the sentences with a word or short phrase.

John Farrant: Sometimes we can hardly believe some of the customers aren't pulling our legs. We once had an elderly gentleman ring up about a car to go to Paris the following morning. We went through the questions and he said he was 69, and it turned out that, although he'd passed his driving test, he hadn't driven for years. He said, 'Is there any way you could give me a <u>refresher course</u> over the phone?' We suggested he let his friend drive.

Travel doesn't always bring out the adventurer in people, though. We had an American tourist ask for a car to drive to Scotland, and who said: 'How many circles are there between London and Scotland?' After some questioning, I realised he meant <u>roundabouts</u>. There are hardly any in the USA – they prefer traffic lights and he'd only ever driven on motorways here before. He only wanted me to work out a route for him!

Now, most people assume that car hire companies make their money from renting out posh, expensive cars like Mercedes and BMWs. This isn't the case – it's the long-term rentals which bring in the money. But of course, it does depend where you go with the car and if you make your intentions clear at the time.

We had one English client book a car for a month. So far, so good. Four weeks later I received a call from him in Spain, saying he was just about to drop off the car. I said, 'Sorry, sir, where are you?' He said, 'Barcelona.' I asked if he'd told the reservations clerk he intended to go abroad with the car, and he said no, really unconcerned. Presumably he didn't realise, or maybe even care, that he hadn't been covered by insurance. I spoke to the supplier afterwards. He said when they got the car back it didn't have any dents or scratches on it but it was so thick with mud it took two days for them to valet it.

Then, we had one gentleman who had a medical condition that meant that he was on drugs that made him semi-drowsy, but he had a certificate from his doctor saying that he could drive. I got a call from the depot manager saying, 'I'm not giving him a car. He can hardly stand up.' We decided he should give the customer a test drive round the block. This guy pulled out of the depot and there was a car coming towards them. He didn't even see it. The depot manager didn't even have time to sound the horn, he had to pull on the handbrake. He said he'd never been so scared in his life.

Other people refuse to believe you're genuinely concerned about safeguarding their best interests. I remember it once took me 15 minutes to persuade a customer that it really wasn't worth hiring a small car, with low power, to go over the Alps. He'd just get stuck and it would ruin his holiday. He simply refused to accept that this type of car wouldn't be up to the job. What d'you do?

We can solve most problems though. We had one gentleman who wanted to go to Oxford. Everything was fine until he suddenly said, 'By the way, I've only got one leg.' I had to call in a few favours, but one of my suppliers managed to get me a car with hand controls.

So, although it may not be straightforward, I enjoy my job on the whole – I guess it's the challenge – every day is different after all!

Unit 16
16.1 pages 134–135
Reading

1 This unit is all about literature and the printed word. As is often the case in the exam, this Reading and Use of English, Part 5 task is taken from a short story.

Possible answers
A short story has few pages and so there is little space to develop characters or plot. The writing must be succinct and 'lean'.
In a novel it is easier to use flashback and other time reference devices. There is much more scope to include long descriptions and/or sub-plots.

2 The significance of the title is that Elizabeth's behaviour and that of her parents shows nothing new or different from previous generations. It is predictable.

Background information
Laurie Colwin wrote five novels and three collections of short stories before she died in 1992. This story appears in her second collection, *The Lone Pilgrim*, a book that includes many stories to do with early experiences of adult life.

3

| 1 C | 2 B | 3 B | 4 A | 5 D | 6 C |

Detailed explanation:
1 The answer (C) is in the words 'was extraordinarily pretty, and such children are never called difficult'. A is wrong, as the text only refers to one child who was older, Nelson Rodker. B is not suggested: the use of 'original' does not imply great intelligence. D is ruled out as there is no evidence of 'painstaking preparation' and only one relationship is referred to (her parents hoped Nelson and Elizabeth might marry).
2 The answer (B) lies in the final sentence of the second paragraph. There is no evidence that she had a 'sense of duty' (A), in fact the reverse is true. C is ruled out as it was Elizabeth who hated the Rodkers, not the other way round. Although it is true that Elizabeth did hide her true feelings ('she learned to turn a cheerful face'), there is no evidence to suggest she disliked doing this (D).
3 The answer (B) is rooted in 'none of her friends wanted to entertain at home'. A is ruled out because the careers weren't always successful ('blacklisted movie producers'). There is no evidence to support C; Holly was the only friend who came home and Elizabeth's mother approved of her, so she would have been unlikely to feel uncomfortable. D is not suggested by the text.

4 The answer (A) lies in the words 'manure was not on her mother's mind' and 'she was much relieved' – presumably her mother had been imagining an illicit relationship with a man at the stables. There is no evidence that Elizabeth's mother begrudged spending the money on the jodhpurs (B). C, though plausible, is not true: her parents 'who felt riding once a week was quite enough' were mildly interested and the mother did arrange the purchase of the jodhpurs. D is likely, but not stated in the text.

5 The answer (D) lies in the final sentence of the fifth paragraph. A is insufficiently rooted in the text: although it implies her parents believed in moderation in reading, we do not know how she was brought up. B is wrong, as Elizabeth's appearance didn't change (only her behaviour at college did). C is wrong as it was other students who 'went wild', while Elizabeth spent time alone in her room.

6 The answer (C) lies in the words 'wanted to enjoy it finally on her own terms' and 'refusing to take a cent of their money'. A is wrong, as she used the bracelet 'as collateral' to borrow money – that is, she didn't sell it but named it as an asset that could be set against the loan if she defaulted on her payments. B is not stated, even if implied by the fact that the daughters of her parents' friends were getting engaged. D is wrong as Elizabeth had always loved New York.

4

The answer is D. A and C are not supported by the reality in the text. B is wrong, as both Nelson and Elizabeth had a good education and in her case, the text shows us it led to other things.
Relevant sentences in the text that support D:
At college, Elizabeth had her first taste of freedom.
Had they known what sort of adult Elizabeth had become, great would have been their dismay.
Elizabeth further puzzled them by refusing to take a cent of their money, although her mother knew the truth: what you dole out to the young binds them to you. To have Elizabeth owing nothing was disconcerting to say the least.

5

a Elizabeth's mother forced herself to sound positive.
b Elizabeth pretended to be happy when really she loathed the Rodkers and her parents.
c Beautiful daughters like Elizabeth are over-protected.
d It might have adversely affected Elizabeth's social life.
e Elizabeth's parents regarded 'adult behavior' as important.

6

Suggested answers
Nelson is conventional, spineless and apathetic.
Opposites for the other words:
articulate / inarticulate
brazen / modest
callous / compassionate
fickle / steadfast
flawed / impeccable
garrulous/ taciturn
trustworthy / treacherous
unflappable / panicky

16.2 pages 136–137
Clauses 2

1 Do you see anything odd about the poem by Bud Weiser? Look carefully: the poet's name, if put together as one word, is the name of a make of beer, which echoes the content of the final line. The poem is a joke!

Background information

Spike Milligan (1918–2002) is perhaps best known for his collaboration with Harry Secombe and Peter Sellers in the BBC radio comedy series *The Goons*, which has influenced many other comedians' work. Gary Snyder (born 1930) is an American poet who was part of the 'Beat Generation' and a friend of the writer Jack Kerouac. Snyder has won the Pulitzer Prize for Poetry and has also translated literature from ancient Chinese and modern Japanese.

2 If you are interested in poetry, it is worth buying a bilingual edition of a poet you enjoy and comparing the original version with its translation.

Suggested answer
Poetry can be translated, but demands additional skills on the part of the translator. It is sometimes impossible to preserve the original rhyme or rhythm. For this reason, a translator should be able to 'take liberties' that the translator of a novel wouldn't contemplate. The first poem contains some idiomatic language (switch off your face, put your love into neutral) that might be difficult to translate within the same rhythm. The first two poems have tightly defined rhythm and some lines rhyme, so perhaps the free verse of Gary Snyder would be easier to translate. On the other hand, some of its nuances are personal to the poet and might be difficult to understand fully and/or get across in another language.

3 The picture is of Eugenio Montale.

1 analysis **2** scholars **3** mistrusted/untrustworthy
4 supposedly **5** imperial **6** imprisons **7** Familiar
8 enigmatic

Style extra

Two of the occurrences of *as* are in the same example.

> **Answers**
> *as* the poet Robert Frost once claimed
> *As* a result
> Familiar *as/though* I was with
> *As* remote *as*
> The change in word order adds emphasis to the fact that it is unlikely.

Turn to page 186 of the Grammar folder after completing the exercise (c and d do not contain concessive clauses).

> **Suggested answers**
> a Greatly acclaimed though this novel is, I find it rather disappointing.
> b As entertaining as the play is, it is lightweight in comparison with his earlier works.
> c As well as being a writer, Romano was a painter.
> d As Robert Frost said, 'A poem begins in delight and ends in wisdom.'
> e Gripping though the storyline of the novel undoubtedly is, its characters lack development.
> f Much as I have tried to get into the book, it remains impenetrable.

Corpus spot

> **Suggested answers**
> a In spite of / Despite the nice atmosphere ...
> OR Although the atmosphere is nice ...
> b ... despite the fact that ...
> OR despite my knowing only ...
> c Although it is not easy ...
> d Despite what she felt ...
> e Although one could see ...
> f In spite of that / Despite that ...
> g Even though I was wrong ...
> h ... in spite of writing ...

4

> 1 even if its/the rhyme is/gets lost OR even if he/she loses the rhyme
> 2 my hand at (writing) short stories, poetry is
> 3 enjoy/like poetry readings, I sometimes take exception to
> 4 as/though the biographer's progress was / had been initially
> 5 strike it lucky with/by creating a bestseller, although/ though/but/whereas/yet
> 6 for fear (that) / out of fear (that) it would/should/ might/could

16.3 pages 138–139

Listening and Speaking

1 The different genres shown are:
Don't Sweat The Aubergine – cookery/food writing
The Flanders Panel – crime/detective fiction
A Bigger Message: Conversations with David Hockney – art/ biography
Matter – science fiction
Mozambique Mysteries – travel writing

> **Possible answer**
> The ingredients in a good book depend on the genre – a good novel might have an intriguing plot, a cast of well-developed characters and be expertly crafted. A good biography, on the other hand, would be informative and accurate, with well-researched details and human interest. A book that is hard to put down usually has a fast-moving plot or suspense of some kind, whereby the reader feels compelled to continue to the end without pausing.

2 The extracts are fairly short, like those in Listening, Part 1. Play them twice if necessary.

> *The Dumas Club* (detective story)
> *Congo Journey* (travel writing)
> **Qualities:**
> *The Dumas Club*: subtle plot (two strands, apparently interlinked), compelling, makes the reader come up with links and suppositions
> *Congo Journey*: more than straight description, brilliant insights into a remote region, meticulous detail on wildlife, superb use of dialogue, funny, moving

Recording script 2 06

Speaker 1: If I had to single out one book from the many I read last year, it would be *The Dumas Club*, by Arturo Pérez-Reverte – that's in translation from the original Spanish. Although I read the opening couple of chapters quite slowly, I soon got completely immersed in the subtleties of the plot, so much so that I quite literally could not put the book down until I had finished it. Some books have this compelling effect on me, and not just detective stories like this one. What is so skilful about the way *The Dumas Club* has been constructed is that there are two strands to the plot, and as a reader, you assume these are interwoven and all the time you're engaging with the text on this basis, making links and suppositions of your own. Well, without giving anything away, there is a masterful twist, which makes this an exceptional book.

Speaker 2: I read loads of travel writing, partly because I have a penchant for travelling myself. That said, I do expect a lot more than straight description and first-hand observation from a truly great travel book. Redmond O'Hanlon's masterpiece *Congo Journey* does not disappoint! Will Self – the author – named it as one of his books of the year and said he felt like starting it again the minute he'd finished it, which is praise indeed! I'll certainly re-read it at some point. It's got brilliant insights into what is a really remote region of our planet. There's meticulous detail on its wildlife and superb use of dialogue … brings the whole thing to life. And then much more besides – it's funny, moving – so you're reading it on many different levels. Above all, though, you marvel at his sheer guts in enduring such a difficult and dangerous journey. Epic stuff.

3　Underline the words for a–h in the recording script in 2.

> **a** immersed　**b** compelling　**c** assume　**d** suppositions
> **e** masterpiece　**f** insights　**g** meticulous　**h** guts

Pronunciation

4　*Subtleties* has a silent 'b'. The silent consonants are underlined in the recording script.

Recording script　2 07

knowledge
wretched
rustle
rhythm
heir
coup
indebted
exhilarating
denouement
pseudonym
doubt
mnemonic
condemn
apropos
penchant

5　The silent consonant is 'b'.

> **Answers**
>
> | 1 | a | p | r | o | p | o | s | | | | |
> |---|---|---|---|---|---|---|---|---|---|---|---|
> | 2 | | | | | c | o | u | p | | | |
> | 3 | m | n | e | m | o | n | i | c | | | |
> | 4 | | | | | p | e | n | c | h | a | n | t |
> | 5 | | | | | p | s | e | u | d | o | n | y | m |
> | 6 | | d | e | n | o | u | e | m | e | n | t |
> | 7 | | | | i | n | d | e | b | t | e | d |

6　Remember that in Speaking, Part 3 you need not cover all the prompts on the card in the exam.

> **a** technological alternatives OR practical advantages
> **b** technological alternatives
> **c** practical advantages
> **d** educational issues
> **e** practical advantages OR technological alternatives

7　Plan your talk, working through the checklist. Record the talk and then analyse it, referring to the checklist.

Writing folder 8 pages 140–141
Part 2 Set text question: Review

Avoid writing at length about the whole plot in the exam – all set text questions ask something fairly specific about the book you have read.

1　Underline the key parts of the question as you read it.

Background information

Matthew Kneale (born 1960) is best known for his novel *English Passengers*, published in 2000, which won the Whitbread Book of the Year and was also shortlisted for the Booker Prize for Fiction. He began writing while teaching in Japan and currently lives in Italy. His other novels include *Sweet Thames* (1992) and *When We Were Romans* (2007). He has also written a collection of short stories entitled *Small Crimes in an Age of Abundance* (2005).

2

> 1 G　2 F　3 B　4 D　5 A　6 C

3

> b C　c B　d E　e C　f B　g E　h B　i E　j B　k E

> **Possible sentences**
> By and large, the author is successful in his portrayal of female characters.
> In much the same way, memories of the past are included as flashbacks.
> As it turns out, Prentice could not have witnessed the event.
> Within a matter of hours, her condition had worsened and she died the following day.
> By the same token, nobody should have been working that day.
> On balance, this is an ambitious first novel, which promises much for this talented young writer's future.

4　Use some of the collocations in your own review later.

> **Possible answers**
> utterly impressive characterisation
> zealously detailed chronicle
> painstakingly accurate depiction
> utterly enigmatic hero
> hauntingly moving images
> intensely compelling narrative
> ingeniously woven plot
> subtly realistic portrayal
> annoyingly pompous protagonist
> exquisitely intricate storyline

5　Write the review, following the advice given on page 141.

Units 13–16 Revision

pages 142–143

Use of English

The aim of this revision unit is to focus on the language covered in Units 13–16, and earlier, as well as extending the work done in Writing folder 7. Specific exam practice is provided for Reading and Use of English, Parts 1, 3 and 4. This Use of English section could be done as a timed test of 30 minutes.

1 The picture shows the WORLDMAP software in action.

> **1** endangered **2** rarity **3** analyses **4** rectangular **5** likelihood **6** patchiness **7** complementary **8** maximise/ize

2

> **1** the outset the man (had) denied
> **2** never saw eye to eye when it
> **3** as I sympathise with / am sympathetic to/towards the line
> **4** as it may seem
> **5** is setting/placing / sets/places great/much / a lot of store on
> **6** came as (something of) a surprise (to us)

3

> **1** B **2** C **3** C **4** A **5** D **6** D **7** A **8** B

Writing

4 The draft proposal has been written as a joke – the date is 1 April, which is otherwise known as April Fool's Day.

Background information

On April Fool's Day, people in Britain play tricks on their friends and work colleagues. Newspapers often carry 'spoof' articles – ones that aren't true. The joke has to be done before midday.

Sample answer

To the Managing Director   1 April

As conscientious members of the IT department, we would like to propose a few amendments to our working conditions. You are aware of our expertise in dealing with computing problems company-wide. Indeed, we think it is fair to say that we are indispensable. To guarantee a rapid response, we have always been willing to work long hours whenever necessary. However, we are not prepared to continue working in this way unless you can put something extra on the table. We would like to suggest the following:

Firstly, it is unreasonable to expect us to travel in on public transport, given that we start very early and stay late. Could we perhaps suggest that the company invests in some stretch limousines (five should be adequate), to cover door-to-door transport. This would clearly lead to better productivity and goodwill.

Secondly, we are rather disappointed with the restaurant downstairs and suggest that it would be more convenient if we had our own chef and facility on this floor. We feel an extended lunch break would be only reasonable, as we work so late into the evenings.

Thirdly, we regret to tell you that the salaries paid by this company are derisory. It would be appropriate for you to offer us a little more at this point, particularly given our track record.

Could you possibly give us some form of response before midday?

With thanks,

Frank McGeek

IT Department

(241 words)

Crossword

This includes some of the idioms, phrasal verbs and other vocabulary from Units 13–16.

Unit 17

17.1 pages 144–145

1

The pictures show, from left to right:
- a girl reading a book in a meadow
- two teenage girls at a funfair
- a father holding his newborn baby
- a mountaineer who has just reached the summit

Sources of quotes (in order of presentation in Student's Book): Thomas Jefferson, Anatole France, Marcus Aurelius, Democritus, Robert Kennedy

Listening

2

> bliss, elation, euphoria, rapture
> contagious, infectious, invasive, virulent
> ephemeral, fleeting, momentary, transient

3

Before playing the recording, spend 45 seconds (the time you will have in Part 4 of the exam) looking at the task. Listen to the recording twice to replicate exam conditions. The underlined parts of the recording script confirm the answers.

> **1** H **2** E **3** B **4** F **5** C **6** B **7** H **8** A **9** D **10** G

Recording script 2 08

Speaker 1

Well, I suppose I would visualise certain snapshots in my life, fleeting moments when I was on cloud nine – the birth of my second child or, more recently, <u>a forest walk on a beautiful morning with the birds singing their hearts out – at times like these, you sort of step outside yourself and think, yes, this is as good as it gets</u>. So it's not about having material possessions or a huge income, though if you have any worries on that front it surely rules out the chance of happiness. <u>It's more to do with personal satisfaction and inner peace.</u>

Speaker 2

For me it's not necessarily a transient feeling. I can recall whole periods of my life <u>when things were basically going right, especially in my career, and I think a positive experience like that works as a catalyst</u>. I suppose I can't have been in the same state of ecstasy from dawn till dusk, but looking back, perhaps through rose-tinted spectacles, it certainly feels that way. But if I had to pick just one event, it would be <u>the elation I felt aged nine on receiving a silver trophy at my first judo contest</u>, something beyond my wildest dreams.

Speaker 3

In my book, <u>it's all to do with shared positive vibes, like infectious laughter rippling through a close family group. Being in a loving relationship is key, as this provides stability</u>. And happiness can be found in small things – <u>the security of a comfortable sofa, curled up with a good book while the wind's howling outside – that's something I remember from my childhood</u>. It may be an old cliché, but it's true, you can't buy it, not at any price.

Speaker 4

Sometimes I've felt <u>a surge of joy</u> in the midst of a perilous situation, and <u>one moment I'll always treasure occurred in the Andes with two fellow-climbers, handling a tricky descent in appalling weather conditions</u>. I hadn't known them that well when we set out, but in that situation, you put yourself on the line and <u>make the impossible happen through mutual trust and cooperation</u>. Others might claim wellbeing is a mental thing, but that's not what really counts. <u>If you're feeling under the weather, you won't experience emotional highs, so it's vital to stay in shape. Well, that's my view, anyway.</u>

Speaker 5

<u>Locations have always been important to me – they seem to contribute so much to a person's mood</u>. A few years ago, I was studying marine activity on a coral reef, part of a close-knit research team on an otherwise unpopulated and <u>stunningly beautiful island</u>. There was one particular day when I'd done three dives, the last at night, and although I was exhausted, I couldn't turn in. So I went back to the beach alone. I lay on the ghostly white sand, gazing at the canopy of stars above me, and <u>saw the most awesome meteor shower – an absolute first for me. It doesn't always take much to tip the balance in favour of happiness, does it?</u>

Idiom spot

Find and underline the idioms in the recording script above.

> **a** be extremely happy
> **b** with a positive view of the past that is unrealistic
> **c** better than anything you could imagine or hope for
> **d** in my opinion
> **e** commit yourself, stand up for what you believe in
> **f** feel ill
> **g** sway (an argument) in one direction

> **Suggested answers**
> **1** In the roomful of people, Jack was the only one to put himself on the line and challenge the speaker.
> **2** Fiona sees her teenage years through rose-tinted spectacles.
> **3** In my book, children should show respect for their elders.
> **4** The fact that the sun was shining tipped the balance and they took the day off.

Vocabulary: Metaphor

4   Some of the possible collocates are given below.

Suggested answers
bruised egos
contagious criticism
fatal dose of scepticism, flaw in the argument
feverish state of activity
healthy bank balance, criticism, dose of scepticism, turnout of voters
jaundiced criticism, sense of humour
sick sense of humour, bank balance
sore loser

5   Metaphors may be easier to learn by topic. A useful book on this area of language learning is *Meanings and Metaphors: Activities to practise figurative language* by Gillian Lazar (Cambridge University Press, 2003).

Answers
a growth/plants   b water/liquid   c fire   d bad weather/storms   e light   f cooking

6   Remember not to mix your metaphors (see second answer below).

Possible answers
The recent wave of violent protests against globalisation has caused many injuries.
A whirlwind of activity sweeps through our house just before we go away on holiday. (*Note: feverish* has been deleted, as this would be a 'mixed' metaphor.)

7

Background information

Gerald Durrell, younger brother of the writer Lawrence Durrell, grew up on the Greek island of Corfu, which is where his interest in the natural world began.

1 B   2 C   3 C   4 D   5 A   6 B   7 C   8 D

8

Similes
as gently and clingingly as pollen
glossy and colourful as a child's transfer
Metaphor
the dark skin of night would peel off
barred with gold

17.2 pages 146–147

Comparison

1   The picture shows a marble bust of the ancient Greek philosopher Epicurus. The word 'natural' in the three headings means that it is understandable for a human being to want such things.

2

1 odds   2 What   3 Few   4 least   5 whose   6 far/further
7 on   8 Such/These

3   Statements a–h exemplify other comparative structures. See the Grammar folder on page 186.

Possible answers
a   I'm actually happier now than I was then.
b   I agree – it's often more enjoyable to eat good food at home in good company.
c   I disagree!
d   Obviously the most important thing to anyone is to be in good health.
e   It depends – sometimes it is easier to hear the songs at home, though it is definitely more exciting to be there on the spot.
f   I disagree – it is far better to watch than play, especially during the winter.
g   It is a remedy, but the best one is to meet someone else who you care for.
h   I'd have to agree with this one – it's not nearly as comfortable being out in a snowstorm as being inside by the fire.

4

Possible answers
c   The more possessions you own, the less satisfied you are.
d   The wider the gap between rich and poor, the greater the inequality of opportunity is for the next generation.
e   The longer you go on buying sweets, the less easy it will be to give them up.
f   The later you tell him about the problem, the worse it'll be for you.
g   The higher you jump, the harder you fall.
h   The more anxious the parents are, the less contented the baby will be.

Vocabulary: Synonyms

5

> **a** WILLING   **b** NOT WORRIED   **c** LUCKY   **d** PLEASED
> fortunate = LUCKY
> ecstatic = PLEASED

6

> **Possible answers**
> PLEASED cheerful, content, merry
> LUCKY opportune, propitious, timely
> WILLING amenable, inclined, prepared

7

> **1** set her sights on visiting / a visit to
> **2** changed his tune / sang a different tune when he
> **3** keep a straight face in OR keep a straight face because/ as/since it was
> **4** on cloud nine at winning/gaining/getting first OR on cloud nine when she won/got/gained first OR on cloud nine having won/got/gained first
> **5** nowhere near as much
> **6** sooner Ralph moves out the better so

17.3 pages 148–149

Reading into Writing: Full Task 1

1 The pictures show:
- a healthy-looking woman riding a horse
- a family walking along a beach
- a desirable house in the sun.

2 Check your understanding of the words and phrases in the box. Many of them are used in the texts below.

3 This lesson looks at a Writing, Part 1 task and analyses a sample answer that has lifted some words and phrases from the texts.

4 Working through the sample answer will make you more aware of the need to reformulate words and phrases. See the rewritten answer on the next page for suggested changes, which are given in italics.

The 'lifted' words and phrases in the rest of the answer are as follows:
Second paragraph: *health and well-being, climate, job satisfaction, aspects, political freedom*
Third paragraph: *healthy, supported by friends and family*

Suggested reformulation
Both texts deal with the concept of 'quality of life' and consider which factors within this umbrella term are the most important in reality. In both cases, *healthiness* is seen as *a crucial attribute*, since *it dictates whether someone can hold down a job* and *therefore influences other 'quality of life' indicators*.
The first text gives an overview of the factors that go to make up a person's quality of life, mentioning *their state of health and general happiness*, social involvement, work, the political status quo and the local *weather conditions*. Not only does it underline the fact that without good health, *being able to work and having* an active and fulfilling role in *society* are impossible, but also, it argues that some *things* cannot be changed *by the individual – how their country is governed* and *any consequent limits on their rights*, for example.
The second text focuses on the annual phenomenon of quality-of-life indexes and, while viewing them as informative, questions the value of their having such prominence in the media. For most of us, it is academic which city in the world has the best quality of life, as we have no real opportunity to uproot our existence and rush to start a new life there. Nor is it necessary, argues the writer, as a good quality of life is still possible, provided that the individual is *physically fit* and *enjoys some stability in relationships*.
While this may be true up to a point, it is nevertheless going to be far more difficult for people trapped in poverty to gain a quality of life equal to that of people at the other end of the wealth spectrum – especially in our materialist society, where possessions seem to count for so much and we are constantly encouraged to wish for more.
(301 words)

Idiom spot

The idiom *make ends meet* means manage on very little money.

> **a** feel the pinch   **b** tighten your belt   **c** keep your head above water   **d** cut corners
> *cut corners* – save time, money or effort by not following the usual procedure
> *down and out* – without hope and usually without a job or place to live
> *keep your head above water* – struggle to survive, usually under pressure
> *feel the pinch* – have less money than previously and suffer as a result
> *in the red* – overdrawn at the bank
> *on a shoestring* – with very little money
> *tighten your belt* – economise
> *a rough ride* – a time when you experience a lot of problems

Exam folder 9 pages 150–151

Listening, Part 1 Multiple-choice questions

1 In the examination there are three different extracts. Here, there are only two. You will hear each extract twice.

1 A 2 B 3 C 4 A

Recording script 2 09
Part 1

You will hear two different extracts. For questions 1–4, choose the answer (A, B or C) which fits best according to what you hear. There are two questions for each extract.

Extract One

Man: Now, from what I can tell from this current album, apparently the singer Lisa Gray is on cloud nine. It's interesting isn't it – the alternative artist who, in her long singing career, has always refused to conform to mainstream notions of musical genres, but who has just made a commercial album which looks set to be a hit. Why the about-face, do you think?

Woman: It looks as if she has now found a kind of fulfilment, after years of swimming against the tide – possibly because of her marriage. After hits like *Needing You* and *Crying Out*, Gray seemed hardly likely to make an album celebrating happiness in love. But, with her new album, that is exactly what she has done and it'll get her a lot of new fans.

Man: Well, she certainly seems to have got over her aversion to pop and with this new album she has definitely proved that she can do it.

Extract Two

Critic: The American artist Dorota Kowalska claims to view her homeland with affection, but the fact that she left the USA and has lived in Europe since 2007 suggests that what might be *Always Fun in the USA* – the title of her latest book of photographs – isn't necessarily something she herself subscribes to. Her images depict largely working-class Americans amusing themselves in ways that only a nation hopelessly committed to the pursuit of pleasure could devise. *Aquapark* gives a bird's-eye view of trippers aimlessly drifting along the concrete waterways on their huge rubber rings. As with most of the characters in Kowalska's eccentric collection, their quest for enjoyment looks naive or perhaps, at worst, even vulgar and trashy. The documentary style in which the photographs show the people contrives derisively to offer the recreational habits of these individuals for our amusement, rather than suggesting a sentimental reaction to such eccentricity.

Listening, Part 3 Multiple-choice questions

2 This is a complete Part 3 question. The underlined parts of the recording script confirm the answers.

1 D 2 A 3 D 4 C 5 A

Recording script 2 10
Part 3

M: You will hear two people, Darren and Helena, talking about Darren's new career. For questions 1–5, choose the answer (A, B, C or D) which fits best according to what you hear.
You now have one minute in which to look at Part 3.

Helena: So, Darren, I hear that you've got a new job working in the voluntary sector. It must have been a bit of a wrench, wasn't it, giving up your high-powered banking job in the City, with those huge annual bonuses and long City lunches? Most people we know thought it was a passing phase, but I always thought you were a bit of a square peg in a round hole, so I've always half expected it. So I guess armed with your degree and a tidy sum put by, you thought you could change careers just like that? But why did it take you two years to make the move?

Darren: I didn't know what I wanted to do; I only knew what I didn't. I was really stuck in a rut until someone I worked with got fed up with me and told me to 'go and do voluntary work or something'. So I decided to take some time off and volunteer for a charity. I reckoned that if I guaranteed them six months, during that time I would be bound to find a proper job, you know a paid one! It wasn't quite as easy as I thought, though. I decided to apply to 12 well-known charities, ranging from overseas aid to homelessness. I put in my applications, but I guess my lack of real conviction and experience was pretty obvious, and they saw straight through me. They didn't even bother to reply.

Helena: Quite right. I don't know why you'd think they would. They need big hitters just like in banking, not people who don't know what they want – I can't imagine why people think that charities should be charitable when it comes to employing people.

Darren: <u>Well, I can see that now obviously</u>. Anyway, I got a lucky break. A friend of a friend had a contact with one of the charities I had applied to. She gave me a name, Anna Rogers, and within days Anna had come back with a proposal. Now, I'm a history graduate and I'd spent two years on a trading floor in the City, so most of her spiel on government research papers went straight over my head, but I did manage to make out that she wanted me to find out about schemes that prevented or alleviated homelessness. <u>I jumped at the chance and handed in my notice at work straightaway.</u> My colleagues told me they'd thought I'd never really do it – they had no idea how desperate I was.

Helena: So how did it go??

Darren: Well, I actually found it a bit on the quiet side, but that was OK. I could hear the tapping of keyboards and conversations on the phone. Even the people were different – they spoke in whole sentences, without the 'yeah, yeah, right, right, offer this, bid that, done' tempo I was used to. I was expecting a collection of meek do-gooders, and I was surprised to find they were OK, and <u>I just got on with things</u>. They were a nice bunch and were only mildly curious as to why I had given up a well-paid job. The biggest surprise, however, was me. I never expected to enjoy it so much.

Helena: So, what about the future?

Darren: Well, that project took five months to complete. That done, I had no real desire to leave and volunteered for another couple of months, writing bits and pieces, even stuffing envelopes. It was novel to be working 14-hour days without moaning for what I once regarded as a pittance. I don't think the City is an easy life. Mind you, this isn't a breeze either – there are still targets here. Equally, <u>the City just wasn't right for me, while this is</u>. I feel pretty stupid that it took me so long to figure that out. I'm just glad I got there in the end and one day I can work on a bigger project where I can start to make a difference to people's lives.

Now you will hear Part 3 again.

Unit 18
18.1 pages 152–153

1 Think about the bulleted points in relation to all parts of the world.

> **Possible answers**
> - Slavery exists in different parts of the world, for example in West Africa.
> - There are many repressive regimes around the world where people suffer these infringements on their personal liberty.
> - I suppose everyone has a nationality, though not always the one they would like – perhaps their country is under the control of another.
> - Religious intolerance is prevalent in many societies; freedom of thought is not always possible under a dictatorship.

Reading

2 The picture shows the tearing down of the Berlin Wall in 1989, which signalled the end of the 'Cold War' and led to the re-unification of Germany.

Carry out the gapped text task, following the advice given in Exam folder 5 on page 83. Remember to underline key words and phrases in both the base text and the paragraphs.

1 E 2 H 3 B 4 F 5 D 6 A 7 G

3

> **Possible answer**
> In general, I believe the future for human rights looks less bleak than it did twenty or thirty years ago. Thanks to the Internet and social media, individuals can find out quickly what is going on around them, and most repressive governments in the world wield less power than they used to because of this 'openness'. Indeed, some regimes have been toppled because they were unable to prevent their citizens from having access to worldwide media coverage. However, it should not be forgotten that human rights abuse still goes on in some parts of the world. And at the same time, increasing globalisation means that we are in danger of losing our cultural identity, which could affect individual freedom too.

4 The words and phrases are all in the text on pages 152–153.

> **a** in limbo **b** a rather faltering endeavour **c** a loosening of the reins **d** a (soft) sideshow **e** dealing a blow to **f** remit

5

Possible answers
a have a lot of influence
b expansion (in the number of)
c made people more aware of
d favourable
e violate
f confirmed in
g put forward by
h under the direction of

18.2 pages 154–155

Modals review

1 The pictures are taken from two animal welfare campaigns run by PETA and Lush.

Possible answer
We share our planet with animals, but it cannot be denied that human beings are the dominant species. So should animals have the same rights as us? It is a complex issue because of our perceived needs. Many people across the world depend on animals for their livelihoods, and domesticated animals provide sustenance for their families. However, the provision of food is one thing, whereas abusing animals in other unnecessary ways is quite another. For me it is unacceptable to cause an animal suffering in the pursuit of a new cosmetics line or even in the development of potentially life-saving drugs. We humans should treat animals with the respect and compassion they deserve.

2 The speaker is against animal testing.

Recording script 2 **11**

Two-and-a-half million animals are used in Australian medical research every year, half a million in Victoria alone. They justify the obscene waste of life like this: animals must be used in order to trial new drugs and treatments safely. But a growing number of doctors and scientists have challenged this line, saying that in fact, animal research is counterproductive. It could in fact be damaging to human health. This is because animals are not like us – their bodies are different, they suffer from different diseases and obviously their reactions to drugs are also different. So animals cannot be used to find cures for humans.

Why does animal testing continue? Answer: it's a huge industry. There are many, many vested interests in animal research, from the big pharmaceutical companies themselves to the manufacturers of the cages that these poor dumb animals end up in. Then, apart from those obvious commercial interests, there are the many scientists who have chosen to base their careers on animal experiments. They would lose their jobs tomorrow if animal testing was stopped, wouldn't they?

Basically, animal research is the ultimate quick fix. In general, it requires many years to monitor the progression of a human disease. Obviously laboratory animals, with their shorter lifespans, tend to decline more rapidly. This means that research projects can be wrapped up quickly. Papers presented, trials successfully concluded, bam, new drugs hit the market. It can't be scientifically sound. But what *should* have been done – full-scale controlled monitoring within a human population – is ruled out as uneconomic. The hard truth is that just about every medical advance has come about either independently from, or despite, animal research. You shouldn't believe everything you hear, right?

Corpus spot

a can be kept … must have
b must/should be changed
c ought to have been / should have been
d correct
e can't have been
f wouldn't have bought
g could live
h wouldn't

3

a shouldn't have   b might have   c must have   d needn't
e don't have to   f shouldn't   g Ought   h Would

4

1 to have put in more
2 have been less humane prior to the establishment
3 put themselves / their job on the line
4 have let us know (about) Lisa's / let us in on Lisa's
5 the record straight about how / about the fact that
6 raise any objection(s) to my/me

5

Background information

The text comes from the book *The New Existentialism* by Colin Wilson, a British philosopher whose most famous book *The Outsider* was written when he was only 24.

1 insignificant   2 evolutionary   3 interminable
4 submissively   5 empower   6 resourcefulness
7 footing   8 natural

18.3 pages 156–157

Listening and Speaking

1 The pictures show:
   • children working in a carpet factory
   • someone making a speech at Speaker's Corner in Hyde Park, London

- a demonstration being broken up violently by the police.

> **Suggested answers**
> Picture A shows a factory where child labour is being used to produce goods. You might call it a sweatshop and it is preventing these girls from gaining a full education.
> Picture B shows a man talking to a crowd of onlookers and he is dressed quite unconventionally! He is probably able to say whatever he wants to in public, but the right to free speech isn't universal and some political regimes would have that man arrested on the spot.
> Picture C shows some kind of civil disobedience, perhaps a protest about something, so I suppose it is illustrating the right to demonstrate in public – there is some form of riot control taking place, though, so maybe this illustrates the lack of such freedom.

2 Look at the pictures as you listen to the first part of the recording. Notice how the man keeps interrupting the woman and doesn't allow her to give her own opinions. He also challenges what she says quite aggressively, which is rather unfair in an interview situation.

Recording script 2 ⑫

Interlocutor: Now, in this part of the test you're going to do something together. Here are some pictures on the theme of freedom. First, I'd like you to look at pictures A and C and talk together about what might have happened just after these photos were taken. You have about a minute for this, so don't worry if I interrupt you.

Man: Er … shall I start?

Woman: Sure, go ahead.

Man: Well, I'll choose the easier of the two. So, if we consider what C shows, it's some kind of demonstration which may have started off peacefully but has obviously turned sour. Er, the police are in there, there'll obviously be lots of arrests, and maybe worse, physical abuse of some kind …

Woman: The … there's a doctor or someone with a medical training there, the armband has a red cross, it doesn't look good …

Man: Yes, yes. The police might take away banners, too, that's what often happens in situations like this. Anyway, what about picture A?

Woman: Well, I'm sure the owners of the factory weren't too happy with the photographer, so perhaps they tried to confiscate the film.

Man: Mm, but we're looking at the photo, so what you suggest can't be true!

Woman: I didn't say they succeeded. Yes, obviously the photographer …

Man: Um, perhaps it was taken in secret? That's what that kind of investigative journalist often does.

Woman: Uh-huh.

Interlocutor: Thank you.

3 Now listen to the second part. The candidates decide to include additional photos to do with education and animal rights.

Recording script 2 ⑬

Interlocutor: Now, I'd like you to look at all three pictures. I'd like you to imagine that they are all going to be used in a book about freedom. Talk together about the aspects of freedom that are shown. Then suggest two other aspects of freedom that you feel should be included in the book. You have about three minutes to talk about this.

Woman: Well, we've already identified political freedom and the rights of children, haven't we? Looking at picture B, I suppose it's illustrating the rights of the individual, isn't it?

Man: Mm, yes. It's taken in Hyde Park in London, the place is called Speaker's Corner and every Sunday …

Woman: I didn't know that. Anyway, the man is holding forth to the crowd about something, so it's all about free speech. He's rather unusually dressed, he's got a mortar board on his head like teachers used to wear, and look, he's wearing a real dog's collar! That's underlining the message of personal liberty – in a liberal society, you can wear what you want.

Man: Yes, that's an important point – you don't have that freedom of choice everywhere. Well, we have to suggest other aspects of freedom to include in this book … um …

Woman: Um, speaking purely for myself, I'd want to include something on education. It's a basic human right. I suppose it's linked to those girls in the factory, they're being deprived of what they should be doing at that age, going to school and learning. If they can't read and write, they'll be trapped for the rest of their lives.

Man: Mm, that's true. But how would you select a photo to show this type of freedom? If you just show a class of schoolchildren, it wouldn't make the point, education's something we take for granted.

Woman: Right, well fortunately, we don't have to worry about which photo is actually chosen, but I do think the book should focus on education.

Man: Oh yes, yes, I, I agree. And then, something else? Mm, freedom of the press maybe? That's part of political freedom, but also the book could focus on how the paparazzi chase after famous people, you'd get a good photo of that!

Woman: I'm not sure that's strictly about freedom, though. And it seems rather flippant, after we've been considering basic human rights like education and freedom of speech. What about including animal rights? It's an important element – we're not the only species on the planet, after all.

Man: But now I'm beginning to wonder what the focus of this book is. I mean, you can't just call it 'Freedom' and put everything in it – there would have to be some limits?

Woman: I don't see why. It would be very interesting. Perhaps a bit long.

Man: Just a little! Er, well, OK, we'll include animal rights. But in my humble opinion, the book will become very unwieldy, an editor's nightmare.

Woman: Maybe …

Interlocutor: Thank you.

Pronunciation

4 Read the Exam spot and then listen to utterances a–f, which have been recorded separately. Repeat after the speaker, paying particular attention to your stress and intonation.

Recording script 2 14

a Anyway, what about picture A?

b I didn't say they succeeded.

c Looking at picture B, I suppose it's illustrating the rights of the individual, isn't it?

d Yes, that's an important point – you don't have that freedom of choice everywhere.

e Speaking purely for myself, I'd want to include something on education.

f I'm not sure that's strictly about freedom, though.

5 Read the task and spend just a few seconds thinking about your ideas – you won't have longer in the exam!

6 The picture shows people protesting peacefully in Cairo during the 'Arab Spring' of 2012.

1 B   2 C   3 A   4 B   5 D   6 C   7 D   8 A

Writing folder 9 pages 158–159
Part 2 Article

1 Before reading the task, look back at the advice given in Writing folder 5 on page 91.

Suggested answers
The article will appear in an academic journal and be read by academics, so it must be formal, serious and impersonal in style.

2 Start with the title. Does it match your answer in 1? Work through the article, underlining any words and phrases that are informal rather than formal, or not impersonal in style.

All content is relevant to the task.

Inconsistencies in style:
use of an informal phrasal verb and chatty tone in title: *Hang on to your rights!* – certain phrasal verbs are appropriate in academic writing, for example *weigh up* in paragraph 1. However, you need to be careful when using phrasal verbs as informal ones stand out and contribute to a negative effect on the examiner (e.g. *help [us] out*).

several instances of *I think …* – an article for an academic audience should avoid use of the first person and adopt an impersonal style.

inappropriate informal use (you rewrite these parts in exercise 4):
really that great (paragraph 1)
the big plus; kids (paragraph 2)
the downside of; 24/7 (paragraph 3)
the Internet gives us the ability to control our lives, right? (paragraph 4)
help us out (paragraph 5)
the big snag (paragraph 6)

3 'Slips' (box 4) are very minor, unintentional mistakes. To achieve a Band 3 or above for Language in *Cambridge English: Proficiency*, you will have to show a high level of accuracy.

Tick the boxes that apply to the sample answer.

Boxes that apply:
Complex ideas are communicated convincingly.
Text is a well-organised, coherent whole.
Errors only occur in less common words and may be slips.
Choice of vocabulary generally shows sophistication and precision.

4

Rewritten answer
(Stylistic changes and spelling corrections in italics)
SOCIAL MEDIA: THE IMPLICATIONS FOR PERSONAL LIBERTY
The prevalence of mobile communication devices together with the widespread use of social networking and the Internet have altered our way of life fundamentally. This article weighs up their impact on individual freedom and assesses whether the outcomes are *unequivocally advantageous*.
Arguably, the main asset of Smartphones and tablets is that friends and family are always contactable. Parents need not be concerned for the *welfare* of their teenage children, as they can keep track of them. This may be beneficial to the older generation, but I think it imposes unfair limits on the liberty of their *offspring*.
One drawback of mobile devices from the working adult's standpoint is that they can be reached *at all times* and the distinction between work and home life becomes blurred. This again places constraints upon the individual, who has fewer opportunities to shut out the stress of everyday life. At the same time, *it is undeniable that* the Internet gives us the ability to control our lives. From booking a holiday to selecting a new home, everything can be done direct, without any middleman restricting what is on offer. So that is an example of greater freedom – the freedom of choice.
As for social networking, the chance to share ideas and communicate more effectively means that nobody need feel alone in the modern world. Furthermore, the role played by social media in disseminating information under less tolerant political regimes shows how networking sites can be used *for the greater good,* contributing to *profound* social change.
However, *the adverse impact of* all this is an inevitable erosion of privacy. People seem happy to display their innermost thoughts and aspirations in a way that would have been unheard of in the previous century, but at what cost? It is impossible to turn the clock back, yet it must be acknowledged that through social media, restrictions have been placed on individual freedom, which society at large may come to regret. (323 words)

5 Use a good monolingual dictionary to extend your knowledge of word families.

a	prevalence	**e**	tolerant
b	contactable	**f**	erosion
c	beneficial	**g**	aspirations
d	constraints	**h**	restrictions

6

a	tolerant	**d**	tolerance
b	intolerance	**e**	intolerant
c	intolerable		

7 Use the mind map to help you plan your ideas. Follow the Exam advice when you write your article.

Sample answer
THE POSITION OF THE INDIVIDUAL WITHIN CONTEMPORARY SOCIETY
How much freedom do we have in modern society? In some ways, we enjoy far more freedom than previous generations, but in other ways, we most definitely do not. This article considers both aspects of this question.
Nowadays, the individual has a strong entitlement to protection under the law, especially in relation to gender and race. Equal rights of this kind seem fundamental to personal freedom. Men and women should earn the same rates of pay for the same job, whatever their age and people of different ethnic backgrounds should be able to attend the school of their choice.
However, at the same time it cannot be denied that some constraints must be placed on the individual if a society is to function properly and these limits are generally enshrined in law. Model citizens recognise that they must abide by the law, in order to protect the weak and vulnerable members of their society, whereas lawless states lack the proper safeguards for these individuals.
In a civilised society, tolerance of others allows free speech and religious freedom. It is vital for individuals to be able to state their beliefs and political views without fear of reprisal. Similarly, everyone should be able to dress as they wish, rather than being attacked for their appearance.
However, there are many limits to personal freedom, not least due to the huge amount of data that exists about us online these days, from our shopping habits to our relationships. Furthermore, in many modern societies, children have less freedom to play unsupervised than in the past and CCTV cameras are everywhere. This undoubtedly affects everybody's freedom in one way, though it undeniably protects us at the same time.
In contemporary society we all carry the notion that we are 'free' but in reality, this isn't always the case. Although 21st-century citizens would probably not want to return to a pre-digital age, the constraints imposed on them are inevitably greater nowadays, largely thanks to the ubiquity of technology. (331 words)

Unit 19

19.1 pages 160–161

Speaking

1 The photo is from the Twilight series of films.

Vocabulary

2 The adjectives refer to personality. Use an English–English dictionary to find the odd one out. You can use any of the words you feel best describes someone who believes in ghosts.

a sceptical The other words all have the idea of 'easy to mislead or deceive'. *Sceptical* means 'doesn't believe things easily'.
b derisive The other words all mean 'easy to deceive'. *Derisive* means 'not worth taking seriously'.
c apathetic The others all have an active meaning. *Apathetic* is passive.
d sensible The other words have the meaning of being aware of things. *Sensible* means 'having common sense – knowing what to do'.
e humble The other words all mean wanting to find out about something. *Humble* means modest.
f upright This is a positive word – the others are all negative.
g eccentric The other words mean 'forceful'. *Eccentric* means 'unconventional'.
h pragmatic The other words mean 'clever' or 'skilful'. *Pragmatic* means 'practical in decision making'.
i impulsive The other words mean 'careful' or 'sensitive'. *Impulsive* means 'hasty'.

Suggested answer
Someone who believes in ghosts is probably gullible, naïve, credulous and susceptible.

Listening

3 Read through the questions and try to predict the answers. Play the recording twice. The underlined parts of the recording script confirm the answers. The story you will hear is true.

1 chains   2 burial   3 crisis apparition   4 patch of mist
5 plumber   6 ladder   7 waist   8 shave   9 dagger

Recording script 2 15

Presenter: Good morning. Today on the programme I'm going to talk about one aspect of the supernatural – ghosts! Now, ghosts have always been with us and are as much of a mystery now as they were in the first century AD, when Athenodorus, a hard-up philosopher, rented a house in Athens which was cheap because of its eerie reputation and noisy neighbours. Sitting working late at night, Athenodorus heard the rattling of <u>chains</u> and, suddenly, the horrifying figure of an old man appeared before him. It beckoned to him and, although Athenodorus tried to ignore it and get on with his work, it refused to let him. So Athenodorus followed the ghost into the garden, where it pointed to a spot on the ground and disappeared. Next day, a hole was dug at the place indicated by the ghost and a human skeleton was discovered. After the remains were given a proper <u>burial</u> and the house purified, the haunting ceased.

This was clearly a ghost with a purpose, but usually the reason for haunting is not clear. There have been a few modern cases where ghosts seemed to have a message, such as a '<u>crisis apparition</u>' of a person, seen by close friends and relatives at the time of his or her death, an event unknown to them until confirmation came later. However, in many ghost sightings, there seems to be no purpose and the ghost's identity remains unknown. Some people are sceptical and do not believe in the existence of ghosts. It is indeed likely that some witnesses who claim to have seen ghosts out of doors have, in fact, mistaken <u>a patch of mist</u> for a human figure, especially if they have been alone and the place was eerie. Other people may have vivid imaginations and 'see' externally something that is really only in their mind.

One of the most vivid apparitions on record was that seen in 1953 by 18-year-old Harry Martindale. Now a retired gardener, but a <u>plumber</u> at the time of the sighting, Martindale was working in the Treasurer's House in York. One day he was at work in the cellar, when, to his astonishment and fright, he saw a Roman soldier step out of the wall. He instantly dropped his tools. What he did not know at the time was that he had put his <u>ladder</u> on the course of an old Roman road. He later described in detail what he had witnessed.

Harry: I heard a sound – the only way I can describe it is the sound of a musical note. At the same time, a figure came out of the wall. And the head of the figure was in line with my <u>waist</u>, and it had on a shining helmet. I was terrified. I got out of the way and scrambled into the corner. And from there, I got a bird's eye view of what it was. It was the head of a Roman soldier. He crossed the room and disappeared into a pillar. Then another soldier on horseback came by, followed by soldiers walking in pairs, side by side.

You couldn't see through them. They were all about one metre five, in want of a <u>shave</u>! Nothing smart about them. They all had the same helmets on, with the plume coming out of the back, down the neck. They all carried a short sword on the right-hand side. I used to think that Roman soldiers carried a long sword, but this was similar to a <u>dagger</u>. And they went as quick as they came. When they were in the centre of the cellar, I could hear a murmuring – no speech, just a murmuring.

Presenter: When the museum curator found the terrified Harry collapsed at the top of the cellar steps, he immediately knew what had happened because he had seen the soldiers himself seven years before. And he knew Harry didn't know that the soldiers' legs were missing because they were walking on the course of the old Roman road, which was beneath the cellar floor.

4

> **Possible answer**
> I think that Harry's experience was probably the result of, maybe, overwork. I can't believe this actually happened.

Style extra

Using onomatopoeic words will help give life to your writing.

> **Suggested answers**
> Chains were described as 'rattling' and the Roman soldiers as 'murmuring'.
> creak – wooden floors
> tinkle – a bell; broken glass
> squelch – mud
> rumble – thunder, train on track
> crunch – gravel or crisp snow when walked on
> slash – an angry person cutting cloth viciously with a knife
> slap – waves on the beach, hand against face
> slam – a door
> click – door lock
> hiss – steam, a snake
> growl – angry dog, people
> screech – parrot, brakes
> drip – a tap
> peal – bells, laughter
> slither – snake moving smoothly, person sliding down or across something smooth
> **a** creaked **b** squelched **c** slashed **d** slithered
> **e** crunches **f** dripping **g** tinkled **h** hissed

> **Possible answer**
> I was lying in bed at home one night – all alone, except for my dog, as, for once, my family had gone out for the evening to a concert. It was a cold, rainy evening and the shutters had begun to bang against the side of the bedroom wall. I could hear the wind getting up and it howling down the chimney. Suddenly, I heard something tinkle, like glass breaking, then a crunch. I turned over, determined not to be spooked by this. Then, there was a creak. This is when I began to get worried, as I knew the third stair from the bottom always creaked. Betsy began to growl softly and then I knew that something was really wrong. I reached for my mobile phone.

5   Read through the text, which explains what a poltergeist is.

> **1** B is correct. A is when something is written in stone or metal; C is written in a meeting; D is for a course or in school.
> **2** A is correct because the text goes on to give the translation of the word.
> **3** C is correct. *Turned over* means 'being put upside down'.
> **4** D is correct because it is the only verb here that is reflexive.
> **5** B is correct because it collocates with 'rules'.
> **6** A is correct because 'spontaneous' is the only one which can be used with an object.
> **7** A is correct because it gives the meaning of 'started'. B, C and D need the preposition 'from'.
> **8** D is correct because it has the idea of future ability.

19.2 pages 162–163
Word order and adverbs

1   Refer to the Grammar folder on pages 187–188. The examples given cover most of the basic word order rules. Some words can change order depending on what you want to emphasise.

> **a** Yesterday I went home on foot. OR I went home on foot yesterday.
> **b** Later she briskly walked up the hill to where, luckily, another coach was waiting.
> **c** Last night I was hardly in the mood to go swimming. OR I was hardly in the mood to go swimming last night.
> **d** Of course he is still lying. OR He is still lying, of course. OR (with the meaning of not moving) Of course he is lying still.
> **e** In fact, Stephen spoke to me in a friendly way the other day. OR Stephen spoke to me in a friendly way the other day, in fact.
> **f** Strangely enough, it rained heavily non-stop all day. OR It rained heavily non-stop all day, strangely enough.
> **g** Apparently, people rarely hide things of value in the attic. OR People rarely hide things of value in the attic, apparently.
> **h** She performed the dance far too slowly.
> **i** To be honest, I think you should get out of the house more often. OR I think you should get out of the house more often, to be honest.
> **j** I saw the comet in the sky only yesterday. OR Only yesterday, I saw the comet in the sky.

2   Make sure you pay attention to punctuation when you do this exercise.

Background information

Uluru (formerly known as Ayers Rock) is a huge red rock in SW Northern Territory, Australia, 450 km SW of Alice Springs. It rises from the desert to a height of 348 metres. It is the largest monolith in the world.

> a Another tells how after a terrible battle …
> b One legend states that Uluru was originally a lake.
> c … that has been sacred to the Aboriginal people for hundreds of years.
> d Many Aboriginal paintings tell important Earth stories.
> e … the time when the world was created.
> f … the Earth rose up in revolt at the bloodshed to form the great blood-coloured rock.
> g They believe that it was made by spirits in the 'Dreamtime' …
> The order is Example, c, g, e, d, b, a, f

Corpus spot

> a He slumped into the nearby velvet armchair, **holding his briefcase tightly** in his hands.
> b **Looked at statistically**, however, the centre has attracted more people, spending more money than before.
> c **Being into contemporary rather than old-fashioned art** I don't find the good old Tate Britain a place I would visit too often.
> d correct
> e I have always wanted to remember **every movie I see and every book I read perfectly**.
> f It goes without saying that **you will seldom OR seldom will you** see a very shy person wearing a bright orange shirt.
> g Kerry is a very green county: you **can hardly** find a road where two cars pass each other.
> h Most of us are aware of the fact that **this solution is not always** economically viable.
> i Before he appeared on the music scene, **'Pop' music hardly existed**.
> j correct

3 Refer to the notes about adverbs and adjectives.

hard means difficult or not soft; *hardly* means not very much

short means not tall; *shortly* means soon

right and *rightly* mean correctly; *right* is only used after verbs and is informal

high is similar to tall; *highly* means a great deal

late is the opposite of early; *lately* means recently

wrong can be used informally after a verb

> a hardly b highly c wrongly/rightly d hard e shortly
> f wrong (also possibly wrongly or right) g lately h right
> i short

4 This text gives background information on how to carry out a ghost hunt.

> 1 make 2 carry 3 of 4 on/forth 5 As/When/If 6 to
> 7 taken 8 any

19.3 pages 164–165

Reading into Writing: Full Task 2

1 The photos are of Abraham Lincoln and John F. Kennedy, both American presidents.

> **Possible answer**
> I think that these coincidences are really very interesting. However, it has been shown that, what people think is 'a once in a million chance' of something happening has a good probability. Take, for example the coincidence of people having the same birthday in a small group. It is actually more common for up to three people to have the same birthday in a group of, say, twenty people, than you would think.

2 These are common expressions.

> Talk of the devil! – said when you mention someone and they then appear
> to have a guardian angel – said about the feeling that there is someone you can't see who protects you
> It's a small world – said about a coincidence involving people known to both speakers
> to have second sight – to be able to know what will happen in the future
> female intuition – a feeling about something that might happen that women are supposed to have
> a feeling of déjà vu – a feeling of being in a place you've visited before or of experiencing something that has happened before
> a sixth sense – a feeling that you have that tells you something isn't quite right – rather like intuition but used by both sexes

3 Read through each text carefully.

4 Look through the texts again in order to find the words and describe which part of speech they are.

> speak out (phrasal verb) outspoken
> anonymity (noun) anonymous, anonymously
> disturbing (adjective) disturb, disturbance, undisturbed, disturbed, disturbingly
> conscious (adjective) unconscious, unconsciously, subconscious, consciousness
> impression (noun) impress, impressive, unimpressive, impressively, impressionable
> dismissed (past participle) dismiss, dismissive, dismissal

5

> a outspoken b dismissive c anonymous d disturbance
> e impressionable f subconscious

6

Suggested improved answer

The two texts discuss the arguments supporting and refuting the idea of coincidence, whether they are evidence of the paranormal or can be explained on a purely rational level. Text 1 puts forward the idea that people react to coincidence in one of two ways. At worst, they are extremely uncomfortable at the thought of being stigmatised as an idiot, or, at best, they are troubled by a worrying occurrence.

Personally, I see myself in the latter category. I heartily agree with the writer that it is important to find out the truth behind a worrying occurrence or coincidence. I think that most people have experienced a feeling of déjà vu, and it can be unnerving, especially if they see themselves as quite sensible, level-headed types. It's hard to know where these feelings spring from, but I tend to think they are past memories of possibly a similar place or occurrence coming to the fore.

Text 2 mentions that people are first of all alerted through their senses to something not being 'quite right'. These feelings are generally thought to be ludicrous, especially given that time has shown that science can explain things which were previously thought to be mysterious.

I'm in two minds about how much science can explain. While I am by no means a gullible person, I still believe there may be room for the unexplained. I have never actually narrowly avoided a plane crash, but I do know people who have escaped serious injury through pure chance. Many coincidences can be easily explained away and the scientific theory of probability has gone a long way to disabusing people of how often some coincidences happen. However, I still believe that there are some things which are not easily explained. (292 words)

Exam folder 10 pages 166–167

Speaking

In the examination there will be two or three students and two examiners. For the purpose of this test you should try to find someone to play the part of another student or the examiner.

Make sure that the timing is correct: Part 1 – 2 minutes, Part 2 – 4 minutes and Part 3 – 10 minutes. There can be anything from one to seven pictures/visuals in the examination. Here there are five photographs.

The photographs for Part 2 are as follows:

A a small car

B a desk top computer

C a book

D a clock

E a refrigerator

Unit 20

20.1 pages 168–169

Speaking

1

Suggested answers

slapstick – silly behaviour like moving a chair when someone is about to sit down – similar to Charlie Chaplin humour

political satire – cartoons in the newspaper or comedy TV programmes on political topics

stand-up – where a comedian is alone on stage telling jokes to the audience

farce – a (sometimes irritating) type of comedy where the audience is aware that the actors are confused about a situation – often within a family

black comedy – making fun of something you shouldn't – like death or murder

Reading

2 Scan the text to find out what impression Bill Bryson gives of life in the USA.

Possible answer

He gives the impression of someone who is fairly happy to be back in his own country, but with reservations. He is enjoying playing with new toys.

Background information

Bill Bryson was born in Des Moines, Iowa in 1951. From 1977, he lived for many years in England with his English wife and family. He then moved back to the States, but has returned to live in England again with his family. His best-selling books include *The Lost Continent* (about America), *Mother Tongue* (about the English language), *Neither Here nor There* (about travelling in Europe), *Notes from a Small Island* (about Great Britain) and *Down Under* (about Australia).

3

Uses of *have*, *get* and *go*

1. **D** is correct because he talks about her enjoying simple pleasures like iced water and she thinks the waitress is just being nice to *her*, not everybody she meets. **A** is wrong because although he mentions food he doesn't say anything about it. **B** is wrong because she does get things for nothing, but nothing suggests that she might not be happy if she didn't. **C** is wrong because he says she is 'slavishly uncritical'.

2. **A** is correct because he thinks a National Health Service is more important. **B** is wrong because he doesn't mention money. **C** is wrong because he doesn't criticise the way things are done. **D** is wrong because he doesn't imply that it is a waste of time, just rather pointless.

3. **A** is correct because it does everything it is supposed to do. **B** is wrong because he doesn't mention anything about free time. **C** is wrong because there is no comparison made between what he thought it would be like and what it is like. **D** is wrong because there is a bit of a fuss when you put in chopsticks and coffee grounds.

4. **C** is correct because he talks about only attempting this when his wife is out of the house. **A** is wrong because he isn't irritated so much as horrified. **B** is wrong because he isn't mending the machine for his wife, but because he himself has been playing with it. **D** is wrong because, although he tries a wider variety of garbage, he doesn't say it should take it.

5. **A** is correct because they make children feel intimidated. **B** is wrong because the incidents do not actually happen. **C** is wrong because there is no competition. **D** is wrong because there is no mention of real arguments.

6. **B** is correct because effusive means enthusiastic. **A** is wrong because he isn't critical of his home. **C** is wrong because nostalgic means thinking fondly about the past and he is talking about the present. **D** is wrong because he isn't angry about anything.

4. Some of these phrases are put in for humorous effect.

   a. I don't want to start being too serious here
   b. a volcano-like eruption
   c. presumably now dead and a skeleton
   d. some young dynamic father
   e. other good things about American household life that are taken for granted
   f. I'll let you know what happens

1. Cartoons which play on words are popular in English.

   The words *tow* and *toe* have the same pronunciation – it's a play on words.
   To give someone a tow means to tow their car for them, i.e. pull it using a rope or chain.
   A *toe* is what you have on your foot. A chiropodist is someone who looks after feet.
   The first driver doesn't want to mend the vehicle himself.

2. You should be familiar with the construction *have/get something done*, so this should be revision.

   a have **b** get **c** got **d** had **e** has/gets **f** get

3. *Go* is often tested in Reading and Use of English.

   a down with **b** in for **c** on **d** over/through **e** for
   f out **g** off **h** with **i** without **j** off
   be spent on = go on
   ebb = go out
   fetch = go for
   enter (a competition) = go in for
   become ill with = go down with
   explode = go off
   match = go with
   go sour = go off
   examine = go over/through
   manage without = go without

4. Remember to count the number of words you write. It must be between three and eight words.

   1. promotion has gone to Penny Stone's
   2. went / kept going over and over (again) in his
   3. went on record as saying
   4. was (ever) allowed to go to waste / (ever) went to waste
   5. didn't (always) go off at a tangent
   6. make a go of her business in spite

Corpus spot

This exercise is error correction. The sentences contain common student errors. Refer to the appropriate Grammar folder if you need further help.

a <u>As it was</u> a wet evening, I stayed at home.
b We would like to know <u>everything that</u> has happened.
c He <u>is already</u> here.
d Only by listening intently, <u>will you hear</u> it singing.
e It would be easier to decide if my son <u>were/was</u> here.
f I have <u>passed</u> my exam this summer.
g It's worth <u>being</u> alive on such a lovely day.
h My family consists <u>of</u> six people.
i That is a mistake I <u>often make</u>.
j Your hair <u>badly needs</u> cutting.
k I suggest <u>doing</u> it immediately.
l This team is the <u>better</u> of the two.
m correct
n My <u>information isn't</u> up to date.
o I <u>have been wanting / have wanted</u> to meet you for a long time.
p I congratulate you on <u>having got / on getting</u> married.
q I wish it <u>would stop</u> raining.
r You can eat as soon as <u>dinner is</u> ready.
s It's a <u>five-mile</u> journey.
t A man came into the compartment to <u>check</u> the tickets.

5 Remember to read the whole text before you do the answers.

1 order **2** before **3** terms **4** no **5** nowhere **6** came/turned **7** All **8** more/other

6

Possible answer
I remember once sitting on a bus on my way to a party. The girl sitting opposite me was dressed rather strangely and I remember staring and thinking that she looked pretty terrible. When I got to the party, there was the girl – she was my friend's new girlfriend. I was embarrassed because I had stared at her rather critically all through the journey.

20.3 pages 172–173

Listening and Speaking

1

Possible answer
I would find the man who played the practical jokes very irritating.

2 Read through the questions and answer the task.

1 B **2** A **3** D **4** C **5** C

Recording script 2 16

Terry: Dr Morris, thanks for lending me that book on eccentricity. I really enjoyed it – especially that bit about Oscar Wilde taking a lobster on a lead for walks and that American-Indian guy who spends his life walking backwards. Oh, and, of course, we all know nowadays from new research that this sort of behaviour has nothing in common with what used to be called lunacy. But <u>it was a bit of an eye-opener that eccentrics are renowned for their longevity.</u> The book reckons that eccentrics don't repress their inner nature and therefore suffer less stress!

Dr Morris: That's right, Terry. They are happier as a result and their immune systems work more efficiently. Anyway, what I've always believed is that human behaviour ranges from absolute conformity, at the normal end of the spectrum, to utterly bizarre non-conformity at the opposite end. Though <u>exactly how much deviation from the norm it takes to qualify as a true eccentric is a bit of a vexed point</u>.

Terry: So, actually we are all eccentrics to a greater or lesser extent?

Dr Morris: That seems to be right. The question of what is normality is pretty personal. We have all had the experience of talking with a friend who tells us that he has just met someone with the most bizarre or risqué habit – only to hear described something which we ourselves routinely do or might wish to do.

Terry: I enjoyed the chapter on innovation in the book. Eccentrics seem to be able to see problems from new and unexpected angles and they can then make imaginative leaps. So, does the man in the street always react negatively to eccentricity?

Dr Morris: Well, <u>we all love eccentrics and yet we are profoundly ambivalent about them.</u> Our collective imagination is piqued by the bizarre behaviour of someone like, for example, Howard Hughes, once the richest man in the world, who lived the last days of his life like a mystical hermit. Eccentrics have thrown off the constraints of normal life to let themselves do exactly as they please – and anyone who doesn't like it can get on with it.

Terry: The book said only about one person in every 5-10,000 is a classic full-time eccentric and most exhibit traits from an early age. They seem to share five traits: being non-conforming; creative; strongly motivated by curiosity; idealistic; and obsessed by one or more hobbyhorses. <u>Non-conformity seems to be the principal characteristic.</u>

Dr Morris: <u>True</u>, though hobbyhorses also feature highly. There was an eighteenth-century aristocrat with a love of animals called Jack Myers. One time havoc broke loose at one of his dinner parties, when he appeared in full hunting costume, mounted on his bear. In the ensuing panic, while his friends jumped out of windows or clambered behind chairs, Myers called out 'Tally-ho' and spurred his mount, which turned impatient and ate part of his leg.

Terry: Amazing! I think I'll have to go into this in more detail now.

Dr Morris: You should. I came across some new findings recently that <u>participants in a study of eccentrics were more likely to endorse what for a better expression we call 'magical thinking' – dreams that portend the future, déjà vu, things like that</u>. They tend to focus their attention on their inner universe at the expense of social or even self-care needs.

Terry: Could you lend me that research, do you think?

Pronunciation

3 You may come across some of the many words English has borrowed from other languages. The ones mentioned here are the most common.

Recording script and answers **2 17**

in lieu of	instead of
ad infinitum	to infinity / without end
ad nauseam	continually so as to bore someone
par excellence	pre-eminently
quid pro quo	something in return
faux pas	a mistake
prima facie	at first sight
niche	recess in a wall, a suitable place, sector
risqué	racy – usually jokes
protégé	someone you have under your wing / a follower
fracas	disturbance
cul-de-sac	street open at one end only
clique	small group of people not welcoming to outsiders
nom de plume	pseudonym used when writing
bête noire	something you dislike
tête à tête	friendly, confiding conversation
hoi polloi	the ordinary people
coup de grâce	finishing stroke

4

> **a** faux pas **b** in lieu **c** nom de plume **d** risqué
> **e** tête à tête **f** ad nauseam / ad infinitum **g** cul-de-sac
> **h** bête noire

5 Read the information in your book. Hesitating, as long as it is in English, is acceptable, as long as it isn't for too long! Time yourself when you do the activity. You have two minutes each on your subject.

> **Possible answer – Task A**
> Personally speaking, I think it is better to conform, as this will help your life go more smoothly. I really admire people who try to be different, who maybe don't get married, but live together, who wear weird clothes or have strange hobbies, but in general you have fewer problems if you conform. If you want to be different, then it's better to live in a large city, like London or San Francisco. There, people don't seem to mind so much that your behaviour may be a little eccentric. If you live in a small village, then everyone will comment on what you do and what you wear and you might end up ostracised by the villagers. This is no way to live your life as you need as many friends as you can get. Having a strange hobby is probably not so much of a problem as not getting married or wearing funny clothes. As long, that is, as you haven't got an anti-social hobby like keeping rats or twenty killer dogs!

Writing folder 10 pages 174–175
Part 2 Articles and Letters

1 In the exam, read each question carefully, to decide what style and tone to use.

> **Functions**
> **A** factual description; speculation; narrative
> **B** factual description; opinion
> **C** opinion; comparison; speculation
> **D** evaluation; opinion
> **E** description; opinion; evaluation
> **Style and tone**
> A should be light-hearted, as this is requested.
> B should be fairly serious.
> C (letter) should be formal; could be fairly light (anecdotal) or more serious.
> D could be either, depending on the set book.
> E (letter) should be formal and polite.

2 This activity should remind you of some of the vocabulary you have learned during the course, which might be relevant to these tasks.

> **Suggested answers**
> **A** adventure, exhilarating, expansion, far-flung, historic, likelihood, multiplicity, unknown, venture
> **B** emissions, expansion, global warming, impinge, intolerable, judicious, multiplicity, perspective, tendency, trend, wipe out
> **C** birthrate, bread-winner, code, domesticity, historic, intolerable, likelihood, morals, patriarch, rules, stress, trend, unemployment
> **D** code, denouement, exhilarating, judicious, morals, perspective, plot, rules, tendency, trend, unmistakable
> **E** context, denouement, judicious, plot, unmistakable

3 You will not have time in the exam to write a rough copy first. Always make a paragraph plan before you start writing your answer.

4 Choose one of the tasks on page 174 and follow the instructions on timing and all the other advice given on page 175.

Units 17–20 Revision

pages 176–177

The aim of this revision unit is to focus on the language covered in Units 17–20, and earlier, and to provide support for the Part 2 letter (see Writing folder 10). Specific exam practice is provided on Reading and Use of English, Parts 1, 2 and 4. These Reading and Use of English tasks could be done as a timed test of 30 minutes.

Use of English

1

| 1 A | 2 A | 3 D | 4 B | 5 B | 6 A | 7 C | 8 A |

2

1 mustn't/shouldn't/can't allow the rumours to carry on OR mustn't/shouldn't/can't let the rumours carry on
2 needn't have helped us do/with
3 come when/whenever he likes as far as I'm
4 to preserve/protect her anonymity, I had the press
5 her sore throat / having a sore throat, Eliza excelled (herself)
6 other than / less than / but a full apology would be acceptable

3

1 with   2 for   3 being/remaining   4 their   5 whether
6 at   7 its   8 needs/has/ought

Vocabulary

4

a click   b peal   c growled   d trusting   e derisive
f head   g waste   h tangent   i faux pas   j fracas

Writing

5

Sample answer
A strange being stood stock still in the middle of the road. There was mist swirling around and it was impossible to make out who or what it was, but I swear I could see horns on its head and a pair of evil, red eyes. As I rammed on the brakes, the radio crackled and went dead. I sat there for a moment, staring in the gloom, trying to work out what was ahead. Then, steeling myself, I sounded the car horn repeatedly and drove towards the ghastly creature, which thankfully bounded off across the moorland as I approached. (100 words)

Crossword

This includes some of the idioms, phrasal verbs and other vocabulary from Units 17–20.

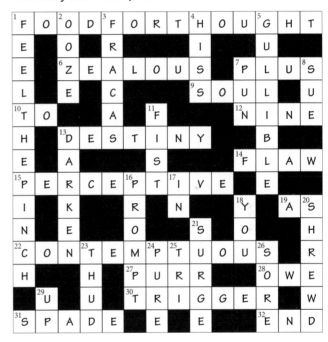

Acknowledgements

The authors and publishers would like to thank the following teachers who reviewed the material:

France: Lesley Joli; Greece: Christina Gravani, Stamatis Papademetriou; Poland: James Cusworth, Dagmara Krakowian; Russia: Natalia Bayrak; Spain: Manuel Padilla Cruz, Richard Pinn; Switzerland: Jean Gibbons; UK: Aleksandra Mrozek, David Tompkins.

The authors would like to give warm thanks to Jane Coates for her constructive comments, patience and thoroughness in the development and editing of this second edition. Thanks also go to Graham Burton for his perceptive comments on the material, to Una Yeung and Charlotte Adams of Cambridge University Press for their support and encouragement, to Hilary Fletcher for her creative flair and tenacity in searching for the right images, to Liz Knowelden for her diligence in monitoring the production stage, and to Alyson Maskell for her work on the original edition.

This product is informed by the English Vocabulary Profile, built as part of English Profile, a collaborative programme designed to enhance the learning, teaching and assessment of English worldwide. Its main funding partners are Cambridge University Press and Cambridge English Language Assessment and its aim is to create a 'profile' for English linked to the Common European Framework of Reference for Languages (CEFR). English Profile outcomes, such as the English Vocabulary Profile, will provide detailed information about the language that learners can be expected to demonstrate at each CEFR level, offering a clear benchmark for learners' proficiency. For more information, please visit www.englishprofile.org

Development of this publication has made use of the *Cambridge English Corpus (CEC)*. The CEC is a computerised database of contemporary spoken and written English which currently stands at over one billion words. It includes British English, American English and other varieties of English. It also includes the *Cambridge Learner Corpus*, developed in collaboration with Cambridge English Language Assessment. Cambridge University Press has built up the CEC to provide evidence about language use that helps to produce better language teaching materials.

The Cambridge Advanced Learner's Dictionary is the world's most widely used dictionary for learners of English. Including all the words and phrases that learners are likely to come across, it also has easy-to-understand definitions and example sentences to show how the word is used in context. The Cambridge Advanced Learner's Dictionary is available online at dictionary.cambridge.org. © Cambridge University Press, 3rd edition, 2008. Reproduced with permission.

Text acknowledgements:

The authors and publishers acknowledge the following sources of copyright material and are grateful for the permissions granted. While every effort has been made, it has not always been possible to identify the sources of all the material used, or to trace all copyright holders. If any omissions are brought to our notice, we will be happy to include the appropriate acknowledgements on reprinting.

Guardian News & Media Ltd for the text on pp. 16–17 adapted from 'The way we travel now' by Alain de Botton, *The Guardian* 4/8/2003, for the text on p. 28 adapted from 'Keep your distance' by Oliver Burkeman, *The Guardian* 14/9/1999, for the text on p. 41 adapted from 'Air Apparent' by Andrew Brown, *The Guardian*, 21/4/2001, for the text on p. 49 adapted from 'Merchant@florence wrote it first 500 years ago' by Philip Willan, *The Guardian* 31/7/2000, for the text on pp. 60–61 adapted from 'Written in the stars' by Jonathan Jones, *The Guardian* 20/7/2000, for the text on p. 89 adapted from 'The whole whack' by Ian Sansom, *The Guardian* 11/11/2000, for the text on pp. 116–117 from 'Wild flowers are nature's anarchists' by Simon Jenkins, *The Guardian* 17/11/2011, for the text on pp. 118–119 adapted from 'Gym'll fix it' *The Observer* 13/7/2008, for the text on p. 119 (Ben) adapted from 'Can the new generation of video games really give you a proper workout in your living room?' by Keith Stuart, *The Guardian* 10/11/2010, for the text on p. 120 adapted from 'Gym won't fix it' by Helen Foster, *The Observer* 21/1/2001, for the text on p. 128 adapted from 'Eyes wide shut' by Kate Hilpern, *The Guardian* 26/2/2001, for the listening exercise on p. 151 adapted from 'Why I dumped the City job with the six-figure salary' by Bruce Robinson, *The Guardian* 3/4/2001, for the text on p. 177 'Lords: rise of CCTV is threat to freedom' by Alan Travis, *The Guardian* 6/2/2009. Copyright Guardian News & Media Ltd 2003, 1999, 2001, 2000, 2011, 2008, 2010, 2009;

Text on p. 25 Copyright © US Geological Survey; text on p. 26 adapted from *Weird Weather* by Paul Simons; Britannica.com for the text on p. 30 from 'Henri Cartier-Bresson' *Encyclopaedia Britannica*. Copyright © Britannica.com. Reprinted with permission; Granta Books and The New Press for the text on p. 32 from *Reef*. Copyright © 1994 by Romesh Gunesekera. Reprinted with permission of Granta Books and the New Press. www.thenewpress.com; Grove/Atlantic, Inc. and HarperCollins Publishers Ltd for the text on p. 34 adapted from *The Rituals of Dinner*, copyright © 1991 by Margaret Visser. Published by HarperCollins Ltd. All rights reserved. Used by permission of Grove/Atlantic, Inc. and HarperCollins Publishers Ltd, Canada; The Irish Times for the text on p. 41 adapted from 'Too much on your plate? Waste not, want not' *The Irish Times* 19/9/2011. Copyright © The Irish Times; Douglas Rushkoff for the text on p. 45 adapted from 'I don't know which of these trainers is me' *The Times* 6/5/2000. Reprinted with permission of Douglas Rushkoff, http://rushkoff.com; The Independent for the text on pp. 50–51 adapted from 'The enduring myth of music and maths' by Tim Gowers, *The Independent* 6/7/2011, for the text on p. 115 (text 2) adapted from 'Is it time to give up on tigers and pandas' by Steve Connor, *The Independent* 9/11/2011. Copyright © The Independent 2011;

BBC Radio 3 for the listening exercise on p. 54 from *Music Machine* originally broadcast 26 January 1999; Robert Hughes for the text on p. 59 from *The Shock of the New* published by Thames & Hudson 1999; Bauer for the text on p. 62 (text 1) from 'Personal View' *Practical Photography*, May 2000. Reproduced with permission; Bernard Venables for the text on p. 62

(text 2) from 'Beauty a force for life' *Birds Magazine*, Summer 2000; Professor Peter Gordon and Professor Harry Richardson for the text on p. 67 from *A Critique of New Urbanism*. Reproduced with permission; Sue Monk Kidd for the text on p. 72 from a synopsis of *The Secret Life of Bees*. Copyright © 2002 Sue Monk Kidd. Reproduced with permission; HarperCollins Publishers Ltd and ICM Partners Limited for the text on p. 74 adapted from *No Logo: Taking aim at the brand bullies*. Copyright © 2000 Naomi Klein. Used by permission of HarperCollins Publishers Ltd and ICM Partners Limited on behalf of the author. All rights reserved; The Times for the text on pp. 82–83 adapted from 'Would I lie to you' by Peta Bee, *The Times* 3/5/2000, for the text on p. 86 adapted from 'Wise up, think global' by Jane Bolton, *The Times* 24/11/1999, for the listening exercise on p. 110 (extract 3) adapted from 'Glad to be a Gaia' by Anjana Ahuja *The Times* 15/5/2000. Copyright © The Times 2000, 1999; David Crystal for the text on p. 84 'Death Sentence' from *The Guardian* 15/10/1999. Reproduced by permission of David Crystal;

Mark Wilbur for the listening exercise on p. 88 (extract 3) adapted from Doubting to shuo www.toshuo.com. Reproduced with permission; Woman Magazine for the text on p. 94 from 'Love on the Internet' *Woman Magazine* 15/1/2000. Reproduced with permission; Tribune Media Services for the text on p. 95 adapted from 'You buzzing at me?' by John McCrone, *New Scientist* 23/12/2000, for the text on p. 108 adapted from 'The Joy of Socks' by Gail Vines, *New Scientist* 23/12/2000. Copyright © Reed Business Information – UK. All rights reserved. Distributed by Tribune Media Services; Penguin Books Ltd and Simon & Schuster, Inc. for the text on pp. 100–101 from *The Fifth Miracle: The Search for the Origin and Meaning of Life* by Paul Davies. Copyright © Paul Davies 1998. All rights reserved. Reproduced with permission of Penguin Books Ltd and Simon & Schuster, Inc.; Helena Paul for the text on p. 105 adapted from 'Dangerous Precedent' from the EcoNexus website. Reproduced by permission of Helena Paul; BBC Wildlife Magazine for the listening exercise on p. 110 (extract 1) from *My Kind of Life* by Sue Beenstock, January 2001; Curtis Brown Group Ltd for the text on p. 113 from *The First Naturalists*. Copyright © Gerald Durrell and for the text on p. 145 from *My family and other animals* by Gerald Durrell. Copyright © Gerald Durrell 1956. Reproduced with permission of Curtis Brown Group Ltd, on behalf of the Estate of Gerald Durrell;

Tanya de Grunwald for the text on p. 128 adapted from 'Interns fight back' 16/5/2011. www.graduatefog.co.uk. Reproduced with permission; Random House, Inc. and Donadio & Olsen, Inc. for the text on p. 134 from *The Lone Pilgrim*. Copyright © 1981 Laurie Colwin. Reproduced by permission of Alfred A Knopf, a division of Random House, Inc. and Donadio & Olsen, Inc.; Spike Milligan Productions Limited for the poem on p. 136 'New members welcome' from *Small dreams of a scorpion* by Spike Milligan. Reproduced with permission; Poem on p. 136 'Cold Mountain' by Gary Snyder; Melanie Jackson Agency LLC for the text on p. 136 adapted from 'Nicholas Jenkins' review of Collected Poems of Montale'. Copyright © 1999 by Nicholas Jenkins. First appeared in *The New York Times Book Review*. Reprinted with permission by Melanie Jackson Agency LLC; The Economist Newspaper Limited for the text on p. 142 adapted from 'Mapping Biodiversity', *The Economist* 23/12/2000. Copyright © The Economist Newspaper Limited, London, 2000; Francesca Klug for the text on pp. 152–153 from *Values for a godless age: the story of the United Kingdom's new bill of rights* published by Penguin. Reproduced with permission of Francesca Klug; Pauper's Press for the text on p. 155 from *The New Existentialism* by Colin Wilson. Reproduced with permission of Mrs Wilson on behalf of Colin Wilson;

University of Washington for the text on p. 157 adapted from *New Study Quantifies Use of Social Media in Arab Spring* by Catherine O'Donnell, UW News & Information. Reproduced with permission; Little, Brown and Johnson & Alcock for the text on p. 163 adapted from *Peter Underwood's Guide to Ghosts and Haunted Places*. Copyright © Peter Underwood, 1996. Reproduced with permission of Little, Brown Book Group and Johnson & Alcock Ltd; The Random House Group and Bill Bryson for the text on p. 168 from *Notes from a Big Country* by Bill Bryson. Published by Doubleday. Reprinted by permission of The Random House Group Limited and Bill Bryson; The Random House Group for the text on p. 171 adapted from *The NSPCC Book of Famous Faux Pas*, edited by Fiona Snelson, published by Ebury Press. Reprinted by permission of The Random House Group Limited.

Photo acknowledgements:

T = Top, C = Centre, B = Below, L = Left, R = Right.

p. 8 (TL): Alamy/© Blend Images; p. 8 (TR): Rex Features/Skye Brackpool; p. 8 (B): Alamy/©Design Pics Inc.; p. 10 (L): © Knit The City http://knitthecity.com; p. 10 (R): © Guardian News & Media Ltd 2006; p. 11 (T): Rex Features/Courtesy Everett Collection; p. 11 (BL): Getty Images/Photographer's Choice/Dan Hallman; p. 11 (BR): Thinkstockphotos/BananaStock; p. 12 (TL, BL): Corbis/Dallas Morning News/Melanie Burford/© Irwin Thompson; p. 12 (TC): Press Association Images/AP/Tony Dejak; p. 12 (TR): Alamy/© Sergio Azenha; p. 15 (T): Getty Images/Stone/ Donna Day; p. 15 (B): Getty Images/The Image Bank/Buena Vista Images; p. 16 (TL): Alamy/© Cristina Fumi Photography; p. 16 (TC): Superstock/© imagebroker.net; p. 16 (TR): Thinkstockphotos/iStockphoto; p. 16 (BR): Thinkstockphotos/Top Photo Group; p. 20: Rex Features/Peter Lawson; p. 21 (L): Superstock/© Steve Vidler; p. 21 (R): Thinkstockphotos/Stockbyte; p. 22 (T): SuperStock/imagebroker.net; p. 22 (B): Alamy/© duncan phillips; p. 24: Thinkstockphotos/iStockphoto; p. 25: Thinkstockphotos/iStockphoto; p. 26 (T): Getty Images/Digital Vision/Donna Day; p. 26 (B): Thinkstockphotos/Creatas; p. 28: Rex Features/Back Page Images; p. 29 (R): Getty Images/Jamie Grill; p. 29 (L): Alamy/Guy Bell; p. 30 (B): Magnum Photos/© Dennis Stock; p. 30 (T): Magnum Photos/© Martine Franck; p. 32 (T): Getty Images/DAJ; p. 32 (B): Thinkstockphotos/Photodisc; p. 34 (B): Alamy/Corbis Super RF; p. 34 (ivory): British Museum Images/© The Trustees of the British Museum; p. 34 (silver patterned): Shutterstock.com/-=Vo=-; p. 34 (smooth silver): Shutterstock.com/Vitaly Korovin; p. 34 (vintage): Shutterstock.com/ffolas; p. 34 (plastic handle): Thinkstockphotos/iStockphoto;

p. 36: Shutterstock.com/Valentyn Volkov; p. 37 (TL): Alamy/Steven May; p. 37 (TR): © Alex Segre/Photographer's Direct; p. 37 (BL): Rex Features; p. 37 (BR): Shutterstock.com/ oliveromg; p. 38: Rex Features/© Warner Br/Everett; p. 40: Thinkstockphotos/Zoonar; p. 41: Getty Images/FoodPix; p. 42 (R): Alamy/ACE STOCK LIMITED; p. 42 (L): Rex Features/BDG; p. 45: © Anthony Cake www.anthonycake.co.uk; p. 46 (L): Getty Images/Image Source; p. 46 (R): Thinkstockphotos/iStockphoto; p. 49: Piazza del Mercato Vecchio, Florence, 1555 (fresco), Straet, Jan van der (Joannes Stradanus) (1523–1605) / Palazzo Vecchio (Palazzo della Signoria) Florence, Italy/The Bridgeman Art Library; p. 50 (L): Alamy/© Radius Images; p. 50 (R): Alamy/© Rider Thompson; p. 53: Getty Images/Hulton Archive/Tim Roney; p. 54: Thinkstockphotos/iStockphoto; p. 55 (a): Rex Features/Sipa Press; p. 55 (b): Thinkstockphotos/Comstock; p. 55 (c): Getty Images/ David Goddard; p. 55 (d): Rex Features/Metal Hammer Magazine/Kevin Nixon; p. 58 (BR): Thinkstockphotos/iStockphoto; p. 58 (TR): Science Photo Library/Martin Dohrn; p. 58 (TL): Thinkstockphotos/Photodisc; p. 59: Sunday Afternoon on the Island of La Grande Jatte, 1884–86 (oil on canvas), Seurat, Georges Pierre (1859–91)/The Art Institute of Chicago, IL, USA/The Bridgeman Art Library; p. 60: Fort Vimieux (oil on canvas), Turner, Joseph Mallord William (1775–1851)/Private Collection/Photo © Agnew's, London, UK/The Bridgeman Art Library;

p. 61: Science Photo Library/NASA/ESA/STSCI/J.HESTER & P.SCOWEN, ASU; p. 62 (L): Shutterstock.com/Linn Currie; p. 62 (TR): Rex Features/PYMCA/Judith Erwes; p. 62 (BR): Thinkstockphotos/iStockphoto; p. 64 (L): Mr and Mrs Andrews, c.1748–9 (oil on canvas), Gainsborough, Thomas (1727–88)/National Gallery, London, UK/The Bridgeman Art Library; p. 64 (R): Henry VII, c.1505 (oil on panel), English School, (16th century)/ National Maritime Museum, London, UK/The Bridgeman Art Library; p. 66 (L): Getty Images/Photolibrary/Phillip Hayson; p. 66 (TR): Getty Images/Workbook Stock/Visions Of Our Land; p. 66 (BR): Alamy/© dbimages; p. 70 (B): Image Source/Robert Harding World Imagery; p. 70 (T): Alamy/© Realimage; p. 72: Rex Features/© FoxSearch/Everett; p. 74: Getty Images/LatinContent; p. 75: Alamy/© South West Images Scotland; p. 76 (TL): Thinkstockphotos/Digital Vision; p. 76 (TC): Image Source/FuseLux; p. 76 (TR): Alamy/© Craig Lovell / Eagle Visions Photography; p. 76 (BL): Superstock/© Lucenet Patrice/Oredia Eurl; p. 76 (BR): Getty Images/AFP/Hassan Ammar; p. 79: © Friends School, Saffron Walden; p. 80 (C, R): Corbis/Rubberball/© Mark Anderson; p. 80 (L): Thinkstockphotos/ iStockphoto; p. 88 (L): Alamy/© dov makabaw; p. 88 (TR): Shutterstock.com/HABRDA; p. 88 (BR): Superstock/© imagebroker.net; p. 90 (MP3): Alamy/© magus; p. 90 (car badge): Getty Images/Bloomberg/Simon Dawson; p. 90 (cans): Getty Images/Scott Olson; p. 90 (phone): Alamy/© Realimage;

p. 92 (L): Thinkstockphotos/Comstock; p. 92 (R): Thinkstockphotos/Photos.com; p. 94: Alamy/© CJG - Technology; p. 96 (T): Rex Features/Jamie Wiseman/Associated Newspapers; p. 96 (B): Thinkstockphotos/iStockphoto; p. 98 (T): Thinkstockphotos/ Goodshoot; p. 98 (B): Thinkstockphotos/iStockphoto; p. 102: Rex Features/Sipa Press; p. 104: © Paul Mulcahy; p. 110 (L): Shutterstock/Thomas La Mela; p. 110 (R): Getty Images/Science Fraction/Karen Kasmauski; p. 111: Science Photo Library/Jacques Jangoux; p. 112: Getty Images/Gallo Images/Martin Harvey; p. 118: Getty Images/ Lane Oatey/Blue Jean Images; p. 119: Corbis/© Paul Burns; p. 120: Getty Images/the Agency Collection/Steve Cole; p. 122 (coffee, cheese, tomatoes, meat, juice, burger, eggs): Thinkstockphotos/iStockphoto; p. 122 (salt): Shutterstock.com/ Andrii Gorulko; p. 122 (sausage): Thinkstockphotos/Hemera; p. 122 (BC): Thinkstockphotos/Hemera; p. 122 (BR): Thinkstockphotos/iStockphoto; p. 123 (L): Thinkstockphotos/BananaStock; p. 123 (R): Thinkstockphotos/Goodshoot; p. 126 (R): Rex Features/Action Press; p. 126 (L): Shutterstock.com/branislavpudar; p. 128: Fi O'Cleirigh/The Guardian; p. 130 (TL): Alamy/© Image Source; p. 130 (TR): Getty Images/The Image Bank/LWA; p. 130 (BL): Press Association Images/AP/Lutfallah Daher; p. 136: Getty Images/Hulton Archive/Keystone; p. 138: MATTER by Iain Banks published by Little, Brown Book Group 2008. Copyright © Iain Banks 2008; p. 138: MOZAMBIQUE MYSTERIES by Lisa St Aubin de Terán published by Little, Brown Book Group 2007. Copyright © Lisa St Aubin de Terán 2007; p. 138: A Bigger Message Conversations with David Hockney by Martin Gayford, © 2011 Thames & Hudson Ltd, London; p. 138: From The Flanders Panel by Arturo Perez-Reverte. Published by Harvill Press. Reprinted by permission of The Random House Group Limited; p. 138: Don't Sweat the Aubergine by Nicholas Clee. © 2012 Transworld Publishers;

p. 141: Front cover of ENGLISH PASSENGERS by Matthew Kneale (Hamish Hamilton 2000, Penguin Books 2001). Copyright © Matthew Kneale 2000; p. 142: Science Photo Library/Natural History Museum, London; p. 144 (L): Thinkstockphotos/Digital Vision; p. 144 (CL): Thinkstockphotos/Brand X Pictures; p. 144 (CR): Thinkstockphotos/ iStockphoto; p. 144 (R): Shutterstock.com/Monkey Business Images; p. 146: Superstock/ © DeAgostini; p. 148 (L): Alamy/© Manfred Grebler; p. 148 (C): Shutterstock.com/ BlueOrange Studio; p. 148 (R): Thinkstockphotos/iStockphoto; p. 152 (T): Rex Features/Sipa Press; p. 152 (B): © Amnesty International www.amnesty.org.uk; p. 154 (T): © LUSH www.lush.co.uk; p. 154 (B): © PETA www.peta.org.uk; p. 154 (monkeys): Getty Images/ Animals-Wildlife/© Comstock; p. 154 (penguins): Getty Images/Just Animals/ © DigitalVision; p. 154 (pigs): Image Source/Herbert Spichtinger; p. 154 (polar bears): © PETA/Tal Ronnen; p. 156 (TR): Rex Features/David Browne; p. 156 (TL): Rex Features/ Frank Monaco; p. 156 (B): Thomson Reuters/Andy Clark; p. 157: Press Association Images/Demotix/Demotix/Mosa'ab Elshamy; p. 160: The Ronald Grant Archive/Summit Entertainment; p. 162: Alamy/© Nic Cleave Photography; p. 164 (TL): Getty Images/MPI/ Henry F. Warren; p. 164 (TR): Alamy/© Pictorial Press Ltd; p. 167 (a): Alamy/© Oleksiy Maksymenko; p. 167 (b): Alamy/© Igor Klimov; p. 167 (c): Alamy/© Ion Prodan; p. 167 (d): Shutterstock.com/Richard Peterson; p. 167 (e): Thinkstockphotos/iStockphoto; p. 177: Shutterstock.com/sculpies.

The publishers have been unable to trace the copyright holder of the image on page 100 and would be grateful for any information to enable them to do so.

Illustrator acknowledgements:

Asa Andersson p. 95; Linda Combi p. 169; John Dillow pp. 69, 113, 114, 145; Mark Draisey pp. 135, 172, 176; Nick Duffy: pp. 18, 52, 149; Clive Goodyer: pp. 37, 85; Julian Mosedale pp. 83, 132, 133, 161, 170, 171; David Russell p. 162; Simon Tegg p. 101; Rory Walker pp. 87, 103

Recordings by Leon Chambers at the Soundhouse Ltd.

Picture research by Hilary Fletcher.